SELLING
& SALES
MANAGEMENT

Sara Miller McCune founded SAGE Publishing in 1965 to support the dissemination of usable knowledge and educate a global community. SAGE publishes more than 1000 journals and over 800 new books each year, spanning a wide range of subject areas. Our growing selection of library products includes archives, data, case studies and video. SAGE remains majority owned by our founder and after her lifetime will become owned by a charitable trust that secures the company's continued independence.

Los Angeles | London | New Delhi | Singapore | Washington DC | Melbourne

Lisa Spiller

SELLING & SALES MANAGEMENT
Developing Skills for Success

Los Angeles | London | New Delhi
Singapore | Washington DC | Melbourne

Los Angeles | London | New Delhi
Singapore | Washington DC | Melbourne

SAGE Publications Ltd
1 Oliver's Yard
55 City Road
London EC1Y 1SP

SAGE Publications Inc.
2455 Teller Road
Thousand Oaks, California 91320

SAGE Publications India Pvt Ltd
B 1/I 1 Mohan Cooperative Industrial Area
Mathura Road
New Delhi 110 044

SAGE Publications Asia-Pacific Pte Ltd
3 Church Street
#10-04 Samsung Hub
Singapore 049483

Editor: Matthew Waters
Assistant editor: Jasleen Kaur
Production editor: Sarah Cooke
Copyeditor: Sharon Cawood
Proofreader: Katie Forsythe
Indexer: Silvia Benvenuto
Marketing manager: Lucia Sweet
Cover design: Francis Kenney
Typeset by: C&M Digitals (P) Ltd, Chennai, India
Printed in the UK

Library of Congress Control Number: 2021937535

British Library Cataloguing in Publication data

A catalogue record for this book is available from the British Library

ISBN 978-1-5297-1258-2
ISBN 978-1-5297-1257-5 (pbk)

At SAGE we take sustainability seriously. Most of our products are printed in the UK using responsibly sourced papers and boards. When we print overseas we ensure sustainable papers are used as measured by the PREPS grading system. We undertake an annual audit to monitor our sustainability.

For John J. 'Midge' DiSalvo

This book is dedicated to my father, John 'Midge' DiSalvo, whose entrepreneurial
spirit and strong work ethic drove him to launch a number of successful small
business ventures during his lifetime. He was the person who first taught me and my
three sisters all about selling and taking good care of the customer. He instilled in us
the need to always strive to exceed customer expectations, whenever possible, and
always operate according to the 'Golden Rule' of treating others as you would want
to be treated. Friendly and outgoing, he was a natural at selling and a people person
who truly cared about his customers. He taught his four daughters, commonly known
as 'Midge's girls', how to create a quality product, serve the needs of customers,
count change, and enjoy the sweet success of selling. His advice to one of my sisters,
as she started a graphic design business, was simple yet stressed the importance of
relationships: 'Do your best for every customer, and then let them talk.' My father
died at the young age of 63, but his passion for engaging with others, working hard
to achieve success, and his entrepreneurial spirit have lived on in my sisters and me.
I cannot think of a finer salesperson and role model than my dear father.

BRIEF CONTENTS

DETAILED CONTENTS

ABOUT THE AUTHOR

Lisa Spiller, PhD is Distinguished Professor of Marketing in the Joseph W. Luter, III School of Business at Christopher Newport University in Newport News, Virginia. She has been teaching marketing courses to undergraduate business students at CNU for 30 years and has helped the Luter School pioneer a major in direct and digital marketing. In addition, Spiller has been a leader in her school's initiatives in sales education. As a member of the University Honors Faculty, she also teaches a course on personal marketing and is passionate about helping her students learn to 'sell themselves' to achieve success in their careers and in their lives.

Lisa Spiller is author of the widely acclaimed textbook, *Direct, Digital, and Data-Driven Marketing*, now in its fifth edition for SAGE. Previous editions of this textbook have been used by colleges and universities in 34 states across the nation and in six countries. Spiller is also co-author of *Branding the Candidate: Marketing Strategies to Win Your Vote* (with Jeff Bergner, Praeger, 2011). Her research has been published in many academic journals and textbooks. Most recently, she was the lead author of a scholarly journal article, 'Sales Education in the United States: Perspectives on Curriculum and Teaching Practices,' which was awarded the Outstanding *Journal of Marketing Education* Sales Education Article of the Year for 2020.

Lisa Spiller has received numerous awards for her teaching, including the Robert B. Clark Outstanding Direct Marketing Educator in 2005 from Marketing EDGE (formerly, Direct Marketing Educational Foundation – DMEF); the inaugural CNU Alumni Society Faculty Award for Excellence in Teaching and Mentoring in 2007; the inaugural Direct Marketing Association of Washington (DMAW) Educational Foundation's O'Hara Leadership Award for Direct and Interactive Marketing Education in 2008; several Faculty Advisor Leader Awards and a Distinguished Teaching Award in 1997 from the former DMEF; and the Elmer P. Pierson Outstanding Teacher Award in 1987 from the University of Missouri, Kansas City. Most recently, Spiller received a Distinguished Alumni Award in 2017 from her Alma Mater, Gannon University, and a Famous Formers Leadership Award from the Girl Scouts of the Colonial Coast in 2019.

As a staunch supporter of her students, over the years Spiller has led numerous student teams to win and place in national and regional collegiate competitions, including the Collegiate Gold ECHO Award from Marketing EDGE and the Collegiate Marketing Award for Excellence & Innovation (MAXI) from the DMAW Educational Foundation.

Spiller received her BSBA and MBA degrees from Gannon University in her hometown of Erie, Pennsylvania, and her PhD from the University of Missouri, Kansas City. Prior to joining academia, she held positions as a marketing director with an international company and an account executive with an advertising agency. Through the years, she has served as a marketing consultant to many organizations. Lisa possesses a true passion for teaching and has been a strong advocate for her students' success throughout her entire academic career.

Lisa Spiller resides in Newport News, Virginia, with her husband. Together, they have three children and three adorable grandchildren. Outside of academia, Lisa enjoys spending time with her family, cycling, golfing, boating, hiking, and reading.

ACKNOWLEDGMENTS

As the author, I am personally responsible for this comprehensive text; however, I must acknowledge the valuable input and assistance I have received from many individuals. While writing this textbook, I was flanked by some of the most giving, patient, and thoughtful people on this planet. There are many people who helped me bring this book project to fruition. First, words of praise cannot do justice to the sincerest appreciation I feel for the following three people. I'm forever grateful to my sister, Cathy DiSalvo, who 'iced each chapter that I baked' by offering a zillion suggested edits and providing the back matter for each chapter; to Johnnie Gray, Technology Services Librarian of the CNU Trible Library, who provided outstanding media, design, and image assistance, and worked with me month after month, enduring my constant pursuit of perfection with humor and grace; and to Susan Barber, Electronic Resources Coordinator, CNU Trible Library, who spent hours expertly searching for and providing relevant and current research material and citation assistance.

I am truly thankful for my two regular 'go to' copyeditors, my loving sister, Tina Fries and dearest friend, Sylvia Weinstein Craft, who never turn down my review requests, regardless of how busy they are – bless you both! Extra thanks to Sylvia for allowing me to include some of her valuable professional etiquette tips in Chapters 2 and 5. And, to two of my other regular supporters, Monica Hill, Associate Director of CNU Alumni Relations, and CNU Alumnus Charles George, who graciously helped me to source numerous images for the book and provided content for particular sections of the book. Special praise to Monica for helping me to obtain many of the opening vignette features from CNU Alumni who work in the sales field.

I am especially grateful to the following people who contributed valuable information to select chapters of this textbook. Many thanks to Dan Schultheis for co-authoring Chapter 6: Listening and Determining Willingness to Buy, Chapter 11: Recruiting, Training and Leading Salespeople, and The Quarry Trucker Negotiation case for Chapter 8. In addition, I'm very grateful to Dan for reviewing and suggesting content edits on other chapters. Special thanks to Linda Ficht for co-authoring Chapter 8: Managing Conflict and Negotiating with Finesse, and for sharing her personal library of resource material with me.

My warmest gratitude goes to my sister, Paula Kosko, for her many valuable contributions of content, images, and examples throughout the book; to Anne Perry for her awesome insight and contributions to several cases and select chapter content; and to Rick Pallen for his expertise and guidance with Chapter 3 and his assistance with the opening vignettes. Special thanks to my brother-in-law, Steven Spiller, for his sales management insight on Chapter 11; to Rachael Judy for her outstanding reviews of select chapters; to Harvey Markovitz for his contributions to Chapter 4 and its case; and to Monique Hunnicutt for her help with the case for Chapter 1. A great deal of appreciation to Bruce Knight for his review and input of chapter material, and his valuable insight, assistance, and contributions in creating the end-of-chapter role-play scenarios, as well as the Self-Selling Appendix.

I am sincerely indebted to the many business professionals who provided valuable input and information to enable me to feature a number of exceptional real-world companies in the cases throughout the book. These companies and individuals include:

- AirBorn – Steven Spiller and Amanda Fuller
- Boston Scientific – Rachael Judy
- Dealbuilders – Pete Ekstrom
- Homefronts by Paula – Paula Kosko
- Pepsi – Kristina Pontillo
- RE/MAX Real Estate Group – Paula Kosko
- STIHL – Nick Jiannas
- Taylor Freezer Sales Company – Rodney van Treeck

Also, I offer special thanks to each of the 39 sales professionals from across the globe who contributed thoughtful perspectives and advice, along with their photos for the opening vignettes to each chapter.

I am sincerely blessed to have family members and friends willing to pitch in and help with my book projects. Special thanks to my models, James Spiller, Suzanne Spiller, Abby Mulugeta, Jack Spiller, Kayla McDade, Rachael Judy, Natalie MacDonald, and Hardik Vora. I also would like to recognize and thank my sister, Cathy DiSalvo, and niece, Amanda Lee, for their help with the Instructor Supplements that accompany this textbook.

I'm extremely grateful to Christopher Newport University for granting me a semester sabbatical leave to allow me to dedicate quality time to creating this textbook, and for the strong support of my academic dean, Dr. George Ebbs, and Department Chair, Dr. Matt Hettche. I could not have completed this book initiative without your support. Thank you.

I extend genuine gratitude for the valuable insight, wonderful support and helpful assistance provided by publisher, Matthew Waters, and assistant editor, Jasleen Kaur, at SAGE Publishing, along with the assistance of Sarah Cooke, Lucia Sweet and Sharon Cawood, on this book.

Lastly, I am most grateful to the following discipline colleagues at various institutions who served as anonymous reviewers and provided valuable comments and suggestions regarding the content and structure of this first edition textbook:

Tim Sellick, University of Worcester

Marianne Collins, Winona State University

Tanya Hemphill, Manchester Metropolitan University

Park Thaichon, Griffith University

ONLINE RESOURCES

Selling and Sales Management is supported by online resources to support instructors in their teaching and assessment, which are available for lecturers to access at study.sagepub.com/spiller

FOR LECTURERS

- **Teaching tips and chapter overviews** will help you **encourage discussion in class.**
- **PowerPoint slides** prepared by the author will allow you to seamlessly **incorporate the chapters into your weekly lessons.**
- **A testbank** of chapter-by-chapter questions will support you in **assessing students and testing knowledge.**
- **Notes for the role play scenarios** can be used as a part of classroom activities to **support the development of practical skills.**
- **Worksheets and suggested course projects** provide **extra resources** to use in workshops.

SECTION 1

The Foundations – 'On the Ground'

1

INTRODUCING ETHICAL RELATIONSHIP SELLING

CHAPTER CONTENTS

PEOPLE, PRACTICES AND PERSPECTIVES FROM THE WORLD OF SALES

Greetings from Nashville, Tennessee. I'm Jack Aldridge, an enterprise account executive with Gartner. I've been with Gartner for seven years and my position responsibilities include consulting with C-level executives to develop and implement an effective, enterprise-wide strategy that maximizes the value delivered by Gartner's products and services, as well as account management. *My advice to you is to sell a product or service you genuinely believe in.* One of my favorite quotes is: 'Do the right things and great results will follow.' (Gene Hall)

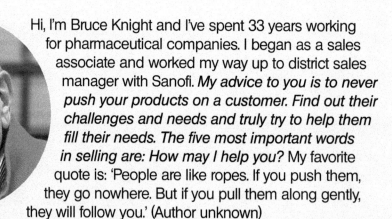

Hi, I'm Bruce Knight and I've spent 33 years working for pharmaceutical companies. I began as a sales associate and worked my way up to district sales manager with Sanofi. *My advice to you is to never push your products on a customer. Find out their challenges and needs and truly try to help them fill their needs. The five most important words in selling are: How may I help you?* My favorite quote is: 'People are like ropes. If you push them, they go nowhere. But if you pull them along gently, they will follow you.' (Author unknown)

My name is Michelle McKenna and I'm a new business sales manager with Open Sky Data Systems in Kildare, Ireland. My position entails seeking opportunities for new business (customers and partners). I've worked in a variety of sales positions for 16 years. I'd like to share this bit of advice with you: *Understand your own values and drivers before applying to an organization – how will you be rewarded and recognized?* Here's a good quote for you: 'A year from now you will wish you had started today.' (Karen Lamb)

Don't make a sale, create a customer!

EYES ON ETHICS

 Keep in mind the following ethical topics as you read through this chapter:

1. Reporting the details of sales encounters accurately.
2. Giving credit to another salesperson when leading a sales team.

INTRODUCTION

Everybody buys. Everybody sells. Everybody wants to feel satisfied and happy. But most people do not want to be 'sold' something. Let's get this straight, this is a textbook about developing skills for successful selling and sales management, yet we are recognizing that people don't like to be 'sold' stuff. Did you misread something? No, that's correct! When people think about 'being sold' something, they associate that with being coerced, tricked, fooled, forced, pushed, or led into buying something that they don't really need, want, or desire. That's the bad rap that the sales profession may have earned decades ago, but it is *not* successful selling in today's modern business world. Successful selling requires you to understand your customer's and prospective customer's needs before you begin any selling activities. There are new rules in selling now that include honesty and integrity, trustworthiness and dedication, and fulfilling the real needs of prospects and customers.[1] Sales ethics must be applied to ensure honesty, responsibility, and fairness in contemporary selling. That's what we'll address in this first chapter, as well as throughout the rest of this book. Let's get started.

MODERN SELLING

Today's modern selling still follows an ordered process which is aligned with the sales funnel (also called 'sales cycle'), which is a graphic that shows that many prospective buyers enter the sales cycle as sales leads; fewer of these progress to prospects once their needs/wants are qualified; and even a smaller number convert to customers once they make the buying commitment (see Figure 1.1). We'll examine the sales funnel more closely in Chapter 4. In addition, we'll overview the stages of the selling process later in this chapter and cover each of them in great depth throughout the chapters of this book. Today's selling process is enabled by digital tools and techniques that make the progression much more efficient, effective, and satisfying for both the buyer and the seller. Digital technology not only enables salespeople to more precisely target prospective buyers, but it empowers those buyers with information and education so that they remain in the driver's seat. Indeed, the modern selling process has evolved over the decades into a rewarding and fulfilling activity for all parties involved.

Figure 1.1   Sales funnel

Understanding the importance of relationships in selling

Successful selling is not about what is sold or bought, it's about satisfying people's needs, wants, and desires. Selling is about solving people's problems. They aren't likely to let you do that unless you develop a good relationship with them and earn their trust. If you truly want to be a part of the problem-solving team, then you have to accept the problems of your customers or your prospective customers (also called 'prospects') as *your* problems. So, in essence, this is a book about how to communicate and really connect with other people, earn their respect and trust, and help to solve their problems by satisfying their needs, wants, and desires. Keep in mind that only relationships built in an ethical manner, with strong integrity will become productive and long term. We'll address the crucial topic of ethics in greater detail later in this chapter, as well as throughout the entire book, but first, let's explore the origins of selling.

Think back to the old days before the invention of modern machinery, communications systems, and modes of transportation beyond horses – that's when selling actually began. Selling started in the form of bartering, where one entity would produce some goods or services of value and would exchange those for the valuable goods or services generated by another entity. These bartering exchanges would satisfy the needs or wants of each party and in the end, the problems of all of the entities would be solved. In those early days, all transactions occurred face to face, likely with the reputations of each individual well established and known by all who engaged in buying and selling exchanges. Back then, if you didn't keep your word, nobody would trade with you. Thus, buying and selling began with the best intentions and integrity. Although our modern world has transformed the simple bartering exchange process, successful selling remains rooted in strong moral convictions and ethical practices.

Confident salesperson

Today's selling is aided by sophisticated databases and analytical tools to help sales-people zero in on those prospective buyers who have a need, want, or problem with which the salesperson can assist. Digital, mobile, text, and social media have led many people to believe that in-person selling is passé – that personal contact is an antiquated notion. However, this is far from the truth. Person-to-person selling puts a friendly, human face on today's digital business world. Think of it this way: a company may create the most brilliant marketing campaign, the cleverest advertisements, the catchiest tweets, and a 'wow' of a website to sell its excellent, need-satisfying products and services, but to land that client account or sell those products or services, its salespeople must come out from behind their desks or laptops and engage with real human beings on a meaningful level. That's where personal selling kicks in.

Personal selling is the interpersonal communication between sellers and buyers or prospective buyers in the exchange of products, services, or something of value, to the mutual benefit of both parties. Personal selling is a feature of the traditional promotional encounter which may take place face to face, by telephone, or via digital channels, such as email, social media, and online conferencing.[2] Some people stereo-typically think of personal selling as 'the art of persuading people to buy.'[3] While persuasion indeed is an important aspect of selling, it does not always lead to mutually satisfying relationships in the long run. Unfortunately, in the past, some overzealous salespeople have used their persuasive talents to be able to 'make a sale' in order to reach a designated sales quota determined by their sales manager. Those situations frequently lead to dissatisfied customers with zero repeat sales potential. Salespeople who are adept at convincing prospects to buy given products/services will only achieve long-term successful customer relationships if they ensure that the products/services being purchased will truly satisfy their customers' needs/wants and solve their problems. Thus, while the ability to persuade is a good skill for salespeople to develop, it can be misused and detrimental when salespeople lack integrity.

Salesperson persuading a prospect

The golden rule in selling today is: *Don't make a sale, create a customer!* Just think about what this saying implies – a sale is just one transaction, but a customer, once created, will potentially purchase from you and your company many times over the years, and if earned, become brand loyal to your company for a lifetime of patronage. Transactional selling, which is a form of selling that focuses solely on completing a deal, is rarely used in today's business world. Rather, relationship selling, which are those activities that aim to develop and nurture mutually satisfying relationships with customers that last a lifetime, is commonly used. Many companies today go beyond building relationships to providing consulting services and forming strategic partnerships with some of their customers via salespeople, providing additional, valuable knowledge and assistance to address specific business needs. This type of relationship selling is called consultative selling or partnership selling, where salespeople are focused on selling long-term value and creating long-term relationships with each prospect and customer as opposed to providing products and services. Thus, the goal of modern selling is to build lifetime relationships and partnerships with customers. How do salespeople achieve this goal? By providing their prospects and customers with something of value or worth.

In a culture of infinite choices and fierce competition vying for a buyer's commitment, salespeople must provide substantial value to their prospects and customers to earn their patronage. Value is the relative worth, utility, or importance of something compared to its cost of acquisition. Value may be offered in different ways, such as providing valuable information, training, serving the customer after the sale, or via the need-satisfying product/service itself. A great example of need-satisfying products are those of Apple, Inc., where many people anxiously await each new version of its innovative products and are quick to buy the latest and greatest technology, regardless of the price. Apple's Steve Jobs embraces this as he describes his company's mission as 'creating products that unleash human potential.'[4] One way or another, salespeople must provide value to their prospects and customers to ensure their satisfaction and cultivate long-term relationships. As such, ethics are fundamental throughout the entire relationship-building and selling processes. Let's now delve into the topic of ethics in selling.

Employing ethical behavior in selling

The first thing that all salespeople must 'sell' is themselves. Simply put, people will not conduct business with people they do not like or trust. Thus, earning the respect and trust of prospective customers is critical to being able to successfully carry out any type of selling activity. There are four key fundamentals of trust:[5]

1. Capability – what are you good at?
2. Dependability – will you meet your commitments and keep your promises?
3. Integrity – will you behave virtuously?
4. Intimacy – how well do I know you?

How can you earn the respect and trust of your prospects or customers? Building trust begins with salespeople believing in their respective company and what it is offering. In addition, you must possess genuine and authentic compassion for your prospects and customers, and sincerely want to help solve their problems. To build trust, salespeople may employ the following strategies:[6]

➤ Be yourself and treat others as you want to be treated.
➤ Establish credibility to enable your prospect to be comfortable with you.
➤ Provide accurate product/service data with complete clarity and transparency.
➤ Share testimonials from previous customers.
➤ Project confidence in what you are selling.

- ➢ Use positive body language when communicating, especially good eye contact, nodding to show understanding, and smiling.
- ➢ Ask open-ended questions to enable customers to provide detailed answers.
- ➢ Carefully listen and respond to consumer needs, wants, and problems.
- ➢ Provide specific deadlines to demonstrate your dependability to meet expectations.
- ➢ Do something unexpected, such as offering additional assistance or performing some thoughtful and helpful action.
- ➢ Mention minor and carefully selected negatives associated with the product/service that may be transformed into positives.

As previously mentioned, some salespeople may be under pressure from their sales managers to close deals by using any means necessary. This can drive some salespeople to make poor decisions and abandon their ethical principles when engaging with prospects. This is never appropriate and will always result in a 'lose-lose' scenario. Numerous research studies have shown that salesperson stress related to ongoing ethical dilemmas decreases job satisfaction and is a leading cause of employee turnover, burnout, and fatigue.[7] Thus, there are negative consequences when salespeople feel forced to behave in a manner that conflicts with their ethical values. For this reason, it is best for salespeople to always live and work by the highest ethical standards. Research shows that businesses with high ethical standards report having higher customer satisfaction, greater customer retention, and more active referrals.[8] The good news is that most companies strive to create a culture of ethical values and to establish realistic sales expectations to positively motivate salespeople without undue stress.[9]

Ethical salesperson

Ethical selling includes a number of different practices that salespeople should exercise on a regular basis. Those ethical practices include:[10]

- Offering truthful information and fair competitive comparisons – speaking honestly about your products and competitor offerings while being careful not to badmouth competitors.
- Handling objections with honesty and sincerity – never overselling your product/service features by promising results that are not feasible, and offering to investigate those questions that you cannot immediately answer.
- Following through on promises and commitments made – giving top priority to honoring commitments in a timely manner and keeping your word on all issues.
- Being accountable for any problems that arise – quickly and honestly taking responsibility for issues and offering potential solutions to remedy a situation.
- Maintaining an ethical-selling based organizational culture – exhibiting ethical behavior on an ongoing basis to all people throughout a company fosters a positive environment.

Thus, all selling necessitates ethical behavior, regardless of who your customers are, the manner by which you're conducting your selling activities, or the channels you are using to interact with prospective customers. Now let's explore the different ways that selling activities may occur.

Exploring different methods of selling

As Figure 1.2 shows, there are two main sales channels – direct and indirect. Direct channels do not include the use of middlemen or any third party such as wholesalers, distributors, or retailers, while indirect channels do use a network of channel partners when selling products/services to consumers. Furthermore, companies may sell to other businesses (formal entities, organizations, associations, or groups who purchase products for further production, use in business operations, or for resale) which is commonly referred to as business-to-business (B2B) selling, or they may sell to final consumers (individuals who purchase products for personal, family, or household consumption) which is commonly called business-to-consumer (B2C) selling. Both B2B and B2C selling may use either direct or indirect channels.

Selling activities typically occur via three different methods – direct, outside, or inside. Let's examine each.

Direct selling is selling products/services directly to consumers via salespeople in non-retail and nontraditional settings. Nontraditional settings include single-level direct sales such as those typically performed one-on-one through in-person or door-to-door presentations, online meetings, or catalogs, host or party-plan selling, or multi-level marketing (MLM), such as network marketing where salespeople, usually called 'distributors', are often required to recruit other salespeople, and compensation is associated with their recruiting results.[11] It is important to note that MLM direct selling is *not* the same as pyramid schemes, which are unethical and illegal. In addition, direct

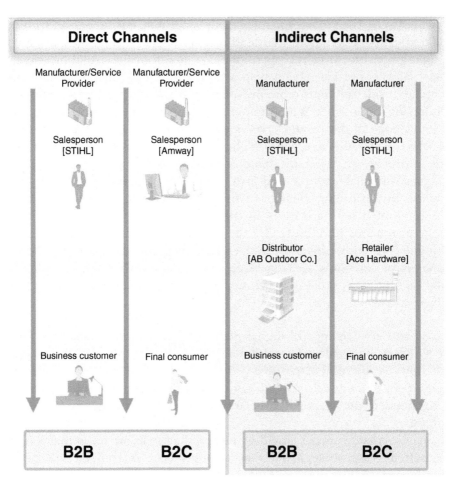

Figure 1.2   Selling channel options

selling is *not* the same as direct marketing since direct selling utilizes salespeople to interact with prospects and customers, whereas direct marketing typically does not. Direct selling may be used for both B2B and B2C selling. Some examples of direct selling are Amway, Avon, Amore Pacific, Herbalife, NuSkin, Mary Kay Cosmetics, Arbonne, and Silpada. For the latest information on direct selling, check out *Direct Selling News* at www.directsellingnews.com.

Outside selling is where salespeople meet with prospects face to face at business meetings, trade shows, conferences, industry events, or other locations. Outside selling is also called 'field sales' (or 'channel sales' when indirect channels are used) because salespeople must leave their offices and go out in the field in order to conduct meetings or sales calls with prospects. Often, outside salespeople earn more than their inside counterparts due to the fact that they bring more experience to the selling situation; however, that depends on the company and industry, as well as whether they earn commissions or bonuses related to reaching or surpassing their specified sales targets or quotas.[12]

Inside selling is where salespeople locate potential customers and guide them through the sales process remotely, instead of face to face. Inside salespeople typically conduct selling activities over the telephone, via email, or by virtual meetings. In the past, inside salespeople have been responsible for selling uncomplicated products; however, today inside selling is more prevalent in many B2B selling situations, as well as in conducting high-ticket B2C transactions.[13] Inside salespeople must command in-depth knowledge of the products/services they are selling since they must be able to explain the functionality and value of their products/services without the benefit of being able to provide an in-person demonstration.

In the past, field salespeople and inside salespeople have traditionally had their own domains, but in today's business world, with rising costs associated with outside selling, coupled with advances in digital technology, the lines between these two selling approaches have blurred. In today's modern world, more field salespeople are interacting with prospects and customers remotely than ever before, and inside salespeople are now serving larger customers with more complex needs.[14] The digital revolution is causing disruption in the use of selling methods in the following three ways:[15]

1. The ease and convenience of digital platforms are enticing consumers to buy via no-cost digital and inside sales methods instead of from outside selling approaches which are typically more expensive.
2. Digital media tools which provide consumers with multiple alternatives for purchasing needed products/services are continually evolving and have become ubiquitous.
3. Data analytics platforms are providing more valuable information that is fueling the selling activities and strategic decisions of both inside and outside salespeople, and sales managers.

Many companies are embracing advances in digital sales tools that enable inside and outside sales collaboration that promotes team rather than individual selling opportunities. Team selling is a collaborative sales strategy where two or more members work together to achieve buying commitments. Examples of how team selling may be used are:[16]

✓ Having two or more salespeople working together on a particular prospective account.
✓ Inviting a sales specialist from another department within the company to address specific concerns a client may have, such as questions pertaining to manufacturing, technical specifications, or customer service.
✓ Building a formal cross-functional team with representatives from sales, marketing, customer service, and senior leadership to collaborate throughout the sales cycle.

Traditionally, the sales function of many companies has created a culture of competition where salespeople are often pitted against one another, with their deal statistics and rankings publicly displayed for everyone in their respective company to see.

Sales team

This competitive selling environment often produced 'star' salespeople who would always drive themselves to win sales competitions among their fellow sales associates. Unfortunately, often these solitary star salespeople would demonstrate 'lone-wolf tendencies' in that they would rarely engage or cooperate with others; dedicated little time and energy to developing interpersonal relationships; and believed that their accomplishments were based solely on individual initiatives and efforts.[17] Just like in the animal world, no wolf can survive for long in the wild when it's separated from its pack. In today's sales environment, the solo salesperson struggles to succeed and typically will only achieve mediocre results.[18] Although the spirit of competition has its merits in other areas, in sales, team selling has been found to be a more powerful sales strategy than individual selling. Team selling offers many key benefits, including:[19]

- Gaining different perspectives and ideas.
- Acquiring contagious energy and motivation.
- Sharing responsibility and accountability, thus feeling less pressure individually.
- Possessing the ability to be at multiple places at one time by dividing and conquering.
- Obtaining unparalleled personal growth, lifelong learning, and skills development.
- Having others to share the victory with.
- Achieving greater selling success.

In order to enjoy the benefits associated with team selling, team members must be carefully selected. Table 1.1 provides some tips to guide you in selecting team members to achieve successful team selling. Later, in Chapter 11, we'll discuss how sales managers can promote a 'we' mentality by employing a 'servant leadership' style.

Table 1.1 Team member selection guidelines

- Possesses good chemistry with other team members
- Shares core values with other team members
- Has an agreed upon team leader to preside over meetings and maintain order
- Has an agreed upon process for resolving potential conflict
- Demonstrates effective communication and transparency
- Shows flexibility and adaptability
- Is reliable and has good follow-through on commitments and promises
- Has a willingness to collaborate
- Possesses effective listening skills
- Is a good team player who possesses a 'we' mentality
- Is knowledgeable
- Applies relevant experience
- Brings unique, value-added capability to the team
- Is persistent in achieving objectives
- Has an excellent work ethic
- Is passionate about the team's common goal

Source: Adapted from Allan Boress, 'Team Selling: Is It Worth It?' (August 20, 2013), www.accountingweb.com/community-voice/blogs/allan-boress/team-selling-is-it-worth-it, retrieved December 9, 2020; Nicki Weiss, 'The myth of the Lone Wolf salesperson,' (September 17, 2018), https://saleswiseacademy.com/2018/09/17/the-myth-of-the-lone-wolf-salesperson, retrieved December 9, 2020.

All salespeople, regardless of whether they are selling solo or on a team, or via outside, inside, or direct methods, rely on their respective company's customer relationship management (CRM) system, which is an integrated system that delivers a single-source transactional database of up-to-date customer information throughout an entire organization to maximize the total value of the customer relationship. We'll discuss CRM in greater detail in the next chapter; however, for now, know that this system provides relevant information on prospects and customers to enable salespeople to build stronger relationships with them, understand their needs and wants, and solve their problems by providing needed products/services. CRM tools and data availability have leveled the playing field for all selling methods as sales metrics can be compared among all methods. Interpreting CRM data can reveal strategic insights that lead to sales-enablement programs and better business results. Sales analytics and sales enablement, which will be more specifically addressed in Chapter 13, are driving the decisions of salespeople in each of the ordered stages of the selling process. Let's now discuss the selling process and overview each of its stages.

THE SELLING PROCESS

Successful selling is typically achieved following a sequential process, with each stage contributing to meeting customers' needs/wants and solving their problems. The selling process progresses in tandem with the customer-buying journey, where the first step is that customers recognize an unfulfilled need/want or problem that needs to be solved. The buyer journey will be discussed in detail in Chapter 2. Keep in mind that the goal of selling today is not to complete as many transactions as possible, but rather, to establish long-term customer relationships. Thus, the selling process continues after a transaction is made.

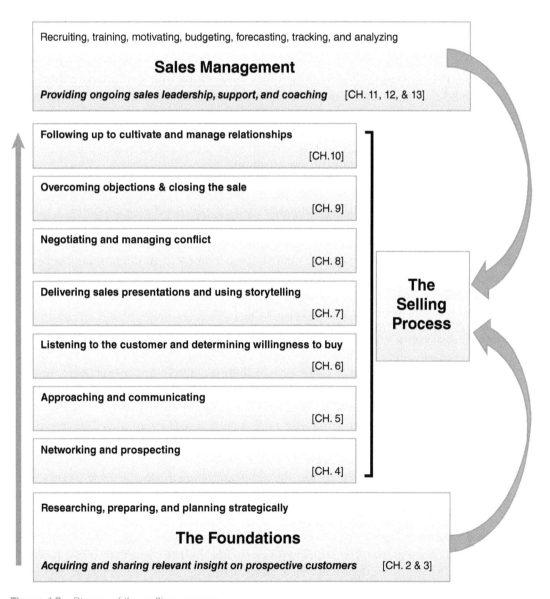

Figure 1.3 Stages of the selling process

Overviewing the stages of the selling process

As Figure 1.3 reveals, the selling process begins by forming a foundation of knowledge from which salespeople can better understand themselves, their company and products/services, and most importantly, the needs/wants/problems of prospects and customers. Successful selling requires an understanding of the dynamic selling situation within which salespeople must operate. Empowered with that knowledge and driven by strategic planning and goals, salespeople begin the ordered stages of selling which are prospecting, approaching, listening and determining willingness to buy, presenting, overcoming objections and negotiating, closing the sale, and following up. Let's briefly examine each of these seven stages:

> **Stage 1 – Prospecting**: This stage involves networking and generating leads with people who may have an interest in the products/services you are offering. In prospecting, salespeople are determining whether there's a fit and a mutually beneficial relationship that's worth pursuing as it may lead to an opportunity to deliver value and earn a buying commitment. The objective in this stage is qualifying leads and cultivating customers through the sales funnel.

> **Stage 2 – Approaching**: The approach stage is where salespeople make initial contact with their prospective customers. This is the meet-and-greet stage of the selling process where the goal is to make a good first impression, establish rapport, build credibility and attain buyer trust, practice good professional etiquette, and communicate effectively to ensure that there is complete understanding between salespeople and customers or prospective buyers. The approach stage of the selling process requires salespeople to master 'soft skills' in order to foster strong business relationships with prospects and customers.

> **Stage 3 – Listening and determining willingness to buy**: This stage of the selling process is often called the needs discovery conversation (NDC) or 'interview' stage and includes asking effective questions, listening actively and proactively, understanding the buyer and their journey, and determining the buyer's willingness to buy (WTB). WTB is a framework that uses a minimally intrusive process that puts potential customers at ease, while the salesperson assists them in self-diagnosis of whether they are ready and able to make a buying decision at that time. If they are, the salesperson would move onto the next stage in the selling process; however, if not, then the potential buyer and the salesperson each decide how to proceed. The salesperson may consider moving onto other sales opportunities that are more likely to come to a buying decision.

> **Stage 4 – Delivering the sales presentation**: During this stage, salespeople will deliver sales presentations to inform and persuade their prospects to move forward in the sales cycle, and eventually close deals. Creating sales presentations necessitates that different approaches and techniques be used to command the prospect's attention and pitch with passion, such as the effective use of storytelling. While

sales presentations comprise a distinct stage in the selling process, in reality they begin with planning and preparing based on prospect research and extend from the moment the appointment is made to the moment the buying decision is made.

Stage 5 – Managing conflict and negotiating: During this stage, conflict or disagreement will likely occur during the selling conversation, along with the need to negotiate or bargain to arrive at a mutually satisfactory sales outcome. Often, buyers raise questions while negotiating with the salesperson. The best salespeople will welcome buyer questions and seek to explore potential areas of conflict. Of course, salespeople must anticipate and be prepared to successfully manage any conflict that may arise during this stage in order to successfully move to the next stage of the selling process.

Stage 6 – Overcoming objections and closing the sale: This stage pertains to obtaining commitments, which may include decisions to advance the sale such as asking for a call-back meeting or to begin the customer relationship by agreeing to buy. Salespeople will encounter both questions and objections from the customer or prospect and they must fully answer each question and overcome each objection in order to continue to earn the buyer's trust. Earning trust during each stage of the sales cycle is needed in order to obtain the buyer's commitment to buy. Based on a thorough understanding of each buyer's unique problem and situation, a particular strategy for closing the sale will be selected and implemented.

Stage 7 – Following up: This stage addresses those activities that are performed after a sale is made, including fulfillment, customer service, and customer relationship management. This last stage of the selling process is crucial to ensure future success and repeat business for your company. Salespeople should conduct follow-up activities with a customer retention focus to strengthen customer relationships and drive future business opportunities.

Most sales transactions tend to move through these seven stages, whether you're consciously aware of it or not, with more complex B2B transactions typically taking longer and involving more people to progress forward than some simple B2C transactions. For example, most consumers will conduct extensive research on automobiles before they decide to visit a car dealership. However, when they do visit a dealership, they signal their interest in buying a vehicle by strolling through the lot or entering its showroom. Salespeople are there to assist prospects in acquiring additional insight and gathering specific information. When salespeople approach prospect to offer assistance, they are able to gather information to understand the prospect's needs and wants and may begin thinking of potential vehicles for that person. By asking the salesperson whether there are any special features, options, accessories, or deals associated with select models of vehicles, the prospect begins evaluating and contemplating making concessions. Some of the prospect's questions may communicate hesitations to move forward with buying a new car. Salespeople will do their best to help their prospects overcome their buying objections. Perhaps the prospect needs more time to decide and opts to leave the dealer-ship. However, if the prospect is willing to make an offer to buy at that time, the salesper-son will likely counter. Alternatively, the salesperson will make an offer to the prospect, who will likely negotiate. If the two can reach a mutually satisfying agreement regarding the terms of the sale, then the discussion will culminate in a commitment to buy.

Car salesperson

After the paperwork is completed and the customer drives off of the lot in a new vehi-cle, the salesperson will likely make follow-up calls and send emails and/or letters. The purpose for this is to thank the customer for the sale and to ensure buyer satisfaction. Typically, the dealership service department will also contact the customer with an invitation to take advantage of free car washes, oil changes, and other relevant services that it provides. At this point, the customer has completed all seven stages of the selling process. In more complex buying situations, several call-backs may be required along with consultations with other people or associates prior to reaching a buying decision. Salespeople are typically responsible for educating prospective buyers about products/

services, building relationships, closing deals, ensuring ongoing customer satisfaction, and performing other related duties that directly impact a company's sales revenues. Let's now examine the different roles that salespeople may perform in greater detail.

Examining the functions in selling

The specific selling activities performed by salespeople vary depending on the salesperson's position, company, and industry. In addition, the roles vary greatly depending on what they are selling, to whom they are selling, and where they are selling. Those people who perform the relevant selling activities may have many different titles, such as sales associate, sales representative, agent, broker, sales manager, district manager, account executive, sales consultant, customer development executive, business development representative, and more. Since there is no standardized system for titling the various sales positions, it is not unusual to find different position titles given to similar selling functions among different companies. However, all selling functions may be placed in at least one of five broad categories:[20]

- Sales representatives – typically entry-level positions that engage one on one with prospective customers.
- Sales management – management positions normally supervise salespeople and sales teams, and often oversee existing client accounts. Sales managers are usually responsible for recruiting, training, and leading salespeople (which we'll explore in Chapter 11); budgeting and sales forecasting activities (which we'll examine in Chapter 12); and performing sales analytics and tracking productivity (which we'll investigate in Chapter 13).
- Administrative sales positions – these positions typically provide services that support salespeople or sales teams, and may include performing clerical functions, analyzing sales data, and acting as a liaison between sales and marketing.
- Account executives and advisors – these positions are associated with account management and tend to require more complex duties, such as establishing relationships with high-value new client accounts, and serving the needs of existing key client accounts by advising, coaching, and providing ongoing customer service.
- Executive-level management – the salespeople in these top-level positions typically hold titles such as 'director' who supervise groups of managers, or 'vice president' who supervise the directors. At this level, they are responsible for strategic planning and achieving the long-term goals of the company.

Depending on the sales function and type of sales-related position, careers in selling normally require a wide variety of skills, including both technical skills (sales training, strategic planning, technology, analytical, and financial) and soft skills (communication, active listening, rapport building, the ability to create an emotional response, and presentation skills).[21] In addition, 'meta skills' (which include communications, critical thinking, interpersonal communications, leadership, and self-management measures, such as taking initiative, managing time, working with others, and mastering the ability to sell ideas) are needed in order to be successful in a sales career.[22]

A career in sales offers several key benefits, including:[23]

✓ High earning potential, with some commission-based positions offering unlimited income potential.
✓ Flexibility in daily schedules, especially in field sales positions.
✓ Job security, since salespeople are typically the last to be cut when business is declining.
✓ A competitive environment with challenges to excel and win valuable bonuses and awards.
✓ The opportunity for self-actualization generated by the emotions felt when sales-people are able to help others.

The sales profession has now become a dynamic and exciting field in which many people find great success and happiness in their career once they decide to pursue it. Keep this in mind as you read this book and explore the wonderful world of modern selling. (To learn more about the various career options in sales, check out Appendix B at the back of this book.)

Selling has always and will always be a numbers game. Thus, individuals who like engaging with both people and data are well suited to a career in selling. In the final section of this chapter, we'll overview some of the key metrics associated with selling.

MONITORING METRICS

Monitoring metrics

Each company has different sales metrics that it uses to measure success. Some metrics are:

• Call totals or averages – number of calls per day, month, quarter, etc., placed to specific prospects or customers.
• Number or percentage of total calls made by contact type (in-person, telephone, virtual, or email).
• Measurement of what content was shown or discussed and how much time was spent on a certain message. When sales calls are completed digitally, these items can be more precisely measured.

- Number of individual or team engagements with customers or prospects.
- Number of events, speaking engagements, or programs conducted and the number of attendees or participants at each.
- Number of suggestions offered by the marketing department and the number or percentage of those suggestions implemented by the salespeople.

Advances in technology have not only reshaped the way selling is occurring in today's world, but also the metrics by which sales activities are tracked and measured. Technology effectively enables manual processes to be automated, meaningful data to be captured and maintained, sales engagements to be personalized, collaboration between departments and salespeople to be improved, sales talent to be developed and coached, and much more. Today, more consumers are comfortable accessing information and purchasing products/services digitally than ever before. This trend will likely continue in the future as consumers are able to access more digital options to help them satisfy their needs and wants, and solve their problems.

Digital disruption doesn't mean that there won't be a role for salespeople; rather, those roles will continue to evolve and be shaped in response to the desires of their customers and the latest digital advances. Consumers, industries, companies, and life in general are always changing. To achieve success in selling, salespeople and sales managers need to stay abreast of those changes, be flexible, adapt when needed, and always keep in mind the end goal of selling: establishing ethical, long-term relationships with customers by providing real value to satisfy their needs/wants and solve their problems. This book was written with that goal in mind and to help you become successful in selling. Remember, everyone sells something even if they don't pursue a formal career in sales.

CHAPTER SUMMARY

- ✓ Note that building good relationships with customers and prospective buyers is more important than making any sale.

- ✓ Position yourself as part of the customer or prospect's problem-solving team.

- ✓ As a salesperson, strive to work well in a team-selling environment.

- ✓ Follow the seven-step selling process routinely as all steps are required for success.

- ✓ Remember that technical skills, soft skills, and 'meta' skills are all required for a successful career in selling.

KEY TERMS

Business-to-business (B2B) selling

Business-to-consumer (B2C) selling

Consultative selling

Customer relationship management (CRM)

Direct channels

Direct selling

Indirect channels

Inside selling

Outside selling

Personal selling

Relationship selling

Sales funnel

Team selling

Transactional selling

Value

REVIEW QUESTIONS

1. While it is important to meet sales quotas, it is not enough to be considered successful in selling. What else do salespeople need to do in order to remain successful in the long term?
2. Describe two different ways that salespeople can provide substantial value to their prospects and customers.
3. Identify three strategies that salespeople can employ to build trust with prospects and customers.
4. Compare and contrast outside selling and inside selling.
5. Describe the benefits that come from team selling as opposed to selling by individual salespeople.
6. Describe four personal characteristics that you believe are most important to consider when selecting salespeople to be on a sales team.
7. Identify and explain the seven steps in the selling process.
8. Name three job positions or functions typically represented in sales organizations. Which appeals to you the most? Why?
9. Identify and provide examples of the three types of skills required to be successful in a career in selling.
10. What benefits are often realized for those making a career in sales?

ETHICS IN ACTION

1. Patrick Muer is a salesman for a large pharmaceutical company. His sales territory was recently broadened when another salesperson left the company. Going forward, he is expected to meet a higher quota

that reflects the larger territory. He has also been challenged to bring in two new accounts by the end of the quarter from the area he has just been assigned. As the months progress, he realizes that there is no way that he can bring on two new accounts while managing his increased workload. He has noticed, however, that one account in the new territory has not been documented in the CRM system. He decides to enter this account as a new customer in CRM. Two months later, he is called to the sales director's office to talk about this particular account. As it turns out, the director noticed that this 'new' account is actually an existing customer who changed the name of the company following a merger earlier that year. What should Patrick say when confronted with this information? What action, if any, should the sales director take regarding Patrick's deception?

2. Jeremy Brady has been a sales team leader for the past five years at an automobile parts superstore. He has always been effusive with praise and recognition for the team members that work with him in opening new accounts. At his last performance review, Jeremy was told by the CEO that while his team members enjoy working with him, the executive team has been disappointed in his lack of individual achievement in closing new accounts. The truth is that Jeremy invests much of his time working with younger salespeople to close and service new accounts. To remedy this misperception, Jeremy claims personal credit for closing the next two new accounts. This behavior shocks and disappoints the rest of the sales team and launches many rumors within the organization. What could Jeremy have done differently when confronted by the CEO? What should Jeremy do now to resolve the rumors and address the dissatisfaction of his team members?

EXERCISE

Everyone buys. Everyone sells. You don't have to be called a salesperson to partake in selling activities. Create a journal for the upcoming week and record each time you engage in buying or selling activities. Keep in mind that the concept of selling includes any time you communicate with other people to provide value that helps to solve their problems by satisfying their needs, wants, and desires. Be sure to address each of the following in your weekly journal:

a. Location or method of buying or selling
b. People involved in the transaction or exchange
c. Type of value provided or purchased
d. A selling and/or buying goal for each transaction
e. Specific sales data that can be tracked and measured per transaction.

READINGS AND RESOURCES

- Alice Alessandri and Alberto Aleo (2015) *Sales Ethics: How to Sell Effectively While Doing the Right Thing*. New York: Business Ethics Press.
- Bob Burg and John David Mann (2010) *Go-Givers Sell More*. New York: Three Rivers Press.
- Dale Carnegie (1936) *How to Win Friends and Influence People*. New York: Pocket Books.
- Michael Maslansky with Scott West, Gary DeMoss, and David Saylor (2010) *The Language of Trust: Selling Ideas in a World of Skeptics*. New York: Penguin Group/Prentice Hall Press.
- Daniel H. Pink (2012) *To Sell is Human: The Surprising Truth About Moving Others*. New York: Riverhead Books/Penguin Books.

CASE STUDY: PHARMACEUTICAL SALES

Note: The names and locations used in this case study have been disguised for confidentiality purposes.

The pharmaceutical sales industry is large and diverse, employing thousands of sales representatives worldwide. Many of these sales reps have enjoyed a life-long career working for several different pharmaceutical companies in different capacities. One such pharmaceutical sales representative is Angela Carr. Angela has dedicated more than 25 years to working for three pharmaceutical companies. She began her pharmaceutical sales career straight out of college and worked as a sales rep for 12 years until she was promoted to a sales manager position. After a few years in her managerial post, she realized how much she missed the regular interaction with physicians, pharmacists, and the medical staff, so she returned to field sales.

Pharmaceutical sales representative

Angela's current sales territory spans approximately 240 miles, encompasses nine cities, in two states, and includes 120 physician offices, 15 pharmacies, and three hospitals. Like most sales reps, Angela specializes in selling a particular type of pharmaceutical drug – in her case, it is the drug Botox. While Botox is sold for both cosmetic and therapeutic indications (treatment of migraines), Angela sells Botox Cosmetic only. She is responsible for providing her medical clients updates about Botox and for achieving her annual sales quotas by encouraging them to prescribe Botox to their patients.

As are most types of selling, pharmaceutical sales are all about relationship building. Regardless of the particular company the salesperson represents, pharmaceutical drug lines that they are selling, or the geographical region to which they are assigned, one thing has stayed constant: educating physicians and medical personnel about the latest pharmaceutical drugs available to most effectively treat the medical needs of their patients. That's the *value* that pharmaceutical sales reps offer their clients. However, *how* pharmaceutical representatives serve their medical practitioner clients has changed greatly over the past few decades. In addition, the rules and regulations that govern pharmaceutical selling vary by country and are constantly changing.

When Angela first started her pharmaceutical sales career, there were limited regulations in place. In addition to regularly visiting her client's medical offices, she was able to organize and host 'dine and dash' dinners, as well as fun events and activities at various sports arenas, circuses, and theme parks for her clients and their families. She was able to distribute free gifts and premiums (pens, hats, mugs, etc.) that included the brand name of the pharmaceutical drug she represented. However, over the years, much has changed. Pharmaceutical selling is now one of the most regulated industries, where reps can no longer leave a pen or notepad at a physician's office if it contains a pharmaceutical brand name or logo.

Today, all pharmaceutical sales reps operate under strict ethical rules where they cannot discuss the clinical trials of a new drug in advance of the 'official clinical approval.' While there is a huge temptation to speak about the new indications, Angela cannot do so as it would be considered an 'off-label' discussion which could cause the pharmaceutical company and the sales rep to incur legal penalties, including substantial fines.

Angela may still host a speaker program dinner; however, her clients cannot bring a spouse or guest, and there are very strict rules in place regarding what the speaker is permitted to say, and also what they must say, about the given pharmaceutical drug. Speakers cannot minimize a side-effect or an adverse event of the drug in any way and they must address safety and indications, among other topics. Speakers must also disclose that they are being compensated for their presentation. If they say something incorrect or break any of the rules of ethics, the sales rep is obligated to interrupt the speaker, correct the dossier, and remind them publicly that they cannot comment on 'off-label' treatments and they must cover the safety issues associated with the pharmaceutical drug. At the conclusion of the speaker program, the sales rep must complete a program-closeout questionnaire and attest to all of the above issues.

Working as a pharmaceutical representative is challenging, but it is highly rewarding and offers a number of perks. Most sales reps work from their home, set their own working hours, drive a company car when calling on the doctors' offices and pharmacies in their respective sales territory, are paid a salary, plus earn commission and bonuses, and sell life-saving or life-improving products. So, if you're seeking an enjoyable sales career where you are making a real difference to the lives of others, consider becoming a pharmaceutical sales representative!

Case questions:

1. What is the primary value pharmaceutical sales representatives give to their clients? How do they provide this value?
2. Explain some of the changes that have occurred in how Angela has carried out her pharmaceutical selling activities over the decades?
3. Why do you think ethics plays a more stringent role when selling pharmaceutical drugs than it does when selling products or services for most other sales industries?

NOTES

1. Phillip J. Brand, 'Sales professionals take responsibility: There are new rules in sales now,' *HCM Sales, Marketing & Alliance Excellence Essentials* (May 2020), 19(5), 29–30.
2. Philip Kotler and Gary Armstrong (2016) *Principles of Marketing*, 16th edn. Boston: Pearson Education.
3. Ralph D. Shipp, Jr. (1980) *Practical Selling*. Boston: Houghton Mifflin, p. 4.
4. John R. Graham, 'Unusual strategies for closing more sales,' *American Salesman* (March 2018), 63(3), 6–10.
5. Sean Callahan, 'We Asked 11 Sales Influencers about How to Build Trust in the Sales Process: Their responses may surprise you' (December 24, 2019), www.linkedin.com/business/sales/blog/management/we-asked-11-sales-influencers-about-how-to-build-trust-in-the-sa, retrieved December 9, 2020.
6. Adapted from Fareeha Afghan, 'How to Establish Ethical Behaviour in Sales' (November 2019), www.simplifie.com/sales-blog/how-to-establish-ethical-behaviour-in-sales, retrieved December 9, 2020; Lestraundra Alfred, '8 Ethical Behaviors to Live and Sell by in Sales,' https://blog.hubspot.com/sales/sales-ethics, retrieved July 16, 2020; and Dennis Rosen, '9 ways to build trust and win sales,' *Sales & Service Excellence Essentials* (November 2016), 15(11), 8.
7. Kristen Bell DeTienne, Bradley R. Agle, Carrolyn McMurdie Sands, Alice Aleo and Alberto Aleo, 'Fostering an Ethical Culture on Your Sales Team' (June 20, 2019), https://hbr.org/2019/06/fostering-an-ethical-culture-on-your-sales-team, retrieved December 9, 2020.
8. Lestraundra Alfred, '8 Ethical Behaviors to Live and Sell by in Sales,' https://blog.hubspot.com/sales/sales-ethics, retrieved July 16, 2020.
9. Kristen Bell DeTienne, Bradley R. Agle, Carrolyn McMurdie Sands, Alice Aleo and Alberto Aleo, 'Fostering an Ethical Culture on Your Sales Team' (June 20, 2019),

https://hbr.org/2019/06/fostering-an-ethical-culture-on-your-sales-team, retrieved December 9, 2020.

10. Adapted from Phillip J. Brand, 'Sales Professionals Take Responsibility: There are new rules in sales now,' *HCM Sales, Marketing & Alliance Excellence Essentials* (May 2020), 19(5), 29–30; and Lestraundra Alfred, '8 Ethical Behaviors to Live and Sell by in Sales,' https://blog.hubspot.com/sales/sales-ethics, retrieved July 16, 2020.

11. 'What Is Direct Selling?', www.thebalancesmb.com/what-is-direct-selling-1794391, retrieved December 9, 2020.

12. Gabe Larsen, 'Inside Sales vs. Outside Sales: How to structure a sales team,' https://blog.hubspot.com/sales/inside-vs-outside-sales, retrieved December 9, 2020.

13. Ibid.

14. Andris A. Zoltners, P.K. Sinha and Sally E. Lorimer, 'Technology is Blurring the Line Between Field Sales and Inside Sales' (October 1, 2019), https://hbr.org/2019/10/technology-is-blurring-the-line-between-field-sales-and-inside-sales?, retrieved December 9, 2020.

15. Ibid.

16. 'There's No "I" in Sales: How to close more deals with team selling,' www.lucidchart.com/blog/what-is-team-selling, retrieved December 9, 2020.

17. Jay Prakash Mulki, Fernando Jaramillo and Greg W. Marshall (2007) 'Lone wolf tendencies and salesperson performance,' *Journal of Personal Selling and Sales Management*, 27(1), 25–38.

18. Nicki Weiss, 'The Myth of the Lone Wolf Salesperson' (September 17, 2018), https://saleswiseacademy.com/2018/09/17/the-myth-of-the-lone-wolf-salesperson, retrieved December 9, 2020.

19. Adapted from Carson Heady, 'Why Team Selling is the Best Selling' (April 18, 2019), www.linkedin.com/pulse/why-team-selling-best-carson-v-heady?trk=related_article_Why%20Team%20Selling%20is%20the%20Best%20Selling_article-card_title, retrieved December 9, 2020; and Nicki Weiss, 'The Myth of the Lone Wolf Salesperson' (September 17, 2018), https://saleswiseacademy.com/2018/09/17/the-myth-of-the-lone-wolf-salesperson, retrieved December 9, 2020.

20. Alison Doyle, 'Sales Careers: Options, job titles, and descriptions' (August 4, 2019), www.thebalancecareers.com/sales-job-titles-2061545, retrieved December 8, 2020.

21. Lisa D. Spiller, Dae-Hee Kim and Troy Aitken (2020) 'Sales education in the United States: Perspectives on curriculum and course materials,' *Journal of Marketing Education*, 42(3), 217–32.

22. D. Finch, J. Nadeau and N.O. O'Reilly (2012) 'The future of marketing education: A practitioner's perspective,' *Journal of Marketing Education*, 35(1), 54–67.

23. Thomas Phelps, 'Why You Should Choose a Career in Sales' (July 22, 2019), www.thebalancecareers.com/why-choose-a-career-in-sales-2918259, retrieved December 8, 2020.

2

RESEARCHING AND PREPARING FOR SUCCESSFUL SELLING

CHAPTER CONTENTS

PEOPLE, PRACTICES AND PERSPECTIVES FROM THE WORLD OF SALES

Hi, my name is Christopher Houghtaling and I am an experienced success strategist, business developer, sales consultant, and team leader based in Horseheads, New York. I have held numerous positions during my career, including the titles of Chief Executive Officer and Chief Operating Officer. I've helped many international companies, including IKEA UK, to transform their sales culture and improve their sales growth. *In my experience, there is nothing more important in sales than researching and preparing each and every sales interaction, regardless of the communications medium used. Without preparation, you are wasting your time and the customer's time. More important, you are telling your customer they are not important. Many customers will see this as an indication that you will not be there when they need you most.*

My name is George Jones, Jr. and I am Director of Personal Lines Sales for Prosper Insurance Company. My primary responsibilities include driving sales performance and compliance for bottom-line growth. While I am based in Virginia Beach, Virginia, I am responsible for a region that includes Virginia, Maryland, Tennessee, and North and South Carolina. I manage a high performing sales team that integrates technology into our processes as we grow. *My advice to you is simple: Be you – it is something I say twice a day. Salespeople can get a bad rap for being too salesy. Being genuine goes far in the sales process.*

Hello, I'm Adam Taliep, Territory Sales Manager with Macmillan International Higher Education. I am based in the United Arab Emirates and responsible for achieving monthly and annual sales targets and growth in six Middle Eastern countries. I have worked in the sales field for 20 years, starting as a consultant and working my way up to management. *My advice to you is to prepare yourself to meet people from all walks of life. Be ready when you do as some will try unconsciously to pull you down to their level, while others are enthusiastic and positive, which is where you will thrive. Stick to what you have learned and apply yourself positively in every situation you find yourself in, within a sales call or opportunity*: 'If you want what you don't have, you got to do what you've never done' (Denzel Washington).

Research drives strategy.

EYES ON ETHICS

Keep in mind the following ethical topics as you read through this chapter:

1. Discovering information on the Web that appears to be the result of a data breach.
2. Hearing politically sensitive information about a customer organization from the buyer.

INTRODUCTION

The subject of this chapter, researching customers and prospective buyers and preparing for selling activities, is of utmost importance for successful selling. It likely goes without saying, but if the goal of selling is to solve the problems and satisfy the needs of customers and prospective buyers, then salespeople must really know their customers and prospects. This is true for both business-to-consumer (B2C) selling and business-to-business (B2B) selling situations. Getting to know customers and prospects requires research. Once salespeople are empowered with valuable insight into their customers and prospects, then, and only then, can they begin to effectively prepare both professionally and personally for their selling activities. Their research and preparation will enable them to have a more productive initial meeting, also called the needs discovery conversation (NDC), which will be addressed in detail in Chapter 6, with each of their prospective customers. By conducting selling activities based on customer and prospect research, salespeople are able to build stronger relationships which lead to loyal customers.

The task of creating and maintaining loyal customers is what customer relationship management (CRM) is all about. An organization with good CRM will develop a customer culture where the focus of all business transactions is on building and strengthening customer relationships. The CRM system creates an invaluable never-ending cycle of research driving strategy. However, the CRM system is powered by detailed customer and prospect research. So, let's get started by exploring customers and prospects!

CUSTOMER AND PROSPECT RESEARCH

Understanding customers and prospective buyers

The heart of selling is the customer. This translates to the need for salespeople to fully understand their customers and prospective customers. Thus, salespeople must gather research on their customers and prospects on a regular basis, since their needs, wants, beliefs, values, interests, worldviews, and so on, are continuously changing. On top of that, most consumers have multiple needs and interests that they are trying to satisfy at any given time, as opposed to just one, so salespeople need to conduct research to truly understand the multi-faceted issues facing customers and prospects. There's so much to investigate, so where should salespeople begin and what data should they gather?

Salespeople should start with existing data that they may have available within their company, such as past customer surveys, customer interviews, customer-support call logs, and so forth.

Salespeople must clearly understand consumer touchpoints, that is how, when, and where the customer or prospect has interacted with their company. A touchpoint is any encounter where prospective buyers engage with the company or salespeople to exchange information; thus, they are scattered throughout the buying decision-making process, also called the customer journey. The customer journey is the set of experiences that a customer goes through, from the moment they become aware of your company or brand. A touchpoint is the first interaction that customers or prospects have with a company, so it's the starting point of the customer journey. Customer touchpoints are not just transactional moments, but are critical interactions within the customer journey that may either build or erode trust, as well as opportunities for information exchange and data collection. Touchpoints reveal the information-gathering techniques used by customers and prospects to learn more about your company or organization.

Some people incorrectly view channels as touchpoints; however, channels are *not* touchpoints. A channel is a passageway, a means of access for the transfer of a product, an idea, or a communication.[1] Channels are a way for salespeople to understand where customers or prospects come from and how they interact with the company or organization, whereas touchpoints are more specific and precise. For example, *online* is a channel, but a *webinar is* a potential touchpoint. A touchpoint can be initiated by the customer or prospect through a variety of mediums, including online and in person. However, not all touchpoints have the same value. Let's examine some of the different types of touchpoints for sales:[2]

- Phone calls – the oldest and most traditional form of touchpoint. Phone calls include both outbound calls, where the customer is on the receiving end, such as in a cold call, and inbound calls, where the customer is originating the call. As we'll discuss later in Chapter 4, cold calling is still a viable technique for salespeople to use.
- Email follow-ups – email follow-up messages are a way to stay in touch with your customers or prospects on a regular basis in order to stay at the front of their minds.
- Social media shares – social media platforms provide ways to engage with customers and prospects by liking and sharing their posts, providing relevant content, or sharing a viewpoint from someone they know and trust.
- In person – connecting with customers and prospects in person is invaluable and will cultivate long-term relationships. Never underestimate the value of the personal touch.

Connecting with customers

Salespeople need to look closely at each touchpoint to understand *why* the customer or prospect interacted with the various touchpoints. In other words, in order to use customer touchpoints for research purposes, salespeople need to explore questions such as:

- What made customers or prospects visit our website?
- What pages did they interact with during their website visit?
- What blogs did they read while they were on our website?
- What resources did they download from our website?

Ultimately, the answers to these questions should shed light on the needs, wants and problems that the customer or prospect is trying to satisfy or solve, thus enable salespeople to follow up in a more meaningful manner. Touchpoints should produce contact information for follow-up. However, sometimes this pertinent data is not provided. In those instances, artificial intelligence (AI) may be used to assist with data collection regarding customer touchpoints. For example, the AI-enabled Prospector tool integrated within Nimble can fill in the contact data gaps in a company's contact records, enabling salespeople to reach out to their customers and prospects without wasting time Googling phone numbers and investigating social media profiles.[3]

Salespeople need to conduct a lot of research in order to determine whether or not they can satisfy their prospects' needs and whether or not their prospects have the propensity to become buying customers. Thus, salespeople must conduct lead research on prospective buyers. This research may include investigating whether prospects are sufficiently qualified in terms of propensity to buy. We'll discuss how to qualify prospective customers in Chapter 4.

One activity worthy of salespeople's time is taking an inventory of customer touchpoints from the customer perspective, to better understand the way the salesperson's own company or organization is viewed. Searching for data within their company, as well as via their stakeholders, such as sales support teams, before seeking to obtain external data about their customers and prospects, will save valuable resources.

Ideally, salespeople should develop a profile of their customers and prospects by gathering descriptive, psychological, and behavioral data via multiple sources, including, but not limited to, transaction data, registrations, interviews, surveys, and online analysis. In order to fully profile their customers and prospects, salespeople will need to investigate geographic, demographic, social, psychographic, and behavioral factors. Let's examine each of these five factors.

Geographic

Potential geographic descriptors may include the consumer's country, state, district, county, trading area, city, town, neighborhood, individual city block, or residential community. In addition, some countries have geographic numerical codes, such as ZIP codes, geocodes, telephone area codes, computer 'match' codes, and territory and route numbers. Often, an important geographic descriptor is that which recognizes the inherent differences among those consumers who reside in central cities, suburban, urban fringe, and rural areas.

Census data is invaluable for research regarding the changing geographic and demographic profile of the American population. The recent Census CD Neighborhood Change Database (NCDB) is a powerful product that presents decades of census tract series data. Additional information about this product is available at www.geolytics.com. Another geographic segmentation tool, the global positioning system (GPS), associates latitude and longitude coordinates with street addresses. Given this information, combined with the technological mapping capabilities of most businesses, salespeople can better determine the business penetration and market potential in certain geographical areas. Today, computer systems are capable of analyzing geographic information systems to help better understand consumer needs related to geographic areas. A geographic information system (GIS) is a computer system capable of capturing, storing, analyzing, and displaying geographically referenced information identified according to location.[4] The GIS software leader is ERSI, which provides a full spectrum of ready-to-use geospatial data products, delivered either as a Web service or as packaged media.[5]

Demographic

Demographics are identifiable and measurable statistics that describe the consumer. Common demographic variables include age, gender, education level, income level, occupation, and type of housing. Salespeople may obtain demographic data by using the following methods: (1) population enumeration, as in a census; (2) registration on the occurrence of some event, such as a birth, marriage, or death; and (3) sample surveys or tabulation of special groups. It is often necessary to research the effect of the interaction of many demographic variables at the same time. For example, it is highly valuable for salespeople to know the marital and household status of a certain 25-year-old male consumer. Just think of two male consumers, both aged 25; one might be married with two children and the other single with no children. These two consumers likely have different buying needs. Often, a single demographic statistic can be misleading. In all cases, the more demographic data you can collect, the better. In addition, currency is the key to the accuracy and validity of demographic data. *Changes* in demography, such as when someone marries or has a baby, have significant marketing implications.

Social

Social factors include a person's culture, subculture, social class rank, peer group references, and reference individual(s). Some types of social factor offer descriptive data, while others provide more attitudinal data. Social factors demonstrate the impact that other people have on our decision-making process and buying activities. For example, reference groups (also called 'peer groups') are those people a consumer turns to for reinforcement. This reinforcement normally comes *after* the consumer makes a purchase decision. However, reference groups may have a direct and powerful influence on buying behavior. A reference individual is a person a consumer turns to for advice. Such persons will influence consumers *before* they make a purchase decision. Therefore, reference individuals normally have a stronger impact on consumer decision making than do reference groups. Social media has driven the importance of these influencers.

Both reference groups and reference individuals may influence buying decisions and are part of the influencer theory, which is based on the idea that a small number of consumers are able to sway the mass market. This theory originated decades ago when Malcolm Gladwell published *The Tipping Point* back in 2000. Most consumers are significantly impacted by the thoughts, opinions, and perspectives of others, particularly those of whom they perceive to be credible and trustworthy. Many consumers believe that salespeople will tell them whatever is necessary to make the sale, while an influencer is considered both an unbiased endorser and a product expert, so their opinion matters. Influencers can be found both off-line and online. For example, specific publications such as *consumer reports*, serve as an influencer for consumers searching for product information and reviews.

In today's digital world, consumers are actively seeking out word-of-mouth, online reviews, and recommendations from those whose opinions they believe they can trust. This influencer marketing is a form of content-driven marketing where the content shared is akin to an endorsement or a testimonial by a third party or potential consumer. Research shows that 91 percent of women consumers look beyond in-person family and friends to tap social networks when they need a recommendation, and 88 percent say they are discerning when it comes to the credibility of online reviewers.[6] Salespeople must research and understand the role and impact of influencer marketing on buying decisions.

Psychographic

Psychographics is the study of lifestyles, habits, attitudes, beliefs, interests, and value systems of individuals. Values represent a person's principles or behavioral standards and can include core human needs, such as the need for security, achievement, health, and freedom. Check out Table 2.1 for a list of common values.

Table 2.1 List of 40 common values

Achievement	Diversity	Involvement	Reputation
Adventure	Fairness	Justice	Respect
Affection	Fame	Love	Responsibility
Authority	Family	Loyalty	Security
Comfort	Freedom	Membership	Service
Commitment	Friendship	Passion	Spirituality
Competitiveness	Health	Pleasure	Success
Contribution	Independence	Power	Teamwork
Cooperation	Integrity	Professionalism	Wealth
Creativity	Intimacy	Recognition	Wisdom

Source: Adapted from Carl Lyons (2007) *I Win You Win: The Essential Guide to Principled Negotiation* (London: A & C Black), pp. 31–2; and Donna Yena (2015) *Career Directions: New Paths to Your Ideal Career* (6th edn, New York: McGraw-Hill), pp. 21–2.

Values are deeply embedded in our unconscious thinking processes and are formed very early on in our lives through our upbringing and other formative influences. Value systems normally provide us with a sense of right or wrong and will directly influence our behavior. Interests often stem from a person's core values, may be influenced by societal norms, and represent the things that a person wants to satisfy or do at the present time. The interests of most people stem from their personality type and basic human needs of what they want to gain, save, avoid, or become. Some examples are the following:

- People want to **gain** self-confidence, an improved appearance, time, professional advancement, increased enjoyment, personal prestige, popularity, praise from others, and financial wealth.
- People want to **save** time, money, and memories.
- People want to **avoid** criticism, physical pain, trouble, discomfort, embarrassment, work, worry, effort, and emotional suffering.
- People want to **become** good citizens, creative, efficient, knowledgeable, good parents, physically fit, influential over others, popular, successful, a recognized authority, and respected.

When salespeople are able to understand the current interests of their customers and prospects, they will have a good sense of their values, as the two are directly related.

As with values, beliefs are convictions that people hold to be true, or an acceptance that something exists. Beliefs are directly related to perceptions. The old saying, 'what is perceived to be real is real in its consequences,' applies to beliefs. That means, what consumers believe to be true, is true in their perception or view. Beliefs directly affect thinking, language, and behavior. However, beliefs will often vary about an issue; therefore, in order to understand consumers and prospects, as well as communicate effectively with them, salespeople must understand their beliefs and perceptions.

Consumer buying behavior is influenced by variables that are often challenging to define, such as lifestyles. Salespeople may obtain psychographic data from external companies, such as Equifax. The Equifax 'Lifestyle Selector' is a large and comprehensive database of self-reported consumer information which is primarily derived from two sources: responses to consumer surveys and product registration cards filled out voluntarily by consumers after they have completed a product purchase. Included for each of the 47 million consumer names and addresses are a variety of demographic characteristics and activities or hobbies. Regardless of how the data is obtained, salespeople need to identify and understand psychographic influences in order to successfully offer value and relevant need-satisfying products and services to their customers and prospects.

Behavioral

The actions taken by consumers are certainly important information for salespeople to research. The specific types of products and services consumers have purchased in the past, the timeframe the transactions took place, the method or location of their purchases, and the method of payment they chose, are examples of behavioral data. Each behavioral factor can indicate a consumer preference. As mentioned earlier, consumer touchpoints will provide additional valuable information about their needs and interests.

Behavioral data may also be generated via 'cookies,' which salespeople may research to examine the online activity of customers or prospects. A cookie is an electronic tag or identifier that is placed on a personal computer. Cookies are a tool for recognizing Web users again after they have interacted with a marketer's website in some capacity. The process is quite simple: whenever a website visitor makes a request to a Web server, that server has the opportunity to set a cookie on the personal computer that made the request. The website host can then use the cookie for tracking beyond the initial click to determine how often that visitor returns to the website, the length of time of each visit, and the particular Web pages visited, which can often detail the specific products or services in which the visitor is interested. Cookies may provide salespeople with valuable insight into the online behavior of their customers and prospects.

Profiling organizational (B2B) consumers

Now that we've investigated each profiling factor, let's discuss the differences between how we might profile organizational consumers versus final consumers. In essence, organizational consumers, also called business consumers, are any formal entity that purchases a product or service for further production, use in its operations, or for resale. We commonly refer to these transactions as business-to-business (B2B) selling. Contrast that with final consumers, who purchase products and services for personal, family, and household consumption, which we refer to as business-to-consumer (B2C) transactions. B2B selling is the process of providing goods and services to organizational consumers and industrial market intermediaries, as opposed to ultimate, final individual consumers, or people like us. Collectively, business consumers consist of public and private companies, government, and not-for-profit organizations. These include small, medium, and large-size manufacturers, wholesalers, retailers, government agencies, and non-business organizations, such as charities, churches, and foundations.

Some of the same profile factors may apply to both B2C and B2B consumers, such as geographic factors, while others may not, such as demographic and psychographic factors. Salespeople should investigate the demographic profile factors of buyers within organizations at the same time as they look at the relevant features of the organizations themselves. In B2B selling, salespeople need to conduct *both* types of research – research regarding the company itself (B2B), and also research on that company's consumers (B2C). Thus, in B2B selling, salespeople are truly incorporating both types of research into their selling strategies. A comparison of descriptive characteristics, contrasting consumer (B2C) and industrial or business (B2B) customers and prospects, is shown in Table 2.2.

Table 2.2   B2C/B2B comparisons

CONSUMER	INDUSTRIAL
Name/Address	Name/Address
Source code	Source code
Age	Year started
Gender	Gender of decision maker
Income	Revenue
Wealth	Net worth
Family size	Number of employees
Children	Parent firm or subsidiary
Occupation	Line of business
Credit evaluation	Credit evaluation
Education	Education of decision makers
Urban/rural resident	Headquarters/branch
Own or rent home	Private or public ownership
Ethnic group	Minority ownership
Interests	Interests of decision makers
Lifestyle of ZIP area	Socio-economics of location
Mail respondent	Mail respondent
Transactions & R/F/M	Transactions & R/F/M

Conducting research to better understand customers and prospects for both B2C and B2B selling situations is the first and most important step in preparing for selling. However, in order for salespeople to be successful, they must fully prepare for the needs discovery conversation (NDC), which includes understanding the business environment they are operating within. The business environment, which is the internal and external factors that influence a company's operating situation, includes the issues of human resources, corporate culture, and power and politics. Understanding the influence of power and politics in a company's environment is the topic of our next section.

Understanding power and politics

What is power and why does it matter in selling situations? Power is described as the capacity to control or direct change.[7] The active form of power is influence. Influence is power in motion and includes any behaviors that represent an attempt to alter someone else's thoughts, attitudes, or behavioral choices. The question is: how will that power be used? Will it be used in an ethical manner? Will it be used for the good of the company? Will it be used in a non-coercive manner to lead others in the pursuit of a goal?[8] Leaders and followers in a totalitarian system, for example, must all conform to the organization's norms in order to contribute to the self-preservation of the system.[9] People adapt to a work situation because they've been conditioned in a certain way. How can the salesperson be successful in the particular company culture unless they understand the nuances that exist?

Salespeople must understand the power and politics at play that affect their prospective customers, including the company culture in existence, in order to effectively interact and provide value. As the salesperson, the better you understand your buyer, their situation, challenges, opportunities, concerns, perspective, business needs, personal motivators, how they are measured, what they value, desired outcomes, their timeframe, budget, obstacles, political allies and detractors, and more – the better you can develop a solution that is relevant, compelling, and creates value.[10] Thus, it is imperative to identify and prepare for the conversation with the main decision makers in advance, to consider which sources of power they may hold and deploy, and to consider who may be influencing their decision-making process. Salespeople need to determine which tactics may be most effective in engaging with that individual. The power and politics of your selling situation will vary based on your different prospective customers.

In summary, understanding the power and politics in play typically leads to better NDCs. Through better NDCs, salespeople have a greater chance of offering solutions that will truly help their prospective buyers solve their problems. Always remember, salespeople are most successful in creating value for their prospective buyers when they have a deep understanding of the total situation their buyers are operating within. Understanding prospective customers and their respective environment has become easier due to digital technology. Let's now explore the use of technology for conducting research.

Using technology to research

Regardless of the different types of consumer profile data that salespeople gather, relying on a single factor to understand and profile consumers and prospects is rarely effective. The old saying 'birds of a feather flock together,' explains the connection between geographic factors and demographic, social, psychographic, and behavioral factors. People with like interests tend to cluster and their purchase decisions are frequently influenced by their desire to emulate their friends, neighbors, and community innovators. Thus, geographic data may provide the means to *identify* clusters of households that have a high degree of *homogeneity*, where prospective buyers are likely to have profiles similar to current customers.

Most salespeople use technology to research multiple profile factors – such as combining geographic data with behavioral data. Several companies, including Claritas, Experian, Acxiom, and MapInfo, combine US census data with consumer lifestyle patterns to profile customers by geographic area. Google Analytics, a Web analytics service offered by Google, tracks and reports website traffic. From the detailed analyses in Google Analytics, salespeople are able to examine their company's website traffic through in-depth customer analysis. The system allows customers to be grouped based on age, gender, affinity categories, and in-market segments. Affinity categories represent individuals' overall interest and lifestyle attributes, while in-market segments represent consumers who are actively searching and have indicated an interest in a product or service.

Digital media has turned the Internet into the largest public data source in the world. Websites and social media offer an abundance of potential research about customers and prospects, but sifting through it to uncover the relevant data for salespeople can be challenging.

Computer work

Web scraping, also called web harvesting or web data extraction, is a technique used to extract structured data from websites.[11] Web scraping is similar to web indexing in that it indexes information on the Web using a bot web crawler, and is a universal technique adopted by most search engines. However, it focuses more on the transformation of unstructured data on the Web, usually in HTML format, into structured data that can be stored and analyzed.[12] Salespeople may utilize customized large-scale web scraping, referred to as web scraping API (WSAPI), a platform that enables companies to extend their existing web-based system to their clients using an application programming interface (API), and provides companies with fresh structured data which is integrated into their system. Uses of web scraping include the following:[13]

- price-monitoring projects to keep track of price changes
- lead generation to download leads information for sales analysis
- outreach to influencers and bloggers to obtain information about name, surname, email address, phone number, etc., usually from a directory of influencers
- research to extract data on any topic and website.

Conducting research on prospects or leads is a common use of web scraping for sales-people. When conducting research on prospects, salespeople will want to obtain as much information as possible on a company and individual contacts prior to reaching out to them. Thus, web scraping may be used to find relevant triggers or action events that sales people may mention in their initial contact with prospects. Salespeople might mention a fundraising event, company milestone, new headquarters or expansion, awards or recognition, new key executive hire, or blog post, and so on.[14]

In summary, web scraping is an essential hacking tactic to mine information on the Internet and to pull together an extensive, highly customized list of leads. More will be discussed on using web scraping for lead generation in Chapter 4. Many salespeople are using a mix of web scraping, web crawling, artificial intelligence, and big data analytics to find content pertinent to their customers and prospects.[15] (See the Readings and Resources section at the end of this chapter to learn more about using online techniques to conduct research for selling.)

Profiling customers and prospects via both online and off-line techniques is an excellent starting point to understand customer and prospect needs. However, these techniques alone will not produce enough relevant information to fully understand consumer needs. Salespeople must also know the stage of the customer journey that their customer or prospective customer is currently at in order to properly serve their buying needs. Let's explore customer and buyer journeys.

Examining customer and buyer journeys

The needs, wants, and buying motives of customers and prospects differ and often depend on where they are in their customer journey. As previously defined, the customer journey refers to the set of experiences that a customer goes through, from the moment they become aware of your company or brand.

These stages include:

1. Awareness stage – during which consumers recognize that they have a problem or unsatisfied need.
2. Consideration stage – during which consumers identify and evaluate possible solutions to their problem.
3. Decision stage – during which consumers make a selection regarding what product or service is the best solution to their problem.
4. Retention stage – during which consumers, who are now *customers*, repeat-purchase and develop a relationship with a given company or brand.
5. Advocacy stage – during which customers develop a strong and vocal relationship with a given company or brand and become an evangelist for it.

Customers may become brand-loyal at the retention stage; however, their loyalty is much stronger at the advocacy stage. The customer journey is viewed from the perspective of the customer and there are many differences between individual customer journeys. In addition, it is virtually impossible to control every aspect of the customer journey, however salespeople seek to enhance all stages of the customer journey, which includes the buyer journey, for all of their customers and prospects.

The buyer journey refers to the stages that a consumer goes through up to their decision to purchase a specific product or service from a specific organization. Thus, the buyer journey only includes the first three stages of the customer journey – awareness, consideration, and decision. It is important to keep in mind that during the buyer journey, consumers are not yet *customers*. They become a customer *after* they make a purchase with a given organization.

Salespeople may create and utilize customer journey maps to organize the customer data they have acquired in their research. A customer journey map is a visual depiction of every interaction and experience a customer has with a company or organization. Each customer's experience begins at the moment of discovery (or awareness) and extends through the lifetime of the customer relationship. Customer journey maps are powerful tools that produce great insight for the entire company. As the example provided in Figure 2.1 shows, customer journey maps can visually tell stories about customers and enable salespeople to engage with their customers and prospects more effectively via customer touchpoints as they progress through the customer journey.

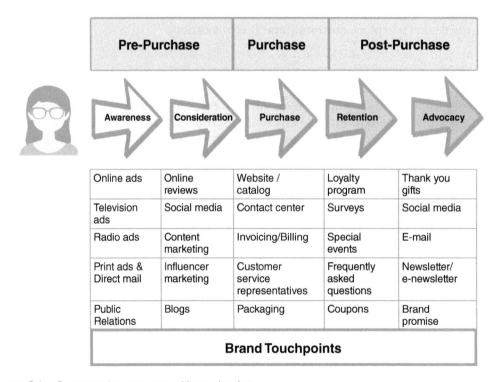

Pre-Purchase		Purchase	Post-Purchase	
Awareness	Consideration	Purchase	Retention	Advocacy
Online ads	Online reviews	Website / catalog	Loyalty program	Thank you gifts
Television ads	Social media	Contact center	Surveys	Social media
Radio ads	Content marketing	Invoicing/Billing	Special events	E-mail
Print ads & Direct mail	Influencer marketing	Customer service representatives	Frequently asked questions	Newsletter/ e-newsletter
Public Relations	Blogs	Packaging	Coupons	Brand promise
Brand Touchpoints				

Figure 2.1   Customer journey map with touchpoints

This knowledge, once distributed throughout the organization to those business units that interact with the customer, such as salespeople, will enable the company to provide an enhanced customer experience. Indeed, customers generate mounds of data about their experiences with a company every single day; however, this data is only valuable if it is captured, organized, analyzed, and shared to deliver effective engagement and improved customer satisfaction from the customer's perspective. The bottom line is that customer journey maps should help salespeople deepen their understanding of their customers' behaviors, thoughts, and feelings across touchpoints in their journey, and they should be actionable.

Actionable customer journeys won't happen unless salespeople are able to offer or propose something of value to customers and prospects. Thus, salespeople must use the research insight regarding what consumers need and want and professionally prepare for the selling process to begin, which is the topic of our next section.

PROFESSIONAL PREPARATION

While there is significant value to be had in mastering the art and skill of the unsolicited sales proposal, there is even more value in taking the time to investigate and understand the prospective customer's needs and wants. In B2B selling, this requires salespeople to navigate the company culture of their prospective customers in order to determine the ultimate decision maker. Salespeople need to find out what is important to that individual (or group if it is a team-based buying decision) to ensure that all of their touchpoints align with those values and issues. Salespeople must identify the key performance indicators (KPIs) for their prospective customers, and if possible, identify their 'pain points.' Salespeople may investigate the pain points of their prospective customers by addressing questions such as 'What issues are keeping their prospective buyers awake at night?' This research and preparation for the initial needs discovery conversation (NDC) will help salespeople prepare to answer any questions their prospective buyers may have, as well as those they don't even know they have.

As previously mentioned, and worthy of repeating, instead of crafting a proposal that you *think* will address the needs of your prospective customers, take the time and do the extra investigative work to arrange a conversation with them. Good preparation takes time and there are no shortcuts. Consider the acquisition of an actual appointment with a prospect as an early victory; and go into such a meeting fully prepared, with your research on their industry, their sector, their company or organization, and their pain points.[16] Check out your prospective customer's social media profiles and conduct research on the person(s) with whom you'll be speaking. Find out if anyone else in your company has already had conversations with this person and learn all you can. Check LinkedIn for any tidbits of information, such as volunteer experience, recent promotion, or that they are a fitness buff, book lover, beach lover or marathon runner. People do business with people, and salespeople must be prepared to connect on a personal level.

It may not be necessary to conduct a full presentation; however, you should be prepared to offer one, and it should be as formalized as possible. By preparing for the NDC, you will demonstrate to prospective customers that you are the person they can trust with their company, their employees, and the potential impacts on their revenues. You must act the part. 'Acting the part' means not only conducting the research, making the telephone calls, or sending the emails needed to get the meeting, preparing the presentation or Executive Briefing, and getting your suit out of the dry cleaners; it also means being prepared to answer questions about your capacity, resources, and prior engagements that demonstrate your capability to serve these prospective customers if you win their business.[17] Part of your preparation, then, should include an up-to-date Capabilities Statement demonstrating effective value creation and documenting your past performance. If you are new to the marketplace, evidence of your effectiveness with previous customers in the form of testimonials, will strongly improve your chances of getting business on your own, especially if you provide contact information for your prospective customer to check.[18] See Table 2.3 for some tips on creating an effective Capabilities Statement.

Table 2.3 *Capabilities Statement tips*

- Conduct background research on your prospective customer and use it when writing your Capabilities Statement.
- Give your Capabilities Statement a title.
- Customize and tailor your Capabilities Statement to your prospect.
- Catch the eye of your prospect by including keywords which match those in your prospect's mission statement and/or request for proposal.
- Include pertinent data: including core competencies, past performance, differentiators, company information, and contact information.
- Ensure that core competencies are benefits tailored to your prospect.
- Include brief testimonials or stories to demonstrate past performance.
- Include unbiased, objective data to differentiate and substantiate your claims.
- Include recent and related awards and accolades, as available.
- Direct readers to your company's website with a call-to-action.
- Ensure that responding to your Capabilities Statement is easy for prospects – 'one-stop concept: one contact, one call.'
- Encourage your prospect's requests for more information.
- Review your Capabilities Statement to ensure it is clear, concise, and able to be easily understood by the prospect.

Source: Adapted from RocketGov, https://capability-statement.com/writing/#:~:text=A%20good%20capability%20statement%20provides%20the%20important%20information,action.%20They%20are%20usually%20written%20as%20a%20command

Lastly, salespeople should be professionally prepared for engaging with prospective customers. That includes reviewing their company's offer or value proposition. In preparing for the NDC, salespeople should begin by reviewing their company's offer to ensure that it is relevant, need-satisfying, and attractive to their prospective customers. Let's explore what the review process entails.

Examining your offer/value proposition

The offer is the value proposition to the prospect or customer, stating what you will give the customer in return for taking the action you are requesting. In essence, it is the terms under which salespeople present whatever they are selling. The offer encompasses both the manner of presentation and a request for a response, which is all created based on the extensive research conducted and needs/wants uncovered, as discussed earlier in this chapter.

Creating need-satisfying offers is a part of ongoing CRM. Without an attractive offer, consumers would not initially commit to buying, and thus the customer relationship would never begin. Without continuous monitoring of customer needs and wants, salespeople could not create appropriate offers to keep their customers satisfied and encourage them to return and purchase again and again. The offer is the all-important 'front-end' activity in the CRM process.

The offer is the element of the sales strategy that can be most quickly and easily revised for an improved result in the selling process. Even the slightest change in the price may produce a dramatic difference in consumer buying behavior. Just think about all of the products that are priced at odd numbers, such as $19.99 or $199.97. These figures are pennies away from the even dollar amounts; however, consumers often perceive them to be far less. Research has proven that odd prices are very effective in generating consumer commitment; therefore, many companies use odd prices in their offers.

To create an effective offer, salespeople must research and really know the target buyers' likes, dislikes, 'hot buttons,' and, most of all, needs and wants. Without this information, it is difficult to create an effective offer. The five components of the offer are product or service, pricing and payment terms, risk-reduction mechanisms, time limits or length of commitment, and incentives (which is optional.) In creating an offer, salespeople should ask themselves four essential questions:

1. What am I selling?
2. Whom am I selling to?
3. Why am I selling this now?
4. What do I want my prospect or customer to do?

The key to effective selling is unlocking the power that comes from knowing to whom you are targeting your offer. It is only by knowing and understanding the target consumer that the offer can be need-satisfying and successful in solving customers' problems. Of course, not all consumers are the same, which often makes creating need-satisfying offerings challenging. The appeal of an offer can be described as its message content that addresses the consumer's needs, wants, or interests, and entices action. The most commonly used appeals are either rational or emotional. The rational appeal targets a consumer's logical buying motives. It presents facts in a logical, rational manner and targets basic needs such as those for food, shelter, clothing, and safety. Rational appeals are normally used for business-to-business (B2B) offers. With B2B offers, salespeople are targeting organizations or groups where often the purchase decision is based on exact specifications and technical data, as well as being made by a buying committee or a team of decision makers. Conversely, the emotional appeal focuses on a consumer's desires and feelings. It targets wants – such as social status, prestige, power, recognition, and acceptance – as opposed to physical needs. Customers and prospects will respond to offers if they provide benefits that appeal to them. Let's examine the importance of benefits when selling.

Converting features to benefits

Benefits may be the physical attributes of a product, translated into terms that meet customer needs. For example, customers don't buy quarter-inch drill bits; they buy the ability to make quarter-inch holes. They don't buy power steering; they buy ease in parking a car parallel to a curb. Salespeople must sell benefits in a manner that matches a customer's motivation, which we described earlier in the chapter. Offers incorporating customer benefits are structured to incite action and overcome human inertia. An analytical technique for identifying benefits, FAB (features-advantages-benefits), appears in Table 2.4.

Table 2.4 Features/benefits example – iPad Pro

iPad Pro		
Features ➡️ (what the product has)	**Advantages** ➡️ (what the features do)	**Benefits** (why customers buy)
Neural engine	Smart and capable	Provides faster and more powerful processing
Face ID	Won't need passwords	Don't have to remember passwords; can unlock and log on with just a glance
A12X bionic chip with neural engine	Excellent performance and efficiency – faster than most PC laptops	Can quickly switch from page to page; easy photo editing and gaming; great for multitasking
Liquid retina display with ProMotion	Better clarity of images	Images look real with true-to-life color; pages feel responsive; easier to read; more enjoyable
Edge-to-edge all-screen design	Larger viewing surface area	Larger picture without larger iPad unit; can do anything you need any way you hold it; easier to read; more versatile
Thinnest iPad ever	Lightweight and exceptionally slender	Easy to hold and tote
Up to 1TB capacity	Ability to store tons of content	No limits on what can be kept
Rounded corners (smooth, yet angular)	Better design	Easy to hold

As demonstrated in Table 2.4, the *features* of the iPad Pro include in its manufacture: a neural engine, face ID, a 2X bionic chip, a liquid retina display, edge-to-edge all-screen design, and the thinnest iPad ever. But what value do these features offer to consumers? Salespeople need to translate these product features into advantages and, then, from these into benefits. For example, face ID capabilities provide the advantage of the iPad being accessed with face-recognition software, the benefits being that users won't have to remember passwords and will have enhanced security. The 12X bionic chip, as another example, provides the advantage of excellent performance and efficiency, the resulting benefit being that users can quickly switch from page to page, which makes reading, photo editing, and gaming easy. Being the thinnest iPad ever offers the corresponding advantages of being extremely lightweight and exceptionally slender, which translate into the benefits of being easy to hold and tote. Converting features to benefits provides salespeople with a useful procedure for understanding the main benefits of a product or service, which is a necessary prelude to selling. Each product or service may have many benefits, so salespeople need to rely on their customer and prospect research to know which benefits are most important to be emphasized when selling. That leads us to the need to discover your unique selling proposition, which is the topic of the next section.

Discovering your unique selling proposition (USP)

There is normally one key benefit for which the brand or company is known. This is referred to as its unique selling proposition (USP) or what it can do that is distinctively better and different than all other competitors vying for the same customers. Salespeople must ensure that their USP matches the main benefits that their customers and prospects desire. Consumer research can aid with this aspect of professional preparation. Once salespeople confirm that the USP of what they are selling is a spot-on target with their customers and prospects, they must be well versed in touting this USP.

However, even if salespeople gather all of the 'right' relevant information about their customers and prospects, understand the influencers, know the stage of the customer journey, have the 'right' need-satisfying value propositions, and present attractive unique selling propositions, they may not be successful in establishing business relationships with prospective buyers. Why not? Because, people do business with people. Let's rephrase that to: People do business with people they like. Let's expand that to: People do business with people they like and trust. Thus, understanding your customer or prospective buyer and getting them to trust and like you are two separate challenges that salespeople must conquer. If the prospective buyer doesn't like and trust the salesperson, then it's not likely that this individual will become a customer. If customers do not like and trust salespeople but like the product or service, they are likely to seek other suppliers for future purchases. If the goal for salespeople is to form lifelong relationships with their customers, salespeople must be both likeable and trustworthy. That leads us to the next section regarding the personal preparation that salespeople must undertake in order to be successful in selling.

As a salesperson, one may ask, how do you get another person to like and trust you when in a business environment? A quote from Charles Green, CEO of Trusted Advisors, encapsulates the approach to developing trust in another: 'People respond positively to a sense that they are being listened to, and to people whom they feel have their best interests at heart.'[19] Thus, to achieve trust, salespeople should use more questions, and fewer statements. The questions asked should not be an inquisition to prospective buyers, nor should they appear that the salesperson is just using a laundry list of specification questions, such as: How big? What color? What delivery time? These questions will be perceived as the salesperson is merely seeking data and information to assist them in making a proposal or selling a product or service. Instead, the types of questions the above quote from Charles Green refers to are those that cause buyers to reflect more deeply on determining why they have made a statement or assumed a position. This is not to debate the prospective buyer's point, but rather to seek further depth on the 'why' behind the 'what.'

Here's an example: If a potential prospect said to a salesperson, 'I'm not interested in any high pressure selling!' Instead of the salesperson responding to this by saying, 'I'm not going to pressure you. I just want to find out if you need what I offer,' The salesperson could say in response to the above statement from the prospect, 'Thanks for being candid with me. Can you tell me why you chose to say that to me at this time?' This latter response invites the prospect to ponder and explain further the motivation for making that statement. The reason, the prospect might state is, 'I've been pressured so much by salespeople in the past, I won't tolerate it again.' This provides an opportunity for the salesperson to expand the discussion further by stating, 'I'm sorry to hear that,' and asking, 'Can you give me an example of when that has happened to you in the past?' With this gentle approach, the process helps prospective buyers to keep reflecting on the motivation behind their statements, as well as enabling prospects to feel that the salesperson is truly trying to understand their perspective better, rather than just reacting to the initial statement in a defensive way. This approach enhances *trust* because, as in the above quote, it keeps the prospective buyer's 'best interests at heart.' As applies to all interpersonal communications, knowledge and understanding of your own personality type, as well as that of your customer's, help significantly in building trust and rapport. Personality types will be explored further in Chapter 8.

PERSONAL PREPARATION

Your success in selling will be a reflection of the quality of your personal, professional, and environmental preparation. Ron Willingham, author of *Integrity Selling*, claims that 'Selling success is more of an issue of *who* you are than *what* you know. While knowledge is necessary, sustained success comes to the person who's driven by strong values and ethics.'[20] Do you have strong values and ethics? Knowing yourself is an important first step toward being prepared to be successful in selling. That requires self-assessment, which is the topic of the next section.

Assessing yourself and determining your own selling style

Knowing what you enjoy doing, what you're good at, how you like to spend your free time, what motivates you to achieve your goals, how you approach tasks, and

Salesperson reflecting

how you interact with other people are all part of understanding who you are. Self-assessment is the process of identifying your values, interests, personality traits, knowledge, skills, behavior/social style, and emotional intelligence. Although we've already discussed some of these earlier in the chapter when discussing research on behavioral factors, let's briefly reflect on them now as they pertain to your self-assessment.

Values are the beliefs and standards by which you choose to live your life. Values aren't necessarily right or wrong, nor are they good or bad. Values determine what is acceptable behavior to you from your perspective, so they affect most of the choices you make every day. Values vary from person to person. So, a behavior or decision that may be unacceptable in your belief system, may be acceptable for another person. Some examples of values are: personal relationships, time with family, social status, financial reward, and community service. In order to identify your values, ask yourself a simple question: What is important in my life? Review and complete the values self-assessment provided in Table 2.5.

Table 2.5 Values self-assessment

Review the 40 common values presented in Table 2.1. Select the top five values that motivate your behavior on a regular basis. Write them down. Next, carefully evaluate this list of values and prioritize them in order of their importance to you. Consider how these values affect the decisions you make in both your personal and professional life. Are your values aligned with selling the product/service you represent?

1. _____   4. _____

2. _____   5. _____

3. _____

Source: Adapted from Carl Lyons (2007) *I Win You Win: The Essential Guide to Principled Negotiation* (London: A & C Black), pp. 31–2; and Donna Yena (2015) *Career Directions: New Paths to Your Ideal Career* (6th edn, New York: McGraw-Hill), pp. 21–2.

Interests are the activities you select to do because you enjoy them. Interests also affect most of the choices we make each day. Interests reveal your likes, dislikes, and motivations. For example, do you like individual or group activities? What hobbies, sports, or leisure activities do you enjoy? Some examples of interests are computer games, dancing, listening to music, photography, reading, and traveling. In order to identify your interests, ask yourself a simple question: How do you like to spend your time? Review and complete the self-assessment of your interests provided in Table 2.6.

Table 2.6   Interests self-assessment

Collecting	Exercise/fitness	Painting	Sports
Computer games	History	Photography	Theater
Cooking	Listening to music	Praying	Traveling
Dancing	Movies	Reading	Volunteering
Drawing/sketching	Musical instrument	Social media	Writing

Select the top three interests that you enjoy the most (or add your own). Write them down. Next, carefully evaluate this list of interests and prioritize them in order of their importance to you. Consider how you choose to spend your free time. Are your interests aligned with selling the product/service you represent?

1._____   2._____   3._____

Source: Adapted from Donna Yena (2015) *Career Directions: New Paths to Your Ideal Career* (6th edn, New York: McGraw-Hill), p. 23.

Personality traits are distinguishing qualities or characteristics that belong to you. Your personality is actually the sum of all of your personality traits combined. Some examples of personality traits are: aggressive, confident, compassionate, honest, impulsive, and risk-taker. In order to identify your personality, you might complete a personality assessment test, such as the Myers-Briggs Type Indicator, listed in the Readings and Resources section at the end of this chapter, which organizes four sets of attributes into a matrix of different personality types. These personality types are: Extroversion/Introversion, Sensing/Intuiting, Thinking/Feeling, and Judging/Perceiving. Each personality type receives a four-letter code with a corresponding profile that describes the characteristics common to people who fit into that respective coded category. Review and complete the self-assessment of your personality traits provided in Table 2.7.

Table 2.7   Personality traits self-assessment

Adaptive	Curious	Impulsive	Passive
Aggressive	Defensive	Inspiring	Persistent
Artistic	Empathetic	Loyal	Positive
Compassionate	Enterprising	Moody	Realistic
Confident	Extrovert	Objective	Risk-taker
Consistent	Honest	Open-minded	Selfish
Creative	Humble	Private	Social
		Passionate	Tolerant

Select the top five that you think best describe you (or add your own). Write them down. Next, carefully evaluate your list of personality traits and rank them in order of strength. Are these personality traits an asset or a liability to your selling success?

1. _____   4. _____

2. _____   5. _____

3. _____

Source: Adapted from Donna Yena (2015) *Career Directions: New Paths to Your Ideal Career* (6th edn, New York: McGraw-Hill), p. 25.

Skills are abilities or activities that you can do that you've acquired through training or experience. You have different types of skills, such as technical skills and functional skills. Technical skills are the knowledge and capability to perform specific operational tasks that typically require some hardware knowledge, such as computer, database analysis, or video-conferencing skills, whereas functional skills are typically those that involve interpersonal skills and are transferable from one task to another. Some examples of functional skills are communicating, summarizing, coaching, counseling, planning, and negotiating. In order to identify your skills, ask yourself a simple question: What are you good at doing? Review and complete the functional skills self-assessment provided in Table 2.8.

Table 2.8 Functional skills self-assessment

Collaboration/teamwork	Health/wellness
Creativity/innovation	Information technology application
Critical thinking/problem solving	Language
Diversity	Leadership
Entrepreneurialism	Lifelong learning/self-direction
Ethics/social responsibility	Oral communication
Financial responsibility	Written communication
Globalization	

Select the top three skills that you believe you have developed (or add your own). Write them down. Next, carefully evaluate your list of skills and rank them in order of proficiency. Which skills can be readily applied to selling? Also, consider which skills are most important in selling, and evaluate your competency in those areas. Where do you have opportunities to improve your skills? What professional development might help you to improve?

1. _____   2. _____   3. _____

Source: Adapted from Donna Yena (2015) *Career Directions: New Paths to Your Ideal Career* (6th edn, New York: McGraw-Hill), p. 32.

In addition to the skills outlined in Table 2.8, you should also assess your behavior or social skills. Social skills help you to relate to people, which is often challenging because no two people are exactly the same. People think, act, listen, desire information, make decisions, and solve problems differently. We'll revisit the important concept of the behavior or social styles of customers and prospects in later chapters; however, for now, let's examine these skills as part of your self-assessment.

By exercising effective listening skills, along with being able to read body language and environmental clues, we will be able to determine the different behavior styles of people, which will allow us to modify our communication to be more appropriate to those people with whom we are communicating. Just think, if we can determine how different people want to communicate with us, we can be more effective in asking and answering questions in a manner that resonates with their particular behavior style. However, we must first understand our own social style before we can adjust our communication behavior.

According to Ron Willingham, people can be categorized into the following four behavior styles:[21]

- **Talkers** are outgoing, friendly, affable people who are easy to approach and fun to be with. They buy from people they like and don't want to disappoint others.
- **Doers** are bottom line, get-it-done people who are action-oriented, decisive, and make quick decisions. They crave respect for their achievements and fear anything that slows them down.
- **Controllers** are reserved and distant. They're logical, unemotional, and want facts and accurate information. They are very analytical and well organized and will only make decisions after carefully digesting all of the facts and data.
- **Supporters** are easygoing, steady, dependable, and loyal. They are detail-minded and don't make quick decisions. They are team players and they like predictability and security, while they avoid taking risks.

Which behavior style best describes you? Most people are a combination of two styles, with one being dominant, the other secondary. Review and complete the self-assessment of your behavior/social style provided in Table 2.9.

Table 2.9 Behavior/social style self-assessment

Talkers	Doers	Controllers	Supporters

Next, think seriously about and evaluate how you interact with other people. Do you fit into one of the four behavior style categories, or are you are a combination of two different styles? Which behavior styles best describe your behavior?

Your dominant style: _____

Your secondary style: _____

Understanding your own behavior style, as well as determining your prospect's style are important when building a relationship. When styles are different, you can modify your style to match that of your prospect. By doing this, you will more readily establish rapport and build trust with the prospect.

Source: Adapted from Ron Willingham (2003) *Integrity Selling for the 21st Century* (New York: Random House), pp. 19–20.

One final area for self-assessment is your emotional intelligence. Emotional intelligence refers to your ability to identify, assess, and manage your emotions. If you are able to manage your emotional intelligence well, then you will likely be more effective in working with other people, solving problems, managing stress, and building positive relationships. Your values, interests, and personality all influence your emotional intelligence. However, your value system will predominantly guide your behavior. Complete the self-assessment of your emotional intelligence provided in Table 2.10.

Table 2.10   Emotional intelligence self-assessment

Carefully read each of the 10 questions and honestly evaluate how you respond to different situations. Then, answer each question according to the scale of 1-4, where:

1 = Never; 2 = Sometimes; 3 = Often; 4 = Always

1. I accept suggestions from others graciously. _____
2. I am able to handle criticism well. _____
3. I am even-tempered despite ups and downs. _____
4. I am able to pick myself up quickly after being rejected. _____
5. I can tolerate uncertainty, while feeling only a small amount of stress. _____
6. I can readily replace my negative emotions with positive ones. _____
7. I can be depended on to take charge in emergency situations. _____
8. I become comfortable and respond readily when a new situation arises. _____
9. I exercise strong self-discipline. _____
10. I can control my anger so that it is invisible to others. _____

How do your emotions affect what you think and say to others? How might you manage your emotional reactions in order to develop stronger relationships with other people?

Source: Adapted from Ron Willingham (2003) *Integrity Selling for the 21st Century* (New York: Random House), p. 6; and Donna Yena (2015) *Career Directions: New Paths to Your Ideal Career*, 6th edn (New York: McGraw-Hill), pp. 35–6.

Completing self-assessments will help you to identify those areas where you are in need of development in order to prepare yourself for success in selling. Your personal growth and development are directly affected by your environment. Thus, the people with whom you are surrounded and connected will also assist in your personal preparation for selling. Let's examine your personal and professional networks.

Evaluating your personal and professional networks

There's an old saying, 'It's not what you know, but who you know.' However, in today's modern world, that saying should be rephrased to: 'It's not what you know or who you know, but who knows you.' In preparation for selling, you need to assess your personal and professional networks and determine who knows you and how your reputation is viewed. The connections you have with people transfer to relationships that matter. Keep in mind that people do business with people they respect and like. So, in order to prepare to be successful in selling, you must be certain that your reputation is solid and spotless, and that you have a supportive network. One quick and easy way to evaluate your reputation is to Google yourself to see what information is publicly available that other people can easily locate about you. You may want to scour your social media platforms as well, to see if they contain any information or photos that are less than desirable.

Networking
© Ben Leistensnider/Christopher Newport University

In evaluating your networks, you may want to conduct an inventory. Your personal networks include your family, friends and acquaintances, with their networking value in that precise order. These networks may include:

- family – immediate family members, relatives
- friends – personal friends, family friends, neighbors
- acquaintances – fellow parishioners, church groups, neighborhood associations, community groups
- your professional networks will vary based on the stage you are at in your career. However, these networks may include:
  - school – professors, advisors, mentors, staff members, counselors, classmates, alumni
  - professional colleagues – current and former bosses, current and former co-workers, association members, customers, suppliers, distributors
  - service providers – doctors, dentists, attorneys, hair stylists, nail technicians, trainers, mechanics
  - volunteer connections – internship contacts, community groups, past and present leaders, and associates from all professional segments.

You may want to assess your digital networks as well, since you will have access to a unique network of people on each social media platform to which you belong. Network connections and opportunities vary by each platform, but most will provide you with an outlet to make quality connections. We'll discuss the use of social media platforms for networking and prospecting in Chapter 4, but for now, make a list of the social networks to which you belong, such as LinkedIn, Facebook, Twitter, Instagram, Snapchat, and so on. Do you belong to any chat rooms? If so, be sure to add them to your digital network list.

Evaluating your personal and professional networks is a good way to prepare for successful selling. However, you will also need to prepare for how you plan to engage and interact with each of these networks. That leads us to the topic of professional business etiquette, which is our next section.

Professional business etiquette

Professional business etiquette includes good personal grooming, effective time management, good interpersonal behavior, and good communications skills, including speaking, writing, and listening. Before we explore each of these areas of professional etiquette, a few words of caution are needed: professional business etiquette varies dramatically around the world. For example, in China, you should bring a small gift from your country to meetings, and in Brazil, it's customary to stand very close to the other person and make physical contact to forge a stronger connection and demonstrate trust.[22] Thus, salespeople must conduct research and prepare to accommodate the unique customs, societal norms, and professional etiquette style of customers from each nation. Being prepared in this way can increase your self-confidence and make prospective customers feel more comfortable with you.

Grooming

Professional etiquette is a projection of yourself. Dressing professionally or appropriately for selling is important as it shows respect for and may help you connect with a prospective customer. Remember, you will never have a second chance to make a good first impression. Although industry appropriate dress codes vary, you will never be wrong if

Figure 2.2 Professional dress
Photo courtesy of Alan Witt. Used with permission.

you take the conservative approach to dressing for business. However, there is a difference between business-professional and business-casual dress codes. As shown in Figure 2.2, business-professional dress implies wearing a suit or similar. Of course, if the dress code is business-casual, you can simply remove your tie and unbutton your collar.

DRESS FOR YOUR DAY

Ferguson is a business casual environment, with occasional needs for professional dress. Field associates are expected to dress appropriately for the job, and our "First in Safety" approach requires associates to wear environment appropriate safety equipment and attire.

While certain events or projects may deviate from the business casual standard at Headquarters, it is expected associates dress for their day every day, regardless of work location or activity. Meetings with vendor partners and customers and training events will have different dress requirements, but all associates should wear appropriate attire for their specific work environments.

ACCOMMODATIONS

Human Resources may make a reasonable accommodation to this policy for those with a disability or medical condition.

APPROPRIATE, PROFESSIONAL AND RESPECTFUL

When selecting business casual attire, remember these three words: appropriate, professional and respectful.

Appropriate: Consider the work environment and day's activities. Business casual attire includes nice denim, slacks, open collar/short-sleeved shirts, polos, sports jackets, skirts, sweaters, etc.

Professional: Ensure proper coverage at the neckline, hemline and waistline. Don't confuse "casual" with "sloppy." Inappropriate dress is anything that is distracting or calls attention away from business.

Respectful: Be mindful of professional goals, how you want to be perceived and how your image can impact that. If you question whether it is appropriate, it probably isn't.

Team leaders not only have the authority to, but are expected to, coach associates who struggle with adhering to this policy. As a manager or associate, if at any time you feel a colleague is not dressed appropriately for the workplace and you do not feel comfortable addressing the situation yourself, please contact your HR Business Partner.

INAPPROPRIATE ATTIRE

- Faded, frayed, soiled or torn attire
- Revealing, tight, short, baggy or oversized attire
- Bib overalls, cargo pants or painter's pants
- Casual or athletic shorts
- T-shirts or shirts with messages across the chest or back
- Jogging suits, sweatpants or sweatshirts
- Flip flops

The Ferguson dress code is an evolving policy that will change over time to stay up-to-date with the needs of our associates.

≋ FERGUSON

Figure 2.3 Ferguson Enterprises' dress code policy
Used with kind permission of Ferguson.

While the dress codes at most companies continue to evolve to reflect changing times, some companies provide very specific guidelines about what is permitted for business-casual dressing (see Figure 2.3 for an example). Generally, salespeople should dress to match the dress codes of their prospective customers. Unless otherwise stated, salespeople should always opt for a business-professional appearance when selling.

Beyond proper clothing choices, good grooming also includes the following: polished shoes; belts that match the shoes (leathers go together); socks that match slacks (fabrics go together); conservative ties (no bright purple, orange or pink) (for males); neatly cut hair and conservative colors (if dyed); clean and clipped nails; light fragrances, if any; fresh breath and clean teeth; concealed body art and tattoos; body piercings limited to only one pair of stud earrings; minimal and tasteful jewelry and makeup; and neutral nail polish (for females) and a clean-shaven face (for males). Some industries and companies may permit males to have a mustache or beard when trimmed neatly; however, the general rule is to remove all facial hair.

Time management

Professional etiquette includes managing time effectively. That means being prompt for appointments and meetings, efficiently using the time spent with the customer or prospect, following up after meetings in a timely manner, and responding promptly to any inquiries from prospective customers. If you are going to be late for an appointment due to something uncontrollable to you, such as an automobile accident or a closed highway, be sure to call ahead and offer the prospective customer the option of rescheduling the meeting. If your presentation to the prospective customer is going to run longer than the allotted time, ask for permission to continue and realistically state approximately how much additional time you may need. Don't assume that you may take more time than the prospective customer has allocated to you without prior permission.[23] Lastly, proper etiquette includes taking the time to be of assistance to fellow salespeople within your company, because at times salespeople may have to team up in order to move the prospective customer through the sales funnel.[24]

Interpersonal behavior

Practicing good interpersonal behavior includes many different activities. Here are some good ways salespeople can demonstrate their politeness and polish:

- Sitting down only *after* you've been invited to do so when entering the office of a customer or prospective customer.
- Introducing yourself properly by standing up to greet someone (by shaking hands or using some alternative type of greeting) who enters the office after you've already been seated.
- Standing and moving around to the front of a desk or table if you are seated behind it to greet prospective customers.
- Asking the prospective customer at the conclusion of a meeting for their preferred way to communicate in the future.

- Properly asking for a future meeting by being clear and specific and including details. For example, instead of asking, 'Do you want to get together soon to follow up on our conversation?' which is a bit vague, ask: 'How about we meet next Tuesday at Smith's Coffee Shop at 10:00 in the morning to continue our conversation?' This includes specific details to which the prospective customer can respond or suggest a different day, time, or place that may work better.

- Using proper table manners when business meetings are conducted over meals. Standard etiquette rules for business meals include: waiting for all members of the party to arrive before sitting down at a table, not ordering the most expensive item on the menu, placing your napkin in your lap when you first sit down and not placing it back on the table until the meal has ended, placing keys, briefcases, folders, and handbags on the floor instead of on the table, keeping your elbows off the table, passing dishes counterclockwise, passing both the salt and pepper shakers at the same time, even though the request may only have been for one of the two, using the proper utensils when dining, not taking leftovers home with you, and leaving an adequate and/or appropriate tip.

- Providing proper introductions by knowing whose name to say first when introducing people. Traditionally, the older person's name is always given first to a younger person. For example: 'Mr. Smith (older), please meet Ms. Jones (younger).' The names of those outside of the company are spoken first before company employees; and senior associates are named before junior ones. For example: 'Mr. Smith, please meet my associates, Vice-President Ann Stafford (senior), Department Manager Charles Blanden (middle), and Northwest territory sales representative Jennifer Jones (junior).' Formal names should be used when making introductions and you should keep the introduction brief, as a complete biography of the person is not necessary.[25]

Table etiquette
© Ben Leistensnider/Christopher Newport University.

Lastly, most etiquette rules are not gender-specific, perhaps with the exception that men are typically required to remove their hats when entering buildings. However, please remember, etiquette rules vary by country, so do your homework and adjust your behavior accordingly. There are many good books available on professional business etiquette, such as *The Essentials of Business Etiquette: How to Greet, Eat, and Tweet Your Way to Success* by Barbara Pachter, featured in the Readings and Resources section at the end of this chapter, and everyone should read more about the rules of proper etiquette for their respective country and practice them regularly.

Much of professional etiquette may seem like common sense. However, savvy salespeople pay close attention to etiquette as they know that the soft skills make a difference in selling. It's not just a matter of knowing good manners; it's a matter of treating the prospective customer with decorum, good taste, and respect.[26] In a highly competitive world, those salespeople who possess poise, polish, professionalism, and preparedness are typically the most productive and successful in conversing with prospective customers. Let's now examine some etiquette tips on how to improve in the area of professional communication.

Communication skills

Good conversational skills are essential to establishing rapport with customers and prospects and thus should be practiced and honed. While we'll discuss communication skills in greater detail in Chapter 5, salespeople should *prepare* for conversations by identifying potential topics of interest to their customers and prospects when conducting their research. Preparation should be done in advance for all conversations, whether they take place in person, on the telephone, or via video conferencing. Communication etiquette includes both verbal skills (how you speak and the words you use) and nonverbal skills (eye contact, gestures, posture, body language). Some of the most important techniques to employ when speaking include: prepare what you want to say ahead of speaking, establish and maintain good eye contact, use proper grammar and word choices, avoid jargon or slang, and speak slowly enough to allow for the processing of what you are saying.

Effective body language is also imperative for in-person conversations. Body language is communication conveyed by certain body movements and expressions and includes facial expressions (smiling, eyes widening, winking, frowning, etc.), poise (composure, self-confidence), posture (sitting up or standing straight and still), and mannerisms (using your hands when speaking, rocking back and forth, tapping your foot, etc.).

An important part of effective communication in selling is the ability to actively listen. Active listening will be addressed in greater detail in Chapters 5 and 6; however, it is important that you understand what active listening is and what it entails. Active listening is when you make a concentrated, conscious effort to hear and understand the words and sounds that surround you; then, respond to and remember the conversation. Paying attention and interpreting the meaning of what is being said is required for active listening. The opposite of active listening is passive listening. Passive listening

Active listening

requires limited or no effort as it is merely hearing what is being said, but not concentrating on what it means at all.

Written communication is another important area of professional etiquette. Professional language, proper grammar, and clear and concise messages are imperative for all forms of written communication, including emails, text messages, posts, and tweets. Salespeople need to be mindful to properly time the delivery of relevant online messages to maximize positive communication impact.

Keep in mind that professional business etiquette is a combination of appearance, mannerisms, behaviors, time management, and verbal and written communications. Customers and prospects are more apt to believe and want to work with salespeople who possess professional business etiquette. As described earlier, good etiquette includes being on time for appointments and meetings, efficiently using the time with the customer or prospect, and following up after meetings in a timely manner. Exercising these good time-management skills will foster stronger business relationships. After all, developing good business relationships with customers is the goal of modern selling.

Now that you know what's included in researching and preparing for successful selling, let's explore how you can assess and measure the effectiveness of these activities.

MONITORING METRICS

Though it is sometimes difficult to specify metrics for each activity in the sales planning process, you may evaluate your success on a regular basis by observing whether or not certain steps in a process were completed or objectives were accomplished. For

Monitoring metrics

example, when monitoring a database or CRM, you can determine how well all customers have been entered into the system. The formula to calculate the percentage of all customers that were logged into the system is: (#customers entered/#total customers) x 100 = %. You may also monitor how often the database is being updated by each user, department, or product line, if consumer touchpoints have been recorded, the number or percentage of consumers at any given stage in the selling process, and so on.

If salespeople record each prospective customer's completion of each of the five stages of the customer journey, the data can be aggregated to reveal the stage at which the majority of consumers are at any given point in time. This can raise awareness of the need to shift more customers from retention to advocacy, to foster future sales. Likewise, if salespeople record whether or not each prospective customer meets the four BANT criteria (budget, authority, needs, timeline), an assessment can be made of which criteria are most often missing when sales do not come to fruition.

As for monitoring your progress with personal preparation, you can measure your progress by answering the assessment questions on a regular basis, using a rating scale such as: most of the time (75–100%) = 4; half of the time (50–74%) = 3; less than half of the time (26–49%) = 2; rarely (0–25% of the time) = 1. The self-assessment questions may include:

1. How often was I able to correctly determine the behavioral type of each prospect or customer?
2. How often was I able to make a good first impression with prospective customers?
3. How often was I able to establish rapport within the first two interactions with a new prospect?
4. How often have I dressed appropriately when interacting with prospects and customers?
5. How often have I been able to actively or proactively listen to prospects?
6. How often have I been able to actively or proactively listen to existing customers?

It is important to note that these questions may also be framed in a negative manner. For example: How often was I unable to make a good first impression? This is helpful when the desired behavior occurs most of the time. The rating scale would then be changed to cover the range of the expected results. You may create additional metrics to assess other behaviors, reflecting areas in which you're working to improve.

CHAPTER SUMMARY

✓ Study existing customers to determine the touchpoints best used to reach prospects.

✓ Apply lead research, influencer marketing and data analyses to target potential prospects.

✓ Consider the political, geographic, demographic, social, psychographic and behavior factors relevant to your prospect before interacting; and document your findings.

✓ Perform a self-assessment of your values, interests, personality traits, knowledge, and skills; and apply new insights to improve your selling process. Know and follow proper business etiquette at all times.

KEY TERMS

Active listening
Appeal
Beliefs
Body language
Business environment
Buyer journey
Channel
Consumer touchpoints
Cookie
Customer journey
Customer journey map
Demographics
Emotional appeal
Emotional intelligence
Geographic information system (GIS)
Global positioning system (GPS)
Inbound calls
Influencer marketing
Influencer theory

Interests
Nonverbal skills
Offer
Organizational consumers
Outbound calls
Passive listening
Power
Psychographics
Rational appeal
Reference groups
Reference individual
Self-assessment
Suspect
Unique selling proposition (USP)
Values
Verbal skills
Web scraping
Web scraping API (WSAPI)

REVIEW QUESTIONS

1. What does the acronym BANT stand for? How can you vet the information determined using BANT data?
2. Compare and contrast the profile factors that apply to B2C and B2B customers.
3. What is web scraping and what data can it provide to aid in selling?
4. Describe the stages of the customer journey.
5. What is a customer journey map and why is it created?
6. What is the appeal of an offer? What are the types of appeals and under what conditions is it appropriate to use each?
7. Why is self-assessment considered preparation for selling? Which areas or characteristics are important to explore during a self-assessment?
8. How do networks affect your ability to sell? Give three examples of each of the three types of networks.
9. What etiquette guidelines should be followed for making introductions when meeting with prospective customers and others from your company?
10. Explain the differences between active and passive listening.

ETHICS IN ACTION

1. While conducting research on the Web for sales leads, you come across information with names, email addresses, and phone numbers for customers of a competitor's product. It is obvious that this data was not purposefully shared on the Web. What will you do with this information?

2. You have a well-established relationship with the buyer of a loyal B2B customer. The buyer tells you sensitive information about an upcoming leadership change that will significantly alter the company's direction and buying strategy. Past leadership's primary goal was high quality; however, future leadership's main focus is immediate cost reduction. What will you do with this information?

EXERCISE

Congratulations! You've been hired by your *favorite* professional sports team to sell corporate sponsorship packages. Your first activity is to conduct research on prospective corporate sponsors. For this exercise, you may select your favorite sport and your favorite professional team, and then determine the research needed in order to prepare for this opportunity. Describe the following:

(Continued)

a. a profile of your prospective corporate sponsors
b. your offer/value proposition
c. the list of features and benefits for becoming a corporate sponsor of the team
d. the desired unique selling proposition (USP) that you should use when preparing for the needs discovery conversation (NDC) with your prospect
e. possible personal network connections who might assist you in connecting with prospective corporate sponsors.

READINGS AND RESOURCES

- Max Altschuler (2016) *Hacking Sales: The Playbook for Building a High-Velocity Sales Machine.* Hoboken, NJ: John Wiley & Sons, Inc.
- Shannon Belew (2014) *The Art of Social Selling: Finding and Engaging Customers on Twitter, Facebook, LinkedIn, and other Social Networks.* New York: AMACOM.
- Mahan Khalsa and Randy Illig (2008) *Let's Get Real or Let's Not Play: Transforming the Buyer/Seller Relationship.* New York: Portfolio/Penguin Group.
- Myers-Briggs Personality Test: www.themyersbriggs.com/en-US/Products-and-Services/ Myers-Briggs.
- Frederick Reichheld (2001) *The Loyalty Effect.* Brighton, MA: Harvard Business School Press.
- Ron Willingham (2003) *Integrity Selling for the 21st Century.* New York: Doubleday.

CASE STUDY: HOMEFRONTS BY PAULA

Paula Kosko is a trained graphic designer who worked for print companies and later for herself in her own graphic design business. The greeting card line she has developed, with help from her sister, is called Homefronts by Paula. Digitally produced, the images faithfully replicate the elegance of a pen and ink or watercolor artwork. (See Figure 2.4 for two sample designs of Homefronts by Paula.)

Paula has created a website, HomefrontsDesigns.com, where customers may place orders for custom Homefronts' design cards and prints. However, she cannot rely on her website alone to attract customers. She plans to proactively sell Homefronts' cards in order to develop long-term business relationships with organizational clients.

Paula has quickly realized that as an entrepreneur, she's spending a major portion of her time and effort involved in the sales process – especially, researching and preparing for selling. Like all entrepreneurs, Paula performs many different roles. She's a business owner, sales manager, business developer, production supervisor, graphic designer, quality controller, accountant, salesperson, and customer service representative. Regardless of whether these different roles are performed by many different people or just one entrepreneur, they are critical to a successful sales model for a business. The functions and activities associated with all of these roles must be carried out with

Homefronts Sample A - Dickenson Law

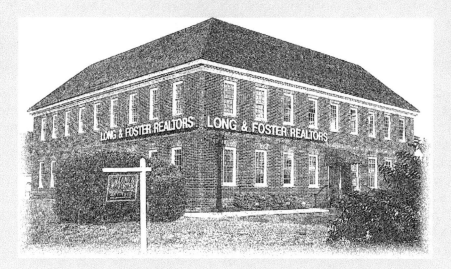

Homefronts Sample B - Long & Foster pen & ink

Figure 2.4 Sample Homefronts' card designs
Used with kind permission of Paula Kosko.

the needs and wants of prospective customers in mind, which requires a great deal of research and preparation.

Prospective business customers for Homefronts' cards could be anyone interested in purchasing business notecards or stationery customized with a rendering of their office building or campus facilities, including builders, contractors, Realtors, businesses, churches, schools, hospitals, and so on. However, based on initial research, Paula has identified a few specific types of prospects (bed-and-breakfast (B&B)

businesses, wedding venues, and Realtors) on which she plans to concentrate her initial prospecting activities.

In preparing to approach these targeted prospective businesses, Paula must conduct additional research. Her background research includes investigating the specific needs, wants, and interests of each of these different types of prospects in order to craft the most effective offer or value proposition that would appeal to each prospective client. Additional professional preparation includes profiling these three types of prospects, identifying the key benefits that each one is seeking, examining their typical buying journey, and determining the touchpoints where she can interact with these different prospects.

For example, when selling to B&B businesses, Paula must first explore how many of these unique businesses exist in any select geographic region, their different geographical locations, ownership information, and the potential uses they may have for Homefronts' cards. Once her initial background research is completed, she may contact several B&B businesses to further explore their needs and to determine whether there is an interest in learning more about her Homefronts' cards. Paula is creating awareness about Homefronts, building relationships, and gathering additional research on a one-to-one basis during this preparation stage of the selling process. Of course, she eventually hopes to be able to move interested prospects through the sales funnel with additional information provided by in-person or virtual sales presentations, via email or postal mail, or directing interested prospects to her website. Paula will need to use a number of different touchpoints in order to successfully sell her entrepreneurial notecards to B&B businesses. Each prospective customer will determine the manner by which they want to be contacted, which will determine the particular touchpoints Paula uses.

In conclusion, entrepreneurial selling is all about building relationships. In order to effectively build relationships with prospective buyers, entrepreneurs must spend much time researching and understanding the needs and wants of prospective customers. Selling entrepreneurial products and services requires preparation, passion, patience, and persistence. Most entrepreneurs are their own very best salespersons. So, if you're planning to own your own business one day, welcome to the wonderful world of selling!

Case questions:

1. What process should Paula use when converting the various features of her custom notecards into benefits for prospective business customers? How can she determine the unique selling proposition (USP) for a given type of prospective business customer?
2. What potential consumer touchpoints should Paula use in her attempt to sell Homefronts by Paula to prospective B&B businesses?
3. How might Paula use digital technology to improve on the manner in which she gathers background research on her prospective business customers?

NOTES

1. www.vocabulary.com, retrieved September 16, 2020.
2. Megan Ranger (2018) 'How Many Touchpoints Does It Take to Close a Sale?' www.nimble.com/blog/touchpoints-sales-funnel, retrieved June 5, 2020.
3. Ibid.
4. USGS, 'What is a Geographic Information System (GIS)?', www.usgs.gov/faqs/what-a-geographic-information-system-gis?qt-news_science_=&qt-news_science_products=0#qt-news_science_products, retrieved September 22, 2019.
5. ESRI, 'Who We Are', www.esri.com/en-us/about/about-esri/who-we-are, retrieved September 22, 2019.
6. Stacy DeBroff, '5 Must-Have Elements for Influencer Marketing Sales Success,' *Promotional Marketing* (November 2016), p. 1.
7. Al Gini (2010) 'Moral leadership and business ethics,' in G.R. Hickman (ed.), *Leading Organizations: Perspectives for a New Era* (2nd edn, pp. 345–55). Thousand Oaks, CA: Sage, p. 352.
8. Ibid.
9. Angela Spranger, personal communication, September 12, 2020.
10. Mike Kunkel, 'The Untapped Power of Sales Discovery Skills' (April 18, 2015), www.mikekunkle.com/2015/04/18/sales-discovery-skills, retrieved September 13, 2020.
11. Ritu Banerjee (2014) 'Website Scraping' (White Paper), http://hminds.campaigntemplate.com/whitepapers/website-scraping.pdf, retrieved June 10, 2020.
12. Ibid.
13. Luca Tagliaferro (2019) 'Data Scraping Tools for Marketers Who Don't Know Code', https://searchengineland.com/data-scraping-tools-for-marketers-who-dont-know-code-319446, retrieved June 10, 2020.
14. Max Altschuler (2016) 'Hacking Sales: The playbook for building a high-velocity sales machine' (ebook), pp. 10–11, retrieved June 10, 2020.
15. Ibid.
16. Angela Spranger, personal communication, September 12, 2020.
17. Ibid.
18. Ibid.
19. Charles Green 'Why Listening to Sales Experts May Be Hazardous to Your Sales,' (2017), https://trustedadvisor.com/trustmatters/why-listening-to-sales-experts-may-be-hazardous-to-your-sales, August 14, retrieved September 12, 2020.
20. Ron Willingham (2003) *Integrity Selling for the 21st Century* (New York: Random House), p. 1.
21. Ibid., pp. 32–4.

22. Aja Frost, 'Business Etiquette: The ultimate guide', https://blog.hubspot.com/sales/business-etiquette, retrieved July 16, 2020.
23. Dave Kahle, 'Seven ways to build rapport with anyone', *American Fastener Journal* (November/December 2016), 32(6), 64–5.
24. Brian Hill (2020) 'Do's and Don'ts for Sales People Etiquette,' https://smallbusiness.chron.com/dos-donts-sales-people-etiquette-52520.html, retrieved July 16, 2020.
25. Patricia M. Buhler, 'Business etiquette: A renewed interest in a lost art,' *American Salesman* (October 2019), 64(10), 13–16.
26. Michael Adams, 'Charm school,' *Sales and Marketing Management* (April 1996), 148(4), 72.

3

PLANNING STRATEGICALLY FOR SUCCESSFUL SELLING

CHAPTER CONTENTS

THE FOUNDATIONS: 'ON THE GROUND'

PEOPLE, PRACTICES AND PERSPECTIVES FROM THE WORLD OF SALES

Greetings from India. My name is Rajarshi Dey Sarkar, and I'm a regional business director for Novo Nordisk India Pvt Limited, leading the business in Eastern India and Bhutan. I have been supporting doctors, nurses and pharmacists in this position for the past six years. *I believe that winning the trust of the customer is the key to successful and consistent sales. Good planning and execution, along with strong product knowledge, a well-practiced sales talk, and respect for customers are vital to developing trust. I describe successful sales persons as 'RAP': resilient, assertive, and passionate.*

Hello, I'm Arthur Harpen, an account executive for Splunk in Washington, DC. I have seven years of experience in sales, progressing through numerous positions serving organizational customers (B2B.) *I've found that preparation, effort and developing a process will help you control what you can and earn your success. Inevitably, there will be things you can't control.* Consider this quote: 'Far better it is to dare mighty things, to win glorious triumphs, even though checkered by failure, than to take rank with those poor spirits who neither enjoy much nor suffer much, because they live in the gray twilight that knows neither victory nor defeat' (Teddy Roosevelt.) Hi. My name is Teddy Pekalski and I'm the senior director of sales for IMC in Vienna, Virginia. I lead a sales team of seven individuals, primarily focused on B2B CPG manufacturers. *To me, sales is a numbers game that requires you to break your annual KPIs into daily and weekly goals that are easy to measure and digest. This helps you to hit those goals every day!* Here's a quote for you: 'Setting goals is the first step in turning the invisible into the visible' (Tony Robbins.)

Long-term success begins with a plan.

EYES ON ETHICS

Keep in mind the following ethical topics as you read through this chapter:

1. Dealing with data that does not support your hypothesis.
2. Responding to an RFP for personal reasons more than professional ones.

INTRODUCTION

In Chapter 1, we described the plethora of digital sales tools available for salespeople to use in today's modern business world. Indeed, hundreds of tools, platforms, devices, and dashboards are now available to capture, analyze, and present data. The result of this digital transformation is the abundance and availability of data. Unfortunately, more isn't always better as salespeople may quickly become overwhelmed and find themselves drowning in the sea of data. Today, what salespeople really need is solid insight or intelligence that is procured from the data to use in actionable ways to strategically plan for successful selling. That is the subject of this chapter. We'll examine the topics of business intelligence, goals and objectives, account planning, business development, and the assessment of strategic planning activities for selling.

How can salespeople achieve success without developing a plan and setting goals to do so? Perhaps luck may enter into the success equation, but they shouldn't count on it. Savvy salespeople ensure their selling success with solid strategic planning based on relevant information. Digital sales tools can produce data, but information gathered from these tools alone isn't enough. Salespeople must understand the 'big picture' of the dynamic environment in which they are operating. This environment includes data about customers and prospects; a company's products, services, brands, and reputation; industry and trends; competitors; supplier networks; and company mission, scope, goals, objectives, and more. Salespeople rely on business intelligence in order to fully understand and operate effectively in their ever-changing environment. Let's explore the concept of business intelligence.

BUSINESS INTELLIGENCE

Business intelligence (BI) is gathering, evaluating, and distributing descriptive information to help make decisions for an organization. BI leverages digital tools to transform data into actional insights that inform an organization's strategic and tactical business decisions.[1] Digital BI tools are used to obtain and analyze data and present analytical findings in easy-to-digest spreadsheets, reports, summaries, dashboards, graphs, charts, and maps to provide salespeople with detailed insight.

Digital charts

It's important to note that business intelligence differs from business analytics in that intelligence is *descriptive* (it summarizes what's happened in the past and what's happening in the present), while analytics is *predictive* (uses past and present data to anticipate trends and outcomes that will happen in the future) and *prescriptive* (it suggests what you should be doing to create better outcomes).[2] Thus, while BI may not tell salespeople what to do or what will happen if they take a certain course of action, it will allow them to examine data to understand trends and derive insights by streamlining the effort needed to search for, merge, and query the data necessary to make sound business decisions.[3] Given that technology is always evolving, Gartner predicts that BI may soon be merged with analytics. This trend is referred to as 'augmented analytics' and it entails machine learning to be infused in the software which will be able to guide users on their queries into the data.[4] BI enables better decision making to occur by producing timely data about the business environment. Let's now investigate the different types of information that BI will produce.

Exploring types of business intelligence

Business intelligence includes information at both the individual salesperson level and the larger, organizational level. BI includes everything from customer analysis to competitive intelligence to business performance management. Some of the specific types of BI include:[5]

- **Customer intelligence** – obtaining data on the characteristics and behaviors of customers and prospects, and to facilitate finding, attracting, and engaging with them, as well as retaining them.
- **Financial intelligence** – collecting and using financial data to generate insights that lead to increased cash flow, profitability, growth, value, and productivity.
- **Competitive intelligence** – anticipating and obtaining information about competitors or the competitive environment that can be utilized as an input to strategic decision making and to develop a competitive edge.
- **Strategic intelligence** – understanding the company's vision, mission, values, strengths, weaknesses, goals, and plans for future success, and communicating these critical success factors with others to encourage organization-wide collaboration while working toward mutual goals.
- **Data intelligence** – creating and communicating easily understood, organization-wide measures, processes, procedures, and systems that promote teamwork and collaboration.

Salespeople can enhance their performance by using data from multiple BI sources, including sales transactions, customer relationship management (CRM) systems, inventory applications, and competitor tracking. BI places 'real time' information at the fingertips of salespeople so that they have valuable insight whenever and wherever they need it. For example, when salespeople are on the telephone or meeting with customers in person, they may have a need to quickly access customer order histories from across all sales channels. BI empowers salespeople with this information with just a few clicks. Salespeople benefit from the ease and availability of intelligence; however, they may also play a critical role in gathering valuable BI as they are on the 'front line' of the organization, interacting with customers and prospects on a regular basis. BI is not a static tool, but rather, it represents a dynamic, iterative cycle that requires salespeople to constantly reevaluate changing conditions. Organizing, synthesizing, and sharing intelligence in a user-friendly manner so that it is actionable for salespeople, are challenging and require ongoing effective communication and collaboration throughout the entire organization.

Computer screen

Examining uses of business intelligence

The potential uses of business intelligence are unlimited and they certainly extend beyond the typical business performance metrics of improved sales and reduced costs. The uses of BI include:

- keeping track of new customer acquisition
- reporting on customer retention
- generating sales reports from customer relationship management (CRM) data
- producing delivery reports
- creating a dashboard to show where prospects are on the sales funnel
- presenting data on salespeople productivity on some incremental basis (daily, weekly, monthly, quarterly, annually, etc.)
- gaining insight into a sales promotion
- revealing which sales promotion worked best with which vendor
- updating 'real-time' sales metrics on product categories
- distinguishing between top- and bottom-selling products or brands.

Data is growing in both volume and complexity; thus, salespeople must learn to cut through the clutter of daily data and collect only 'useful' information that provides needed insight in serving their customers. There are five criteria that salespeople may use for judging the usefulness of information. These criteria are:

1. **Accuracy** – the degree to which the information reflects reality.
2. **Availability** – the degree to which the information is accessible when needed.
3. **Sufficiency** – the degree to which there is enough information available.
4. **Currency** – the degree to which the information is recent and up to date.
5. **Relevancy** – the degree to which the information is pertinent and applies to the situation.

While all five criteria are important to use in evaluating the usefulness of data, the most important criterion is *relevancy*. Regardless of whether or not the information

Examining data

is current, accurate, and available, it will not be applicable or helpful in the decision-making process if it is not relevant.

Business intelligence software is only as good as the people who use it. Salespeople must master the digital tools for fishing relevant data from the river of constantly moving information, and channeling the stream of useful information that is of strategic and tactical value to their selling activities. Business intelligence is useful information that can assist salespeople in making decisions pertaining to setting goals and objectives as well, which is the topic of the next section.

GOALS AND OBJECTIVES

Salespeople using business intelligence must first have a complete understanding of what they are trying to accomplish – which are their goals – before they can make good business decisions. Business intelligence is the tool that helps salespeople make good decisions while executing their strategies to reach their goals. Salespeople are trying to achieve a number of sales goals or desired outcomes at any given point in time. Some examples are goals established for qualified sales leads, sales calls, sales volume, profitability, new client accounts, customer retention, customer service, and sales territory coverage. These sales goals usually motivate individual salesperson performance, both in the office and out in the field. However, all goals are not the same. Let's explore the different types of goals.

Distinguishing between types of goals

There are different types of goals that salespeople may establish. They include:

- Short-term goals – these goals are those incremental activities that salespeople desire to accomplish in a time period of one year or less. *Example: Secure three new client accounts during the third quarter of this fiscal year.*
- Long-term goals – these goals specify future accomplishments and they normally have a time period of 1–10 years, with five years being the norm, for the desired outcome to be achieved. *Example: Penetrate at least three new sales territories within the next five years.*
- Milestone goals – these goals are major accomplishments or benchmarks along the way to reaching long-term goals. Milestone goals may also be considered short-term goals. *Example: Obtain 20 qualified leads each month during the first quarter of this fiscal year.*
- Individual goals – these goals are specific personal outcomes a salesperson desires to achieve, as opposed to company-wide goals. *Example: Complete my digital certification training by the end of this calendar year.*
- SMART goals – SMART stands for specific, measurable, achievable, realistic, and timebound. These goals are challenging, but realistic, and include timelines by which they must be achieved. SMART goals are phrased in terms of outcomes, not actions. *Example: Achieve sales volume of $800,000 by the end of this fiscal year.*

For salespeople, SMART goals are the most effective type of goals to establish because they are very specific and enable progress to be measured and tracked. Smart salespeople will make each of their goals SMART, regardless of whether the goal is being set for themselves, an account, their company, or an entire sales territory. Check out Table 3.1 to see how SMART goal statements provide much greater clarity than other types of goal statement.

Table 3.1 Vague versus SMART goal statements

Vague	SMART
To increase company sales revenues	To increase sales revenue of brand X in each territory by 10 percent this fiscal year over last year
To increase product sales	To sell 10 percent more volume of product X in each territory during the third quarter compared with the second quarter of the current fiscal year
To generate new customers	To acquire five new B2B customer accounts per sales team in October of the current fiscal year
To improve company communications	To implement a new company-wide communications system and complete and document beta testing of each interface in the system by the end of the fiscal year
To introduce a new product	To provide 500 samples of product X to the residents of 12 specified urban markets by the end of the fiscal year
To improve the storytelling capabilities of our staff	To hold five weekly training sessions for all sales associates hired in the past 12 months, on the topic of storytelling and to obtain two manager-approved customer success stories from each of these sales associates by the end of the fiscal year

Salespeople should place all of their goals in writing and share them with anyone who may be affected by or contributing to them. In addition, by sharing written goals with others, salespeople may be held accountable to achieve their goals, which often serves as additional motivation.

Exploring the relationship between goals and objectives

Goals specify the desired outcomes to be achieved. By setting goals, salespeople can plan and prioritize their work activities, including how to effectively manage their time. Objectives are sub-goals that are smaller and more easily attained. For every goal established, there may be two or three objectives that will need to be achieved in order to reach the overall goal. Objectives are similar to milestone goals as they are benchmarks that demonstrate progress toward a long-term goal. Of course, in order to reach stated goals and objectives, strategies need to be employed. A strategy is a course of action or an action plan that details what activity needs to occur in order to achieve an objective. Several specific strategies may need to be implemented in order to accomplish an objective. Once again, salespeople must plan and prioritize their action plans since their time is a limited resource. Lastly, in implementing strategies, salespeople need resources or tools, which are referred to as tactics. Salespeople may employ a variety of tactics when implementing their strategies. Useful information, obtained via business intelligence, is one of the most valuable resources salespeople can use to support their selling activities. Other tactics include financial resources and human resources.

Figure 3.1 shows the relationship between goals, objectives, strategies, and tactics. Every customer and sales situation brings unique challenges for salespeople. Therefore, salespeople must constantly update, modify, or alter their action plans according to the changing needs of their customers. Note that making progress toward goals is an ongoing activity for salespeople, and requires the regular modification of strategies and tactics.

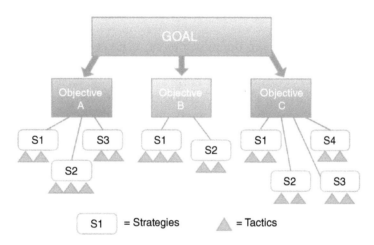

Figure 3.1 Strategy flowchart

Of course, it's important to differentiate between results that salespeople may not be able to directly control versus those that they can directly control. For example, a goal with a measurable result of 'establishing three new accounts in six months' is only partly under the control of salespeople. Compare this to a goal with a measurable result that is entirely under the direct control of salespeople, such as 'dialing the telephone at least 25 times per day' or 'sending out at least 25 emails or text messages to prospective customers per day.' Salespeople can completely control the second goal, but not the first. Now, the number 25 was achieved by 'back solving' from the resulting goal of three new accounts in six months. For this example, back solving includes referencing metrics from prior experience for each of the following questions:

1. How many proposals are typically needed to obtain three new accounts?
2. How many meetings/discussions with prospects are typically needed to be able to present a proposal to the prospective customer?

3. How many telephone calls traditionally need to be made (or text messages, or emails sent) to find a prospect willing to have a discussion meeting?
4. How many dialing attempts does the salesperson usually have to make to connect with one prospect?

This back-solving process thus results in the number of 'dials' of the telephone (or text messages/emails) that salespeople can anticipate needing to make (which is in their total control) to meet the desired goal of three new accounts in six months. This provides a sequencing framework that can be adjusted up or down for the number of dials if the actual results differ from the anticipated number. This process is ALWAYS a trial-and-error one; however, it helps to set an expectation of the resources and time needed to get the desired results. This is a significant improvement over just doing 'more' dials and hoping for the result of three new accounts in a given time period.

Salespeople must always keep their customers at the center of each and every strategic decision that they make as they strive to reach their goals, fulfill their business vision, and uphold the core values or guiding principles of their respective company. In the next section, we'll explore how salespeople can actively partake in account planning initiatives to better serve their customers.

ACCOUNT PLANNING

Once salespeople have gathered the relevant business intelligence and have determined their goals, objectives, strategies, and tactics, what do they do with all of this valuable information? They create an account plan, of course! An account plan is the output or document that is created on the basis of the account planning process. Account plans may range in length from a single page to an entire report. Keep in mind that plans are nothing; it's the *process* of planning that is of critical importance. Account planning is a company-wide collaborative effort toward conducting in-depth assessments of current relationships and activity with customers, as well as with future prospects, to determine where value can be added. In other words, account planning is the integrated effort to create a synergy among the entire organization based on the intelligence gathered, in order to help solve the problems of customers.

The roles of the people involved in the account planning process vary depending on the company; however, normally the account team includes senior sales management, salespeople, and customers. In addition, some companies will include strategic partners or industry experts in their account planning process. Account planning can and should be conducted at both upper and lower levels of a company; thus, individual salespeople should be actively involved in account planning. However, since the primary role and value of most salespeople is to be out in the field selling, most companies streamline their account planning process to keep it simple and efficient for salespeople.

Planning meeting with client

For example, Rachel Judy, a field sales representative at Boston Scientific, a manufacturer of medical devices with locations in 40 countries around the world, is responsible for creating and managing an account planning system for each one of her 15 accounts (physician offices) in her sales territory. However, her corporate team at Boston Scientific is also actively conducting account planning at the corporate level. Involving customers or clients in account planning is an additional opportunity for salespeople to reinforce business relationships while out in the field.

Account planning originated in the United Kingdom in 1965 and spread to the United States and beyond in the early 1980s.[6] Account planning has been practised for more than 50 years as part of a multi-billion pound, dollar, euro, and yen marketing communications industry.[7] While account planning technically began in the advertising industry, it is now a critical practice within the strategic planning cycle of most high-performing sales organizations.[8]

Account planning is really all about producing strategies that provide innovative solutions to meet the needs of customers to strengthen relationships and grow the account value. Account plans also provide a structure to help salespeople determine what's important and what's not when pursuing customers and prospects.[9] Thus, account planning can help salespeople to determine which accounts to focus on for growth and development and which to resign. Those involved in account planning should take into consideration the Pareto principle, which states that 80 percent of your business typically comes from the top 20 percent of your accounts. Thus, salespeople must recognize the worth of each account and allocate their valuable resources, especially their time, accordingly. Not all accounts are alike, thus different types of account plan are needed. Let's consider the different types of account plan.

Investigating different types of account plan

Mark Donnolo, author of *Essential Account Planning*, one of the Readings and Resources listed at the end of this chapter, states that there are four different types of account plan. According to Donnolo, these are:[10]

1. **Strategic** – this is the most common type of account plan which is created and used for large, complex accounts that are usually national or global in scope. Strategic account plans are designed for growth and development. These plans are developed for high revenue-generating accounts that require large account teams and much buy-in on the part of the contributors to the plan.
2. **Tactical** – this is a simplified version of a strategic account plan that is used for mid-sized accounts that require shorter and less comprehensive plans. Tactical plans are commonly used by companies that sell all products or services through a transactional sales process. These plans are appropriate for companies that generate the bulk of their revenue from mid-sized accounts.
3. **Aspirational** – this type of account plans focuses on game-changing growth. Unlike the other types of account plan, aspirational account plans do not plan incrementally, rather they begin with a long-term goal or vision. For example, instead of planning for 10 percent growth each year for the next five years, these plans state an increase in revenue of 50 percent by a specified date. These plans often require the account team to seek out partners in order to reach the aspirational goal(s) established.
4. **Pursuit** – this type of account plan is designed for new customers. While it has the same basic structure of a strategic account plan, obviously it does not contain the same amount of history or performance details. Pursuit account plans require more ongoing effort to gather the needed research since a prior relationship doesn't exist.

Here's a good example of *strategic* account planning. Computer giant Hewlett-Packard Co., which does business in more than 100 countries, requires a robust sales process that can accommodate cultural diversity, local requirements, and the varying experience levels of its sales teams. Account planning at Hewlett-Packard Co. is used to aggregate information into a clear view of expected business over a specified period of time, such as one to three years.[11] According to Jeff Schmidt, worldwide account business planning lead at Hewlett-Packard Co.: 'with the assistance of talented HP staff in each region, we've successfully re-engineered the company's account planning process, making it one of our strongest tools for driving breakthrough thinking and finding growth opportunities.'[12] Using a clear vision and a flexible planning model with globally consistent templates and timelines, the results have been excellent. During the first year of account planning implementation, the number of account plans submitted by account managers increased from 50 to 1,500.[13]

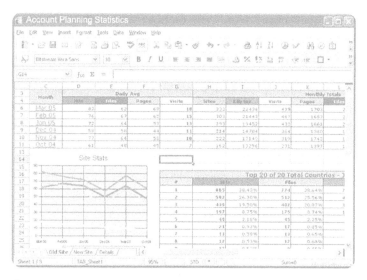

Planning reports
Screenshot of Microsft Excel used with permission from Microsoft.

Account planning leads to increased accountability, improved sales performance, and more satisfied customers when implemented effectively. Now let's examine what is included in the account planning process.

Examining the components of account plans

Account planning entails mini-strategic plans to be created for each customer or prospect. The actual content of the plan will vary based on the company, the customer, and the type of plan being created. Check out the Cooper International case study at the end of this chapter for an example of an account plan. In general, account plans typically include the following seven components:[14]

1. **Profile and position**. This section should include data such as the history of the account, including the strategic relationship with the customer and past transactions; key customer values, needs and goals; and the competitive landscape.
2. **Needs mapping and alignment**. This section describes customer needs and the manner by which your company will align itself to serve this customer. The section may include a summary of how your account team will use its resources to provide value to the customer in a dynamic business environment.
3. **Goals and objectives**. This section details the goals and objectives for the account. These include benchmarks or milestones that the account team plans to accomplish for the customer.
4. **Action plan**. This section details the strategies or courses of action that the account team needs to implement in order to achieve account milestones and goals.

5. **Team support**. This section details the tactics for how the company needs to come together in order to support the account plan. The section identifies tools for implementing the strategies and performing the activities needed in order to reach the specified account goals. These tactics may include internal commitments as well as the external uncontrollable variables that need to be addressed.

6. **Performance dashboard**. This section includes a dashboard to record the metrics and measurements that track the account team progress, along with help to identify any revisions that may be needed to better serve the customer.

7. **Organizational structure/Title search and assessment**. This section should include all of the known (and unknown) people at the target account that will be involved in the buying decision as either decision makers and/or influencers. Not only is it best to actually draw an organizational chart schematic, but also to fill in as many titles and names as are known at any one time; along with reporting structure, knowledge of the people in the various roles, and their level or degree of support (advocate/neutral/inhibitor) for the proposed account plan for the company. Of course, when this is first created there will be many open boxes on the organizational chart, as well as unknowns for who is against (inhibitors) and who is for (advocates) the proposed account plan. These open boxes and unknowns should be completed while developing and presenting the plan to the account. This then allows the account team to more directly focus their contact meetings so as to complete the 'advocate/neutral/inhibitor' account sales team organizational structure chart.

New digital sales tools have become available to assist those involved in account planning to contribute to account plans and collaborate with one another throughout the account planning process. For example, Salesforce partner Altify now offers features, such as TeamView dashboards, that track status against opportunity plans for all accounts from early deal qualification to the development and execution of mutual close plans.[15] Keep in mind, even with modern digital tools, that the best account plans are worthless if they are not used to serve customer needs. Of course, in order to be relevant, account plans must also be regularly revised and updated to adapt to the inevitable changes that will occur in each customer's needs and position.

Account plans may be used by members of the account team or even by anyone throughout the entire company who may have a role in strengthening customer relationships and serving the needs of customers. Account plans may be used to determine relevant offers and promotional message content, develop effective promotional materials and need-satisfying sales proposals, create portfolios, craft sales scripts, and compose relevant stories and customer testimonials. Account plans may also be used to drive new customers, which is commonly referred to as business development. That's the topic of the next section.

BUSINESS DEVELOPMENT

All salespeople seek to grow their business by acquiring more customers, however not all prospective customers are a good match for what they are offering. Helping to evaluate the goodness of fit of prospective customers is where business development merges with the selling process. Although the specific role and function may vary by company and industry, traditionally business development encompasses the tasks of generating new business opportunities for salespeople. It's important to note that in some companies, especially smaller sized ones, salespeople perform their own business development tasks and activities. However, in many larger companies where business development activities are separated and not handled by salespeople, business development representatives are responsible for qualifying leads and prospecting through existing business accounts to engage with prospective buyers.[16] So, think of business development as *prospecting* for new customers, which, in and of itself, is not a *selling* activity.

We'll discuss prospecting and qualifying leads in much greater detail in Chapter 4, but for now, think of business development staff as performing the first part of the sales process and salespeople performing the second part. When the two parts come together effectively, they create a synergy where the output is much greater than the sums of its parts. In other words, business development representatives run the first leg of the relay race and then pass the baton to salespeople who sprint to the finish line by nurturing the relationship and ultimately closing the sale and obtaining commitment. Let's now explore the activities involved in business development and how they are similar yet different from selling.

Person working at computer screen

Analyzing business development activities

Business development representatives perform valuable activities such as making cold calls, sending emails, and leading high-level discovery calls with prospects in order to book sales appointments for salespeople to follow up. While business development activities commonly fall under the sales umbrella at most companies, these may divert the focus of salespeople from selling. Salespeople sell. Traditionally, salespeople close deals, obtain agreements, and create customers. Business development representatives do not close deals. Instead, business development supports the activities of salespeople so they can spend more of their time out in the field doing what they do best – selling. So, the main differentiator between salespeople and business development representatives is whether or not they close deals.

Business development representatives spend time qualifying leads for salespeople, so that salespeople will have greater success in closing a sale and earning a commitment. Salespeople must be able to assess the 'urgency' and 'capability' of the sales lead in order to make a decision on how to proceed. Without clearly assessing urgency and capability, salespeople cannot differentiate easily between the 'suspects' who they think *should* ultimately become customers from those that actually *will*. We will describe how to assess these urgency and capability factors further in Chapter 6.

Remember, the primary function of salespeople is to generate sales revenue for their company by satisfying customer needs. Thus, sales revenue is the best measure of salespeople's effectiveness. However, sales revenue is not typically a metric used to evaluate business development representatives in most companies. As stated previously, salespeople in some companies are responsible for both selling and business development. Common metrics to evaluate business development activities include the number of cold calls made, outbound emails sent, or appointments booked, and the amount of sales pipeline generated.[17] As in the game of hockey, business development representatives may get credited with an 'assist' in creating a customer and generating sales revenue, but their performance is not normally directly measured by it. As previously discussed, digital tools make it easy to track data for all of these metrics. Using customer relationship management software, the data can be analyzed and presented via a sales dashboard at any time.

Salesperson working

Acquiring more customers is certainly one strategy to achieve business growth; however, retaining current customers may be an even more profitable strategy. Did you know that it costs (on average) about 8–10 times more money to acquire a new customer than it does to keep a current one? Thus, salespeople may be better served by directing their efforts toward retaining and achieving business growth through the customers they already have. Let's compare the two business development strategies of customer acquisition versus customer retention.

Retaining customers versus acquiring customers

There are two basic ways to increase business – sell more to current customers or acquire new ones. Selling more to current customers may include selling larger quantities, up-selling to more expensive items, or selling more frequently. Focusing on current customers and strengthening relationships with them will lead to business growth and even greater profitability because salespeople already have a relationship with their current customers, thus some degree of customer affinity or loyalty can be expected. As we discussed in Chapter 2, loyal customers generate greater profits for an organization over their lifetime of patronage due to the fact that they cost less to serve, spend more over time, are less price sensitive, and may generate valuable referrals which will lead to new customers.

Successful salesperson
Used with kind permission of Rachael Judy.

Thus, savvy salespeople and business development representatives will seek business growth from customers both inside and outside of the company. As presented in Chapter 2, all of the customer research gathered and stored in customer databases, should be readily accessible to salespeople and business development representatives. A customer database is the key to developing strong customer relationships and retaining current customers. It is the vehicle through which a company documents comprehensive information about each customer. This information might include the consumer's past purchases (buying patterns), demographics (age, birthday, income, marital status, etc.), psychographics (activities, interests, and opinions), and much more. Salespeople use this information to direct all future interactions with each customer on an individual basis. For example, the customer database is used for such purposes as lead generation, lead qualification, sale of a product or service, and promotional activities. Armed with this information, salespeople are able to develop a closer relationship with each customer on a personalized basis. The stronger the relationship with each customer, the more likely it is that the customer will continue purchasing from the company, as well as provide valuable referrals.

The task of creating and maintaining loyal customers is what customer relationship management (CRM) is all about. In an attempt to retain current customers, companies invest in activities to create and enhance customer loyalty. These activities may include capitalizing on cross-selling, continuity selling, and referral opportunities. Cross-selling refers to selling your current customers' products and services that are related (and even unrelated) to the products/services they currently purchase from your company. By analyzing the products and services your customers have purchased from you, you can identify and capitalize on numerous cross-selling opportunities. Continuity selling, which has also been referred to as 'club offers' or 'subscription offers,' is where consumers purchase on a regular basis – either weekly, monthly, quarterly, or annually. Another very effective activity to generate sales with current customers is a referral program. Salespeople can provide incentives to current customers to encourage their relatives and friends to become customers as well. Many salespeople provide a 'forward to friend' option in their email communications with customers.

Data analytics

In addition, data analytics of transactional data may be performed to reveal additional opportunities for business growth. Database analytics is where customer information housed within the customer database is analyzed to draw inferences about an individual customer's needs. This relies on customer profiling, modeling, and data mining. Data mining uses statistical and mathematical techniques to extract knowledge from data contained within a database. It is the process of using software tools to find relevant information from large amounts of data, typically an enterprise data warehouse, and using the results for strategic business decision making.

By analyzing the data contained in a customer database, profiles of a company's average customers and its best customers can be created. Armed with this information, salespeople and business development representatives can seek out new customers who may have needs and wants similar to those of their current customers. This also enables prospecting via renting lists of prospects that match the profile of their best customers and targeting them with offers to attract new customers. This is a much more effective and efficient way to generate new customers than generic lead-generation activities, such as merely blanketing the mass audience with advertisements in the hope that someone with a need or desire for the product/service will respond. More specific details on prospecting will be presented in Chapter 4, but for now, understand that analyzing the customer database enables salespeople to conduct more precise prospecting activities. Keep in mind that the more data salespeople have about their current customers, the more effectively they can serve them. For that reason, salespeople regularly update customer records and, whenever possible, incorporate new information into their customer records. Most salespeople recognize the need to both retain and grow the value of current customers, as well as acquire new ones. Achieving business growth is not solely limited to one strategy versus the other, but rather, a combination of the two methods.

Salespeople and business development representatives who focus outside of the company to acquire new business often do so via lead-generation activities, which will be addressed in Chapter 4. In some industries, it is a common practice for companies to present new business opportunities by outsourcing projects where they offer interested business development representatives and salespeople a chance to bid on publicized projects via a request for proposal (RFP) process. Research shows that almost 60 percent of businesses use outsourcing to reduce their expenses.[18] Let's explore RFPs.

Responding to requests for proposals (RFPs)

A request for proposal (RFP) is a formal announcement issued by companies or organizations specifying a particular project for which they are outsourcing and seeking potential bids for a contract to be awarded for its completion. RFPs allow companies to collect offers from vendors and select the vendor that can best meet the criteria that the company sets forth in the formal proposal request. RFPs normally specify the following information:[19]

- brief overview or background of the company
- project goals and scope of tasks to be completed
- anticipated schedule for selection and announcement of proposal award
- time and place for submission of proposals
- timeline for project completion
- elements that must be included in the proposal submission
- due dates and method for submission of proposal
- required and desired elements of the proposal such as a cover letter, resumes of the key account team, and potential partners
- evaluation criteria which will help eliminate unqualified vendors from submitting a proposal
- potential uncontrollable variables that may inhibit a vendor from submitting a proposal; and
- budget – which specifies the amount available to pay for a vendor to complete the project.

Salespeople and/or business development representatives who believe their respective companies have the expertise and capability needed to complete the posted project will need to write a proposal and respond to the RFP in a timely manner. Salespeople should differentiate their proposals by offering their unique selling proposition (USP) in order to stand out from the competition. Some differentiating characteristics include being the foremost technical expert in the relevant field, providing local or unique staffing capabilities, offering superior project management, or employing innovative processes.[20] Beyond featuring their respective competitive edge in their proposals, salespeople and business development representatives may also include their RFP team collaborations. Just as closing a sale usually takes a team, responding to RFPs usually involves several different people. Winning proposals often include input from subject matter experts, partners, various salespeople, and the management team.[21] RFP teams also spend time researching the business opportunity, including key internal stakeholders and decision makers at the company posting the RFP. Visiting the company's website and exploring the frequently asked questions (FAQ) page is a good starting point to obtain background research. Figure 3.2 provides an example of an RFP.

When a sales team receives an RFP without prior involvement with the requesting organization or knowledge that an RFP is even coming, the odds that they will be chosen typically decline. This is because most RFPs are built on the authors or issuers of the RFP and their knowledge of an already successful solution in other similar organizations. This often, unfortunately, reduces the likelihood that the RFP authors or issuers will choose anyone but the solution provider for which the RFP structure and requirements were initially created. This is not to say that salespeople or business development associates should not respond to an RFP in which they were not involved in the RFP development, it is merely a factor to consider in assessing the likelihood of being selected as the winner in the RFP process and ultimately being awarded a sales contract.

Responding to RFPs and writing proposals require a great deal of salespeople's available time, which is an important consideration. Therefore, creating proposals

Request for Proposal [SHORT FORM]

RFP: **[Project Name]**	Proposal Due By: **[Date]**	**[Company Name]**
Project Overview: [Insert Project Overview]		
Project Goals: • Goal 1 • Goal 2 • Goal 3		
Scope of Work: [Describe Scope of Work in Greater Detail]		
Current Roadblocks and Barriers to Success • Roadblock 1 • Roadblock 2 • Roadblock 3		
Evaluation Metrics and Criteria • Criteria #1 • Criteria #2 • Criteria #3		
Submission Requirements • Requirement #1 • Requirement #2 • Requirement #3		
Project Due By: **[Enter Project Due Date]**		Budget: **[Amount]**
Contact: **[Enter Name]**	Email: **[Enter Email]**	Phone #: **[Enter Number]**

Figure 3.2   Sample RFP form

should be moved to the latter end of the sales process, if at all possible, as opposed to being the first action taken. Why? Because, philosophically, a proposal should be merely a documented record of what has already been agreed to in the meetings with the prospect when they developed the requirements and reasons to buy. Too often, salespeople use the proposal phase too early because they use it as a talking document to fine-tune their solution, rather than as a summary of their conclusions after interacting with the prospect. If a proposal is not placed in the proper position during the sales process, it winds up being an unsuccessful effort. This is reflected in one of the metrics used to measure sales teams, which is the percentage of closes to proposals made. Usually, this number is well under 20 percent and almost always under 50 percent. To improve performance against this metric, proposal writing should be a task assigned to business development associates as opposed to wasting the precious selling time of salespeople.[22]

Along with RFPs, sometimes companies may issue other requests, such as a request for a quote or a request for information. These requests may be in conjunction with RFPs or separate. Either way, answering questions can be a time-consuming and challenging activity for salespeople and business development representatives. Discussing and determining the best possible answers is important since the answers to the questions are typically scored by the evaluating team. Table 3.2 provides some tips on answering questions. In addition, Tom Sant, author of *Persuasive Business Proposals*, which is one of the recommended Readings and Resources listed at the end of this chapter, offers many excellent tips for responding to questions.

Table 3.2 Techniques for answering questions

- Don't change the order of questions asked or attempt to rewrite them, as it will make the evaluator's job more difficult.
- Repeat each question word for word, then provide the answers in a different font or color of type immediately after each question, so the answers stand out.
- Include a compliance matrix or a table that lists the requirement or question, your level of compliance, and the page number in your document where the answer is fully addressed.
- Never send the evaluator off to another part of your proposal to locate an answer by stating 'see above' or 'see Section 2' as this may make you seem lazy or inconsiderate.
- Answer each question each time it is asked, even if the question seems redundant to another question that you have already answered.
- For important answers, acknowledge that the question is significant, make a persuasive statement about what you've done in this area, and substantiate any claims with details and relevant data.
- Keep it simple, but avoid one-word answers. For dichotomous (yes/no) questions, reply with either 'yes' or 'no' and then provide a brief explanation to expand on your answer.

Source: Adapted from Tom Sant, 'Winning proposals', *Sales & Service Excellence Essentials* (June 2010), 10(6), p. 7.

In summary, achieving business growth through prospecting for new customers is a part of every business development representative's job and may be one of the responsibilities of many salespeople. Acquiring new business by responding to RFPs requires business development representatives and salespeople to stay alert to industry opportunities and respond quickly when an RFP is announced. Of course, responding to RFPs also requires conducting additional research and writing and submitting effective proposals. All these activities are a necessary prelude to calling on prospective customers. These strategic planning activities, when completed well, will lead to greater selling success. Of course, customers, prospects, industries, and the marketplace environment are constantly changing, thus continuous assessment is needed to ensure that the strategies in place remain relevant. That is the topic of our last section for this chapter.

MONITORING METRICS

The difference between selling and successful selling is effective planning and decision making. Effective planning and decision making require adequate and timely research

Monitoring Metrics

insight or business intelligence that is continuously updated to ensure that it is relevant to the strategies being executed. Monitoring strategic planning activities to be sure that these courses of action will lead to the achievement of goals and objectives, is what assessment is all about. Let's investigate this important topic.

Salespeople must constantly evaluate and revise their strategies to adapt to the ever-changing business world in order to reach their established goals and objectives. Beyond re-evaluating and revising strategies, salespeople need to carefully allocate and safeguard their most precious resource – their time. This means that they need to determine what strategies are working and which are not. In addition, salespeople need to recognize that not all strategies, activities, customers, or accounts have the same potential impact to contribute toward achieving strategic goals. Thus, salespeople need good business intelligence to be able to allocate their time wisely or most efficiently. This is where measurement enters into the assessment process. As you can see, remaining flexible, open to change, and accepting of critical feedback are essential to becoming a successful salesperson.

Key performance indicators (KPIs) are significant factors that companies use to measure and monitor their own performance against. For each factor, a level is established that indicates success for the company.[23] KPIs help to quantify goals and objectives and enable progress to be measured. KPIs are measurable and reflective of whatever self-defined success goals are established, thus they are excellent in motivating salespeople to reach their specified objectives. However, KPIs may also facilitate the monitoring of shared goals and objectives, both within and across company departments and units.[24]

The measurement and analysis of KPIs can lead salespeople to re-evaluate their strategies and potentially revise them to better align with achieving specified goals and objectives. KPIs can also be established for the ongoing monitoring and measuring of customer relationships. Steve Anderson, president and founder of Performance Methods Inc., notes that relational factors are at work in creating the opportunities for value creation that fuel the increase in revenue.[25] Thus, measuring sales revenue as the sole KPI may be too limiting and may not provide an accurate assessment of relationship selling strategies. By measuring consumer trust and perceived credibility, companies can effectively align their account team members with the customer team members to maximize authentic long-term relationships that will maximize the value for both the customer and the company. Anderson calls this team-to-team alignment and he has developed four distinctive levels of alignment to use when assessing relationships: vendor, preferred supplier, planning partner, and trusted advisor.[26]

In conclusion, measuring, re-evaluating, and revising strategies to meet the customer's needs and maximize value are imperative activities for salespeople to conduct on a regular basis. To be successful in selling, savvy salespeople obtain business intelligence, establish SMART goals and objectives, conduct account planning, pursue business development opportunities, assess their strategic plans, and make adjustments as needed to best serve their customers. All of these activities may be considered 'pre-selling' or 'pre-approach planning' and they are critical to the success of the selling process.

CHAPTER SUMMARY

✓ Before interpreting data, you must consider the accuracy, availability, sufficiency, currency, and relevancy of that data.

✓ Ensure that all goals, whether personal or organizational, meet the SMART criteria.

✓ Use account planning to ensure a company-wide, collaborative effort to solve customer problems.

✓ Create proposals to RFPs at the latter end of the sales process to be most efficient with salespeople's time.

✓ Monitor success using customer-focused KPIs that are meaningful within departments, as well as across the company.

KEY TERMS

Account plan	Data mining
Account planning	Goals
Business development	Key performance indicators (KPIs)
Business intelligence (BI)	Objectives
Continuity selling	Request for proposal (RFP)
Cross-selling	Strategy
Database analytics	Tactics

REVIEW QUESTIONS

1. Name and describe the five types of business intelligence.
2. What are the five criteria that salespeople may use for judging the usefulness of information? Which criterion is the most important?
3. List the characteristics of a SMART goal. Give an example of one SMART goal.
4. Discuss the relationship between goals, objectives, strategies, and tactics.
5. Compare and contrast the four different types of account plan.
6. What are the seven components typically included in an account plan?
7. Compare and contrast cross-selling, continuity selling, and a referral program.
8. Define the acronym RFP and provide four pieces of information that should be specified within it.
9. State three tips for effectively completing a request for proposal (RFP).
10. What are KPIs? Why isn't sales revenue alone enough to determine the success of the sales team?

ETHICS IN ACTION

1. You have been the sales director for a retail sporting goods store for more than five years. You've personally hired the sales managers for each of the departments. As you continue to monitor sales revenue performance, you identify that a particular department has underperformed for the last two months. You've been told by the sales manager that staff turnover is the cause. You reported that to the CEO last month. However, now when you look more closely at the available data, you see that there is really only one salesperson who is underperforming and he isn't a new hire. What conversation do you have with the department manager? What would you recommend that he do? How do you present a different cause of underperformance to the CEO next month?

2. You have been a salesperson for the same company for all 10 of the years it has been in business. You have many loyal customers. While your job has been rewarding, you've identified another company you'd rather work for. You see that your target company has an RFP out that you could respond to on behalf of your current company. Though working on this RFP will take some of your time away from existing customers as well as other prospects, it is a great opportunity to make connections at the target company. How do you approach your manager to discuss this? How much time and effort do you devote to convincing your manager that this is worthwhile for the company?

EXERCISE

Congratulations on your promotion! You're now a member of the account planning team responsible for working on the Rochester Corporation account, which is your company's largest client. The senior executives at the Rochester Corporation are seeking to diversify and enter a new consumer market with their robotics technology. In the past, the company has been very successful in selling globally throughout the airline industry, but now seeks to target the automotive industry instead. You've been charged with preparing the initial overview for this account plan. First, specify the type of plan you will create. Then, document the details of your plan, addressing each of the following items if/as pertinent:

- profile and position
- profiles of targeted prospective customers
- needs mapping and alignment
- goals and objectives
- action plan
- team support
- performance dashboard.

READINGS AND RESOURCES

- Mark Donnolo (2017) *Essential Account Planning: 5 Keys for Helping Your Sales Team Drive Revenue*. Alexandria, VA: ATD Press.
- Alan Melkman and Ken Simmonds (2006) *Strategic Customer Planning* (London: Thorogood Publishing), https://thorogoodpublishing.co.uk/product/details/478/strategic-customer-planning.
- Tom Sant (2012) *Persuasive Business Proposals*, 3rd edn. New York: AMACOM.
- 'How to Write an RFP,' www.thebalancecareers.com/how-to-write-an-rfp-2276025.
- 'A Valued Tool Still Has Unmet Potential,' *CIO Insight* (October 2005), 58, 61–72.
- '24 Best Business Intelligence (BI) Tools List in 2020,' www.guru99.com/business-intelligence-tools.html.

CASE STUDY: COOPER INTERNATIONAL

Note: The names and locations used in this case study have been disguised for confidentiality purposes.

Cooper International (CI) is a multinational conglomerate headquartered in Toronto, Ontario, Canada, that produces fire, HVAC, and security equipment for buildings. The company employs more than 100,000 people in about 2,000 locations across six continents. One of those employees is Bill Craft, director of sales for the Business Technologies Group. Bill manages a sales team of 13 field sales representatives. At the end of every fiscal year, which is September 30 for his corporate accounts, each of his sales representatives must submit an account plan for a minimum of six major accounts (valued at more than $100,000 each in new revenue) on which they are currently working. These accounts represent major collaboration projects under one comprehensive CI program.

CI's account planning process requires salespeople to document and share a variety of data, including customer intelligence, competitive intelligence, and strategic intelligence, gathered at the salesperson level to better access customer needs and wants. This, in turn, aids Bill in strategically planning for his sales team to more effectively serve its customers and maximize both productivity and profitability for CI. Figure 3.3 provides a sample CI account plan for one of its government accounts, which includes sections on current account status and customer overview, current fiscal year metrics, key business drivers and outcomes, sales process (operations, steps, timeline), and lessons learned. In addition, the CI account plan includes outlook data for the next fiscal year, including projected metrics, account trends, account roadblocks, key milestones and execution items, planned meetings, the overall strategic approach (who, what, where, why, and when) for serving the account, notes for action items, and a summary of current issues or areas of concern with the account.

Account planning, when properly implemented, provides CI (at the corporate level), Bill (at the managerial level), and salespeople (at the field level) with several key strategic benefits, including increased accountability of their sales activities, improved sales performance, and more satisfied customers. Bill solemnly attests to the value of account planning as he recognizes how it has helped his sales team to become highly successful.

As Bill leads a breakout session at CI's annual corporate retreat in Montreal, he recalls a story of where account planning made the difference between success and failure for one of his team's largest accounts, Belt Brothers Corporation (BBC). The date was October 15 and the new fiscal year had recently begun. Jim River, the field sales representative assigned to the BBC account, had identified both intense direct competition and changing border laws to enter the United States, as challenges to business success in his annual account plan for BBC. Sure enough, one warm and sunny Sunday afternoon while Bill was enjoying a cookout with some close friends, he received a telephone call from Jim, explaining that his support materials for the trade show in New York City he would be attending were not going to clear the US border due to new documentation rules. Jim needed those materials with him in New York City as he was planning to share them with the new BBC buying agent and other BBC representatives at a scheduled meeting while attending the trade show.

Thanks to the prior alert that Jim's account plan had provided, Bill was able to quickly diffuse the situation by ensuring that additional paperwork needed by the US border officers was prepared in advance and ready to be downloaded on an if/as needed basis from the CI portal. Jim downloaded the paperwork and the materials arrived at the trade show on time. Both the meeting with BBC and the trade show were a great success. Not only did the new buying agent and representatives from BBC place a sizeable order for CI's new security equipment line, they also provided on-the-spot endorsements that served to

Account Name	Gov't Account Q Smart	2019-2020 Review					

Current State: 2019 Overview

QSmart is the Global authority in airborne persistent surveillance solutions. Founded in 1969, QSmart takes pride in offering complete surveillance solutions at a low operational cost. Minimal transactions based off of 2018 performance. Security spending was under a watchful eye this year. They are headquarterd in Toronto, Ontario, Canada. so it allows me/us to meet and conduct business with all of the important players & POC'S in the game.

FY 2020 Target NSP	Actual to Date NSP	Year End Prediction	Variation (Target to EOY)	Impact Factor (% of your Plan this Account Represents)		Trend (drop down box)	
150K	48K	500K	0.0%	Six Percent			

Key Drivers (Outcomes of 2019 Predicted/Actual)	Sales Process (Account Operations, Steps, Timeline)
Government contracts drive security spending.	
Sustainability is a competitive drive for Q Smart. Being able to set themselves apart from the rest of the pack is a competitive driver.	This customer has a strong Canadian presence with offices in Toronto, Windsor, and Montreal. All security decisions are made locally from the Toronto office by lemma decision maker who is the facilities Security officer. On large scale projects there is joint decision making.
The purchasing steps are two fold. They sometimes buy the equipment outright and at other locations where they have a lease they negotiate CI owned transactions.	

Lessons Learned	
keep pipeline full as some forecasts don't' play out as we first thought.	
IT department is slow to act and has caused issues on new jobs that need their assistance. Jobs go over due to repeat trips.	
This customer has been setting unrealistic deadlines on all of the projects so far. Not one has been completed on time.	

2020 Outlook							

Predicted Outright Sale	Predicted RMR	Year over Year Growth/Decline	Impact Factor (% of your Plan this Account Represents)	Estimated Customer Visites (Monthly)	Projected Annual Travel Spend (Site Map Needed)	Call Frequency
150K	25K	10% / 0%	20%	5	650	1
						Monthly

What is trending in the Account?	Road Blocks (Internal/ External)
Security Spending has increased	Only road block I can see is they brought on a new security advisor that does not have any loyalty to us. Have to be careful when pricing up jobs as he already has shown he will shop us.
Upgrading and converting aging Access systems. Have already started the ball rolling on replacing their facility Commander access system with CCURE 9000.	Customer start dates and deadlines are unrealistic. Might lose projects due to earlier than usual start times.
Customer trust has increased due to providing a more hands on approach.	

First 90 Day Plan (Key Milestones and Execution items, Planned Meetings)	2020 Strategy (Overall Approach - Who, What, Where, Why, When)
Identify if they have a security budget and what it is. Are there any potentail roadblocks that might prevent us from conducting business as usual, I.E new procurement procedures, budget, approval process.	Create a unique value proposition that explains how Cooper International products can solve their problems, improve their situation, and state why they should continue to buy from us and not the competition.The customer has already made a good decision by choosing CI and are enjoying the benefits of the protective services we have given them. We have an in with this client so instead of just stopping at winning the work we won, use this as the starting point to look for additional opportunities to help them achieve their Corporate objectives.

Notes	

Action items		Owner
Complete the outstanding installation issues at the SIL.		Art Boyteam - Sirus Co.
Convert the remaining GE access readers to to SWH and CCURE9000		Donald Pellen

Figure 3.3 Cooper International account plan sample

influence two new client accounts to be obtained. As Bill wrapped up his presentation, he concluded that during times of uncontrollable and dynamic situations, account planning can provide the needed insight to effectively serve customers in a timely manner.

Case study questions:

1. Which type of account plan does CI require its salespeople to submit to their sales manager each fiscal year? Use details from the case study to support your answer.
2. Describe the five Ws of the information gathered for the account planning process.
3. Describe one commonality that you might find in multiple prospect account plans and explain why that item is important for account planning.

NOTES

1. Mary Pratt, 'What is Business Intelligence? Turning data into business insights,' *CIO Framingham* (October 2019).
2. Ibid.
3. Ibid.
4. Ibid.
5. Adapted from Valeh Nazemoff, 'Rewire your brain for business success,' *Home Business Magazine: The Home-Based Entrepreneur's Magazine* (May/June 2015), 22(3), 38; Ron Price, 'Strategic intelligence,' *Sales & Service Excellence Essentials* (July 2009), 9(7), 14; and Seena Sharp, 'Competitive intelligence: Incorporate new perspectives,' *Sales & Service Excellence Essentials* (February 2010), 10(2), 16.
6. Margaret Morrison and Eric Haley, 'The role of account planning in US agencies,' *Journal of Advertising Research* (March 2006), 46(1), 124–31.
7. Keith Crosier and David Pickton, 'Marketing intelligence and account planning: Insights from the experts,' *Intelligence & Planning* (Bradford 2003), 21(7), 410–15.
8. Mark Donnolo, 'Account planning for SALES,' *Talent Development* (May 2017), 71(5), 48–53.
9. Ibid.
10. Ibid.
11. Jeff Schmidt, 'Re-engineering strategic account planning at Hewlett-Packard: Five lessons from the front line', *Velocity* (2009), 11(1), 46–9.
12. Ibid.
13. Ibid.
14. Adapted from Mark Donnolo, 'Account planning for SALES,' *Talent Development* (May 2017), 71(5), 48–53; and Dan Schultheis (2020), personal communication.
15. David Needle, 'Beyond CRM? Altify touts CRO as next big enterprise aspiration,' *eWeek* (February 2019).
16. Izabelle Hundrev (2019) 'What Does a Business Development Representative Do? (+Job Description)', https://learn.g2.com/business-development-representative, retrieved July 13, 2020.

17. Ibid.

18. Caroline Forsey, 'Don't Just Set it Adrift and Hope: Best practices for a request for proposal', *OfficePro* (July/August 2020), pp. 12–16.

19. Ibid.

20. Tara Landes, 'Proposal writing: Choose your battles', *Canadian Consulting Engineer* (March/April 2013), 54(2), 34–7.

21. Katie Flanagan, 'Why collaborating helps you win more RFPs: Winning proposal teams know they need to collaborate with each other, subject matter experts, and sales', *HCM Sales, Marketing & Alliance Excellence Essentials* (July 2019), 18(7), 22–3.

22. Dan Schultheis and Phil Perkins (2018) *The Willing To Buy Coach* (Bloomington, IN: Author House), pp. 64–6.

23. Adam Rapp, Joe Calamusa and Daniel G. Bachrach (2014) *Transformative Selling: Becoming a Resource Manager and a Knowledge Broker* (Bronxville, NY: Wessex), p. 100.

24. Ibid., pp. 100–1.

25. Steve Anderson, 'The keys to effective strategic account planning,' *Velocity* (2012), 14(1), 23–6.

26. Ibid.

SECTION 2

The Selling Process – 'Out in the Field'

4

NETWORKING AND PROSPECTING WITH EFFECTIVENESS

CHAPTER CONTENTS

PEOPLE, PRACTICES AND PERSPECTIVES FROM THE WORLD OF SALES

Hello. My name is Sami Hamad. I'm a sales account manager for Topgolf, located in Virginia Beach, Virginia. I have nine years of experience in sales. My primary focus currently is corporate clients with whom I work directly to execute the ideal event experience. *I have found that a best practice for building relationships is to DO IT NOW when responding to clients and customers. When you get a lead, call them immediately. When someone emails you, respond instantly. Responding in a timely fashion goes a long way in building client relationships.* One of my favorite quotes is 'A salesperson's ethics and values contribute more to sales success than do techniques or strategies' (Ron Willingham.)

Hi, I'm Andy Kemp, Head of Sales & Marketing for The Bakery Worldwide Limited in London, UK. I am responsible for sales/marketing strategy and delivery, which includes creating our value proposition, understanding our audience, and creating suitable campaigns to reach, engage, and convert our target audience. *My favourite and most useful technique is 'value selling.' My advice: don't forget to be yourself and be a good person as people like that.* 'Profit for a company is like oxygen for a person. If you don't have enough of it, you're out of the game. But if you think your life is about breathing, you're really missing something' (Peter Drucker.)

Hi, I'm Monique Pirrone. My career in pharmaceutical sales and management has spanned 30 years. I've found networking has been the glue that continues to solidify my career throughout those years. *Without networking, we cannot grow in our roles, get to know our customers and what's important to them, and help them gain access to the resources they need. The easiest way to do this is to just ask. Like I always say, 'You don't ask, you don't get!'*

It's all about relationships.

EYES ON ETHICS

Keep in mind the following ethical topics as you read through this chapter:

1. Committing to a mentoring partnership.
2. Responding to frustration and anger when cold calling.

INTRODUCTION

The subject of this chapter, networking, generating leads, and prospecting effectively, is really all about building relationships with people. As discussed in Chapter 2, people do business with people they like and trust. Therefore, regardless of whether you are selling to final consumers (B2C) or business consumers (B2B), you still need to focus on making connections and then nurturing relationships with other people. Savvy salespeople are always networking, searching for leads, and prospecting because sales is a field that requires people to be at the top of their game all day, every day. They use each and every resource, strategy, technique, and tactic available to network and prospect in order to develop relationships. Let's first explore making connections via networking before we delve more deeply into building and managing relationships.

Business people networking
© Ben Leistensnider/Christopher Newport University.

NETWORKING

Networking is defined as using a supportive system for sharing information and services among individuals and groups that have a common interest.[1] In other words, networking entails strategically identifying and connecting with people to create visibility with those who might support you and/or your company. In the selling context, networking is a necessary skill for making a variety of contacts, identifying new prospects, and finding new customers. However, it is critical that salespeople do not approach networking as an opportunity to make some quick sales by 'working the room' gathering business cards. The primary benefit to be gained from networking lies in the opportunity to establish business relationships or friendships with people.[2] Networking is not a one-time event; rather, it's an activity that salespeople should perform on a regular basis. Salespeople should establish goals before participating in each networking, social, or business event or activity. Salespeople should address these types of questions: Why do you need to build a network? What do you want your network to do for you? What are *you* going to do *for* your network?

The term 'networking' implies that it takes work to engage with others; however, when effectively carried out, it can be pleasant and fun. After all, what could be more enjoyable than connecting with new acquaintances and friends? However, networking does take time, patience, skill, and effort to be effective. Let's now examine how to be effective in networking.

Examining and implementing effective networking strategies and techniques

Effective networking is a skill that needs to be developed and practiced in order to achieve a level of ease or comfort when interacting with other people, especially with people who you have recently met. Based on one's personality type, some people tend to be more prone to enjoy engaging with others (extroverts), while other personality types (introverts) require more time, patience, and practice in order to enjoy conversations. However, introverts tend to be excellent listeners, which naturally makes them very good at networking – regardless of whether or not they truly enjoy the activity.

Effective networking focuses on three tactical areas:

1. **How potential networking contacts are identified**. Identifying the 'right' group(s) of people with whom you want to associate is critical to successful networking. Examples of target groups are your family, relatives, friends, neighbors, church groups, fitness buddies, co-workers, industry colleagues, and online social networks such as LinkedIn, Facebook, and Twitter. One digital platform for finding in-person community events or networking opportunities is *meetup.com* where you can connect online with groups and then later meet in person. While the list of potential networking opportunities is nearly endless, you might expand your target groups by the following:

   - associating with and adapting to a target group that you naturally like and have an affinity with anyway[3]
   - joining groups that serve the people in your target market, and attending as many meetings as possible[4]

- volunteering for nonprofit organizations, school activities, and neighborhood associations
- getting involved in community events or alumni activities
- attending trade shows, conferences, workshops, career fairs, or other types of formal professional events
- looking for opportunities in unexpected places (holiday events, parties, happy hours, exercise classes, school groups, etc.).

2. **How to engage with people when you first meet them**. There are some common sayings about first impressions that are on target in networking. First impressions are the lasting ones; you never have a second chance to make a good first impression, and people are often judged on their first impression. Therefore, you need to be approachable, sincere, authentic, and polite when you first meet someone.[5] Excellent eye contact and a warm and friendly demeanor are crucial to making a good initial impression. Dressing appropriately and giving a good handshake – if prospective buyers offer their hand to you first – are important. Then, exercising good listening skills and only focusing on the person in front of you by giving that person the purity of your attention, is critical. While conversing, thinking about what you can do to serve them instead of how they might help you, is key to building a relationship. You must remember the golden rule of effective networking: *Give first*.[6] Here are some strategies that will serve you well when engaging with other people:[7]

- offering something of value to people to increase their desire to meet with you
- being patient and avoiding jumping into sales mode right away
- remembering that relationships take time
- focusing on building rapport and increasing the level of trust
- demonstrating a sincere personal interest in the other person
- concentrating on learning more about the person and the person's business.

3. **How you choose to follow up after you meet someone**. Regarding appropriate follow-up, there are some obvious actions that you should take right after you meet someone, such as saying 'It's been a pleasure meeting you' and thanking them for the conversation. In addition, you should exchange business cards and mention a future time, place and/or date when you might see them again. Then, following up within 24 hours with an email to thank them again for their time and conversation, is important. As an alternative to email, sending a hand-written letter provides a more personal touch and shows your attention to detail. In today's digital world, sending a personalized letter via the postal mail will make you stand out from others and make you even more memorable. If you have offered to provide additional information or assistance to the person during your conversation, either include that information or specify when and how you will be providing it. Thus, the recipient knows that you will be following up on all of the details from your conversation in a timely manner. When appropriate, connecting the recipient to other people in your network may also be mutually beneficial.

When following up, you should keep in mind that you are nurturing each new relationship by providing value. You should go the extra mile to serve others. By adopting the mentality that you want to help others to achieve their goals, you will be more likely to achieve your own networking goals. Networking is not about building a network and feeling confident that you have it established, but rather, it is about continuously building relationships and improving your networks to get them to work for you.[8] You must keep replenishing your network as job changes, layoffs, and retirements will constantly chip away at your circle of contacts.[9]

Sometimes, your network of contacts may produce the most valuable connections to people with whom you want to develop an even closer business relationship or friendship – such as a partner or mentor. That's the topic of the next section.

Business partners/mentors
Used with kind permission of Monica Hill.

Identifying and establishing partners and mentors

Through business relationships, salespeople may become aware of the level of knowledge and expertise that the contacts in their network possess on various topics or subjects. A natural alliance may form with some of these people as the relationships develop over time. Thus, salespeople may become more closely aligned with particular people and their relationships may progress from awareness to respect to admiration to affiliation to partnership. Research shows that networking with peers at industry events is one of the most frequently used paths to find and create strategic alliances.[10]

Given today's digital world and the rise of influencer marketing, salespeople may seek out partnership relationships with key influencers in their field. Influencer marketing is a form of content-driven marketing where the content shared is akin to an endorsement or a testimonial by a third party or potential consumer. 'Influencers' can be anyone, located anywhere. All influencers have one thing in common: they are influential because of their large followings on social media platforms and the Web.[11] In influencer marketing, an influencer or 'social media celebrity' is paid to promote a specific item or brand. This creates a cross between the traditional celebrity endorsement and the modern content-driven campaign. Some influencers got their start on online platforms, while others began their journey by becoming specialists in their field and leveraging social media to their benefit. Influencers can be utilized to promote a specific product in a manner that connects with audiences by identifying a trusting and familiar face with a brand or product.

Influencer marketing is not limited to any social media platform and may be executed in both B2C and B2B situations across all applications available in digital marketing. The bottom line is that influencer marketing is very effective in swaying the behavior of large groups of consumers. Salespeople should be transparent and share information and metrics with influencers that they partner with so that trust is created and mutually beneficial relationships are cultivated.[12] Salespeople should give influencers material that will help them to better understand the benefits of the solution being offered, so they can more effectively influence the *right* prospects. When selecting influencers as partners, salespeople should not fall victim to selecting an influencer with the highest number of followers because it's really about partnering with the *right* influencer, based on the product or service being sold.

A mentor is a trusted friend, counselor, or teacher. A mentor is usually a more experienced person who is willing to assist you in your professional development. Mentors can assist salespeople to advance their careers, enhance their education, and/or build their networks. What do mentors provide? They may provide expertise, guidance, resources, positive reinforcement, constructive criticism, and connections. Good professional mentors are supporters through both successes and failures. The best mentor relationships are long-term and reciprocal. Giving back to your mentors will strengthen the relationship as supporters should always be supported. Mentors are the strongest part of your network and will always be there to assist you. Typically, your mentors will want to share their networks with you, often providing an introduction along the way, so that your potential networking connections increase quickly with assistance from your mentors.

Acquiring valuable mentors takes time. Mentor relationships normally develop out of the pool of contacts from your network. Thus, making connections with people who have similar interests or are like-minded is important when networking. LinkedIn, a valuable professional social network, has made researching, locating, and connecting with people having similar interests quick and easy. In Appendix C, we'll explore how LinkedIn can be effectively used by college students to connect with alumni even before they enter the business world. Of course, all social media platforms are vital channels for networking, generating sales leads, and prospecting. Let's now examine what's involved in the lead-generation and prospecting stage of the selling process.

LEAD GENERATION AND PROSPECTING

Lead generation is a method of getting inquiries from potential customers.[13] Lead generation is often considered the first step in the selling process as it works hand in hand with prospecting. A sales lead is an individual or a business that is suspected to have an interest in the products or services you are selling.[14] A sales lead is commonly referred to as a suspect, in having the potential to become a prospect. It's important to note that sales leads do not become prospects until they've been qualified to determine their level of interest and fit as a potential customer.

Prospecting is engaging in activities or conversations with suspects to inquire, assess, discover, educate, and determine whether there's a fit and a relationship that's worth pursuing which may lead to an opportunity to deliver value and earn a commitment.[15] As we discussed in Chapter 2, prospects are 'hand-raisers' who have identified themselves as having an interest in your company or organization. Prospects may have visited your website or have become a qualified lead. Let's now discuss the process of how sales leads are qualified to become prospects.

Qualifying leads and cultivating customers through the sales funnel

The magical question that all salespeople seek to answer is this: Will a given sales lead become a buying customer? While there's no crystal ball to make that prediction with 100 percent certainty, there are some criteria that salespeople may use to determine whether or not suspects qualify as prospects. Opinions vary; however, at a minimum, most salespeople use the following two criteria:[16]

1. Do the sales leads have a need or want for the product or service? In other words, will the suspects benefit from buying the particular product or service?
2. Can the sales leads afford the product or service? Regardless of whether the suspects have a need of or want what's being sold, if they do not have the ability to pay for the product or service, they cannot be further considered as a prospect.

During the lead-qualification process, salespeople must conduct lead research on prospective buyers which may include investigating BANT criteria.[17] BANT stands for:

- **B**udget – Does the suspect have the resources to buy?
- **A**uthority – Does the suspect have the ability to make the buying decision?
- **N**eeds – What are the biggest problems that the suspect is seeking to solve with the respective purchase?
- **T**imeline – How soon is the suspect desiring to purchase?

Keep in mind that the specific BANT criteria will vary from one company to the next, but investigating this type of data about prospects will enable salespeople to more efficiently use the BANT criteria to qualify sales leads, which will enable salespeople to allocate time well and not waste time on leads that don't qualify as serious prospective customers.

BANT is a very useful acronym for performing a gross assessment of a 'suspect.' A suspect is someone that you *think* may have a need or want for your company's products or services. To make the transition to a real 'prospect,' it is necessary to explore whether the need is just an 'interest' or an 'urgency.' This is typically vetted by direct, personal, face-to-face interaction with the suspect (such as during a needs discovery conversation) or via some form of visual connection with them. Once urgency is determined, the salesperson can truly qualify the suspect as a legitimate 'prospect' that is likely to make a decision (assuming the B, A, and T have been obtained).

In order to make the BANT process even more effective, it is useful to define the BANT of the composite of an *ideal* suspect who from past experience has proceeded through the prospect phase to become a customer. This will provide a general template from which we can filter all the BANT information on likely suspects, to provide another factor that increases the odds of finding a new customer more effectively.

In many companies and organizations, the marketing department and/or business development associates are in charge of lead generation, while salespeople typically do their own prospecting via their personal network of connections and via online tools. Some companies have separate lead-generation personnel whose main responsibilities are to produce leads for the sales department to follow up. Often, salespeople are sent lists of leads from their respective marketing or business development departments, who they should contact and initiate the selling process with. In some companies, there has been a discrepancy between the quality and quantity of leads provided. That's why some salespeople make a distinction between a marketing qualified lead (MQL), which is a sales lead whose engagement levels suggest that he is likely to become a customer, and a sales qualified lead (SQL), defined as a sales lead that indicates immediate interest in a company's products or services.[18] Besides the source of the lead, the main difference between MQLs and SQLs is the *urgency* of the lead. With SQLs, salespeople should follow up quickly, within 24 hours of discovery if possible. Thus, in addition to BANT criteria, salespeople must be able to assess the 'urgency' of the suspect to make a buying decision when qualifying leads and prioritizing prospects, which will be addressed further in Chapter 6.

There are a wide variety of lead-generation techniques that have the potential to produce a number of qualified prospects; however, not all sales leads are of equal value. Sales leads may be classified and prioritized based on their 'quality' or potential to be converted into a buying customer. The quality of the lead is often described as being hot, warm, or cold. These different lead quality levels can be described as follows:[19]

- **Hot leads** – these leads are ready to buy and have the available budget to close the deal. These leads have become qualified prospects. They are considered high-quality leads.
- **Warm leads** – these leads are actively seeking to make a purchase. They may have expressed an interest in buying and may have used the product/service on a trial basis. Warm leads are actively examining and comparing competitor offerings or

they may be currently engaged in a contract with another supplier and seeking to make a switch.

- **Cold leads** – these leads may not possess awareness of your company or products/services and are not ready to buy something at the current time. They are considered low-quality sales leads.

As is likely obvious based on their descriptions, hot leads are the most valuable leads for salespeople, followed by warm leads, while cold leads are not desirable to most salespeople.

While lead quality is vital, the quantity of leads generated is also important. There is often a trade-off between the quantity and the quality of sales leads generated. The quantity of sales leads is important because salespeople typically cannot close on each and every lead they obtain. Here's an example of how the metrics, or 'theory of ratios', work:

A salesperson with 100 warm quality leads might be able to make 10 appointments, out of which four will be converted into customers. If that salesperson has a quota of 40 sales per month, 1,000 warm quality leads per month will be needed just to be able to meet the minimum number of required sales.[20]

Thus, while both quantity and quality of sales leads are important, quality is much more important. Salespeople cannot waste their valuable time and effort in pursuing cold leads that do not possess a good chance of becoming prospects and ultimately customers. Thus, cold sales leads are not usually pursued by salespeople. Salespeople should seek to understand their potential prospects and their needs in order to determine whether there's a fit between the needs of the suspects and what they are offering. If not, the salesperson should disqualify the suspect and focus their prospecting efforts elsewhere, with sales leads who may be able to move through the sales funnel. Let's examine the process that will help salespeople to move suspects through the sales funnel.

Understanding and employing lead generation and prospecting

Following a lead-generation system or process will normally produce high-quality suspects that will qualify and become prospects. Let's consider the following five-step lead-generation process:[21]

1. Identify your target audience – you cannot effectively reach and sell to your ideal customers if you don't articulate exactly who they are, along with background research on their needs, wants, problems, and so on. As we discussed in Chapter 2, understanding your customers and prospects is key to successful selling, including effective lead generation.
2. Pick your promotional methods wisely – in order to generate sales leads, you need a promotional plan that will get your products and services in front of members of your target audience. Thus, selecting the appropriate communication channels or contact methods to reach and engage with your target audience is important.

3. Create a sales funnel – in order to collect contact information to follow up on, you need to have all prospects complete a standard form or landing page, often in return for some value-added incentive. In addition to providing contact information, the standard form helps you to compare and contrast prospects.

4. Follow up to build relationships – following up via telephone, email, or an e-newsletter, are effective ways to cultivate those relationships that you've just made in order to guide them from the lead stage through to the commitment stage of the selling process. Consistent communication via an e-newsletter or other media vehicles, is a cost-effective method to strengthen relationships.

5. Leverage social media to connect and engage – social media provides a number of opportunities to create conversations with prospective customers and develop even more leads. You will need to determine which social media platform(s) to use based on insight into which platforms your target customers are using, as well as create value to entice them to engage with you socially. Some techniques to attract more followers are running social media contests, creating online lead quizzes, including fun videos, showing quick replies to inquiries, posting conversations in their field, and updating your posts on a regular basis.[22] We'll discuss social media platforms in greater detail, later in this chapter.

Before the digital revolution, lead generation and prospecting primarily occurred at places such as trade shows where visitors to a company's booth would speak with the salespeople manning the booth and complete cards with their contact information, which would later trigger a call from that company's sales team.[23] Trade shows are still an effective lead-generation and prospecting technique for some companies and industries; however, today there are many other techniques that may be used

Generating sales leads

118

as well. Some of the different sources for generating sales leads and prospects are marketing and advertising, referrals, social media, networking and outreach, project trials, and consultations.[24]

Most salespeople and business development representatives use a variety of both offline and online techniques to generate good sales leads and prospects. Let's first examine some of the common offline techniques that salespeople use in generating leads and prospecting for new customers, and then we'll explore the common online techniques.

Using offline lead-generation and prospecting techniques

There are many offline techniques that may be effectively used to generate suspects and prospects; however, the first and foremost starting point for all lead generation and prospecting is analyzing a company's customer database. Analyzing current customer data is done to enable salespeople to develop profiles of their best customers versus their average customers. Armed with this information, salespeople can seek out new customers who may have needs and wants similar to those of their current 'best' customers. Using this customer profile, salespeople improve their accuracy in identifying and targeting prospective customers. Some common offline lead-generation and prospecting techniques are:

Current customers. Customer retention is typically a very productive and profitable strategy to increase sales revenue because salespeople already have valuable relationships developed with these customers. Salespeople should communicate with their current customers to thank them for their business, encourage repeat sales, and increase the value of these relationships by capitalizing on cross-selling opportunities. Cross-selling refers to selling products and services to your current customers that are related (and even unrelated) to the products/services they currently purchase from your company. By analyzing the products and services your customers have purchased from you, you can identify and capitalize on numerous cross-selling opportunities.

Referrals. The most effective way to generate leads from current customers is to obtain referrals. Research shows that sales leads that come from referrals convert to customers faster, have lower costs of acquisition, and have higher customer lifetime values than any other leads.[25] With referrals, salespeople ask current customers to provide a recommendation to encourage their relatives, friends, and business acquaintances to become customers as well. Salespeople may also send them offers to entice them to provide referrals. In addition, salespeople may provide a 'forward to friend' option in their email communications with their customers. Of course, salespeople should *earn* the referral by providing excellent 'above and beyond' customer service, industry insight, and value throughout the selling process with each of their current customers. When customers provide referrals, they often include a brief introduction for the salespeople to follow up on, thus a 'warm entry' is established. Communication with current customers should both thank them for their patronage and invite valuable referrals at the same time.

Endless chain. Another technique that may be used with current customers is where salespeople ask current customers to identify other potential buyers who might possibly be interested in purchasing the same or a similar product or service. Think of a chain letter or email – the process should be ongoing and never-ending if each new customer provides names of additional potential buyers. However, unlike referrals, customers normally do not provide any introductions to the potential buyers, just their names and contact information.

Inactive customers. Second to current customers, inactive customers are likely the next most valuable source for lead generation and prospecting. Why? Because of the previous relationship or affinity that salespeople may have with these customers. Inactive customers may be people who have once purchased from your company but are not currently doing so, or they may be those who have inquired or have been referred but have not bought. For example, such people may have received a product demonstration and were interested in buying, but the timing wasn't right for them to buy. Salespeople should touch base with these inactive customers to see if their situation has changed. Salespeople may investigate why these inactive customers stopped buying and encourage them to purchase again. Salespeople should stay in contact with inactive customers to ensure they will have 'top of mind' recall for these customers. To do this, salespeople may periodically send inactive customers relevant information or personalized emails. Remember that, as inactive customers, they are already qualified prospects who can use their network to generate sales leads.

Networking organizations. Joining formal networking organizations that are specifically designed for networking is an excellent technique. For example, you might join a Business Network International (BNI) chapter. BNI is the world's largest referral organization and you can visit its website at www.BNI.com to locate a group near you.[26] However, BNI allows only one member from a professional industry classification to join each chapter, with the sole purpose of generating more business for its members.[27]

In addition, some specific networking organizations are available for select industries or types of contacts. For example, a couple of recommended female networking organizations are:

- **FABWOMEN** – this is an organization started by Shanna Kabatznick in 2014. The purpose of FABWOMEN is for women to make deep connections, experience personal and professional growth, and enjoy laughter together. The organization started with 20 women meeting monthly. Today, FABWOMEN is an international women-focused membership organization. It is a high energy, inviting group of women that come together to learn, laugh, and connect. Through purpose-filled events, members develop personal and professional relationships that engage one another and enrich their lives. FABWOMEN is about more than women in business; it is also about the business of women. Visit https://fabwomen.me to learn more.
- **eWomen Network** – this is another female business networking organization whose mission is to help one million women entrepreneurs each achieve one million dollars in annual revenue. To support this goal, the network helps women grow their influence, recognition and impact significantly by providing resources,

business networking, marketing, promotion, coaching, events, podcasts, speaking opportunities, scholarships, grants, and assistance with video production. Check out www.ewomennetwork.com for more details.

Networking event
© Ben Leistensnider/Christopher Newport University.

Networking events. Salespeople should participate in as many relevant networking events as possible in order to grow their lead list. As previously discussed, networking is all about face-to-face mingling with others and applying an 'always be helping' philosophy. Exchanging contact information via business cards is excellent, but remember that the goal is to make relationships, not to merely collect business cards.

Trade show

Salesperson public speaking
© Ben Leistensnider/Christopher Newport University.

Trade shows. Select industries offer periodic trade shows or exhibitions where salespeople can set up booths or exhibits to feature their respective products/services. These events are designed to provide an opportunity for visitors at each booth to meet face to face with representatives from the various companies participating at the trade show, and to be able to learn about the products/services being featured. Salespeople gather high-quality leads at these events.

Trade associations. Trade associations comprise groups of people or companies that operate in a specific industry, so salespeople will find many relevant leads by actively affiliating with appropriate trade associations. Trade associations exist to provide value to their members; thus, salespeople can contribute to that value by offering to write articles for their newsletters, websites, and member events. Salespeople who do this will quickly become known and perceived as an expert in their field, which in turn will generate sales leads.[28]

Public speaking opportunities. Similar to writing articles for a trade association, taking advantage of relevant public speaking opportunities will also position salespeople as authorities or experts on a given subject matter, which, in turn, will generate leads. Most trade associations and community groups, such as the Rotary Club, are in constant need of speakers for their regular meetings. The key is to put together and deliver a presentation that addresses relevant topics, solves problems, and offers value. Of course, salespeople should also use that platform to share information about their company and its products and services, along with contact information. At the end of their talk, salespeople should invite members of their audience to take a business card and contact them for follow-up assistance.

Personal networks. The personal networks of salespeople are broad, diverse, and invaluable! They include family, friends, classmates, exercise buddies, fraternity brothers, sorority sisters, alumni, and so on. The personal networks of salespeople are so valuable because they already have built-in trust established. Most salespeople have a number of separate personal networks that don't interact with one another, yet you, that salesperson, have a relationship with all of them. You are the common denominator to help connect people in your various different personal networks to one another.

Thus, using your personal networks to make connections can generate valuable leads, while providing a real service to those in your inner circle.

Bird dogs. Bird dogs, also called *spotters*, are people hired to provide leads to salespeople. Some people naturally make excellent bird dogs due to their professional position requiring them to interact with people on a regular basis. These types of people include bartenders, cocktail waiters, door attendants, bellhops, delivery people, hair stylists, nail technicians, fitness instructors, secretaries, and hospitality workers.

Sales letters. Writing sales letters can be an effective lead-generation technique if the letter is written effectively and sent to the appropriate targets. Effective letters will capture the reader's attention, be read quickly, and generate a response. There are a number of tactics, such as personalization, an attention-grabbing headline or opening, the use of appealing letter formulas, layout, photographs, and stories, and so on, that may be used to increase the likelihood of the receiver engaging with the sales letter.[29] Intrigued? Check out *The Ultimate Sales Letter*, a book by Dan Kennedy (featured in the Readings and Resources section at the end of this chapter), for more information.

Telephone. To those who know how to use them, the interactive features of the telephone are, in many cases, replacing the face-to-face contact of a salesperson's visit to a prospect. The phone removes the need for travel and makes it possible to talk *with*, and not just to, customers and prospects. Telephone applications may be categorized as inbound calls where the initiator of the communication is the customer or prospect calling to place an order, to request more information, or for customer service. The second category encompasses outbound calls where the salesperson is the initiator of the marketing communications. Outbound calls commonly deal with lead generation, appointment setting, market research, database verification, database appending, and, of course, sales. Outbound calls are generally longer in duration and require more experienced/higher-paid personnel than inbound calls. In addition, outbound calls have become extremely regulated due to various legal regulations. The laws vary by country and salespeople must know the consumer privacy laws that pertain to their geographical location.

Video calls. These are similar to telephone calls, but provide more personal interaction than telephone calls because all parties can see each other. Visual clues provide valuable information as you are talking to and getting to know someone. Normally, these are exploratory calls that last between 30 and 60 minutes. The purpose of the call is to see how both parties can be of assistance and help one another. Zoom calls may be automatically scheduled with a button on a website that initiates an electronic calendar to set up an appointment.

List rental. Salespeople may rent lists of leads and prospects that match the profile of their best customers, and target them with promotional offers to attract new customers. There are lists available for almost everything. Just name it, and there's a list for it! The challenge for most salespeople is to locate appropriate lists that will enable them to communicate with prospects that are likely to have a need or desire for their products or services. Fortunately, this task has become much easier due to advances in technology, the availability of lists, and companies like NextMark.

NextMark, headquartered in Hanover, New Hampshire, is a leading provider of list commerce technology. NextMark offers a free media list finder service to provide access to insider information on virtually every list on the market – which totals more than 60,000 lists! As revealed in Figure 4.1, a simple click on the Find Media tab on NextMark's website will take you to the list finder. Simply type in the keyword for the kind of list that you wish to locate and voilà – an entire page of lists pertaining to your keyword is likely to appear! What happened? NextMark's list finder search engine identified the most relevant and popular lists based on your keyword. Each of these lists will have an associated rank – which indicates the 'relevance' or fit of the data card to the specific set of search criteria used, and, in addition, the type of channel for which the list is available, such as postal mail, email, telephone, insert, or stuffer. Next, click on the list that you want to further explore and, in seconds, a data card appears for that particular list. Each data card includes detailed information about the list, along with buttons to request additional information and to place orders.

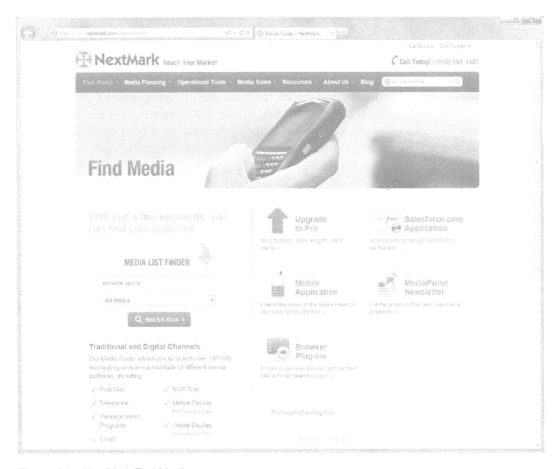

Figure 4.1   NextMark Find Media screen page

List rental, especially when used with the other offline techniques, such as sales letters or telemarketing, is a much more effective and efficient way to generate leads and locate prospects than merely blanketing the mass audience with advertisements in the hope that someone with a need or desire for the product/service will respond. Salespeople may contact a list broker in order to rent a list if they do not want to use a digital list finding service such as NextMark.

In summary, while the collection of lead-generation and prospecting techniques addressed above is not an exhaustive list, they represent the most commonly used offline methods. Now let's examine some common online techniques for generating leads and prospects.

Utilizing online lead-generation and prospecting techniques

Before we begin describing the online techniques, let's reflect for a moment on how our modern digital world has dramatically transformed lead-generation and prospecting activities for most businesses and industries. However, always remember that technology is only a tool which will never replace human intelligence and the unique capabilities of salespeople. While examining the commonly used online techniques, keep in mind that computers may be better at math, but they don't come close to the creativity and ingenuity of the human brain.[30] Having a personal connection to prospects, understanding what they want, and delivering problem-solving results is what salespeople do much better than computers. However, digital lead-generation and prospecting techniques offer great precision and assistance for salespeople when generating leads and prospecting for new business.

Similar to offline techniques, the most valuable online lead-generation and prospecting techniques are those associated with current customers. Some common online lead-generation and prospecting techniques are the CRM system, online reviews, search engine optimization (SEO), online advertising, webinars, blog posts, email, web scraping, and social listening. These are detailed below.

CRM system

The first digital technique that should be used for lead generation and prospecting is the company's customer relationship management (CRM) system, as it will enable salespeople to analyze existing customer data to identify the defining characteristics and behaviors of current customers. Salesforce, IBM, and other companies offer artificial intelligence (AI) tools to interface with CRM systems to produce valuable predictive analysis. This data will enable effective digital targeting of sales leads via other digital techniques, including email blasts, online advertisements, and social media platforms.

For example, a Harley-Davidson dealership located in New York City used Albert, an AI-driven marketing platform offered by a firm called Algorithm's, to analyze existing customer data from the dealership's CRM system to drive in-store traffic by generating leads. For Harley-Davidson, leads were defined as customers who express interest in speaking to a salesperson by completing a form on the dealership's website. The results were outstanding as the dealership quickly went from getting one qualified lead per day to 40 per day. By the third month, the dealership's leads had increased by 2,930 percent.[31]

Online reviews

Salespeople can encourage their current customers to leave online reviews which may serve as potential leads and future referral opportunities. In addition, online reviews provided by customers on platforms such as Google, Yelp, and Facebook can enable a company to get higher search engine rankings, which in turn will also lead to a greater number of sales leads and prospects.[32]

Search engine optimization (SEO)

Optimization is the *process* of improving website traffic by using search engines. In general, when a link to a website is listed higher in position on a search engine results page, the user is more likely to view it. Thus, search engine optimization aims at moving the link to be one of the top ones on the results page.

In today's digital world, most prospective customers will conduct background research before making important buying decisions, with the majority of these prospects using search engines to find information online. In fact, some prospects may be searching for companies prior to companies looking for them. Because of this shift in prospect behaviors, it has become very important and valuable for a company to have its products and services or a company website show up on the *first page* of search engines for a particular keyword that describes or will benefit their business. How important is it to be on the first page of Google? The number one position on Google search achieves an average of 58.4 percent of all clicks from users, according to a study from Optify. Websites ranked number one receive an average click-through rate (CTR) of 36.4 percent; number two has a CTR of 12.5 percent; and number three has a CTR of 9.5 percent.[33] Thus, the closer the company is to the top, the more traffic they will receive from the organic search listing.

There are three components to getting a site ranked in most search engines, and specifically in Google. They are: content, links, and activity. Content refers to how relevant the content on the site is to the actual domain name and how relevant it is to the keyword search. For instance, a site with the domain www.dogtraining.com is likely to have a #1 ranking based on a keyword search on Google if it has current, relevant information about dog training, content is added and updated regularly, and the site has a large number of high-quality backlinks. Any other sites competing on the same 'dog training' keyword will be hard pressed to knock www.dogtraining.com out of the number one spot on Google. When prospects search for information, it's important that the data they find is relevant, accurate, and consistent across all media channels and digital formats. When prospects visit a company's website, they should see a concise attention-grabbing value proposition. In addition, the salesperson's contact information should be listed on each and every webpage in the same format. This is easily achieved by adding the contact information to the footer of the website. The number of links is a count of how many electronic links are formed to the website, and can be thought of as a popularity contest. This metric is based on the premise that the more valuable a site is, the more people will link to it. The end result of linking is twofold. First, if the content is good, it will establish the author as an expert across multiple directories in various media. Second, it will create traffic from each of these directories back to the website. This leads to the third part of Google's triad for getting a site ranked, which is activity. Activity refers to the average length of time people stay on a website and how they are interacting with the website. Activity also includes a measure of how often a site is updated – daily, weekly, or monthly – the more often the better. Given that most prospective customers will search for information, salespeople must embrace SEO and integrate a strong digital presence into their lead-generation and prospecting activities.

Online advertising

Advertising through digital platforms, especially via social media such as Facebook, Twitter, LinkedIn, and Instagram, have come a long way over the past decade. Sales-people don't need to have big budgets to reach their targeted prospect. Facebook ads comprise more than 20 percent of global, mobile digital ad spending as these ads are very user friendly, work well on almost any budget, and provide substantial analytics for tracking.[34] In fact, you can import a list of email addresses within Facebook to create ads that will show only to that specific list of consumers.

Plus, Facebook allows you to create custom audiences based on people's actions and how they engage with your company – for instance, people who land on a particular website or a specific page on a website, people who like, comment, or share on a Facebook page, people who add products to a shopping cart, but do not finish purchasing, and so on. Over time, salespeople can add consumers to each audience, target ads to the various audiences, and run retargeting campaigns.

Once a custom audience grows to 1,000 consumers, Facebook allows you to create a lookalike audience based on the custom audience. Lookalike audiences are unique to your custom audiences. Plus, each custom audience can create multiple lookalike audiences. With lookalike audiences, you can create additional audiences based on the top 1%, 2%, 5%, 10%, and so on, of each custom audience. Facebook uses its analytics and builds each lookalike audience based on consumers who have interacted with your site or page. Lookalike audiences are considered cold traffic, but the conversion rates are normally higher than would otherwise be expected. This is due to the fact that each audience was created based on people who have already interacted with your website or Facebook page.

The laser focus of this targeting makes online ads a highly effective lead-generation and prospecting technique.[35] We'll discuss social media platforms more a bit later in the chapter, but for now, keep in mind that salespeople should include using online ads in their arsenal of tools for generating new customers.

Resources are available to train salespeople and others on how to use online ads effectively. For example, PublishToThrive.com, an entrepreneurial business venture developed by Charles George, focuses on training non-fiction authors, speakers, coaches, consultants, bloggers, and course creators to build an online business (see Figure 4.2). This resource teaches clients how to implement digital marketing strategies to build an email list, engage the list with email newsletters, and then monetize the list. To generate leads, Charles offers a free downloadable report, *101 Ways to Increase the Size of Your Email List*. To build the list, he uses paid media buys, such as Facebook ads and solo emails. All paid media traffic is sent to a landing page, where suspects can either opt in to download the report or leave. Charles monetizes the list with paid ads, affiliate marketing, product sales, workshops, coaching, and services. Here are a few metrics that Charles tracks to grow the business and ensure the business is profitable:

→ **Cost per lead**: on average, it costs between $2.00 and $3.00 per web-based opt-in leads.
→ **Landing page conversion rate**: currently, the landing page is getting a 43.6 percent conversion rate from cold Facebook ad traffic.
→ **Email open rates and click-through rates**: these metrics reveal how engaged the email list is. Currently, the email list averages a 36.8 percent open rate and a 5.6 percent click-through rate.
→ **Value of a customer**: Charles measures this number at three, six, nine, and 12-month intervals.

The reason for this? To determine when the break-even point between cost per lead and revenue will occur. If Charles knows the media buys will break even within the first three months, then the customer will be more valuable at six, nine, and 12 months. Knowing these metrics creates more leads, customers, and a more accurate estimate of future revenue.

Tracking this data allows Charles to grow and then monetize the list. Plus, it tells him which media buys are profitable and allows him to scale the company, and gain revenue quickly by increasing the size of the prospect email list.

Publish to
THRIVE

Figure 4.2 PublishToThrive.com logo
Used with kind permission of PublishToThrive.

Webinars

A webinar is an online presentation held via the Internet, usually in real time.[36] The concept behind webinars is similar to public speaking in that salespeople can provide an informative presentation about a problem that a group of prospective customers may be facing and then offer assistance to help solve the problem. Webinars are very flexible and enable salespeople to speak on a wide range of topics, from the comfort of their home if desired. In addition, the software, such as Go to Webinar, Zoom and ReadyTalk, is inexpensive and easy to use.[37] Salespeople can invite prospects to attend their webinars via email communication, social media advertisements, trade association announcements, and other means of communication.

Webinars are commonly used in B2B selling and can be effectively used to generate leads and build a prospect list. Let's examine a four-step process for doing so. The steps are:

1. The presenting company, A, sets up an affiliate link for the promoting company, B.
2. Company B sends an email to its list with the affiliate link, asking its customers to join them on the webinar to learn about some topic of interest to those on the list.
3. The link in the email that Company B sent to customers on its list is a link to the opt-in page for the webinar.
4. When people opt in to the webinar, those names and email addresses become an asset of Company A, because they can be downloaded from the webinar software and inserted into an email program, such as Icontact. This allows Company A to directly communicate with these people via email at any point in the future.

Traditionally, companies will use a separate opt-in email form for people to actually log in to the webinar when it is being delivered. This serves two purposes. First, it allows Company A to measure who registered for the webinar and how many people actually logged in. The company can then look at this number to determine its close rate and how many people actually purchased. Second, the company can segment the people who did not log in or purchase, into separate lists and email a link to the recorded version of the webinar, or details of the webinar will be rebroadcast.

Blog posts

A blog is a web log that contains informally written information and journal-like entries. There are many types of blogs, varying from those chronicling personal experiences to informational, article-like pieces from experts. Blogs also vary in scope. Some blogs are about a very specific topic, such as 'A beginner's guide to Microsoft Word software,' while others can cover a much wider subject, such as computers. Still others have no stated subject at all. For salespeople, blogging is really about communicating, offering information, and having a means to connect with prospective customers, whether they follow the blog, submit questions, or post comments to various entries. When writing blogs, salespeople should provide answers to frequently asked questions (FAQs) about their product. All company-based blogs that aim to sell their product or service should create a type of discussion board to drive interaction with prospects. Salespeople may also contribute informational blogs to other websites, such as social networking websites like LinkedIn. As previously mentioned, increasing the number of links to and from your website will increase the SEO rankings of the site. Thus, blogs with links to your website are a valuable technique for prospecting and lead generation.

Email

Email is similar to traditional direct mail in that it is conducted on a one-to-one, personal basis. However, email costs a lot less than traditional mail and therefore enables sales-people to communicate on a more frequent basis. In addition, email is much faster and prospects respond more quickly to email than to direct mail, with replies normally coming within hours from the time they received the message. Likewise, this sets expectations to receive timely responses from salespeople when they send email requests or inquiries. Multiple studies reveal that it typically takes only three seconds for prospective customers to decide whether to open a marketing email in their inbox.[38] Salespeople need to make a connection in the subject line to get the prospects who are scanning emails to click on the subject line. With solid background research, email allows salespeople to send tailored and personalized messages to specific customers, based on needs. This method is most effective when it is database-driven and customized to match the needs of customers within specific market segments. This is true for both B2B and B2C email.

Research shows that sales leads should receive an email sequence with multiple follow-up emails, each containing an appropriate call-to-action (CTA) to move them through the sales funnel.[39] However, solo emails may work to generate lead traffic when used with targeted email lists where the people on those lists are accustomed to receiving, opening, and clicking on emails. Plus, if used correctly, there is either a direct or an implied endorsement when buying email addresses from a particular company. Essentially, you are leveraging the relationship the list owner has with the customers on the list, which makes the contact a warmer lead. For example, say you rent a segment of 2,500 subscribers from a total list of 50,000 and send a solo email to that segment. If the response is good, then you might rent the whole list and distribute a solo email to generate even more leads. If the email is effective in generating leads with the entire list, then you may purchase multiple mailings at a discounted media buying rate (which is normally negotiable). So, solo emails also work well to test lead lists and determine their effectiveness.

Finally, banner ads, text message ads, and solo emails are sold on the basis of either a flat rate or a cost per thousand (CPM). Solo emails are typically the most expensive and can range anywhere from $30/M to $200/M (M is the Roman numeral for one thousand). When sending either e-newsletters or solo emails, you may include several hyperlinks within the email; however, they should all take the customer to the same website destination or landing page.

Today's salespeople use marketing automation or software platforms and technologies designed to effectively carry out email blasts. Marketing automation has multi-channel capabilities and has stemmed from the use of auto responders, emails that have been set up to be sent automatically when triggered by a predetermined variable or some particular event. Auto responders enable salespeople to create and set up an email system and then remain hands-off as it sends out electronic messages. Triggers may include the purchase of a new product, an opt-in to a new list, the registration for a webinar, or pretty much any other activity that has an electronic signal associated with it.

Here is a typical scenario for how salespeople use auto responders for generating leads and prospects:

A. Prospects opt in to a new list.
B. They are immediately sent an auto responder welcoming their communication and providing them the information they requested.

C. Two days later, each prospect receives a second email with additional content linked to a teaser video.

D. On the third day, these prospects receive a third email with a link to another video. This video may be a current customer providing a testimonial.

Salespeople may use auto responders to generate leads and prospects, to build prospects' familiarity with a product or service, and to provide information that prospects will perceive as valuable – all with the goal to increase sales. Most email software providers offer auto responders as part of their packages and services. As far as measuring response rates, most email service providers can do this. Typical metrics that can be measured include deliverability rate, open rate, click-through rate, bounce rate, and the unsubscribe rate. Salespeople need to be aware of and adhere to the legal regulations which typically vary by country and may apply to their geographical area, regarding using email to generate leads.

Computer screen with digital data

Web scraping

As discussed in Chapter 2, web scraping is a technique used to extract structured data from websites.[40] Web scraping is a universal technique adopted by most search engines to index information on the Web using a bot web crawler. In essence, web scraping is a hacking technique to mine information on the Internet and to formulate highly customized lists of leads.

An example of the use of web scraping is using Connectio.io, which is Facebook ad software that allows you to connect Facebook lead ads to your email provider's CRM system. It also helps you find hidden Facebook interests to target ads. It creates custom audiences based on specific auto-responder lists, and it will automatically turn a page's most engaged posts into ads.

One of the most common uses of web scraping is conducting research on prospects or leads and downloading information for sales analysis.[41] When researching potential leads and prospects, salespeople will want to obtain as much information as possible on a company and individual contacts, prior to reaching out to them, and web scraping is an effective technique for doing so. In addition to Connectio.io, which was mentioned in the above example, Table 4.1 reveals a number of software tools that may be used for web scraping.

Table 4.1 List of web-scraping software

Import.io – Is great to use if you can clearly describe your customer or prospect so that Import.io will know where to find relevant information about that target customer or prospect on the Web.

Datanyze – May be used to either prospect or gather information about current customers and notify salespeople on day one a customer has added a competitor's technology, which enables them to reach out to that customer before it's too late.

BuiltWith – Is a website profiler tool that allows salespeople to see all websites that are using certain Web-based services or integrations, which enables lead lists to be created.

InsideView – Provides salespeople with updates on all business and social events that are happening for each prospect and can also provide a real-time dossier on every prospect listed in the salesperson's company CRM system.

FunnelFire – Is an online sales intelligence platform that continuously tracks keywords across thousands of news sources, allows users to filter prospect-related online data, and offers CRM system integration so that the lead profiles are generated in real time for salespeople.

DiscoverOrg – Is a sales and marketing intelligence platform that gathers company and market information, follows trigger events and job changes, figures out an organization's structure, provides contact information, and integrates with many CRM systems.

Followerwonk – Is an analytics tool on Twitter which offers many features including audience targeting.

Little Bird – This software helps salespeople find influencers by using select keywords, seeing which potential buyers connect with, as well as who is connecting.

Parsehub – This tool enables salespeople to conduct advanced data segmentation and collect information about calendars, comments, infinite scrolling, infinite page numbers, drop downs, etc. on big publications and blogs.

Octoparse – With the free Octoparse account, salespeople can scrape up to 10,000 records, or for a one-time fee, unlimited records.

Grepsr – This platform offers salespeople the opportunity to manage their data-scraping projects with a project management tool, as well as automation, whereby once it is set up and a rule is set, the software will perform regularly scheduled scrapes.

BKLNK.com – This software finds relevant Amazon categories to make it easier to get your book ranked in Amazon's search. For instance, it lists similar categories and shares how competitive the category is.

Longtail Pro – Longtail Pro helps you identify keyword phrases and provides metrics on each keyword by how difficult it is to rank for the keyword.

InterestExplorer.io – The purpose of this software is to help discover new Facebook ad interest that is not normally displayed in the ad managers' searches.

Source: Max Altschuler (2016) *Hacking Sales*; Charles George, personal communication; and Luca Tagliaferro, 'Data scraping tools for marketers who don't know code' (July 15, 2019), https://searchengineland.com/data-scraping-tools-for-marketers-who-dont-know-code-319446, retrieved June 10, 2020.

Social listening

Social listening is monitoring social media platforms to learn: what is being said about a particular company's brand, what topics are relevant to the company, and what insight can be gained from the content communicated by that company.[42] The content may include direct mention of the brand, customer feedback, and discussions about competitors, industries, or any related keywords, hashtags, and topics. Social listening is not just assessing social media mentions; it also entails analyzing the content to identify potential areas for generating new business opportunities. Looking for areas of customer needs that are not presently being met is a strategy that can generate new leads and prospects.[43] Also, social listening gives salespeople an opportunity to understand what is being said about their company, engage in conversations with their brand's audience, and respond to questions and issues as they arise.[44] Salespeople may see someone talking about a problem that they can solve, so they can offer valuable advice and suggestions.[45] Salespeople may use tools such as Google Alerts, BuzzSumo, Mention, or SproutSocial.com to begin social listening.

Summary

In summary, new online techniques for generating leads and prospects arise regularly and salespeople must keep abreast of innovations. For example, while social media has become a regular and standard mode of communication for most businesses and individuals, these platforms are constantly offering new features. Social media lead-generation and prospecting techniques are critical for salespeople today and they will be explored in our next section.

Exploring social media platforms for developing leads and prospecting

In today's digital world, most, if not all, salespeople use social networking for generating leads and prospecting. Wondering why? The reason is likely obvious: it works. Social media networks offer salespeople the opportunity to reach a huge diverse audience, given that more than 45 percent of the global population is active across different social media platforms.[46] Social networking sites reach more than 82 percent of the world's online population and 75 percent of B2B buyers have said that social media would influence a future purchase.[47] Research also shows that social media is the most effective technique used worldwide for improving lead-generation quality.[48] In addition, viewing on mobile devices represents two out of every three digital media minutes and up to 60 percent of this time is spent on social media apps.[49]

Salespeople need to determine which social media platform will work best for generating leads and prospects. Typically, the best platform for generating leads is the platform their customers use because salespeople need to engage with customers and prospects where they live. However, research shows that the best social media platforms for B2B lead generation are Facebook and LinkedIn.[50] Let's briefly explore these two social media platforms.

Facebook icon

Facebook

Research shows that 82 percent of B2B marketers believe that Facebook is the best site for social media lead generation.[51] Why? For starters, more than 2.45 billion people use Facebook every month, which gives the platform the largest social networking population.[52] Facebook also offers some helpful tools to gather leads on its platform, including segmenting, retargeting, and creating lookalike audiences. In addition, Facebook offers excellent advertising products that provide an immersive experience, including canvas ads and carousel ads.[53] With Facebook ads, salespeople can boost posts, send people to a website, increase conversions on the platform, give video views, gather data about leads, and more.[54] Facebook dynamic lead ads are basically promoted forms designed to gather customized information about leads that can be automatically uploaded to a company's CRM system or downloaded for salespeople to follow up.[55] Facebook dynamic ads can be aligned based on people's interests and the lead-generation form encourages people to take action. Facebook ads are user-friendly, work well on almost any budget, and provide substantial analytics for internal tracking and assessment.[56]

Salespeople may want to create a Facebook group, which is similar to an online forum that encourages members to become more active and engaged. Members of a Facebook group can post questions, answer questions, offer advice to others, and share their brand experiences. Of course, salespeople need to start discussions and provide relevant content for their Facebook group members. In addition, salespeople may use Facebook to generate sales leads via Facebook events. Facebook events enable salespeople to plan, coordinate, and distribute announcements and invitations to events in order to encourage people to attend. Salespeople can easily engage with their audience via Facebook's calendar connection, which most people have on their smartphones, and may include compelling event photos, descriptions, maps, details, partners, and more. These are just some of the ways that salespeople may use Facebook for lead generation and prospecting. New features are emerging constantly which make Facebook a very effective social media platform for salespeople to use to identify and engage with sales leads and prospects.

LinkedIn icon

LinkedIn

LinkedIn is the number one professional social networking platform available, so it makes perfect sense for salespeople to use this networking site to identify and engage with prospective customers. LinkedIn has more than 675 million users, with more than 70 percent of those outside of the United States. In addition, 94 percent of B2B marketers use LinkedIn to distribute content, and 80 percent of B2B leads come from LinkedIn.[57]

Similar to Facebook, LinkedIn offers Lead Gen Forms, which is a pre-fill form ad format just for lead generation. These dynamic lead-generation ads are available as Message Ads and Sponsored InMail on the LinkedIn platform, and feature direct calls to action that can help generate leads.[58] Research shows that the average conversion rate on a LinkedIn Lead Gen Form is 13 percent, which is very high considering a typical website conversion rate is 2.35 percent.[59]

Thus, LinkedIn is an ideal place for salespeople to identify prospects, decision makers, and influencers to generate leads. How do salespeople find leads on LinkedIn? Here's a five-step process:[60]

Step 1: Create a client-facing profile. This should be a compelling LinkedIn page that contains the profiles of the key executives of the company and is written in a manner that provides thought-provoking information to prospective customers.

Step 2: Provide free relevant content. This content may be a blog post, e-book, video, etc. that demonstrates expertise, targets a specific audience, and includes a call-to-action.

Step 3: Search for prospects using the advanced search option. The filtering options include keywords, job title, company size, geographic location, first name, and last name. Additional filters, such as company size, interests, and years of experience, are available with a premium LinkedIn account. Sales Navigator is one of LinkedIn's premium plans that is specifically designed for lead generation.

Step 4: Send a personalized invitation to connect. This initial outreach will begin the conversation. However, with a free LinkedIn account, salespeople will only be able to send an InMail message to those people that they are already connected with. However, they can connect with all leads when using a premium LinkedIn account, such as the Professional Plan. This plan currently permits 20 InMail messages per month and allows companies to store 1,500 saved leads and more.[61] Salespeople should be sure to include who they are, why they're reaching out, and why it's worth responding (the value) in their initial communication.[62]

Step 5: Reply to warm leads. Salespeople should engage with those LinkedIn users who replied to either the content or the call-to-action they distributed. Timely replies are needed for all effective lead generation and are especially critical when using social media platforms.

An additional step that salespeople should take when using LinkedIn for generating leads and prospecting is reviewing the 'Who's Viewed Your Profile' section of their company's LinkedIn account. This section will provide an instant list of 'warm' prospects since the LinkedIn visitors listed there have been inspecting the salesperson's or company's profile on the platform, thus indicating that they may already have an interest.[63]

Regardless of the social media platform, salespeople must use effective strategies to obtain more leads and engage with prospects on social media. Some of these strategies are:[64]

- providing profile data and clear contact details
- creating links and call-to-action buttons such as sign-up, book, get, and reserve
- creating clickable and click-worthy content, especially sharp images, compelling copy, and videos that will entice the user to take the requested action
- developing and following a regular posting schedule of relevant and valuable content in order to keep followers interested and obtain more leads
- developing relevant and user-friendly landing pages to provide users with a clear path that is as easy to follow as possible
- using the respective social media advertising form that is available within most social media platforms
- offering attractive incentives such as contests, sweepstakes, discounts, special codes, gated or invite-only content or whitepapers, etc., to give people a reason to share their information with you
- personalizing your offer to tailor it to a particular sales lead by taking advantage of the targeting tools available on the respective social media platforms which may include gender, occupation, or age level
- using GIFs, which are animated images, to provide greater visual impact and creative style to the content, as most people use GIFs and other visuals, such as emojis, in their online communication
- utilizing a website meeting scheduler, such as Calendly, to allow prospects to be able to conveniently schedule appointments with salespeople. This direct scheduling eliminates the series of back-and-forth emails otherwise needed to select a date and time that works based on people's availability
- using a contact management program to record all interactions and track all touchpoints with sales leads, document preferred contact methods of prospects, and ensure timely and appropriate follow-up
- maintaining close alignment with the marketing department to take full advantage of any information shared on sales leads.

Salespeople must understand the differences between the various social media plat-forms as well as consider using both 'cold calling' and warm-calling techniques when generating leads and prospecting. We'll examine the differences between warm and cold calling in the next section.

Analyzing and employing cold calling

Making the initial contact with a prospective customer is one of the most difficult challenges that a salesperson has and may be the most critical to establishing a long-term relationship between the potential customer and the company or sales organization. Various means are employed to begin a relationship. The most productive method using media is to contact prospective customers using direct mail or LinkedIn Sales Navigator. The communication should include a branding message about the company and ask prospects to reply with an indication as to their level of interest in the company and its offerings. That way, the prospect becomes aware of the company and the value provided to its customers. As dis-cussed earlier, networking is also critical to meeting prospects. To prepare for networking, salespeople should develop a short summary statement about themselves and the value they can provide to the prospect (the 'elevator pitch'). Delivering this pitch along with cre-ating an opportunity to meet the prospect outside of the networking event is known as a 'warm calling' opportunity for the salesperson. The prospect is aware of the salesperson's organization and its benefits, so when the salesperson phones the target it is a warm call. The challenge that the salesperson has is what to say when they call the prospect.

Salesperson on telephone

Some companies use a method called 'cold calling' to make initial contact with a prospect. Cold calling, also referred to as cold canvassing, is defined as making an unsolicited call to a potential sales lead or prospect with whom the salesperson has had no prior contact nor gathered any lead qualification information. Cold calling differs from warm calling, which typically involves salespeople gathering background research using direct mail and LinkedIn prior to contacting potential prospects on the telephone.

With cold calls, the likelihood of the lead or prospect moving through the sales funnel and qualifying as a customer is unknown. The success rate for the salesperson to even have a conversation with a potential prospect during a cold call, is typically less than 3 percent.[65] In addition, unsolicited cold calls are very expensive. Even when using direct mail, digital platforms, and social media such as LinkedIn to establish contact, the salesperson must still spend time on the telephone to begin a dialogue that may lead to a sale.

Cold calling is used by sales teams at some major companies, including State Farm Insurance, Granite Telecommunications, Gartner, IBM, Paychex, NY Life, and Xerox, to name a few. It is a very popular method for creating an initial contact with prospects and is used successfully in business-to-business (B2B) marketing. Cold calling is typically done by telephone as opposed to in-person, such as canvassing door to door. Salespeople can be successful in using cold calling when they realize that the primary objective of the cold call is to make the prospect aware of the possibility that working with them may provide a better solution or eliminate a recurring problem they've experienced.[66] Since it is a one-on-one direct conversation, there is a mutual exchange of information that takes place during the phone call. This allows the salesperson to suggest a follow-up meeting to present possible solutions to the prospect.

The challenge of cold calling is that the salesperson must reach and get the attention of the decision maker. Most B2B prospects are generally busy multi-tasking and ignore attempted sales pitches over the telephone in a cold-calling situation. Such decision makers have no idea who the salesperson is, nor the patience and attention span needed for a salesperson to introduce a potential solution to the perceived prospect's problem, without prior qualification. Salespeople must respect the fact that although their prospects multi-task all the time, there are so many different issues vying for their attention. One cold call interrupts their attention span and their busy day. Their tendency may be to hang up the phone on the caller. Therefore, the strategy in cold calling must relate to these obstacles.

The purpose of the cold call is *not* to sell. The objective of a cold call is to set a follow-up meeting. Typically, salespeople must hold the prospect's attention for at least 10 uninterrupted minutes in order to gain a commitment to a follow-up meeting. During this time, the salesperson can qualify the prospect, show understanding of their problems, and demonstrate how they can solve the problems together. To achieve the cold-calling objective, the salesperson must be strategic and follow an ordered process. Table 4.2 reveals the step-by-step process for conducting a 'Gold' call, along with tips for conducting successful cold calls.

Table 4.2 10 steps to successful 'Gold' calling

1. Define the company's unique selling proposition. What is its uniqueness for solving the prospect's challenge? (NOTE: Do <u>not</u> sell on the phone. Your mission is to get the appointment, not make a sales call.)
2. Use an ice breaker to introduce yourself and define how long the call will take. 'I am **hoping** (emphasis is critical) I can get 10 seconds to explain why I am calling.' (NOTE: 52.8% are likely to respond to this statement to continue the conversation.)
3. Take the USP and solve the problem: 'Lemonade quenches thirst.' Lemonade stand statement: 'We sell lemonade to quench thirst.' (NOTE: 76.5% are likely to respond to this statement to continue the conversation.)
4. Use a focus question to connect prospects to the need: 'How much personal focus do you have in solving challenges to train your students or salespeople to be more effective on the phone or on LinkedIn?' (NOTE: 61.8% are likely to respond favorably and will continue the discussion.)
5. Use an attention question to pose the solution to a challenge the prospect has: 'Suppose that we have a simple way to train your students or salespeople to convert leads to customers, would I get your attention?' (NOTE: 79.4% are likely to respond favorably to a phone call from a salesperson with this statement.)
6. Use a decision-maker question to reveal the decision maker: 'If you are not the person in charge of making the decision, could you direct me to the person who is?' (NOTE: 61.8% are likely to continue.)
7. Use a trial close: 'Could we schedule a time next week to speak again, either on the phone or in your office, to see where we may be a fit?' (NOTE: 70.6% are likely to respond favorably.)
8. Use a closing question to schedule a follow-up meeting. There are several alternatives to ask the same question. '<u>When</u> can I have more of your attention? Is Tuesday at 3:00 or is Wednesday at 4:00 better?' (NOTE: 72.5% are likely to respond favorably.)
9. Provide meeting confirmation information: 'May I have your email address? I will send you a meeting invite.' 'I won't call to confirm but should you have a need to change, just drop me a note.' (NOTE: 73.5% are likely to respond favorably.)
10. The sales meeting is where you NOW have the prospect's attention to present and sell.

Source: Research conducted by Professor Harvey Markovitz. who interviewed 100 sales executives, asking: 'What is the likelihood that you would continue the conversation when asked this question?' (Used with permission of Harvey Markovitz.)

There is no time during a cold call to give a 'pitch' for the business or discuss a value proposition. There's no time to give an elevator pitch or provide a business solution, knowing that the target is not interested in talking on the telephone because that person has other pressing issues. Salespeople must be prepared to handle this. Salespeople must grab the attention of their prospects in only 2–5 seconds to make a great first impression. Salespeople must be careful not to set off their prospect's trigger by asking for too much information. What should the salesperson say once the phone is answered by someone at the prospect organization?

Salespeople must prepare a short (10 words or less) statement that describes the benefit that they can provide to the prospect. This is a statement of your company's unique selling proposition (USP), and a simple short statement of the end result of how you solve problems. You must define the uniqueness of your business and then describe what problems you will solve, how you will solve them, and what's in it for your prospect to listen to what you have to say. For example, 'We help companies solve international shipping challenges,' or 'We train salespeople and students to be more effective in converting LinkedIn and telemarketing leads to customers.' Be sure to describe your business in simple terms, such as the following lemonade stand statement: 'We sell lemonade to quench thirst.'

The salesperson needs to make an appointment and confirm it. It must be kept simple as any complications decrease the likelihood of the appointment being made. You should ask the 'focus' question to be sure that you are speaking with the *right* person, the decision maker, at the prospect company. The focus question will establish the connection between the prospect and the need or problem. For example, 'When it comes time to training students, how much personal involvement do you have with that part of your business'? Next, you must gain the prospect's attention by asking another simple question: 'Suppose I was in a position to train your students at a much lower cost and get them up to speed quicker. Whose attention would I need to get to see if there is a fit?' And, 'If you are not the person, could you direct me to the person who is?' Once the prospect has been qualified, expressed an interest, and indicated desire to go to the next stage, you are ready to move to asking the closing question and scheduling the appointment.

Cold calling works. For example, professional speaker Troy Harrison found success in using cold calling to set up appointments and have conversations with prospects, who then went to his social media to view all of his posts, YouTube videos, testimonials, and so on. His prospects used social media to assess his reputation, which led them to book him for a speaking engagement.[67] This example demonstrates that cold calls worked for Harrison in generating leads and prospects when social media supplemented his initial cold-calling efforts.

Strategies to increase the effectiveness of cold calling include following up several times after the initial contact, using a carefully crafted personalized script for each communication effort, and contacting the appropriate person within the targeted company.[68] Scripts should be customized for each of the various steps of the selling process. For example, Pete Ekstrom has been in the business of cold calling for more than 30 years and has used his successful cold-calling process to create *The Gold Call Script Builder Kit* (see Figure 4.3) which he sells commercially. Companies, such as Oracle, Xerox, Google Apps for Business and NY Life Financial Advisors, among others, have adopted *The Gold Call Script Builder Kit* to train their salespeople in cold calling.

Figure 4.3 The Gold Call Kit logo

As demonstrated above, *The Gold Call Script Builder Kit* includes sharing the steps of how to build an effective outbound Gold Call script, script composition strategies, effective questioning techniques, and personal coaching sessions with Pete Ekstrom. Sound appealing? You can learn more by investigating *The Gold Call Script Builder Kit*, featured in the Readings and Resources section at the end of this chapter.

Both warm-calling and cold-calling methods may be successfully used to generate sales leads and prospects. However, all lead-generation techniques are not equally effective. Salespeople must monitor and assess the effectiveness of prospecting approaches and activities to determine which techniques work best to generate prospects and customers. That's the topic of our final section.

MONITORING METRICS

Monitoring metrics

Essential metrics to assess in lead generation and prospecting include cost per lead and close rates. Let's examine each of these metrics.

Cost per lead (CPL)

CPL is the most important metric to understand in lead generation. Regardless of whether you are generating leads offline at a trade show or online via social media, calculating CPL will help salespeople to more effectively allocate their lead-generation budgets. As Figure 4.4 shows, CPL is calculated by dividing the amount of budget spent on lead generation by the total number of qualified new leads acquired. CPL varies by industry, product/service, and channel.

For example, let's say a salesperson has $1,000 to spend on an AdWords campaign. If this salesperson obtains 100 qualified leads from that campaign, then the corresponding CPL is $10 ($1,000/100). By calculating the CPL for each of the lead-generation techniques, channels, or platforms used, salespeople can compare CPLs and use this comparative analysis to identify those techniques, channels, or platforms that provide the best return on investment (ROI). Some channels, such as SEO and email, typically outperform other channels, such as television advertising and display ads in print publications.[69] CPL assessment will help salespeople to determine where they should focus their lead-generation efforts.

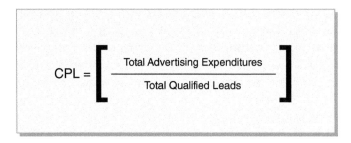

Figure 4.4 Formula for calculating CPL

Close rates

A close rate or ratio is the number of sales a salesperson closes compared to the number they tried to close. Think of it this way: Of all the leads in a salesperson's pipeline, how many of them led to a sales commitment? Close rates are calculated by dividing the number of customers that came from a group of leads by the total number of leads generated over a period of time. The result of this calculation is typically less than 1.00. The result is then multiplied by 100 in order to express it as a percentage of the total number of leads. Once the close rate has been determined for a given lead-generation method, it can be used by salespeople to determine the number of leads they need to generate to meet a given sales quota. To do this, they simply divide the number of customers they need by the close rate to calculate the number of leads they need to generate. For example, let's say a salesperson closed 10 deals out of the 40 they were working. The close ratio in this case is 0.25 or 25 percent. The higher their close rate, the more effective salespeople are at converting opportunities in the pipeline into sales revenue. Also, the higher their close rate, the fewer leads they will need to generate to meet a given sales target.

Once salespeople calculate their close ratio, they can compare it to industry benchmarks and targets. Sales close rates vary by industry; thus, the following benchmarks are only representative of a few industries. Research conducted by Hubspot on the close rates of more than 8,900 companies' sales organizations across 28 industries, revealed the following sales close rates by industry:[70]

- Biotechnology industry: 15%
- Business & industrial industry: 27%
- Computer software industry: 22%
- Computers & electronics industry: 23%
- Finance industry: 19%

Research also shows that social media platforms and strategies work to generate and nurture leads through the sales funnel. For example, the average lead capture rate of a social media quiz is 31.6 percent; videos shared on social media platforms get 66 percent more qualified leads; and one in three people who participate in a social media contest agree to receive further information.[71] Of course, salespeople must be quick to respond to inquiries via social media. Research shows that more than 85 percent of customers expect salespeople to respond to their questions and inquiries on Facebook within six hours.[72] Social media platforms enable one-on-one customization and personalization in advertising to and contacting prospects, which increases the impact of the communication. For example, LinkedIn ads that directly address someone have a 19 percent higher click-through rate and a 53 percent higher conversion rate than ads that don't.[73]

Salespeople who use social media to collect leads will also be collecting valuable analytical insights as well. Salespeople should use Google Analytics to track leads to their company's website, which will enable them to determine where the majority of their leads are coming from. For example, if the metrics show that LinkedIn is generating more leads than Facebook, Instagram, or Twitter, then the salesperson should place greater efforts on LinkedIn.[74] Salespeople may also use sales analytics tools to determine the type of content, including both images and messages, that performs best. For example, UK retirement community developer McCarthy & Stone found that images of apartment exteriors received more clicks than computer renderings. By using this insight, McCarthy & Stone was able to generate 4.3 times more sales leads and lower costs per lead in its next campaign.[75]

In conclusion, salespeople should use a variety of lead-generation and prospecting techniques and customize their use to what works most effectively given their industry, company, and target market customers. In today's ever-changing world, salespeople should always be on the lookout for new places to find sales leads and prospects. Remember, the process for lead generation and prospecting is all about cultivating mutually beneficial relationships that help salespeople build their network and, ultimately, grow their customer base.

CHAPTER SUMMARY

✓ Note that a strong network and a supportive mentor are success factors in your career.

✓ Qualify leads to optimize the return on investment for your time.

✓ Use social media effectively to generate leads and engage with prospective customers.

✓ Remember that your primary goal when cold calling is to secure an appointment.

✓ Evaluate, monitor and work to continuously improve your cost per lead and close rate.

KEY TERMS

Auto-responder	Networking
Blog	Optimization
Cold calling	Outbound calls
Cold canvassing	Prospecting
Cross-selling	Prospects
Customer relationship management (CRM)	Sales lead
	Sales qualified lead (SQL)
Inbound calls	Social listening
Influencer marketing	Suspect
Lead generation	Warm call
Marketing automation	Webinar
Marketing qualified lead (MQL)	Web scraping
Mentor	

REVIEW QUESTIONS

1. What is a professional mentor and how do you find one? What are the benefits of having a supportive mentor? As you consider your current contacts, who might be a good mentor for you?
2. Compare and contrast MQL and SQL.
3. Name and describe the three components evaluated when a website gets ranked by Google and most other search engines.
4. What are auto responders and why are they used? Typically, when salespeople use them to generate leads and prospects, what does the consumer experience when they opt in to a new list?
5. What is social listening and why should salespeople do this?
6. Describe the five steps of the process used to generate leads using LinkedIn.
7. List at least four effective strategies that can be used to obtain more leads and engage with prospects on social media.
8. What is the purpose of a cold call and what strategies can be used to improve the effectiveness of cold calling?
9. What is CPL? How is it calculated and why is it important to know this information?
10. What is close rate? How is it calculated and why is it important to know this information?

ETHICS IN ACTION

1. Through the course of your college studies, you met and entered into a mentoring relationship with Mr. Tom Rivers, the CEO of a small, local company. After graduation, you land a sales position with a global competitor of Tom's company. While Tom has expressed interest in your career growth in the past, his interest currently seems limited to any insider information you might share. Meetings with him have become uncomfortable for you. What do you say to Tom to address this issue? Will you continue to meet with him in the future?

2. You have spent the entire day making cold calls for a new product being introduced by your company. You are frustrated that your efforts so far have been futile. It seems that no one will take the time to hear you out. On the next call you make, you reach a man who asks for more information about your company. As you begin to reply, he interrupts you abruptly and begins ranting with anger over how he was treated by your company when working for a different employer. What do you say or do to respond to his criticism? Is it worthwhile to try to continue a discussion at this point?

EXERCISE – NEXTMARK PROSPECTING

Do you like to travel? If so, you are among the millions or billions or perhaps zillions of people who do. Tourism is a powerful industry that affects many different businesses, including hotels, restaurants, retail outlets, attractions, transportation providers, and meeting facilities. Tourism is also an industry made up of many different types of consumers with vastly different needs, wants, and desires to which tourism marketers must strategically appeal. Congratulations! You have become a sales development representative for your favorite vacation destination. Your main responsibilities are to generate leads and prospects for the businesses associated with your tourist attraction. Critically think about your business development challenge and address each of the following questions:

A. How will you begin to tackle your business development challenge? Why?
B. Which lead-generation and prospecting techniques will you use? Why?
C. What prospective customers will you pursue? Why?
D. What specific metrics will you measure and monitor to determine the effectiveness of your lead-generation and prospecting techniques?
E. Do you think that your business development activities will be successful? Why?

(Continued)

ROLE-PLAY

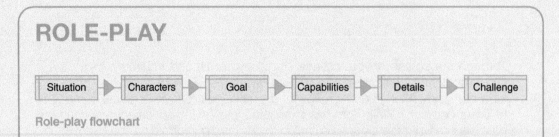

Role-play flowchart

Situation: You work as a sales professional for a local Honda dealership. It is December and your boss is putting a lot of pressure on the sales force to have a big month so the dealership can end up in the black for the year. There are a huge number of new 2021 models in and a modest number of remaining 2020 models that the sales manager wants to get off the lot. There are also a large number of used cars recently traded in that are models between 2016 and 2019.

Characters: You have two years of experience working for the Honda dealership and you have earned 'Top Salesperson' for five different months during the past year. A couple in their late 30s with three young children, aged 3, 5 and 6, comes into your dealership. Their 2005 SUV has 220,000 miles on it and is on its last legs. The dad is an engineer for a local manufacturing plant and earns a decent salary. The mom, once an elementary school teacher, quit her position to care for the children. The couple met in college and have been married for 10 years.

Selling goal: All prospective customers who visit the dealership are not qualified. You must qualify their buying capability and determine the best fit for a 'win-win' selling situation. The selling goal is for the salesperson to qualify the prospect and ultimately obtain a buying commitment.

Product/service capabilities: Honda automobiles are known for their excellent craftsmanship, reliability, and value. Consumer Reports routinely ranks Honda models among the top in its respective classes of vehicles. Honda has a medium-to-high price range and its vehicles are known not only to last a long time but also to hold their value for resale better than vehicles from most manufacturers.

Sales call details: The couple is very wary of high-pressure selling tactics, having just come from another dealership where they had to endure two hours of a very pushy, very high pressure, salesperson. Needless to say, their defenses are up. They have modest income and savings so buying a new, fully loaded model is probably beyond their comfortable reach.

Selling challenge: Role-play how you would approach this couple. How do you find out their needs and find the right fit for them without coming across as too pushy? How far can you move the couple along in the sales funnel?

READINGS AND RESOURCES

- Charles George (2020) 'Publish to Thrive: 101 ways to increase the size of your email list,' https://publishtothrive.com/lead-gen.
- Mike Jones and Ken Guest (2019) *Digital Prospecting: Finding, Nurturing and Closing Sales with Social Technologies.* Owing Mills, MD: Sandler Systems, Inc.
- Dan Kennedy (2006) *The Ultimate Sales Letter*, 3rd edition. Avon, MA: Adams Media.
- Ivan Misner, David Alexander and Brian Hilliard (2010) *Networking Like a Pro*. Irvine, CA: Entrepreneur Press.
- Andrea Nierenberg (2002) *Nonstop Networking: How to Improve Your Life, Luck, and Career.* Sterling, VA: Capital Books, Inc.
- Dayna Rothman (2014) *Lead Generation for Dummies*. Hoboken, NJ: John Wiley & Sons, Inc.
- 'The Gold Call Script Builder Kit,' https://thegoldcall.com.

CASE STUDY: CASHEDGE® AND DEALBUILDERS

CashEdge® provides innovative, online financial applications for banks, credit unions, and wealth management firms. The company serves more than 175 financial institutions in North America, including such leading institutions as Citibank, Royal Bank of Canada, and The Vanguard Group. CashEdge has offices in New York, Silicon Valley, and India. With CashEdge, financial institutions are able to create compelling online offerings that attract customers, generate revenues, and reduce costs. Cash Edge offers the following services:

- **Open Now-Fund Now:** online banking; automated account opening and funding
- **Advisor View:** wealth management; online investor account aggregation
- **Compliance View:** electronic collection of investor statements domiciled at other firms.

A few years ago, CashEdge established an objective to build a structured sales organization to sell its investor account aggregation solution to the independent advisor channel of retail brokerage firms. Before hiring any outside salespeople, CashEdge sought to first build a prospect pipeline of qualified leads that would be used by its newly-hired sales representatives. Pete Ekstrom, president of Dealbuilders (Figure 4.5), and his sales development team were contracted to work as direct representatives of CashEdge. Pete and his team handled all of the activities associated with qualifying prospects for CashEdge. They coordinated the scheduled meetings with key decision makers at prospective client firms, and built the sales pipeline for the new sales representatives at CashEdge.

Pete's team served as a prospector of new business for the online account aggregation solution that CashEdge offers to retail brokerage firms and other wealth management firms. **Cold calls** were made to key contacts within targeted companies, such as: Vice

Figure 4.5 Pete Ekstrom, president of Dealbuilders

President of Sales, Vice President of Advisory Services, Vice President of Recruiting, Chief Technology Officer, Chief Marketing Officer, and Chief Executive Officer.

Pete and his Dealbuilders team qualified prospects on the basis of whether there was a priority interest in helping the advisory channel strengthen the relationships they had with high net worth and institutional investors through the Web. Once the prospect was qualified, the team scheduled an in-person meeting or conference call on behalf of CashEdge.

Dealbuilders also qualified prospects for a CashEdge compliance solution ('Compliance View') that helps the legal and compliance areas of financial institutions comply with established US Securities Exchange Commission (SEC) and National Association of Securities Dealers (NASD) regulatory guidelines regarding the supervision of outside investment activities by employees and immediate family. CashEdge provided a means to electronically collect the duplicate copies of a firm's employees' statement of accounts domiciled away from the firm which employed them. This ensured that a firm would meet current legal requirements.

The business development team at Dealbuilders made cold calls to the General Counsel, Chief Compliance Officers at Wall Street's largest investment banks and brokerage firms, including CSFB First Boston, JP Morgan Chase, Morgan Stanley, and Goldman Sachs. Prospects were qualified on the basis of their expressed belief that the manual, mail-in processes used to collect duplicate statements are inefficient and that they would rather replace their current paper-based system with an electronic process. The electronic process would reduce operational costs and mitigate the possibility of securities fraud such as 'trading ahead.'

The Dealbuilders team, through cold calling, also qualified prospects for the CashEdge online account opening and funding solution called 'Open Now-Fund Now.' The CashEdge account opening solution automates the new account opening process and electronically transfers funds cleared through the Automated Clearing House (ACH) into the new accounts set up through the banks' web interface. Pete's team made cold calls to the senior executives of retail banking and credit unions and to those who manage the online banking system for their financial institution. His team scheduled meetings on behalf of CashEdge senior management

Since contracting Dealbuilders, Pete and his team have scheduled more than 100 meetings and conference calls with prospective clients, and have helped to generate more than $1 million in new software license sales for CashEdge.

Case questions:

1. For what reasons did CashEdge seek out the services of Dealbuilders? What business development challenges did Dealbuilders assume for CashEdge?
2. How valuable were the cold-calling, lead-generation activities conducted by Pete's team? What did they produce for CashEdge?
3. Had CashEdge not contracted Dealbuilders, how else might the company have effectively generated leads?

NOTES

1. Toni Harris, 'Becoming a networking success,' *Advisor Today* (March/April 2016), 111(2), 46.
2. Landy Chase, 'Networking: Why too many sales people just don't get it,' *American Salesman*, Burlington (January 1998), 43(1), 22–8.
3. Richard Weylman, 'In networking, relationships come before sales,' *National Underwriter* (Life, health/financial services ed.), Erlanger (February 1993), 97(5), 14.
4. Ibid.
5. Amanda Visser, 'How to build valuable networks,' *Finweek* (November 2017), pp. 52–3.
6. Toni Harris, 'Becoming a networking success,' *Advisor Today* (March/April 2016), 111(2), 46.
7. Adapted from Richard Weylman, 'Turning visibility into sales,' *National Underwriter* (Life, health/financial services ed.), Erlanger (August 1999), 103(31), 21–2.
8. Amanda Visser, 'How to build valuable networks,' *Finweek* (November 2017), pp. 52–3.
9. Jim Lucy, 'Sales tips that still matter: An ace salesperson can sometimes sell you some good life lessons,' *Electrical Wholesaling* (January 2019), 100(1), 4.
10. Kathryn Mayer, 'Peer networking key to finding sales,' *Benefits Selling*, New York (July 2012).
11. Influencer Marketing Hub, 'What is Influencer Marketing: An in depth look at marketing's next big thing', https://influencermarketinghub.com/what-is-influencer-marketing, retrieved May 15, 2019.
12. Colleen Garland, 'How to measure the value of influencer marketing: By applying the principles of growth marketing to influencer marketing, brands can now effectively track the success of an influencer partnership,' *Global Cosmetic Industry* (June 2018), 186(6), 22–5.

13. Wendy Connick, 'Why Lead Generation is Critical to the Sales Process' (December 8, 2018), www.thebalancecareers.com/what-is-lead-generation-2917375, retrieved July 15, 2020.

14. Dan Tyre, 'How to Find Sales Leads Online,' https://blog.hubspot.com/sales/how-salespeople-can-generate-their-own-leads, retrieved July 15, 2020.

15. Keith Rosen, 'The secret to prospecting success,' *Sales & Service Excellence Essentials* (November 2014), 13(11), 36–7.

16. Anthony Urbaniak, 'Prospecting systems that work,' *American Salesman* (January 2016), 61(1), 27–30.

17. Izabelle Hundrev, (2019) 'What Is Business Development? (+ How It's Different from Sales),' https://learn.g2.com/what-is-business-development, retrieved July 13, 2020.

18. Liz Fulham, '10 Top Tips on How to Generate Sales Leads' (December 9, 2016), www.b2bmarketing.net/en/resources/blog/10-top-tips-how-generate-sales-leads, retrieved July 15, 2020.

19. Ibid.

20. Wendy Connick, 'Why Lead Generation is Critical to the Sales Process' (December 8, 2018), www.thebalancecareers.com/what-is-lead-generation-2917375, retrieved July 15, 2020.

21. Adapted from Alyssa Gregory, 'How to Generate Sales Leads in Your Small Business' (August 6, 2019), www.thebalancesmb.com/how-to-generate-sales-leads-in-your-small-business-2951792, retrieved July 15, 2020.

22. Angela White, '7 best ways to attract customers through social media: Attracting more followers and qualified leads,' *HCM Sales, Marketing & Alliance Excellence Essentials* (January 2020), 19(1), 26–8.

23. Wendy Connick, 'Why Lead Generation is Critical to the Sales Process' (December 8, 2018), www.thebalancecareers.com/what-is-lead-generation-2917375, retrieved July 15, 2020.

24. Dan Tyre, 'How to Find Sales Leads Online,' https://blog.hubspot.com/sales/how-salespeople-can-generate-their-own-leads, retrieved July 15, 2020.

25. Jennifer Schiff, '9 proven methods for generating sales leads,' Lonoff. CIO; Framingham (Feb 23, 2017).

26. Brian Offenberger, '5 ways to generate more sales leads,' *SDM: Security Distributing & Marketing* (July 2016), p. 56.

27. Brian Offenberger, '3 ways to generate sales leads,' *SDM: Security Distributing & Marketing* (January 2020), 50(1), 33.

28. Brian Offenberger, '5 ways to generate more sales leads,' *SDM: Security Distributing & Marketing* (July 2016), p. 56.

29. Dan Kennedy (2006) *The Ultimate Sales Letter*, 3rd edition (Avon, MA: Adams Media), pp. 46–70.

30. Joanne Black, 'Stop overlooking this if you really want qualified leads,' *HCM Sales, Marketing & Alliance Excellence Essentials* (April 2019), 18(4), 34–6.

31. Brad Power, 'How Harley-Davidson used artificial intelligence to increase New York sales leads by 2,930%,' *Harvard Business Review* (Digital Articles) (May 30, 2017), pp. 2–5.

32. Brian Offenberger, '5 ways to generate more sales leads,' *SDM: Security Distributing & Marketing* (July 2016), p. 56.

33. Smart Insights, 'SEO analytics', www.smartinsights.com/search-engine-optimisation-seo/seo-analytics/comparison-of-google-clickthrough-rates-by-position, retrieved May 15, 2019.

34. Jamie Izaks, 'Incorporating social media into your lead gen strategy: Pervasive as it is, social media is still the "final frontier" for many franchise lead generation campaigns,' *Franchising World* (August 2017), 49(8), 48.

35. David Morgan and Alex Chavez, 'Facebook vs. LinkedIn for lead generation: Who wins?' *SDM: Security Distributing & Marketing* (July 2017), pp. 36–8.

36. Brian Offenberger, '3 ways to generate sales leads,' *SDM: Security Distributing & Marketing* (January 2020), 50(1), 33.

37. Ibid.

38. Rosalie Donlon, 'Finding the right prospect,' *Property & Casualty*, 360 (July 2017), 121(7), 46–7.

39. Dan Tyre, 'How to Find Sales Leads Online,' https://blog.hubspot.com/sales/how-salespeople-can-generate-their-own-leads, retrieved July 15, 2020.

40. Ritu Banerjee, 'Website Scraping' (White Paper) (April 2014), http://hminds.campaigntemplate.com/whitepapers/website-scraping.pdf, retrieved June 10, 2020.

41. Luca Tagliaferro, 'Data Scraping Tools for Marketers Who Don't Know Code' (July 15, 2019), https://searchengineland.com/data-scraping-tools-for-marketers-who-dont-know-code-319446, retrieved June 10, 2020.

42. Swetha Amareson, (2020) 'What Is Social Listening and Why Is It Important?', https://blog.hubspot.com/service/social-listening, retrieved August 15, 2020.

43. Brian Offenberger, '9 steps to realizing leads with social media,' *SDM: Security Distributing & Marketing* (November 2019), 49(11), 33.

44. Jennifer Schiff, '9 proven methods for generating sales leads,' *Lonoff.CIO; Framingham* (February 23, 2017).

45. Angela White, '7 best ways to attract customers through social media: Attracting more followers and qualified leads,' *HCM Sales, Marketing & Alliance Excellence Essentials* (January 2020), 19(1), 26–8.

46. Ibid.

47. Jamie Izaks, 'Incorporating social media into your lead gen strategy: Pervasive as it is, social media is still the "final frontier" for many franchise lead generation campaigns,' *Franchising World* (August 2017), 49(8), 48.

48. Katie Sehl, 'How to Get More Leads on Social Media' (February 2020), https://blog.hootsuite.com/how-to-generate-leads-on-social-media, retrieved July 16, 2020.

49. Jamie Izaks, 'Incorporating social media into your lead gen strategy: Pervasive as it is, social media is still the "final frontier" for many franchise lead generation campaigns,' *Franchising World* (August 2017), 49(8), 48.

50. 'State of social lead generation,' *Social Media Today and Sharpspring* (November 4, 2019), www.eMarketer.com-E, cited in Katie Sehl, 'How to Get More Leads on Social Media' (February 2020), https://blog.hootsuite.com/how-to-generate-leads-on-social-media, retrieved July 16, 2020.

51. Ibid.

52. Katie Sehl (February 2020) 'How to Get More Leads on Social Media,' https://blog. hootsuite.com/how-to-generate-leads-on-social-media, retrieved July 16, 2020.

53. Jamie Izaks, 'Incorporating social media into your lead gen strategy: Pervasive as it is, social media is still the "final frontier" for many franchise lead generation campaigns,' *Franchising World* (August 2017), 49(8), 48.

54. Steve Anderson, 'Let's get social,' *Property & Casualty 360* (March 2016), 120(3), 14.

55. Katie Sehl (February 2020), 'How to Get More Leads on Social Media,' https://blog. hootsuite.com/how-to-generate-leads-on-social-media, retrieved July 16, 2020.

56. Jamie Izaks, 'Incorporating social media into your lead gen strategy: Pervasive as it is, social media is still the "final frontier" for many franchise lead generation campaigns,' *Franchising World* (August 2017), 49(8), 48.

57. Omnicore, 'Linkedin by the Numbers: Stats, demographics & fun facts,' www. omnicoreagency.com/linkedin-statistics, retrieved July 16, 2020.

58. Katie Sehl (February 2020), 'How to Get More Leads on Social Media,' https://blog. hootsuite.com/how-to-generate-leads-on-social-media, retrieved July 16, 2020.

59. Ibid.

60. Adapted from John Nemo, 'The best place to find "warm" leads on LinkedIn: How to spark 1-on-1 engagement with someone who has you on his or her mind?' *HCM Sales, Marketing & Alliance Excellence Essentials* (April 2018), 17(4), 32–4; and Mike Renahan, 'How to Find Sales Leads on LinkedIn & Twitter: A step-by-step guide,' https://blog.hubspot.com/sales/how-to-find-sales-leads-on-linkedin-twitter-a-step-by-step-guide, retrieved July 16, 2020.

61. Kalin Kassabov, 'Tips to Generate Leads on LinkedIn,' *Forbes* (March 27, 2020), www.forbes.com/sites/theyec/2020/03/27/tips-to-generate-leads-on-linkedin, retrieved July 16, 2020.

62. Mike Renahan, 'How to Find Sales Leads on LinkedIn & Twitter: A step-by-step guide,' https://blog.hubspot.com/sales/how-to-find-sales-leads-on-linkedin-twitter-a-step-by-step-guide, retrieved July 16, 2020.

63. John Nemo, 'The best place to find "warm" leads on LinkedIn: How to spark 1-on-1 engagement with someone who has you on his or her mind?' *HCM Sales, Marketing & Alliance Excellence Essentials* (April 2018), 17(4), 32–4.

64. Adapted from Katie Sehl (February 2020), 'How to Get More Leads on Social Media', https://blog.hootsuite.com/how-to-generate-leads-on-social-media, retrieved July 16, 2020; John Nemo, 'The best place to find "warm" leads on LinkedIn: How to spark 1-on-1 engagement with someone who has you on his or her mind?' *HCM Sales, Marketing & Alliance Excellence Essentials* (April 2018), 17(4), 32–4; and Dan Tyre, 'How to Find Sales Leads Online,' https://blog.hubspot.com/sales/how-sales-people-can-generate-their-own-leads, retrieved July 15, 2020.

65. Ken Guest, 'Does cold calling still work? Prospecting in today's business world,' *HCM Sales, Marketing & Alliance Excellence Essentials* (June 2019), 18(6), 5–7.

66. Keith Rosen, 'The secret to prospecting success,' *Sales & Service Excellence Essentials* (November 2014), 13(11), 36–7.

67. Troy Harrison, 'How to use social media in successful prospecting,' *eMPS* (April 2016), 18(4), 20–1.

68. Ken Guest, 'Does cold calling still work? Prospecting in today's business world,' *HCM Sales, Marketing & Alliance Excellence Essentials* (June 2019), 18(6), 5–7.

69. Kalin Kassabov, 'Tips to Generate Leads on LinkedIn,' *Forbes* (March 27, 2020), www.forbes.com/sites/theyec/2020/03/27/tips-to-generate-leads-on-linkedin, retrieved July 16, 2020.

70. Hubspot, 'Sales Close Rate Industry Benchmarks: How does your close rate compare?', https://blog.hubspot.com/sales/new-sales-close-rate-industry-benchmarks-how-does-your-close-rate-compare, retrieved July 16, 2020.

71. Angela White, '7 Best ways to attract customers through social media: Attracting more followers and qualified leads,' *HCM Sales, Marketing & Alliance Excellence Essentials* (January 2020), 19(1), 26–8.

72. Ibid.

73. Katie Sehl (February 2020) 'How to Get More Leads on Social Media,' https://blog.hootsuite.com/how-to-generate-leads-on-social-media, retrieved July 16, 2020.

74. Ibid.

75. Ibid.

5

APPROACHING AND COMMUNICATING WITH SUCCESS

CHAPTER CONTENTS

THE SELLING PROCESS: 'OUT IN THE FIELD'

PEOPLE, PRACTICES AND PERSPECTIVES FROM THE WORLD OF SALES

Hi, I'm Michelle Caldas, Regional Sales Director for Flight Centre Travel Group in New York City. My responsibilities include managing and developing sales strategies for a team of account executives and facilitating collaboration with Sales Enablement, Product Marketing, Talent Acquisition, Human Resources, Operations, and Suppliers to drive team productivity and prospect/client engagement. Over my eight-year career, I've found that adaptability is a critical trait and that adaptive selling techniques are needed as use of the Internet, social media, and the marketplace itself constantly change. Consider this quote: 'Always do your best. What you plant now, you will harvest later.' (Og Mandino)

Hello, I'm Katherine McPhaden, a Sales Counselor for National Church Residences in Columbus, Ohio. Through my 20-year career in sales, and particularly when working with nursing homes, I've found that I do more listening than talking. Instead of feature dumping, my advice is to focus on the person's needs, wants, and interests. After you have a clearer picture of what is important to that person, then you can match their needs/desires to what you have to offer. This personalization will let them know that you offer a good value and that whatever it is they are buying is worth it to them.

Greetings. I'm Boris Wiedemer, Account Manager for Amazon Web Services – Germany. I have three years of experience providing Account and Territory Management for organizational consumers. *My advice is to be customer-obsessed, to deliver speed and action as it's required, to ask the right questions, and to listen carefully. Remember that it's not about selling, it's about helping customers achieve their long-term goals.* Here's a quote for you: 'Always be closing,' from the movie *Glengarry Glen Ross*.

You'll never have a second chance to make a good first impression.

EYES ON ETHICS

Keep in mind the following ethical topics as you read through this chapter:

1. Making a good first impression while under emotional duress.
2. Applying adaptive selling when you are unclear about the prospective customer's social and behavioral style.

INTRODUCTION

This chapter addresses important 'soft skills' that salespeople must possess in order to be successful in selling. The skills addressed include establishing rapport, making good first impressions, building credibility and attaining buyer trust, practicing good professional etiquette, communicating effectively by using verbal and nonverbal techniques, adaptive selling, neuro-linguistic programming, and lastly, evaluating or assessing communication effectiveness to ensure that there is complete understanding between salespeople and customers and prospects. The approach stage of the selling process requires salespeople to master soft skills in order to foster strong business relationships with customers and prospective buyers. This chapter will provide many strategies, techniques, and tips for doing so.

APPROACHING

In selling, approaching entails salespeople making the initial contact with prospective customers. This is the meeting-and-greeting stage of the selling process. The goal of approaching is for salespeople to establish rapport with their prospective customers.

Establishing rapport

Rapport is defined as a close and harmonious relationship in which the people or groups concerned are 'in sync' with each other, understand each other's feelings or ideas, and communicate smoothly.[1] Rapport entails salespeople forming bonds or personal connections with their prospective customers to establish mutual understanding. Have you ever experienced the feeling that you've known a person your entire life, yet you've only just met this person and have spent a mere few minutes conversing? You might not be able to explain why you feel this way, but you just do. That's rapport. Sometimes these bonds form immediately and naturally, with salespeople just 'hitting it off' with certain prospective buyers with whom they have things in common. However, at other times, achieving rapport takes some time and effort.

Elevator meeting & greeting

What can salespeople do to develop rapport with prospective buyers if it doesn't occur quickly and naturally? Using the background research that salespeople gather in preparation for approaching prospective customers, they are able to apply a number of strategies that may help to build rapport. These strategies include:[2]

- **Be enthusiastic**. Enthusiasm, just like a smile and laughter, is normally contagious and may work to get the prospective buyer to open up and share the enthusiasm.
- **Be totally transparent**. This entails having complete integrity in sincerely wanting to form a relationship with the prospective buyer, not just wanting to make a sale.
- **Be empathetic**. This involves truly relating to the needs, motives, and desires of the prospective buyer.
- **Take the high ground**. Here is the opportunity to be open, honest, and have the strength of moral character to tell prospective buyers when a product or service will not truly meet their needs. Losing sales in the short term due to taking the high road will quickly gain rapport and earn trust, and may even work to build valuable long-term relationships that lead to future sales.
- **Ask perceptive questions**. Asking questions of prospective buyers and paying close attention to the answers can enable salespeople to probe and ask more follow-up questions. Subtly digging for additional information, even personal preferences, can reveal information about interests, hobbies, and other areas where some connection or common ground may be established.

- **Use the prospective customer's name**. The name of each and every prospective customer is unique and wholly and completely owned by the person. Names offer a clear way to distinguish between people. People like to hear their name spoken and it can work to help to form a connection with them.
- **Offer a sincere compliment**. By noticing and complimenting prospective customers (or their respective company), salespeople are expressing their attention to detail and their sincere interest. Compliments may also serve as conversation openers to ease into a relationship.
- **Identify a personal connection**. Salespeople who have something in common with prospective customers are wise to mention it. This commonality doesn't need to be profound, as it could be as simple as having a common hobby or fitness activity, attending the same university, or volunteering for the same non-profit organization. The goal is to create a connection on a human level which requires a bit of investigative work on your part. Mentioning what you have in common with the prospective buyer will move both the introduction and the relationship forward.
- **Tell a short personal story**. When salespeople tell a very brief authentic or real story about something personal, it adds a measure of warmth, reality, and humanity to the introduction. Personal stories reveal that we are all human and likely have something in common. Storytelling will be discussed in much greater detail in Chapter 6.
- **Mirror the buyer**. Mirroring entails behaving similarly to the prospective customer by subtly copying that person's body language, posture, traits, and moods. Most people are more comfortable and more likely to open up with people whom they perceive to be like themselves. Thus, salespeople can purposefully behave similarly to their prospective customers. However, salespeople must make a genuine and honest attempt to understand their customers and their behaviors in order for mirroring to work.
- **Exercise pacing**. Hand in hand with mirroring is pacing. Pacing involves the speed by which the salesperson moves through the sales process. Salespeople should allow prospective customers to set the pace and follow accordingly, to effectively connect and engage. We'll talk more about mirroring and pacing later in this chapter as they are both techniques in adaptive selling.

In summary, successful salespeople do not skip the 'small talk' and get right down to business with their prospective customers. They begin by building rapport. Salespeople are much more successful when selling to prospective customers with whom they resonate and get along. For example, Tom Davenport was very successful in easily establishing rapport when selling to the various winery owners throughout his sales territory. Why? Because of Tom's family background in farming, he could naturally relate to and understand the unique needs, wants, and concerns of the grape growers at all of the different vineyards. Establishing rapport is the foundation to good relationships. And, as you know by now, relationships are the key to successful selling.

Establishing rapport

Approaching may sound quite simple and natural; however, it takes preparation and effort to be successful in your approach. During the approach, salespeople may need to 'break the ice' in order to deal with and overcome potential barriers or shields that some prospects may create to protect or guard themselves when meeting someone for the first time. An effective approach gets prospective buyers to let down their guard and open their minds. According to Ron Willingham, author of *Integrity Selling*, featured in the Readings and Resources section at the end of the chapter, an effective approach sets the stage and prepares clients, customers, or prospects to listen to the salesperson.[3] Willingham proposes four 'action guides' for salespeople to follow to successfully approach prospective customers. These four action guides are:[4]

1. **Tune the world out and your prospects in**. Salespeople must give their prospective customers pure, 100 percent attention and focus in order to be successful in approaching.
2. **Put them at ease and make them feel important**. All human beings have the innate need to feel valued and important. Salespeople must recognize this need and find ways to address it when engaging with each and every prospective customer.
3. **Get them talking about themselves**. Salespeople should utilize the background research that they've conducted on their prospects and ask meaningful and relevant questions in order to spark conversation and get their prospects to open up about their situation.
4. **Hold eye contact and listen to how they feel**. Holding eye contact while actively listening to a prospective customer enables a strong emotional connection or bond to form. Of course, appropriate active listening gestures, such as using facial expressions or nodding to show understanding, should be used as well.

By practicing and following these action guides, salespeople help their prospective customers to lower their defenses, open up, and engage in productive conversations. Of course, salespeople will be much more effective in successfully approaching prospective customers and gaining rapport if they make positive initial impressions, which is the topic of our next section.

Creating memorable first impressions

First impressions are critical because they form very quickly, last a very long time, and directly affect both perceptions and buying decisions. In addition, salespeople will have a very difficult time trying to change negative or less-than positive first impressions. Thus, anything less than a positive first impression is lethal to relationship-building success with prospective customers. Indeed, first impressions, which are typically formed within the first three seconds of an initial meeting, are the lasting ones.[5] You have only one chance to make a good first impression. There can be no second chance to make a good first impression.

The approach is where salespeople have a face-to-face opportunity to make a positive impression with the prospective customer and to project positive vibes about both themselves and their respective company. However, in today's digital world, most prospective consumers will check out the company's website, browse online customer reviews, read blogs and case studies, and so on, *before* they meet with salespeople. Fair or not, a company's online content will factor into the formation of the initial impressions of salespeople. Thus, salespeople should review the online content of their company's website to be sure that it projects a positive impression.

A good first impression is one of the factors that will set you, the salesperson, apart from everyone else in today's business environment. However, being able to effectively sell face to face is not a natural talent – it's something that is developed, not inborn. You may have to videotape yourself or get in front of a mirror to practice meeting and greeting to be natural and effective, and to master it with confidence.

Given that first impressions are so important, let's explore how salespeople create memorable first impressions. First, introductions are key and salespeople must know how to properly introduce themselves to the people they meet. This includes both selecting the right words and using appropriate gestures when meeting and greeting someone. Always strive to begin conversations on an upbeat and positive note. Table 5.1 provides some tips on unproductive greetings that you should avoid.

Table 5.1 Unproductive greetings to avoid

Avoid being negative.

Avoid: Hi, Mr. Smith. It's so hot out there today that I'm melting away.
Better: Hi, Mr. Smith. What a beautiful hot summer day we have today.

Avoid being too casual.

Avoid: Hi, Jan. It's great to see you, my favorite girlfriend client.
Better: Hi, Ms. Jones. It's very nice to see you again.

(Continued)

Table 5.1 (Continued)

Avoid being too generic.

Avoid: Hi, Mr. Johnson. What's new? How's business?

Better: Hi, Mr. Johnson. Have you had an increase in business recently due to the summer tourists?

Avoid being direct and aggressive.

Avoid: Hi, Ms. Brink. So, are you ready to give me some business?

Better: Hi, Ms. Brink. Have you had an opportunity to look over my proposal?

Avoid insulting your customer when visiting without an appointment.

Avoid: Hi, Mr. Ball. I just happened to be out in the area so I thought I'd drop by.

Better: Hi, Mr. Ball. I wanted to stop by to drop off these samples that I mentioned to you during our last meeting.

Source: Adapted from Ralph Shipp, Jr. (1980) *Practical Selling* (Boston: Houghton Mifflin), pp. 215–16.

Let's now examine the words and gestures needed for effective greetings which will lead to good first impressions.

Words

What should salespeople say when they meet a prospective customer for the first time? They will need to carefully prepare and select words to very briefly introduce themselves. These words may be considered their introductory sound bite, which should simply roll off the tongue with ease and confidence. Although salespeople will need to briefly introduce themselves, they should keep it short and simple. Remember, the focus is on the prospective buyer. Salespeople should emphasize only those aspects of their profile that relate to the interests and values of their prospective customers. According to Dorie Clark, author of *Reinventing You: Define Your Brand, Imagine Your Future*, featured in the Readings and Resources section at the end of the chapter, 'It's useful to have a "trusted cabinet" of friends and colleagues who can help you understand "how you come across to the world" … You can ask them what they see as your strengths, your best traits, and the most likable things about you so you can emphasize those things when you're meeting someone new.'[6]

When preparing two or three talking points, salespeople should keep in mind that while they should showcase the value that they can offer to the prospective client, their talking points should present *evidence* of their expertise and value, as opposed to trying to impress the prospect with their vast knowledge and expertise.[7] Wise salespeople understand that the goal of the first impression is not to dazzle the prospective customer, but rather, to create a memorable and engaging conversation that makes the prospect feel comfortable and good about entering into a relationship.

Gestures

Regarding gestures when greeting someone, it may seem elementary, but it is important to actually *practice* a handshake. A poor handshake is lethal to a good first impression.

When shaking someone's hand, only one or two hand pumps is appropriate.[8] It is generally said that one should have a 'firm' handshake. You know when you are shaking the hand of an unpracticed person because the experience is akin to being handed a limp, damp fish. Yuck! However, the term 'firm' may tend to make people overcompensate and crush perfectly good knuckles. A good handshake should be warm, energetic, and inviting. It should be the recipient's first indication of your interest in them. However, as shown in Figure 5.1, it is very important that salespeople shake hands *only* when their prospective buyers extend their hand *first*.

Figure 5.1   Buyer extending his hand first to salesperson

Given the recent world COVID-19 pandemic, social norms have changed. Handshakes, which were once a standard element of meeting and greeting, may have come to an end in many selling situations. Salespeople are wise to be prepared with alternative ways to greet prospective buyers. As shown in Figure 5.2, there are some alternatives to sharing a handshake when greeting someone. These are the:[9]

- **Fist bump**. While extending a fist of closed knuckles still entails contact between the salesperson and the prospective buyer, the contact is very brief.
- **Elbow bump**. Similar to a fist bump, the salesperson and buyer tap extended elbows.
- **Forearm bump**. Similar to a fist bump, the salesperson and buyer tap raised forearms.
- **Extended nod**. Tipping your head forward and holding it there for a few seconds resembles a subtle bow.
- **Heart tap and palm point**. Here, you would touch your heart with your open palm for a second or two and then extend your open palm toward the person you are greeting.
- **Heart tap, nod, and palm point**. With this one, you are adding a nod while touching your heart for a few seconds and then extending your open palm toward the person you are greeting.

- **Thumbs up**. This entails having one or both of your thumbs extended upward with your arm raised slightly for emphasis. Giving a thumbs up is a widespread and universal show of acknowledgment as well as approval.
- **Peace sign**. Raising your arm slightly and flashing the 'V' with your pointer and middle fingers on one hand is known as the 'peace sign', another widespread and universal show of alliance.
- **Hand wave**. This involves bending your elbow and raising your hand up in front of your chest with an open palm facing the person you are greeting; then gently moving your hand back and forth after it is raised. You may opt to tilt your head while doing so.

Keep in mind that the prospective buyer should initiate and dictate the type of greeting gesture, and the salesperson should follow along accordingly. Also, each of these alternatives should be paired with a genuine smile and appropriate words of greeting, such as 'It's so nice to meet you, Mr. Smith.' If the prospective buyer does not initiate a greeting gesture, salespeople should use one of the non-contact gestures, as opposed to a handshake, a fist bump, or an elbow bump.

The rules of introduction when first meeting someone include: maintaining good eye contact, smiling, and above all, carefully listening to what is being said. Listen carefully to people's names when they're being introduced to you and if you aren't certain that you've heard the name correctly, then simply request a restatement of it. You might say, 'I'm sorry, I didn't catch your name; can you please repeat it?'[10] Remember the individual's name and use a memory aid if it's helpful. For example, try to remember to repeat that person's name at the initial introduction, then say the name again during the brief first conversation. If the opportunity is there to repeat the individual's name before leaving, try to use it again, as without repetition, the name will be easily forgotten. As Dale Carnegie, author of the highly influential book, *How to Win Friends and Influence People*, states, 'a person's name is to that person the sweetest and most important sound in any language.'[11]

Figure 5.2A Elbow bump

Figure 5.2B Fist bump

Figure 5.2C Forearm bump

Figure 5.2D Wave

Figure 5.2E Peace sign

Figure 5.2F Heart touch

Figure 5.2G Thumbs up

Figure 5.2 Series of handshake alternatives

Salesperson listening to buyer

As mentioned earlier in this chapter, the best gift you can ever give someone is the purity of your attention. If you can master the art of making all those people you talk with feel that they are your one and only audience, you will achieve guaranteed success in approaching. In today's busy world where cell phones and Apple watches constantly buzz and beep, it's sometimes easy to become distracted. Salespeople should silence all disruptive electronic devices before meeting with a prospective customer. Salespeople must also be mindful to stay 'in the moment' and shut everything else out. Concentrating solely on the conversation is especially needed when meeting with a prospective customer in a busy place, such as in a restaurant or outer reception area, where many different people are coming and going. Complete attention and focus on the person you are speaking with should be maintained throughout the entire conversation. Keep in mind that when meeting and greeting, it's all about the prospective customer – not about you. The approach stage is essentially an introduction and is simply an exchange of information; however, it will be the last exchange unless you are successful in making a good first impression and establishing rapport when meeting and greeting.

People do business with people they like and can relate to. According to Jeb Blount, author of *People Buy You*, a recommended book listed in the Readings and Resources section at the end of this chapter: 'being likeable and remaining likable is sort of like "relationship glue." Likeability impacts how others perceive you, their willingness to engage in conversations, and their openness to answering your questions.'[12] Being likeable and establishing rapport are very important; however, alone they do not equate to obtaining the prospective customer's credibility and trust. Credibility and trust must be earned.

Earning credibility and securing buyer trust

Prospective customers are more apt to listen to and do business with salespeople that they believe are credible and can trust. While this statement is logical, it is not always easily accomplished. Let's first dissect the terms. *Credibility* means a salesperson is reliable and possesses integrity. When people *trust* someone, that means they have faith, belief, hope, and conviction in that person. Credibility and trust go hand in hand, and to be successful, salespeople must work to establish both qualities in the eyes of their buyers. Salespeople should follow the Platinum Rule, which is 'Do unto others as they would have you do unto them, not as you would have them do unto you.'[13]

Savvy salespeople will step into the shoes of their prospective customers and apply empathy to truly understand their needs and wants, as well as to offer relevant solutions that will solve their problems. However, promising solutions alone is not enough. Prospective customers must be able to rely on salespeople to *deliver* on the promises that they make. As a general rule, most people sincerely want to trust others to follow-through on promises and offers. As Blount notes: 'Most people, however, given enough consistent evidence that you keep your word and do what you say you'll do, will begin to trust you.'[14] An excellent principle that all salespeople should practice is to *under-promise and over-deliver*. In other words, salespeople should strive to exceed expectations on a regular basis. By exceeding customer expectations, salespeople will generate positive word-of-mouth communication and referrals, which in turn, is one sure way to establish credibility, earn trust, and build an outstanding reputation.

Beyond being likeable, demonstrating authentic concern, delivering on promises made, and exceeding expectations, salespeople should convey their expertise and potential value to their prospective customers in order to establish credibility and earn trust. Salespeople should share their expertise via valuable, relevant, and need-satisfying information in an *objective* manner. For example, when meeting and greeting prospective customers, salespeople may offer to share testimonials, success stories, online reviews, performance metrics, and so on, from current or former customers via blogs, newsletters, e-newsletters, webinars, white papers, and so on, whenever possible.

In summary, being attentive, providing valuable information, and following through on promises made will contribute to building rapport, establishing credibility, and creating buyer trust. However, it goes without saying that if these qualities are not combined with good professional etiquette at all times, salespeople will not be successful in approaching and building rapport.

As you learned back in Chapter 2, professional business etiquette requires salespeople to present a professional image, to manage time well, and to communicate effectively at all times to increase the likelihood of successful selling. More specifically, professional business etiquette includes areas of good grooming, effective time management, good interpersonal behavior, and all forms of communications skills, including speaking, writing, and listening. Proper etiquette is also influenced by the unique customs and societal norms in various countries, so preparation is needed to ensure the best approach for each customer.

In summary, having a professional appearance and practicing good and appropriate professional etiquette can increase salespeople's self-confidence and help prospective customers feel more comfortable with them. Likewise, customers and prospects are more apt to believe and want to work with salespeople who project a positive 'can do' image and attitude. Salespeople must first believe in themselves and the value that they are offering to prospective customers. Salespeople must focus on what they can control and refrain from fear or fretting over the uncontrollable or unknown. Confidence in selling comes from salespeople being properly prepared to meet prospective customers and being able to manage their emotional intelligence when engaging with them, which is the topic of our next section.

A confident 'can do' attitude

Using emotional intelligence

As discussed in Chapter 2, emotional intelligence refers to your ability to identify, assess, and manage your emotions. The ability of salespeople to perceive *how* they are feeling, understand *why* they are feeling the way they are, and then be able to *adjust* their behavior to achieve desired outcomes, is of chief importance in successfully approaching, establishing rapport, and engaging with prospective customers. Often, the root cause of salespeople incurring poor sales performance is not their lack of selling skills, but their inability to manage their emotions, think clearly, and react effectively.[15]

According to Colleen Stanley, author of *Emotional Intelligence for Sales Success: Connect with Customers and Get Results*, listed in the Readings and Resources section at the end of the chapter, 'Emotional intelligence bridges the "knowing and doing" gap.' Most salespeople know what to do; however, under difficult selling situations, they often buckle and default to non-productive behavior.[16] Stanley believes that there are three emotional intelligence skills that may be taught to avoid having salespeople buckle under pressure from a tough prospect or customer. They are:[17]

1. **Emotional self-awareness**. This is teaching salespeople to reflect on a previous conversation in order to recognize their own emotions and analyze why their emotions had a negative impact on their actions. They might ask themselves questions such as: Why was I intimidated? How could I have prepared better? What could I have done to improve my concentration and active listening?

2. **Assertiveness**. Being assertive enables salespeople to state what they need or want without becoming either too aggressive or pushy, or too passive. Being assertive enables salespeople to become good at moving prospects through the selling process, or at disqualifying them when they aren't a good fit with the company.

3. **Empathy**. Relating to prospective buyers on an emotional level is just plain smart. Salespeople who empathize with other people show compassion and understanding. Empathy leads to both rapport and trust with prospective buyers.

Stressful moment

Emotional intelligence and understanding the what, why, and how of emotions is best discovered through self-awareness and self-discovery by scheduling downtime, creating a technology-free zone, and naming the specific emotion.[18] Stanley explains how some salespeople not trained in emotional intelligence, may experience a 'fight or flight' response when meeting with a hostile prospective customer who clearly does not want to engage in a conversation. The 'fight' would entail the salesperson becoming aggressive toward the prospect, talking faster and louder, and getting defensive – all harmful to rapport and relationship building. Flight responses are equally destructive in that the salesperson might ignore the hostile prospect, fail to obtain needed information, and/or abruptly end the conversation without an adequate way to move forward.[19] The good news is that salespeople can improve their emotional intelligence skills through practice and commitment.

Specific ways to increase your emotional intelligence skills include:[20]

- **Responding instead of reacting to conflict**. Staying calm during stressful situations, avoiding the temptation to make impulsive decisions, focusing on conflict resolution, and aligning nonverbal responses with words are productive ways to respond to conflict.
- **Utilizing active listening skills**. Listening for clarity, understanding what is being said before responding, paying attention to the nonverbal details of a conversation,

allowing the prospective buyer time to respond, and showing respect are included in active listening.

- **Maintaining a positive attitude**. Having an awareness of the surrounding moods, knowing what needs to be done in order to keep an optimistic outlook, and monitoring one's attitudes help to keep one's emotions in check.
- **Taking critique well**. Avoiding becoming offended or defensive, understanding where the criticism is coming from, understanding how the critique is affecting others or self-performance, and determining how to resolve the issue develops emotional intelligence.
- **Utilizing leadership skills**. Setting high standards, serving as an example to others, taking initiative, and applying solid problem-solving and decision-making skills help ensure a productive response to situations as they arise.
- **Being approachable and sociable**. Smiling, using appropriate social skills, projecting a positive presence, and commanding strong communication and interpersonal skills are keys to building strong relationships.

Thus, salespeople who are able to manage their emotional intelligence well will likely be more effective in approaching and communicating with other people. As Coach John Wooden advocates in his book, *Wooden on Leadership*, manage your emotions or they will manage you.'[21] His advice pertains to salespeople as much as it does to college basketball players. Emotional intelligence skills may be considered soft skills; however, they are sure to produce good hard results in selling.

In conclusion, approaching entails using a wide variety of 'soft skills' to successfully meet, greet, connect, and engage with prospective customers. Successful approaching leads to meaningful and productive conversations with prospective buyers. Of course, conversations require salespeople to possess effective communication skills, which is the topic of our next section.

COMMUNICATING

Communication skills are typically ranked first among the skills that salespeople must possess in order to be successful in selling. In selling, communication occurs constantly via many different formats, including in-person, written, telephone, digital, and so on. Good communication, which includes effective speaking (oral), writing, and listening skills, are imperative to being able to interact with clients, customers, and prospects. Let's discuss each of these areas in turn.

Speaking effectively

Salespeople must be engaging speakers; however, to be effective in communicating orally, they must command excellent verbal, nonverbal, and vocal skills. In fact, the actual words they speak are not nearly as important as their body language and how they articulate their message. As Figure 5.3 shows, when people communicate in person orally,

55 percent of communication is nonverbal, 38 percent will be conveyed by vocal tone, and 7 percent through the words that are being used.[22] Congruence is of critical importance in effective oral communication. Congruence means that your body language, words, and tonality of voice are all aligned and in sync with one another.[23] For example, if you are agreeing with someone, your head should be moving up and down and not from side to side, or else there would be incongruence. Another example is that when you give someone a compliment, you should do so with a smile and a pleasant voice to match your words of praise. Let's now examine in greater detail what's included in each of the three dimensions of oral communication: verbal, nonverbal and vocal skills.

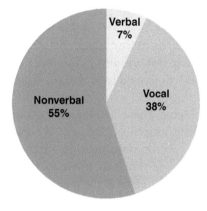

Figure 5.3 Communication skills pie chart

Verbal skills

Verbal skills pertain to the words you choose to use when speaking. Some of the most important techniques to employ regarding verbal skills include preparing what you want to say ahead of speaking, using proper grammar and word choices, and avoiding jargon and slang. Salespeople should prepare for conversations by identifying the potential topics of interest to their customers and prospects when conducting their research. Of course, controversial topics, such as politics and religion, should be avoided. Salespeople should prepare in advance for conversations which may take place in person, on the telephone, or via video conferencing.

It goes without saying that salespeople must always remember to be aware of their manners when speaking. This includes remembering to say 'please' and 'thank you' at the appropriate times. Saying 'No problem' is not an acceptable substitute for saying 'You're welcome,' nor is 'Have a good one,' an adequate way to say 'Thank you.' Typically, you should never use your prospective customer's first name unless the individual tells you to do so. North America is the only culture where using someone's first name is sometimes acceptable.[24] Asking permission to use someone's first name is especially important when your prospective customer is older, more highly educated, or more established than you. This may seem 'old school' to you; however, manners matter when communicating.

Nonverbal skills

Nonverbal skills pertain to body language and include eye contact, gestures, and posture. Body language is communication conveyed by certain body movements, posture, expressions, and tone of voice. As described in Chapter 2, body language includes facial expressions, poise, posture, and mannerisms. Techniques for effective body language include maintaining good eye contact and posture, nodding to show understanding or agreement, using facial expressions to convey appropriate feelings, and appearing confident and in control.

Salespeople must carefully observe body language in their prospective customers in order to understand what they are thinking. Two basic clues that are easy to notice are *open* body language, which may signify that the prospective customer has an open favorable position, versus *closed* body language, which denotes a more negative or resistant position where they may be unwilling to change their minds. Closed body language is typically characterized by crossed legs, folded arms, clasped hands, or the body turned away, whereas open hands and arms usually indicate open body language.[25] In addition, when prospective customers are leaning *forward*, their body language is communicating that they are listening carefully, actively engaged, and interested. Those who are leaning *backward* may be communicating that they are only passively listening, or not interested.[26] Salespeople need to learn to read and understand body language in order to be able to communicate effectively with their prospective customers.

According to Carl Lyons, author of the book *I Win You Win: The Essential Guide to Principled Negotiation*, prospective customers typically possess one of the four basic modes of body language:[27]

1. **Responsive** – very interested, actively receptive, listening and learning.
2. **Receptive** – interested, but not yet actively accepting; may need additional information, may consider incentives, needs time to think and consider.
3. **Resistant** – actively resisting, may show emotions, not interested.
4. **Non-responsive** – totally disengaged, not mentally present.

Figure 5.4 shows a series of photographs demonstrating some of the various styles included in the four modes of body language. Certain body movements provide clues regarding which mode of body language the prospective customers are conveying and how they may be thinking or feeling. Examples of these body movements are listed below.[28]

Responsive mode:

- **Being engaged**. Leaning forward, open body, arms and hands, and good eye contact are signs that the prospective customer is actively listening to the salesperson.
- **Appearing eager**. Leaning forward, opening legs and up on toes, as in a sprint position, typically indicates that the prospective buyer is very interested in what the salesperson is offering.

Figure 5.4A Attacking

Figure 5.4B Evaluating

Figure 5.4C Rejection

Figure 5.4D Disengaged

Figure 5.4 Series of body language modes

Receptive mode:

- **Listening**. Nodding their head up and down in agreement, tilting their head sideways, and blinking often indicate that the prospective customer is in a positive and receptive listening mode.
- **Evaluating**. Placing a hand, pen, or eye glasses to the mouth, rubbing chin, and crossing a leg with ankle on knee are signs that the prospective customer is considering and evaluating, and needs more time or more information to form a decision.

Resistant mode:

- **Wanting to speak**. Finger tapping, foot tapping, or staring are signs that the prospective customer is in a resistant mode and wants to speak because they have a point to make.
- **Attacking**. Leaning forward, finger pointing, and clenching fists are signs that the prospective customer is angry or opposes what is being said and wants to attack.
- **Being defiant**. Frowning and standing up with hands on hips indicate that the prospective customer is in a resistant mode whereby they clearly disagree with what is being said.

Non-responsive mode:

- **Seeming disengaged**. Closing papers or binders, putting their pen down, staring out the window, looking around the room, or glancing at their watch or cell phone indicate that prospective buyers want to end the conversation or meeting.
- **Rejecting**. Moving back in the chair, with arms folded, legs crossed, head down, and frowning indicate that the prospective buyer is rejecting what the salesperson is saying.

Keep in mind that while the above body movements offer clues to how the prospective customer is feeling or thinking, these clues are not always consistent or accurate. Communication is a mixture of verbal and nonverbal signals, so salespeople need to use the body language clues in conjunction with what the prospective customer is saying. For example, as Figure 5.5 shows, when prospective customers are looking over their eye glasses at a salesperson, it typically indicates that they are judging and scrutinizing what the salesperson is saying. Is this positive or negative? It could go either way. The prospective customer could verbally respond with, 'Yes, that just might work well for our company!' or 'No, I don't think that will work for our company.'

Figure 5.5 Buyer looking over glasses at salesperson

Vocal skills

Vocal skills relate to the rate, pitch, tone, and articulation of speech. Some tips to improve your vocal skills include varying the tone and tempo of your voice to keep the listener's attention, pronouncing your words clearly, fully completing sentences and not dropping the end of a sentence, and speaking slowly enough to allow the listener to process what you are saying. Regarding the tone and tempo of your voice, it is extremely important for you to be aware of your voice inflection. Have a high-pitched voice? Work to lower that tone. You will be more believable and creditable with a strong, solid voice than a squeaky, high-pitched sound. If your normal speech is peppered with unintended filler words, such as 'er,' 'um,' 'ah,' 'like,' or 'you know,' it is critical to eliminate those habits before you begin conversing with prospective customers.

Exercising strong vocal skills is also critical when communicating via the telephone. Salespeople should present a voice that is upbeat and enthusiastic so that the prospective customer can sense genuine interest, empathy, confidence, and success. Unless salespeople are using FaceTime or some other video-conferencing option instead of a regular voice call, facial expressions will not factor into the communication. However, the temperament and attitude of salespeople will come across loudly and clearly. Therefore, salespeople's voices should indicate that they are smiling on the other end of the call. Lastly, salespeople should be wary about over-using scripts that turn salespeople into an automated machine when embarking on telephone calls with prospective customers. In today's digital world, many prospective customers actually want to speak with a living, breathing human being, so salespeople should customize and personalize their telephone calls and use their vocal skills to engage with each individual caller.[29]

Good conversational skills are essential to establishing rapport with customers and prospects, and thus should be practiced and honed. Now, let's explore communicating by the written word.

Writing well

Regardless of whether the mode of written communication is online or off-line, when salespeople communicate in writing, all of the normal aspects associated with face-to-face communication are gone. The myriad factors that contribute to making a good first impression with a prospective customer are stripped away and the written word stands alone to represent you. Thus, you are what you write/type. Professional language, proper grammar, and clear and concise messages are imperative for all forms of written communication, including emails, text messages, posts, and tweets. As Laura Simonds, managing editor of *Small Business Computing*, once said, 'We live in an era of sound bites and 140-character messages, but good writing still matters when it comes to the business world.'[30]

There are a number of techniques that salespeople can use to become more effective in their written communication. Some common writing techniques are:[31]

- **Keep your readers in mind**. Before writing anything, determine how much your prospective customers care about the subject, how much they may already know about the subject, and why they are reading what you're about to write. Salespeople should offer relevant information that is of value to prospective customers. Be sure to customize your writing to your prospective customers.
- **Be yourself**. You should always write the way you speak. Show your personality and be genuine. Your writing should reflect your unique personality because the prospective customer will warm up to you faster this way, enabling you to generate greater rapport.
- **Use the active voice**. Active voice sentences are more concise, direct, and engaging than passive voice sentences. As business writer Grace Carter states: 'Sentences written in the passive voice use more words and generally don't read as decisively. They're the literary equivalent of a weak handshake.'[37]
- **Follow a writing formula**. Following a writing formula can help you develop a connection as well as a more logical flow. There are many writing formulas that salespeople may opt to follow. For example, **A-I-D-A**, of unknown origin, is a formula that has been used by direct response copywriters for many years. The formula is to: Attract **A**ttention, Arouse **I**nterest, Stimulate **D**esire, and Call for **A**ction. Another formula is the **KISS** principle. Also of unknown origin, this creative copywriting formula stands for 'keep it simple, stupid!' The KISS copywriting formula has been effectively used by creative geniuses for centuries. The basic premise is to keep the message simple and easy to understand and remember.
- **Write concisely**. Be considerate of your prospective customer's time and keep your message brief. Your goal is to write in a clear and easily understood manner. You are writing to persuade your prospective customers, not to impress them, so your communication should be written with that goal in mind.
- **Consider different attitudes and points of view**. Your prospective customers may have different attitudes and opinions. You must keep this in mind when making word choices so that you write in a manner that is in sync with the perspectives of your target prospective customers. When you write in a way that resonates with your prospective customers, you will build rapport, create greater trust, and nurture your relationships.
- **Be accurate**. Written communication, especially in a digital format, can be easily checked for inconsistencies and inaccuracies. Thus, you must be careful to double-check your sources and validate the accuracy of your written communication.
- **Use correct spelling and good grammar**. If your writing is filled with errors in spelling, grammar, sentence structure, word use, etc., your credibility will be negatively affected. You should always use a spell-check tool. However, please remember that spell check will not catch all of the writing errors. To ensure clarity of communication, you should read your writing several times, aloud if necessary, or have someone else read it, and edit it as needed.

When writing sales letters, you should take the advice of Dan Kennedy, author of *The Ultimate Sales Letter*, who offers the following six steps to get you started in your writing:[33]

1. Don't be intimidated by the idea or process of writing as there's no magic or genius required.
2. Recognize the value and power of your unique understanding of your business, products, services, and customers.
3. Assemble and organize ideas, samples, and good reference materials into an easy-to-access file.
4. Think 'selling' when you write inasmuch as the sales letter is akin to a sales presentation in print.
5. Apply your thoughts to paper and remember that your initial draft can be revised and edited later.
6. Avoid perfectionism because in most businesses, the sales letter does not need to be perfect in order to achieve good results.

When sending written communication to prospective customers, salespeople should consider a handwritten personal note instead of a formal typed letter. A personal note will impress the prospective customer, provide a sense of being special, appreciated, and acknowledged, as well as make you memorable.[34] A personal note can be personalized and written on unique stationery, such as the note cards produced by Homefronts. As Figure 5.6 shows, Homefronts cards are customized note cards featuring a digitally produced rendering of a business building that faithfully replicates the elegance of a pen-and-ink drawing or watercolor artwork. These note cards will enable your note to stand out from other letters a prospective customer receives. Salespeople should strive to be creative and unique in their written communication.

LIGHTHOUSE BUILDERS, INC.

Figure 5.6 Homefronts' notecard example
Used with kind permission of Paula Kosko.

Lastly, a few special considerations may be needed when you write for online communication. Netiquette refers to the etiquette of electronic communication. Online communication is usually provided in a written format unless salespeople use a video-conferencing tool, which enables the prospective customer to hear their voices and see their faces. When composing email communications, you must be sure to include a specific subject line that is both eye-catching and interest piquing in order to entice the prospective customer to click on and read your email. A few specific tips for effective email communication are the following:[35]

- Email should be used for more informal communication and should be kept brief.
- A greeting and a closing should always be used.
- Upper-case messages should be avoided since they tend to resemble shouting.
- Replies should be sent within 24–48 hours.

In addition, salespeople need to be mindful of properly timing the delivery of relevant online messages to maximize the positive communication impact.

Overall, all of the tips for writing well apply to online as well as off-line content. Good writing skills are imperative to effective communication and successful selling, as are exceptional listening skills which is the topic of our next section.

Listening carefully

All salespeople need to develop an exceptional ability to carefully listen in order to be successful in selling. As we covered in Chapter 2, salespeople must understand and use

Salesperson actively listening to buyer

active listening techniques to ensure effective communication. Techniques for effective active listening include: having good eye contact, taking notes, using body language to demonstrate your understanding of what is being said, and asking relevant questions that show you comprehend what was said. To ensure you are actively listening, avoid the temptation to check your phone, text while talking, or perform any other multi-tasking activity. Doing any of these types of activities will convey the message to your customers that you are not focused on them.

Of course, each and every prospective customer has a unique personality, set of preferences, motivations, and habits; thus, each one will communicate differently. These differences add up to their social or behavioral style. The key to successful selling is learning to carefully listen to each prospective customer and to vary your communication according to the social style of that person. That leads us to the topic of our next section, adaptive selling.

Applying adaptive selling techniques

Just as each prospective customer possesses a unique social style, each salesperson has an individual style in communicating as well. However, the salesperson's unique style will not resonate with *all* customers or prospects. The practice of **adaptive selling** refers to salespeople recognizing and changing their selling message and behavior based on the unique characteristics of each customer or prospect and the selling situation.

Salespeople who possess the ability to be versatile and flexible, and to adapt their approach and communication style to that of each of their prospective customers, will be much more successful in selling. In doing so, salespeople are able to deliver a unique and need-satisfying experience adapted to each customer's unique social style. The ability to get your communication style in sync with those of others, maximizes your effectiveness in all aspects of life, especially in selling. Without these skills, both personal and professional relationships may become conflict-prone because you are failing to fully deal with the fact that each person communicates differently.[36]

Have you noticed that you get along better with some people than others? That happens in selling as well. Often, the reason that salespeople find it easier and more natural to interact with some prospective customers is because they likely share the same social style with those prospects. Unfortunately, that natural connection occurs with only about 25 percent of prospective customers, while there is a disconnect when communicating with the other 75 percent.[37] Therefore, versatility, the ability to understand differences in communication styles and preferences and to adapt to make interactions more productive, is critical in selling.[38] The good news is that versatility can be learned, practiced, and perfected by understanding and applying adaptive selling techniques.

Adaptive selling relies on two things: knowledge of the selling situation, and emotional intelligence. First, knowledge of the selling situation includes information about products, services, company, industry, and competitors, as well as knowledge about prospective customers, which is the most important type of information. Salespeople rely on research using many different sources to gather these facts prior to approaching prospective customers. Second, strong emotional intelligence can help salespeople to communicate at an appropriate volume and pace, which helps them adjust their tone and control their impulse to try to move a conversation forward too quickly. For example, some prospects enjoy a cheerful communication tone, while others seek a more reserved or laidback style. Some prospective customers are extroverts who are very sociable, with loud enthusiastic voices, while others are introverts who tend to be quiet and shy.

As far back as Hippocrates, humans have sought to understand and classify people's psychological preferences and behaviors. Most notably, decades ago, Carl Jung and other social scientists formalized frameworks for categorizing people according to their preferences and behavior. In the 1940s, psychologists Isabel Briggs Meyers and Katharine Briggs completed a landmark study on personal style and behavior, known as the Myers-Briggs Type Indicator, which determined four basic preferences that may describe an individual's psychological type. They are Extrovert/Introvert, Sensing/Intuition, Thinking/Feeling, and Judgement/Perception. Thus, there are 16 different personality types that may be used to classify people. This research study led to the development of social or behavioral styles that cluster behavior around four overarching styles.[39] While there are several different social style models or classifications, they all depict the same four basic social style categories. Some of these models follow.

According to psychologists David Merrill and Roger Reid, the four social styles are: Analyticals, Drivers, Expressives and Amiables.[40] As the model in Figure 5.7 shows, the four social styles vary in terms of behavior, reflecting the following two dimensions:[41]

1. **Power or assertiveness** – the degree to which individuals assert themselves, control and present themselves and their ideas with confidence, strength, and assurance. This dimension may be characterized as the 'tell versus ask' dichotomy.
2. **Emotion or responsiveness** – the degree to which individuals reveal themselves, their emotions, feelings, and impressions. In other words, this dimension classifies one's orientation as 'people versus task' and gauges how 'open' the person is.

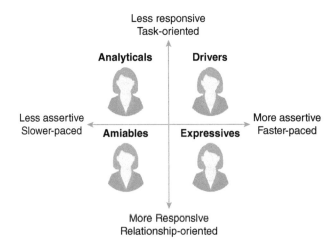

Figure 5.7 Merrill & Reid's social style model

Another model, which was briefly described in Chapter 2, is that developed by Ron Willingham. His model states that people can be categorized into the following four behavior styles: Talkers, Doers, Controllers, and Supporters.[42] As the model in Figure 5.8 shows, the four social styles reflect combinations of two different dimensions: the need for recognition versus the need for security, and the tendency to be process oriented versus results oriented.

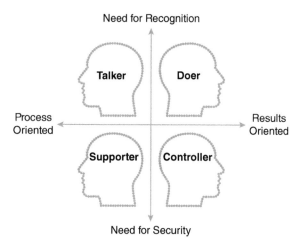

Figure 5.8 Willingham's social style model

Lastly, Dr. William Marston, a Harvard-trained psychologist, outlined the four communication styles as: Dominance, Influence, Steadiness, and Conscientiousness.[43] This 'D-I-S-C' system, also referred to as the Personal Profile System, has been developed by Carlson Learning Company as a guide to salespeople in understanding their clients better.[44]

Adaptive selling based on the four basic social style classifications can be very effective; however, it only works when salespeople *first* determine their own social style via self-assessment. Once they understand their own style, they can evaluate the social styles of their prospective customers and use style flexing, which is adjusting behavior to mirror or match another person's social style, to interact more effectively with each of their prospects. How can salespeople determine their prospective customer's social style? They use clues to be able to classify prospective customers into one of the four different social style groups.

The descriptions of each of the four different social styles are very similar across the three different models, as are the clues for classifying the style of prospective customers. They are as follows:[45]

- **Driver (Doer/Dominant)**. These are achievers, bottom-line, get-it-done people who are action-oriented, goal-oriented, results-driven, decisive, competitive, efficient, disciplined, practical, and who make quick decisions. They crave respect for their achievements and fear the loss of power. They tend to display controlled facial expressions and a rigid body posture. They are often surrounded by trophies, awards, and plaques – all attesting to their achievements. (See Figure 5.9.)

Figure 5.9   Office of a driver

- **Analytical (Controller/Conscientious)**. These are reserved and distant. They're logical, unemotional, task-oriented, quality-focused, slow-paced, and want facts and accurate information. They are very analytical and well organized and will only make decisions after carefully digesting all of the facts and data. They tend to be reserved and won't express their opinions readily. They typically display a closed posture and hard-to-read facial expressions. They are surrounded by orderliness. Their desks may be loaded with paperwork, but it's all stacked in neat piles. (See Figure 5.10.)

Figure 5.10   Office of an analytical

- **Expressive (Talker/Influence)**. These are outgoing, friendly, affable people who are easy to approach and fun to be with. They're frequently thought of as 'people persons' who are upbeat, optimistic, and enjoy interacting with others. They tend to speak quickly, use animated expressions, and share their feelings easily. They buy from people they like and don't want to disappoint people. They are more daring in their dress with colors and jewelry. They will often have trinkets, fun gadgets, and photos in their somewhat cluttered office. (See Figure 5.11.)

Figure 5.11   Office of an expressive

- **Amiable (Supporter/Steadiness)**. These are easygoing, steady, honest, dependable, and loyal. They are stable, detail-minded people who are unhurried and slow in decision making. They are team players and they like predictability and security, while they avoid both conflict and taking risks. They work hard and focus on doing a good job versus the end results. They are usually the first ones to work in the morning and the last ones to leave in the evening. They focus on opinions rather than facts and speak slowly and softly. They have a more casual posture, often leaning back while talking, and they avoid making direct eye contact. They typically have homey offices displaying family photos, plants, and other, related items. (See Figure 5.12.)

Figure 5.12 Office of an amiable

The social style classification process is not always clear cut. Most people are a combination of two social styles – one being dominant, the other secondary. The majority of salespeople are Expressives, while the top 5 percent are Drivers.[46] While no single social style is 'better' than the other, prospective customers possessing each style respond best to information presented in the particular manner best suited to their style. This is true because customers of different styles have different ways of considering and reaching buying decisions. Lastly, determining a prospective customer's dominant social style takes practice and exceptional active listening, and even more work is required to match or mirror their behavior. Listening carefully to identify, classify, and respond to a person's dominant communication mode is what neuro-linguistic programming entails, which is the topic of our next section.

Understanding and utilizing neuro-linguistic programming

When conversing with prospective customers, salespeople will receive lots of information, such as clues as to the prospect's dominant social style. In addition, salespeople will discover that the way their prospects speak and the words they use vary from prospect to prospect. Neuro-linguistic programming (NLP) is a technique for enhancing one's ability to detect personality types through an increased awareness of verbal and physical cues.[47] NLP was initially developed by researchers John Grinder and Richard Bandler in 1975 in order to help therapists develop greater trust, rapport, and understanding with their clients. Thus, NLP is another social science technique that salespeople may use to build rapport and communicate more effectively with their current and prospective customers.

NLP has three essential elements. They are:[48]

1. **Neuro**: 'related to the brain' – refers to the mind and how we organize our thoughts and process information through our five senses.
2. **Linguistic**: 'pertaining to language, general body language' – concerns language and nonverbal communication systems, how we use language, and how it is coded, ordered, and given meaning.
3. **Programming**: 'conditioning the brain' – pertains to our sequences of repetitive behavior and our ability to organize our communication and neurological systems to achieve specific desired goals and results.

Thus, NLP details the connections among our thoughts, our speech, and our behavior. NLP maintains that although people have five senses, most people have three dominant sensory modes in terms of how they communicate – visual (V), auditory (A), and kinesthetic (K); or seeing, hearing, and feeling.[49] These three senses (V-A-K) comprise the three modalities of NLP. People tend to favor and use certain words when speaking based on each person's dominant mode of communication (V-A-K). Here's how it works:

- **Visual (V)** people think in terms of pictures, recalling and remembering information in terms of mental images, and imagining everything in terms of pictures. Visual people use visual language, such as see, appear, look, show, picture, and envision.
- **Auditory (A)** people think in sounds, remembering all things in terms of sound, and recognizing people from the sound of their movements. Auditory people use auditory words, such as hear, listen, sound, resonate, and loud and clear.
- **Kinesthetic (K)** people think in terms of feelings, remembering people from their touch or feel, and tending to be touchy-feely kind of people who often touch people while talking. Kinesthetic people use tactile phrases, such as feel, touch, grasp, get hold of, get to grips with, and get a handle on.

Salespeople can be trained to carefully listen for cue words and phrases (see Table 5.2) when prospective customers are speaking in order to identify each one's dominant V-A-K mode of communication based on the words they are using. Determining each prospect's dominant mode of communication takes training and practice.

Table 5.2 NLP predicate words and phrases

VISUAL (V)		
Words:	horizon	survey
analyze	idea	vague
angle	illusion	view
appear	image	vision
clarity	inspect	watch
clear	look	witness

(Continued)

Table 5.2 (Continued)

VISUAL (V)

cognizant	notice	Phrases:
conspicuous	obscure	appears to me
demonstrate	observe	in light of
dream	obvious	looks like
draw	perception	mental picture
examine	perspective	well defined
focus	picture	
focused	scene	
foresee	see	
glance	show	
hazy	sight	
hindsight	sketchy	

AUDITORY (A)

Words:	mention	tell
announce	noise	tone
articulate	oral	utter
audible	proclaim	vocal
communicate	pronounce	voice
converse	remark	Phrases:
discuss	report	be all ears
dissonant	resonate	clear as a bell
divulge	roar	give an account of
earshot	rumor	loud and clear
enunciate	say	unheard of
gossip	shrill	word for word
hear	silence	
hush	sound	
inquire	squeal	
interview	state	
listen	talk	

KINESTHETIC (K)

Words:	hold	tied
active	hustle	touch
affected	intuition	unbearable
bearable	lukewarm	unfeeling
charge	motion	unsettled
concrete	muddled	whipped
emotional	panicky	Phrases:
feel	pressure	get hold of
firm	sensitive	make contact

flow	set	get a handle on
foundation	shallow	come to grips with
grasp	softly	cool, calm, and collected
grip	solid	get the drift of
hanging	structured	too much hassle
hassle	support	so soft
heated	tension	

Source: Adapted from William Nickels, Robert Everett, and Ronald Klein, 'Rapport building for salespeople: A neuro-linguistic approach,' *Journal of Personal Selling & Sales Management* (November 1983), 3(2), 1–7.

Salespeople need to speak the language of their prospective customers in order to effectively communicate and establish rapport. This entails mirroring or matching, as mentioned earlier in the chapter. Mirroring is the process of matching certain behaviors, such as a person's tone or tempo of voice, body posture, gestures, facial expressions, breathing patterns, and so on. Using words from each of their prospective customer's dominant mode of communication is the primary NLP technique for salespeople to mirror or match their prospects. Of course, in order to apply NLP, salespeople must first understand their own dominant (V-A-K) mode. As Figure 5.13 displays, there are three steps to applying NLP to improve effective communication. Once salespeople determine their own dominant mode, they can work to identify the dominant modes of each of their prospective customers, and then modify their language to get in sync with each of their prospects.

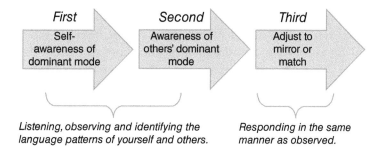

Figure 5.13 Flowchart of the three steps in the NLP process

Applying this three-step process should enable you to communicate more effectively with people, regardless of their unique personalities and varying communication styles. But how do you know if your communication is effective? This question leads us to our final section of this chapter which addresses how you can ensure that you are communicating successfully. There are some assessment techniques and measures that you may use to ensure that you are communicating effectively with your target audience.

MONITORING METRICS

Monitoring metrics

Being a successful and effective communicator doesn't just happen, nor are people born with good communication skills. Being able to communicate effectively and persuasively requires training, practice, and assessment to ensure that your communication is clear, concise, relevant, and engaging.

Evaluating communication effectiveness

Assessing your communication style and working to improve where indicated is imperative to becoming an effective communicator and achieving success in selling. So, let's examine some ways that you can evaluate your communication skills.

Identify and understand. As mentioned earlier, self-assessment is required in order to identify and understand your own unique social style and NLP-dominant mode of communication before you can become a really effective communicator. Are you a Driver? Are you Expressive? Do you think in terms of images and use visual words when you speak? Or, do you have a hands-on approach to life and use words that are associated with touching and tactile feeling? You may complete a self-assessment by videotaping yourself multiple times and then evaluating those tapes to determine your own personal style. Once you know your own personal communication style and have determined your prospective customers' styles, you will be able to tell what adjustments to make in order to mirror or match the styles of each of your prospects.

Practice and perfect. Practicing interpersonal communication skills by partaking in role-plays with fictitious prospective customers will help you to sharpen your skills and increase your confidence level. The more role-plays you carry out, especially with different people, the better you will become in determining the social styles and NLP-dominant mode of communication of each person with whom you converse. Multiple role-plays will enable you to gain experience in adjusting your communication style to mirror the style of each prospective customer. Practice makes perfect!

Observe and learn. Video-taping your role-plays and reviewing those tapes to critically observe yourself and identify areas of needed improvement, are always helpful.

While reviewing tapes, evaluate your speech pattern, your vocal skills, and your body language. You'll be able to determine whether you are truly mirroring your prospective buyer's behavior and communication style, or you just think you are doing so. As Figure 5.14 reveals, without proper mirroring, a disconnect in communication may occur. Of course, you may always ask someone else to listen to and/or watch your role-plays and provide evaluation and suggestions. Savvy salespeople are always learning and continuously striving to improve their communication skills.

Figure 5.14 Different dominant NLP modes

Certain aspects of communication may be evaluated and scored using metrics to serve as a baseline for monitoring improvement. The final section in this chapter will address the communication metrics which may be tracked.

Evaluating speaking skills

You may evaluate your speaking skills, knowledge of content, appearance, and ability to meet set time limits on a regular basis using a rating scale, such as, Excellent = 4;

Good = 3; Fair = 2; Poor = 1; Not observed = 0 as a scoring mechanism. For some items, such as the number of filler words that you use when you speak for a specific period of time, counting the raw number and comparing it to previous evaluations will be meaningful. (If you speak for varying amounts of time, calculate the *rate* of using filler words in a selected amount of time.) You should document your scores to gauge your improvement over time. Some specific items you may evaluate are listed below.

Speaking skills:

* clarity of speech, including any mumbling and any mispronounced words
* pace of speech
* volume of speech
* use of filler words, such as 'um' and 'like,' and upspeak/uptalk, such as a rising inflection as if you are asking a question at the end of a declarative sentence
* frequency of eye contact with the audience
* frequency and appropriateness of gestures, body language, facial expressions, posture, and poise
* energy level, including expression, varied intonation, engagement with subject matter, and being passionate about the topic
* appropriate use of grammar.

Command of content:

* evidence of prior preparation, including ownership of the material that you are providing
* effective use of notes or notecards for details, but not being completely reliant on them
* ease of understanding key points by the audience
* clarity of explanation for any visual aids used to support the message
* ease of providing greater details than what the supporting materials contain
* ability to effectively and confidently answer questions.

Attire: attire appropriate for the audience.

Time limit: speaking length is within the allotted time as set by the prospective customer.

In conclusion, salespeople must be engaging communicators and exceptional listeners. They must pay close attention to their prospects and adjust both their behavioral style and NLP communication approach to that of their prospects. Rapport is achieved faster when salespeople are able to match their social style and NLP communication mode to that of their prospective customers. Adaptive selling increases the ability of salespeople to consistently build productive and trusting relationships with many types of prospective customers, which is the best predictor for obtaining second appointments, acquiring referrals, and securing buyer commitment.[50] Conducting ongoing evaluations of their communication effectiveness will help salespeople to become even more successful in selling.

CHAPTER SUMMARY

✓ Prepare and practice to make a good first impression; request critiques from others.

✓ Know your own personality style and pay attention to customers' speech and behavior to determine their styles as well.

✓ Flex your style to be in sync with your customer's social style to enhance communication and build rapport.

✓ Determine metrics for your sales presentations and conversations, and work to continuously improve the impact you make when speaking.

KEY TERMS

Adaptive selling
Approaching
Body language
Congruence
Emotional intelligence
Mirroring
Netiquette

Neuro-linguistic programming (NLP)
Nonverbal skills
Rapport
Style flexing
Verbal skills
Versatility
Vocal skills

REVIEW QUESTIONS

1. Describe five ways to build rapport with a prospective customer.
2. What is the goal of a first impression? What will you do to ensure that your first impression is positive, successful, and memorable?
3. Describe at least three alternatives to the traditional handshake and reasons why you might use a different method.
4. What are the three emotional intelligence skills described by Colleen Stanley that help salespeople when dealing with a tough prospect or customer?
5. According to Carl Lyons, there are four basic modes of body language that prospective customers typically possess. Describe the characteristics of each.
6. Following the KISS principle, list at least three writing methods that you will use to ensure proper writing technique.

7. What is adaptive selling and why is it important?
8. What are the four different social style groups? Which group are you in?
9. What is NLP? Describe the three senses that indicate people's dominant mode of communication?
10. Name four metrics you can use to determine the effectiveness of your speaking skills.

ETHICS IN ACTION

1. Judy Thomson had been trying to set up an initial visit with a prospective customer for five months. The visit will finally take place this Friday. On Monday, she was notified of the death of a cousin she was particularly close to. She is very upset and totally distracted as she mourns her loss. She is unable to move the appointment to a date in the near future and is very uncomfortable with any other salesperson representing her at this meeting. As her manager, what would you advise her to do about this situation? Should she keep the appointment? If so, do you recommend that she mention the situation she is currently in to the prospective customer? What can she do to keep the potential sale progressing, while honoring her need to grieve?

2. As a salesperson, you have learned to determine prospective customers' behavioral and social styles. This does not come naturally to you, so you've been practicing making determinations of friends and family members. You confirm your assessment with each person and have been told you've been correct each time. In an initial sales discussion with a prospective customer, you quickly determine the prospect is Expressive (Talker/Influence), a friendly, affable person who is easy to approach, upbeat, optimistic, and doesn't want to disappoint people. You adjust your sales presentation and mannerisms accordingly. At the end of the discussion, the prospect states his disappointment at the lack of supporting data and product details you provided. You suddenly realize that you misread his behavioral style. How do you recover from this mistake and prove that you value all that information as well? What can you do to decrease the likelihood of making a similar error in the future?

EXERCISE

It's time to have a conversation! For this exercise, you are to engage in a conversation in which you will proactively listen and analyze the neuro-linguistic programming (NLP) modality of yourself and your conversation partner. So, select a conversation partner and agree on the topic to be discussed, and be ready to time your conversation for

10–15 minutes. Be sure to review the NLP cue words (Visual, Auditory and Kinesthetic) for assessing a person's dominant mode of communication provided in this chapter, before beginning your conversation.

You must be aware of your language while speaking to identify the NLP cue words that you are using when conversing. While you speak, your partner will proactively listen. Then, at the conclusion of your conversation, both you and your partner should document what you believe your dominant NLP mode is based on the predicate words you used while speaking. After that, enter into another conversation where your partner speaks while you actively listen. Once again, at the conclusion of that conversation, both you and your partner should document what you believe your partner's dominant NLP mode to be based on the predicate words that your partner used while speaking. After both conversations are concluded, compare notes and analyze your conversation from an NLP perspective, including:

a. Agreement on your dominant NLP mode.
b. Agreement on your conversation partner's dominant NLP mode.
c. Comparison of both your and your partner's dominant NLP mode of communication and body language used while conversing.
d. Identification of what (if any) adjustments you should make in order to match the NLP-dominant mode of communication, as well as mirror the body language of your communication partner, in order to maximize overall communication effectiveness.

ROLE-PLAY

Role-play flow chart

Situation: You are a pharmaceutical sales representative who has been calling on a particular physician for five years. This doctor is always swamped with patients and his office is understaffed. He averages seeing more than 40 patients a day where the typical physician sees 25 patients a day. His most challenging patients are his diabetic patients. Many of them have multiple physical problems (high blood pressure, high cholesterol, overweight) in addition to having diabetes. To complicate matters further, many of his diabetic patients do not fully comply with treatment.

(Continued)

Characters: You have been a pharmaceutical sales representative for 12 years now, specializing in diabetes drugs. You love your position and have excellent relationships with all of the physicians you regularly call on. Dr. Miles is a 52-year-old well-respected internal medicine physician. He has had a thriving office practice for more than six years now. You've noticed that Dr. Miles has numerous photos of his wife and children in his office and he has mentioned how proud he is of his eldest son's Eagle Scout achievement.

Selling goal: To communicate the value of your pharmaceutical company's products and services and obtain commitment to allow you and your company to take a more active role in helping his staff improve the care of his diabetic patients.

Product/service capabilities: Your company has a new, long-acting insulin that may become state-of-the-art treatment for Type 1 diabetics. Your pharmaceutical company has diabetes educators that can be scheduled to visit medical offices and teach patients about diabetes and about medications upon request.

Sales call details: The problem is that patients don't like to give themselves shots every day. The staff doesn't have time to properly educate patients about diabetes and how to give themselves these medications. The doctor is wary of any new medications that could complicate things for his patients or his staff.

Selling challenge: How do you approach this physician? Can you determine Dr. Mile's social style? If so, what adaptive selling techniques might you use when interacting with Dr. Miles?

READINGS AND RESOURCES

- Jeb Blount (2010) *People Buy You*. Hoboken, NJ: John Wiley & Sons, Inc.
- Dorie Clark (2013) *Reinventing You: Define Your Brand, Imagine Your Future*. Brighton, MA: Harvard Business Review Press.
- Joseph O'Connor and Ian McDermott (1996) *Principles of NLP*. New York: HarperCollins.
- Barbara Pachter (2013) *The Essentials of Business Etiquette: How to Greet, Eat, and Tweet Your Way to Success*. New York: McGraw-Hill Education.
- Colleen Stanley (2012) *Emotional Intelligence for Sales Success: Connect with Customer and Get Results*. New York: AMACOM.
- Ron Willingham (2003) *Integrity Selling for the 21st Century*. New York: Doubleday.

CASE STUDY: PEPSI

Note: The names and locations used in this case have been disguised for confidentiality purposes.

Upon graduating from college, Abby Riley was swiftly immersed into the sales world as a field sales representative for Pepsi. After a week of intense sales training with the soft drink giant, she began calling on the 75 7-Eleven franchise and corporate-run stores located in her sales territory, which encompassed the southeast region of the USA. Abby dressed daily in khakis and a Pepsi polo to match her customer profile, as all of her store managers also wore polos and slacks. On a weekly basis, Abby visited each store where she met with a variety of customers who possessed different buyer styles, interests, and languages (see Figure 5.15).

Figure 5.15   Pepsi sales rep stocking shelves
Used with kind permission of Kristina Pontillo.

Abby quickly learned how to adapt to each individual buyer style in order to form good working relationships, the key to effective selling. Yes, the numbers behind any sale are vital; however, growing the number of Pepsi cases doesn't happen easily, nor in the same manner, for any one customer.

Most of Abby's stores were owned or managed by people of Indian ethnicity, so learning the cultural, religious, and business styles of Indian clientele assisted in her relationship-building and selling abilities. In addition, she had to learn which franchise owners were the key influencers throughout her sales territory, as those customers had connections that influenced the buying decisions of other franchisees. Naila, for example, owned one of the busiest 7-Eleven stores in one large coastal city. She was a feisty woman and had connections to almost every store in the region. If Naila was upset, she wasn't going to buy your product; nor would other stores. When Naila had an issue, Abby tended to her right away, regardless of whether or not it was an off-schedule sales day visit.

One of the biggest encounters Abby was challenged with was a driver issue at 5:00 a.m. one Tuesday. Naila called Abby, explaining that the Pepsi delivery driver had parked his truck in the incorrect spot and he wasn't delivering the product correctly. The Pepsi driver and Naila got into a verbal altercation and she made the driver leave her store. Abby drove to Naila's 7-Eleven store to deflect the situation. Her successful efforts made it possible to have the delivery team send a new driver to Naila's store so the Pepsi products could get checked in and the sales transaction could be completed. Even though Abby spent an extra two hours of her morning at Naila's store, it was worth it to keep her customer happy and their business relationship intact. Thus, Naila's future buying decisions, as well as those of other franchise owners who were influenced by Naila, were not affected by the delivery mishap.

Throughout Abby's territory, there were multiple franchisees with managers who would run the store whenever they were not there. However, it was typically the franchise owner who placed the orders. Abby always kept her schedule flexible in order to interact with each of the key decision makers throughout her territory. At another location in her region, Abby had a very narrow window of time where she could visit for only 30 minutes with Rana, the store owner. This was because Rana's store had a small parking lot, so she didn't want any sales reps at her store during the 7-Eleven coffee rush – the first few hours of the morning, which are the most profitable time for most stores. In addition, Rana attended a weekly class later in the morning. In order to build strong relationships, Abby had to understand each of her customers and respect their individual situation and availability. Rana also requested her delivery window be altered because of other deliveries and the limited size of her parking lot. Changing the Pepsi delivery schedule pleased Rana. Abby took time to work with Rana, resulting in new Pepsi products and increased total volume and distribution for the store. Being able to assist customers with their requests strengthened Abby's relationships with her customers, leading to greater success in selling.

Case questions:

1. Why was it important for Abby to tend to Naila's store issue immediately, even though it was not Abby's scheduled sales day to be there? Was the time that Abby lost that day worth any potential business in the future? Why?
2. Why is being flexible with customers important? How does flexibility impact business success in the long term?
3. Describe way(s) that Abby improved the business relationship between Rana and Pepsi. How did Pepsi benefit from the strong business relationship between Abby and Rana?

NOTES

1. Wikipedia, 2020.
2. Adapted from William F. Kendy, 'The importance of building rapport,' *Business Insights: Essentials* (Feb./Mar. 2014), 47(2/3), 6–7; and Dave Kahle, 'Seven ways to build rapport with anyone,' *American Fastener Journal* (Nov./Dec. 2016), 32(6), 64–5.
3. Ron Willingham (2003) *Integrity Selling for the 21st Century* (New York: Random House), p. 5.
4. Ibid., pp. 5–6.
5. Hank Darlington, 'The importance of first impressions,' *Supply House Times* (October 2018), 61(8), 50–3.
6. Dorie Clark (2013) *Reinventing You: Define Your Brand, Imagine Your Future.* Quoted in Rebecca Knight, 'How to make a great first impression,' *Harvard Business Review* (Digital Articles) (September 12, 2016), p. 3.
7. Rebecca Knight, 'How to make a great first impression,' *Harvard Business Review* (Digital Articles) (September 12, 2016), pp. 2–6.
8. Patricia M. Buhler, 'Business etiquette: A renewed interest in a lost art,' *American Salesman* (October 2019), 64(10), 13–16.
9. Adapted from 'With virus, skip the handshake,' *Administrative Professionals Today* (June 2020), 46(6), 6.
10. Aja Frost, 'Business Etiquette: The ultimate guide', https://blog.hubspot.com/sales/business-etiquette, retrieved July 16, 2020.
11. Dale Carnegie (1936) *How to Win Friends and Influence People* (New York: Simon & Schuster), p. 88.
12. Jeb Blount, 'Start connecting: Stop trying to build rapport,' *Sales & Service Excellence Essentials* (August 2010), 10(8), 6.
13. William F. Kendy, 'The importance of building rapport,' *Business Insights: Essentials* (February/March 2014), 47(2/3), 6–7
14. Jeb Blount, 'Start connecting: Stop trying to build rapport,' *Sales & Service Excellence Essentials* (August 2010), 10(8), 6.
15. Ibid.
16. Colleen Stanley, '3 emotional intelligence skills to teach,' *Northern Colorado Business Report* (December 2012), 18(6), 15.
17. Ibid.
18. Colleen Stanley (2012) 'Emotional Intelligence for Sales Success: Connect with customers and get results' (ebook) (AMACOM), pp. 33–8.
19. Ibid., pp. 43–4.
20. Adapted from Sabrina Brawner, 'Increase your emotional intelligence,' *Personal Excellence* (August 2016), 21(8), 20.
21. John Wooden (2005) *Wooden on Leadership* (New York: McGraw-Hill), p. 144.
22. Carl Lyons (2007) *I Win You Win: The Essential Guide to Principled Negotiation* (London: A & C Black), p. 86.

23. Ibid., p. 87.

24. Kahle, 2015-ET-H.

25. Carl Lyons (2007) *I Win You Win: The Essential Guide to Principled Negotiation* (London: A & C Black), p. 88.

26. Ibid.

27. Ibid., p. 89.

28. Adapted from Carl Lyons (2007) *I Win You Win: The Essential Guide to Principled Negotiation* (London: A & C Black), pp. 90–3; and John Boe, 'Sit up straight and pay attention,' *American Salesman* (March 2019), 64(3), 20–6.

29. Jeff Davidson, 'Are sales slipping through the phone? The most basic tenets that you don't want to overlook,' *HCM Sales, Marketing & Alliance Excellence Essentials* (April 2017), 16(4), 17.

30. Lauren Simonds (April 19, 2013) 'Good writing can help you succeed,' *Time Business*, https://business.time.com/2013/04/19/good-writing-can-help-you-succeed, retrieved October 11, 2020.

31. Adapted from Grace Carter, 'The art of the written word,' *Training Journal* (October 2018), pp. 32–3; and Landy Chase, '"Netiquette" for sales professionals,' *Official Board Markets* (September 2011), 87(36), 20.

32. Grace Carter, 'The art of the written word,' *Training Journal* (October 2018), pp. 32–3.

33. Adapted from Dan S. Kennedy (2006) *The Ultimate Sales Letter: Attract New Customers; Boost Your Sales* (Avon, MA: Adams Media), pp. 5–6.

34. Eileen Brownell, 'How to make yourself memorable,' *The American Salesman: Burlington*, (March 2010), 55(3), 24–8.

35. Adapted from Patricia M. Buhler, 'Business etiquette: A renewed interest in a lost art,' *American Salesman* (October 2019), 64(10), 13–16.

36. Deanne DeMarco, 'Get your communication styles in-sync,' *Training and Development in Australia: Surry Hills* (April 2005), 32(2), 26–30.

37. Michael Leimbach, 'Sales versatility: Connect with customers every time,' *Sales & Service Excellence Essentials* (January 2010), 10(1), 10.

38. Ibid.

39. Susan Croft (2002) *Win New Business: The Desktop Guide* (London: Thorogood Publishers), pp. 71–84.

40. Ben Janse (2019) '*Merrill Social Styles Model*,' www.toolshero.com/communication-skills/merrill-social-styles-model, retrieved October 11, 2020.

41. Susan Croft (2002) *Win New Business: The Desktop Guide* (London: Thorogood Publishers), pp. 71–84.

42. Ron Willingham (2003) *Integrity Selling for the 21st Century* (New York: Random House), p. 19.

43. Deanne DeMarco, 'Get your communication styles in-sync,' *Training and Development in Australia: Surry Hills* (April 2005), 32(2), 18–20.

44. Susan Foster, 'What's your client's style?' *Sell!ng* (December 1998), 6(5), 8.

45. Adapted from Ron Willingham (2003) *Integrity Selling for the 21st Century* (New York: Random House), pp. 18–20; Susan Foster, 'What's your client's style?' *Sell!ng*

(December 1998), 6(5), 8; Jonathan Farrington, 'The 4 social styles,' *LifeHealthPro: New York* (May 2013); and Scott Ritchey, 'The four social styles in sales,' *Supply House Times: Troy* (October 2016), 59 (8), 68.

46. Jonathan Farrington, 'The 4 social styles,' *LifeHealthPro: New York* (May 2013).

47. William Nickels, Robert Everett and Ronald Klein, 'Rapport building for salespeople: A neuro-linguistic approach,' *Journal of Personal Selling & Sales Management* (November 1983), 3(2), 1.

48. Susan Croft (2002) *Win New Business: The Desktop Guide* (London: Thorogood Publishers), p. 81.

49. Carl Lyons (2007) *I Win You Win: The Essential Guide to Principled Negotiation* (London: A & C Black), p. 83.

50. Michael Leimbach, 'Sales versatility: Connecting with customers every time,' *American Salesman* (November 2015), 60(11), 20–5.

6

LISTENING AND DETERMINING WILLINGNESS TO BUY

Lisa Spiller and Dan Schultheis

CHAPTER CONTENTS

PEOPLE, PRACTICES AND PERSPECTIVES FROM THE WORLD OF SALES

Hi! I'm Yvonne Cochrane and I have worked in sales and business development for more than 30 years. Although my sales experience lies mainly in printing, I have dipped my toe in a few other industries such as pharmaceuticals, oil and gas, telecoms, holistic therapies, ending up in academic publishing. My sales territories are Scotland and Ireland. My advice to you regarding listening is: *To always listen actively (and reply with empathy) to get the information you need to meet the customer's needs. Listen for specific information that you have asked for and observe verbal or behavioural indicators that demonstrate that something is important to the customer.* A quote that sticks in my mind and works for me is: 'People buy people so build that rapport ... a proven method to see your sales soar' (Author unknown.)

Hello, my name is Bryan Higgins and I'm a regional sales manager for Anheuser-Busch InBev (Devils Backbone Brewing Company). I'm based out of Nashville, Tenneessee where I manage a regional team of sales professionals that communicate brand strategies to our wholesaler partners. I'm involved in the production logistics, pricing, distribution, and program execution throughout our portfolio and footprint. My advice to you based on 14 years of sales experience is this: *Be sure to fully understand who your customer is. Their goals, problems, opportunities, and strengths will all shape the solutions you present to them. This is accomplished by asking the proper questions and actively listening to your customer.*

Hi, I'm Tisha Lim, a sales associate with Bloomberg Industry Group. I support three relationship partners throughout a full sales cycle by scheduling new business demos, identifying up-sell opportunities, ensuring meeting completion, and performing daily outreach to prospect for clients in the Western and Eastern regions of the US.

I believe that a great sales professional is one who is always curious. By that, I mean to always ask your prospect or client questions. Let them tell you their pain points, let them explain their needs and priorities, and let them lead you to the solution. I've learned that there are only two reasons to interact with a client: 1. To get information; 2. To get commitment.

To listen well is as powerful a means of influence as to talk well.

– An ancient Chinese proverb

EYES ON ETHICS

1. Respecting all prospects equally, while needing to prioritize business opportunities.
2. Reporting data on your performance in meeting the intent of the four pillars of the Willing to Buy framework.

INTRODUCTION

The topic of this chapter is on listening to the customer and determining a willingness to buy, often called the needs discovery conversation (NDC) or 'interview' stage of the selling process. In this chapter, we'll examine the activities and techniques involved during the interview stage, which includes asking effective questions, listening actively and proactively, understanding buyers and their individual journeys, and finally, determining each buyer's willingness to buy.

By this point, you, the salesperson, have researched prospective buyers (Chapter 2), strategically planned for successful selling (Chapter 3), and networked and prospected for potential customers who might have a need/want for whatever you are selling (Chapter 4). In addition, you've approached your prospective buyer and have established good rapport (Chapter 5). This chapter explores the next stage of the selling process – what transpires when the salesperson is sitting down with the prospective buyer. Of course, effective conversation is what needs to occur, but how does this happen? How do salespeople begin this conversation? What techniques should they use to keep the conversation going and moving in the *right* direction?

After salespeople effectively gain rapport with their prospective buyer, how do they transition from the approach stage to the interview stage? First and foremost, they need to stay focused on their prospective buyers and their needs, wants, interests, goals, and so on. Offering a suggestion to continue the conversation is an effective way to move the ball forward. While there aren't any 'magic' words that salespeople should use, here's an example of what salespeople might say:

Based on my research, I believe that what I have might be a good solution for you, however I cannot be certain until I fully understand your needs and goals. So, if it's OK with you, I'd like to ask you a few questions to obtain additional information, so that I'll know if what I have is indeed a good fit for your needs.

An alternative might be:

Based on my research, I have some questions that may help to identify what situations(s) in your organization you're trying to change, and what impact that might have on your organization. So, if it's OK with you, I'd like to ask you those questions and get an understanding of what you may be dealing with.

Note that the difference between these two approaches is that the first one is presumptive, in that the salesperson thinks they know what a solution might be before asking questions about the problem the prospect is experiencing. Also, using the word 'needs' suggests that the prospect has already done some work on the problem and is now ready to articulate what the requirements are for the solution. The second approach only seeks to understand what the person is experiencing currently and what the impact of changing or not changing that situation may be. Also note that both of these statements emphasize the prospective customer's needs and allude to the previous research that the salesperson has conducted on the prospect. These statements also request permission to begin the interview process. When sincerely professed, authentic statements like these may cause prospective buyers to unfold their arms, physically and emotionally, open their minds, and be more receptive to continuing the conversation with you.[1]

Another alternative is to talk only about the *problem* and the pain or discomfort the prospect is experiencing, associated with that problem. Lastly, salespeople should always verify that they have heard their prospects correctly prior to beginning to discuss a solution. That requires effective questioning and listening, which is the topic of the next section.

EFFECTIVE QUESTIONING AND LISTENING

Interviewing is the single most important step of the selling process and it is the heart of customer needs selling.[2] During the NDC or interview stage, the Pareto principle should be applied. As applied to customer interviews, this principle indicates that salespeople should be listening 80 percent of the time, while talking only 20 percent of the time. When salespeople do speak, they should do so for the expressed purpose of either asking questions for additional information or paraphrasing back to the prospect what they have said in order to assure proper understanding. *Stop Selling and Start Listening*, the title of a book by Chip Cummings listed in the Readings and Resources section at the end of this chapter, is applicable here. His point is that *listening* to the prospective customer is paramount to successful selling. However, this isn't as easy as it sounds. What if the prospective buyer isn't talking? How can salespeople listen if buyers aren't describing what they need? That's why requesting prospective buyers' permission to ask them questions at the beginning of this stage is a good technique to use. Let's now discuss questioning in greater detail.

Using effective questioning

The skillful use of questions is one of the simplest and most powerful ways to elicit the values, interests and perceptions of the prospective buyer. Asking questions is the most effective way for the salesperson to determine what the prospective buyer really wants.

The right questions may open up communication lines and encourage conversations that increase the level of trust the prospective buyer has in you and whatever you are selling.[3] The salesperson should ask prospects exploratory questions that require them to expand on their previous answer. For example, the salesperson may ask, 'What is a pressing issue you are dealing with in your company?' The customer may reply, 'I want to improve my accounts receivable.' An appropriate follow-up question to expand on this might be, 'What are the reasons that caused you to pick accounts receivable as your answer?' This allows prospects to reflect on how the accounts receivable became a problem and thus give more context to their initial answer. In other words, seeking to have the prospect explain the 'why behind the what' is critical in effective needs discovery conversations. A list of questions should be planned and prepared in advance; however, salespeople should be able to be spontaneous and ask additional relevant questions when and where needed. Effective questions will focus on the needs, wants, interests, and so on, of prospective buyers and will of course vary depending on what salespeople are selling.

In addition, the salesperson should use another line of questioning in parallel with the needs analysis questions. These are questions that assess the level of urgency prospects feel to make a change and implement a new way of addressing their concerns. These types of questions will approach the issues by asking:

- What will happen in your environment if you don't change the current situation?
- Why is now the time to make a change to your current environment?

There are many different types of questions that the salesperson may ask in different ways. Here are five categories of questions to explore:[4]

1. Indirect questions. These are open-ended questions which allow the buyer to express their feelings and opinions without limiting the direction of their answers. Example: *What are you thinking about this option?* Alternatively: *What impact would changing your current environment have?*
2. Direct questions. These questions ask for an expansion or evaluation of a specific area. They limit the buyer to focus on a precise topic. Example: *What are the areas that concern you the most?* Additionally: *What made you choose these areas rather than others to address?*
3. Empowering questions. These questions are solution-oriented and focus on what positive actions can be taken. Example: How might this particular option work to solve your problem? Alternatively: How would your environment change if you addressed and fixed this problem?
4. Disempowering questions. These questions are problem-focused questions and are concerned with barriers to making progress. Example: Why do you think this option won't work for you? Alternatively: What obstacles do you see in your workplace environment that would prohibit you from addressing this problem?
5. *Possibility questions.* These questions are useful in generating ideas or options. They normally begin with 'What if ...?' Example: *What could you do if you were able to*

reduce your operating costs by 30 percent next year? However, this question is presumptive on the part of the salesperson in that the prospect would assume that 30 percent improvement is totally feasible. Rather than leading with this type of question, it is typically best to start with a more general question, such as: *If you could eliminate this problem, what two or three improvements would you notice in your workplace environment?*

Salesperson speaking to the buyer

Keep in mind that questions must also vary based on the behavior style (Talker, Doer, Controller, Supporter) of the prospective buyer, as discussed in previous chapters. This means that salespeople will need to pick and choose from their list of questions based on the specific social style of the prospective buyer with whom they are conversing. Let's explore some potential questions that might work well with each of the four different behavior styles of prospective buyers.[5]

Talkers, who are concerned with how others feel, and want to please others, might respond well to questions such as:

* How do you think others will feel about what I'm offering?
* What do you think others will say about this?
* Who else might need to be involved in the purchase decision?

Doers, who are more focused on getting results and less focused on details or the need for social approval, might respond well to questions such as:

* How can I help you to reach your objective?
* What problems do you have that I can be of assistance with?
* How might this help you to achieve your goals?

Controllers, who are very interested in facts, logical processes, organization, and efficiency, and motivated by logic, instead of emotion, will not want to spend much time conversing. They may respond best to questions such as:

- What would help your organization operate more efficiently?
- What's your target return on investment?
- What business risks do you want to avoid?

Supporters, who are stable and dependable, may be willing to spend more time conversing with you if they trust you are stable and dependable. Therefore, you may be able to ask more questions, including some of the following:

- What might help you do your job better?
- What's worked well for you in the past?
- What additional details may I expand on for you?

Notice how the suggested questions vary based on the behavior style of the prospective buyer. Salespeople must be prepared for interacting with all four different social style types of customers. As presented in Chapter 2, salespeople should know the behavioral style of their prospective buyers *in advance* in order to properly prepare for face-to-face NDCs. Salespeople should not wait and try to analyze the behavior style of their prospective buyer during the actual meeting because that could detract from their ability to listen to the prospect. However, while it is generally a good practice to prepare for the NDC by thinking about the role and potential communication style of the prospect, salespeople run the risk of over-preparing and trying to fit the prospect into a 'style box.' Thus, too much preparation and rigid scripting may result in losing the intimacy and variability of the person-to-person dynamics that enhance any natural interpersonal communication.

Table 6.1 Techniques for effective questioning

- Research your prospective customer to understand their background, needs, wants, interests, etc. The more insight you obtain, the more prepared you will be, and the more relevant your questions will be in obtaining more details about your prospect during the needs discovery conversation.
- Select and word your questions wisely. Be sure to interview your prospective buyer, not interrogate them. Carefully wording your questions will enable your prospect to open up and share information freely.
- Use direct questions to obtain specific information. Follow these with other types of questions, such as indirect, empowering, or possibility questions. This will create a natural flow to your conversation.
- Ask clear and simple questions that are easy to answer. Avoid personal questions or questions that pertain to anything that may be controversial or sensitive to your prospect.
- Use questions to provide the prospective buyer with additional information. Whenever appropriate, convert statements into questions that encourage your prospect to respond with more details. For example, 'Did you know our company has been ranked among the top five customer service providers for the past 10 years?'
- Use questions to clarify and summarize the buyer's need, wants, interests and situation. Details matter, so you want to be certain that you've both correctly heard and understand their answers.

Source: Adapted from John Patrick Dolan, 'Discover exactly what your sales prospect wants in the negotiation process,' *American Salesman* (2017), 62(9).

Salespeople should create different questions and uniquely plan for the questioning process for each and every prospective buyer. Some techniques for carrying out the process of effective questioning include planning your questions ahead of your conversation with prospective buyers, seeking the their permission to ask them questions, and beginning with broad, simple questions before moving on to deeper questions as the conversation continues.[6] Check out Table 6.1 for some tips on effective questioning.

Questioning is a productive process to encourage prospective buyers to actively engage in conversation with salespeople. Of course, salespeople need to take the time to really listen to the answers provided and respond accordingly, which is the topic of the next section.

Employing active listening

Listening is not the same as hearing. People often confuse the physical act of hearing with the emotional art of listening.[7] Hearing is a biological function. Hearing is passive, whereas listening is an activity, an action, and a learned skill. Thus, salespeople cannot passively listen, but rather, they need to be trained to actively and proactively listen. Let's review the terms.

Passive listening, also known as assumptive listening, requires limited or no effort at all. With passive listening, our ears naturally hear the sounds that surround us without any mindful focus. Many things that passive listeners hear are based on assumptions of what they believe they will hear. So, passive listeners hear what they believe or assume they will hear. Passive listeners often start to cut others off during mid-sentence and don't ask questions to validate their assumptions, which may be inaccurate. Passive listening can be destructive to relationships.

Active listening is when you make a conscious effort to hear and understand the words and sounds that surround you. Thus, active listening requires a higher level of conscious attention and a deeper level of concentration on the communication – both verbally and nonverbally. So, active listeners will listen with their eyes, as well as their ears. They read body language, facial expressions, gestures, posture, and so on, as well as factor in tone, pitch, and rate of voice of other people, all important aspects of communication which were detailed in Chapter 5. Active listeners give their audience their complete, full, and undivided attention, which builds trust and rapport, and thus supports and enhances relationships.

Proactive listening, also known as intentional listening, is transformational in that you are present, focused, and engaged with your audience so deeply that you are no longer listening *to* someone but you are listening *for* select information.[8] Proactive listening is active listening taken up a notch. Proactive listeners will listen for key insights, opinions, or cues that might subsequently trigger particular questions that they should ask to help move the conversation forward. Proactive listening encompasses not only verbal and non-verbal communication, but also written communication. Proactive listeners take time to really understand the other person's point of view before sharing their own. They are focused on getting to the root cause of a challenge or objectives

Active listening and using body language

that are most important to the other person. Proactive listeners know how to leverage what they've heard as they have the ability to take what they learn and craft powerful, relevant follow-up questions that move the conversation forward with greater clarity. The laser-sharp focus of proactive listeners is completely on their audience, which reinforces, strengthens, and maximizes relationships.

Now that we've considered the three types of listening, let's examine both the need for and ways in which salespeople can improve their listening skills. Were you ever formally trained to listen? Most likely, your answer is 'no' as very few people have been formally taught effective listening skills. To listen actively or proactively requires concentration, hard work, patience, objectivity, and the ability to interpret the verbal and nonverbal communication of others.

Salespeople need to learn how to listen. Why? Well, people remember only about 25 percent of what they hear when they passively listen, as opposed to about 85 percent when they actively listen.[9] On average, we spend about 50 percent of our working hours listening to other people, which is more than any other single activity in which we partake.[10] Studies consistently show that a salesperson's active listening behavior leads to strong sales performance.[11] This makes sense, as naturally, salespeople who actively listen will be able to be more responsive to the needs of the customer, which strengthens relationships. Beyond that, when people actively listen to what someone is telling them, they are likely to receive a much more positive reaction when it's their turn to speak.[12]

There are many ways that salespeople can improve their listening skills. A good starting point is to complete a self-assessment to identify and recognize your own mistakes that limit your ability to listen. Here are some questions to begin your self-assessment. Do you give your audience your complete, undivided attention, or are you a multi-tasking listener, that is, doing something else while listening? Do you remove background noises when you are conversing or do you allow these distractions to remain? Are you attentive to eye contact, gestures, body language, tone, and voice inflections when you are listening or not? Do you practice selective listening and hear only what you want to hear or are you truly open to learning new ideas? Are you listening with the intent to understand other people's point of view, or are you trying to force your own opinions on them? You may continue your self-assessment by examining the common listening mistakes provided in Table 6.2, to see if you are guilty of any of them.

Table 6.2   Common mistakes that limit our proactive listening

---

✓ Listening through a personal perspective lens that filters what you focus on when you listen. For example, do you hear and process information from a perspective of trust or distrust? Openness or resistance? Acceptance or judgement? Fact or assumption?

✓ Listening while multi-tasking, which basically conveys to the other person that 'You're not important enough for me to stop what I'm doing to give you my full and undivided attention.'

✓ Interjecting your point of view at inappropriate times by not listening and not waiting for a pause in the conversation.

✓ Cutting people off in the middle of their sentences, which limits our ability to be able to hear the person's complete point of view.

✓ Not staying quiet while the other person speaks, which inhibits your ability to really focus on and hear what the other person is saying.

✓ Pretending to listen while you conjure up in your mind what you want to say next.

✓ Selectively listening only to those points you agree with or want to hear.

Source: Adapted from Keith Rosen, 'Proactive listening – Part II: 14 mistakes that kill productivity, sabotage coaching and result in sales loss,' *HCM Sales, Marketing & Alliance Excellence Essentials* (2017), 16(9).

Active and proactive listening require a methodological process. Salespeople should internalize this process and practice it whenever they are communicating with a prospective buyer. According to John Asher, author of *Close Deals Faster*, salespeople should follow three quick and easy steps to become a better listener. These steps are:[13]

1. *Totally focus on the prospective buyer's point of view*. Remove distractions and anything that might hinder the flow of information or make the prospect uncomfortable. Don't allow outside factors to steal your attention from your prospective buyer.
2. *Ask permission to take notes and then take notes*. Before starting to take notes, be sure to ask your prospective buyer's permission, which is polite and displays your respect. Taking notes also shows that you are actively listening and makes you appear more engaged and professional. By writing things down, you will improve your retention rate of the details.
3. *Summarize the client's needs and repeat them back to get an agreement*. To show further respect for your client, verbally share the key points of your notes. If the points are completely accurate, this will demonstrate your listening and understanding. If the points need adjusting, the client can assist you in doing so, which will lead to collaboration.

In addition to using an effective listening process, salespeople should practice a number of techniques to ensure that they are listening actively or proactively to their prospective buyers when they are speaking. These techniques include the following:[14]

- ✓ Open your mind and ears. Switch off all negative thoughts and be receptive to whatever message your prospective buyer is conveying to you.
- ✓ Listen from the first sentence. Put aside anything that you might be preoccupied with at the time of your interaction with the prospective buyer. Concentrate fully from the first word to the last one.
- ✓ Analyze what is being said. Don't try to figure out or anticipate what your prospective buyers will say, but rather, pay attention to exactly what they are saying. Analyze that content only.
- ✓ Listen, don't talk. Don't just appear to be listening, but really and truly listen to each and every word. Listen with your ears, eyes, and heart, while providing feedback to let your prospective buyer know that you are listening. A smile, nod, or simple gesture can convey feedback without using your voice or words.
- ✓ Be responsive. Get your whole body into a listening mode by facing your prospective buyers, looking directly into their eyes, and using facial expressions to show that you are listening.
- ✓ Never interrupt, but always be interruptible. Obviously, interrupting your prospective buyer is rude and should not be practised. However, if you encourage your prospective buyers to interrupt you at any time, that shows that you truly care about their understanding, questions, and opinion.
- ✓ You must learn to be patient and exercise patience. That may include waiting a few seconds after your prospective buyers finish speaking to be sure that they have completed their thought.
- ✓ Ask questions. As mentioned earlier in the chapter, asking questions to clarify your understanding of what your prospective buyer means is a good technique to use in conversations. Asking questions for further clarification can reinforce the fact that you are truly listening.
- ✓ Learn to control your emotions when you feel them rising. Emotions may negatively affect your behavior and prevent you from proactively listening to your prospect.
- ✓ Stay cool. You should be completely relaxed throughout your conversation with your prospective buyer in order to create a stress-free environment. This calm environment will hopefully rub off on your prospective buyers and get them to relax and enjoy the conversation.

Once salespeople have learned how to become better listeners, they will be able to more effectively use questions to obtain greater clarity and input from their prospective buyers. This technique is called probing, whereby a question is asked to uncover a more detailed response. Often, salespeople use a series of continuous questions to explore a particular topic. Proactive listeners are masters at the 'art of phraseology' in

Active listening

that they always ask critical questions to seek deeply-held information.[15] Some examples are:

- When you say 'The customer is pushing back,' can you provide more details about that?
- I heard you say that you're feeling a bit overwhelmed by your current situation. Can you tell me more about that?
- Based on what you've said, I understand that your first priority is to maximize customer satisfaction. Can you expand on the measures that you will use to assess this?

Listening for key phrases and responding with relevant probing questions are techniques successful salespeople should regularly practice. However, this is often easier said than done. For example, what happens if salespeople hear the prospective buyer say something that they *know* to be incorrect? In those situations, the salesperson is faced with a dilemma – as it is likely that simply disagreeing with the prospective buyer or offering a correction will put the prospective buyer on the defensive. Perhaps a wiser course of action is to wait and listen, *really listen*, to what the prospective buyer has to say about the situation. Even when salespeople are confident in the accuracy of their information, it is still possible to actually be wrong. Given a different perspective, there may be at least one other, equally plausible analysis of the situation, so that both parties are correct. Keep in mind that selling is all about relationships and helping customers solve their problems, so building and safeguarding the trust of your prospective buyers by actively and proactively listening to them, are critical to successful selling.

Effective listening enables salespeople to both assist their prospective buyers in solving their problems, while helping them to move through their buying journey. The buyer journey is the topic of the next section.

BUYER JOURNEY

Exploring the buying journey

The primary objective of salespeople during the interview stage or needs discovery conversation is to help prospective buyers make need-satisfying decisions that will solve their problems. However, salespeople cannot successfully accomplish this objective without a complete and accurate understanding of prospective buyers and where they are in their buying journey. As previously discussed in Chapter 2, in order for salespeople to connect with their prospective buyers, they must fully comprehend the needs of each of their prospective buyers at any given time. Of course, these needs are constantly changing. This is why it is imperative during the interview stage for salespeople to clarify the previous research that they have gathered about their prospects. All prospective buyers are unique and may be in different places along their buying journey; thus, salespeople cannot use a 'one size fits all' approach. Let's review the buying journey and the consumer decision-making process presented in Chapter 2 to explore how salespeople may be able to assist prospective buyers during the interview stage of the selling process.

As you likely recall, the buyer journey refers to the stages that a consumer goes through up to their decision to purchase a specific product or service from a specific organization. As Figure 6.1 reveals, this journey includes the following three stages:

1. *Awareness stage*, during which consumers recognize that they have a problem or an unsatisfied need.
2. *Consideration stage*, during which consumers identify and evaluate possible solutions to their problem.
3. *Decision stage*, during which consumers make a selection regarding what product or service is the best solution to their problem.

Figure 6.1   Buyer journey stages flowchart

It is important to remind you that during the buyer journey, consumers are not yet *customers*. They become customers *after* they make a purchase with a given organization; however, salespeople must form valuable relationships with consumers during all stages of the buyer journey and beyond.

Salespeople should consider the stage in the buying process each prospective buyer is currently at – and segment them based on the stage, instead of according to their needs/wants. This new segmenting strategy enables salespeople to develop more relevant questions in order to explore each prospect's needs and unique situation, as well as deliver more pertinent problem-solution data to each prospect.

For example, consumers in the awareness stage may be just beginning to conduct research regarding problem-solution options. They may need more rudimentary information, such as descriptions and information regarding frequently asked questions. In addition, when prospects are in the awareness phase, salespeople should conduct an 'impact' and 'urgency' review to ensure that they are in the same stage of the buying process as their prospects who initiated the investigation. In conducting that review, salespeople can then observe and assess the importance, urgency, and impact of the sale. This assessment should not only include an assessment of the impact that making the change (buying the product/service) would have on the prospect's organization, but also the perceived impact of NOT changing the current condition that started the investigation.

Salespeople should expect consumers in the consideration stage to know more about a particular field and the competitive options available. So, they will be seeking additional information beyond what they have already gathered. To serve these consumers, salespeople might provide buyer guides regarding what to look for when comparing options. Lastly, consumers in the decision stage who are ready to buy will seek details regarding the specific benefits of how the salesperson's company and services may directly solve their problem(s) and contribute to their success. Detailed cost-benefit data and case studies of other clients may be provided.

While the typical buyer journey may differ slightly for final consumers (B2C) versus business consumers (B2B), both buyer journeys have changed in recent years and have become more complex. Let's examine how the buyer journey has changed and how salespeople must learn to adapt.

Understanding the changing role of the buyer

Long ago, salespeople were the consumer's first contact to obtain information and education about a product or service. Typically, salespeople would initially meet and engage with prospective buyers when they were in the awareness stage of the very first buyer journey. Fast-forward to today where digital and social media has enabled consumers to have a wealth of information at their fingertips at any moment of their choosing. Consumers today are educated and empowered. Consumers have taken control of the buyer journey process and salespeople have less opportunity to influence the decision-making process of their prospective buyers. Consumers don't normally interact with salespeople until *after* they have conducted plenty of research and have determined that connecting with salespeople will add value. That means that many consumers won't engage with salespeople until the third and final stage of the buyer journey. However, the fact that there is much information available to prospects before they reach out to salespeople for a solution, does not preclude (and may even necessitate) the need for salespeople to conduct a review with their prospects of the 'urgency' for and 'impact' on their organization. Full consideration must be given to the anticipated effects of making a *change* (buying decision), as well as the impact if a change is NOT made.

Consumers researching

The buyer journey is less linear and predictable than it once was, and is more complicated due to the presence of multiple media channels, online platforms, immediate research potential, and the ease of drawing comparisons between competitor options.[16] Thus, often consumers no longer proceed through the buyer journey in any one logical, ordered manner as they once did. The buyer's role has changed and so must that of salespeople. This is especially true in the B2B buying process.

Gartner research reveals that when B2B buyers are considering a purchase, they spend only 17 percent of that time meeting with potential suppliers. Also, when buyers are comparing multiple suppliers, they spend only 5–6 percent of the time with any one sales representative. Additional Gartner research shows that the typical buying group for a complex B2B solution involves six to ten decision makers, each armed with four or five pieces of information they have gathered independently.[17] In addition, the number of options and solutions that prospective buyers might consider is expanding as new technologies, products, suppliers, and services emerge.[18] These facts confirm that selling in today's modern world is more complex and that the roles of both buyers and sellers have changed.

To better understand how to help B2B prospects advance through a complex buying process, Gartner research has identified six B2B buying 'jobs' that consumers must complete to their satisfaction before they finalize their purchase decisions.

These buying jobs include: problem identification, solution exploration, requirement building, supplier selection, validation, and consensus creation.[19] These buying jobs don't happen sequentially, but more or less simultaneously, often with consumers engaged in 'looping' or revisiting each of the buying jobs at least once.[20]

Regardless of whether the prospective buyer is a business consumer (B2B) or a final consumer (B2C), salespeople today need to constantly demonstrate their value while they make it as easy as possible for consumers to guide themselves through the buyer journey stages. Today, salespeople have become consultants in the consumer buying journey as opposed to being the primary leader. The new role of salespeople is referred to as sales enablement, whereby the salesperson becomes more of a guide as the consumer moves through the buyer journey. Research shows that 62 percent of high-performing salespeople foresee a bigger role for guided selling in the future.[21] Salespeople should provide information that is clear and easily digestible, and make the next steps in the buying process easy to take.[22] Salespeople must work more closely with marketing associates and take greater advantage of marketing automation and all of the buyer data that marketers gather.[23] Salespeople can gain valuable insight by knowing how prospective buyers have previously interacted with their company, such as via website visits, LinkedIn interactions, chat sessions conducted, or webinars attended, as well as what the prospect might already know about the products and services. Lastly, salespeople must understand the myriad influences that affect consumer decision making today.

In today's modern world, the buyer journey of most consumers is significantly impacted by the thoughts, opinions, and perspectives of others. As you may recall from Chapter 2, the concept of influencer marketing is changing the traditional role of most salespeople. Influencer marketing is a form of content-driven marketing where the content shared is akin to an endorsement or testimonial by a third party, loyal customer, or potential consumer. Throughout all phases of the buyer journey, consumers are actively seeking out word-of-mouth, online reviews, and recommendations from others whose opinions they believe they can trust.

Influencers may offer salespeople new opportunities for relationship and partnership building. Building relationships with influencers may be constructive activities for salespeople. Finding out what influencers are saying about given products and services is critical for salespeople to know how and where to use this information to add value to the journeys of their prospective buyers. Salespeople need to figure out how and where they can authentically meet consumers along the buyer journey in this new environment. Salespeople must also know how to recognize and determine when a consumer is not likely going to progress along the buyer journey. This entails determining consumers' willingness to buy, which is the topic of the next section.

WILLINGNESS TO BUY[24]

As an introduction, there needs to be a level setting on what Willing to Buy means, how it is additive to the typical selling process, and finally, the components of the

Willing to Buy (WTB) framework. The WTB framework uses a minimally intrusive process that puts potential customers at ease while, together with salespeople, self-diagnosing whether they are ready and able to make a buying decision at this time. The fundamental premise for the WTB framework is to assess, at the outset of a sales opportunity, whether there is likely to be a decision made early enough to stop applying unnecessary effort in trying to make the decision happen. This allows the salesperson to 'move on' to other sales opportunities more likely to come to a decision. This is an important component to anyone who wants to have a successful sales career, since the most successful salespeople are able to determine which sales opportunities are *not* likely to close in a timely fashion. Determining this early, then, enables salespeople to conserve one of their most important assets – their time.

In pursuing any sales opportunity, WTB is used to determine the 'whys, whos, and hows' of making a decision, independent of the content or fit of a proposed solution. Most people, when first hearing of the WTB framework, likely will wonder: Why should it work? Let's expand on that thought with the following questions:

1. Why would a prospect share with you their deep-seated reasons for wanting to buy from you, or from anyone, for that matter?
2. Why would they share with you the amount of money they are willing to spend? (Note that we realize asking for the budget numbers is in every salesperson's playbook. It's a tough business and can be delicate. We'll spend time on this a bit later.)
3. Who, after all, decides if the justification for buying your products, services, or consulting experience is clear and evident at all?
4. And if you are speaking with a buyer's gatekeeper, why would they share the intimate details about *who* would be involved in the decision? After all, the gatekeeper usually guards against access to the people at the top.

The WTB framework is not intended to be difficult or overly academic. Every concept shared here is based on human psychology, in addition to some sociological implications. In fact, most of the concepts introduced in this chapter are based on precepts that most people already know and acknowledge, but perhaps have never organized in quite this way. So, let's begin.

'Framework' versus 'system'

For many years, sales management professionals and learned authors have professed to have the ultimate selling and/or sales management system. Books on boosting sales line the racks at Barnes and Noble, Amazon, and so on. Every year, there are myriad offers for books, CDs, and DVDs guaranteed to increase a salesperson's sales performance astronomically. Podcasts and online courses are current ways to deliver messages about the latest system. Before we go any further, a discussion about the difference between a system and a framework is warranted here.

So, let's talk about what a system is, and then we can talk about what it isn't. When one searches the Internet, a definition reveals that a system is a set of principles or procedures according to which something is done, an organized scheme or method. That seems fairly promising, doesn't it? Based on this definition, we might conclude that a sales system would provide us with a set of step-by-step procedures that, if followed precisely, would lead to increased sales effectiveness. That often turns out not to be the case. There really is no step-by-step system for sales success because, when dealing with people, no 'system' can be invented that allows for the variability of people, problems, and solutions that always work. So, in that sense, success in this profession can seem like a mystery.

A framework is a set of assumptions, concepts, values, and practices that constitutes a way of viewing reality. Back in the 1960s and '70s, there was an old saying: 'Reality, what a concept!' But in business you are better served facing reality, no matter what decision you are trying to make or opportunity you intend to pursue.

Therefore, the Willing to Buy (WTB) concept is best defined as a framework, a tool to help both the sales professional and the sales manager discover and face reality. Once the cold light of day shines on an opportunity, they can take steps to either abandon the time-consuming deals unlikely to produce sales results, and/or invest more time and effort into those that will. Thus, the WTB Framework is an approach by which salespeople can interrogate all of the important criteria that separate opportunities that will come to a decision from those that won't.

The four pillars of the Willing to Buy framework

Before we go any further, it is important to identify and position what we call the four pillars of the WTB framework (see Figure 6.2). The salesperson needs to be aware of the role each plays in assisting both the sales rep and, as appropriate, sales managers in correctly identifying winnable business and disqualifying those opportunities that really aren't winnable.

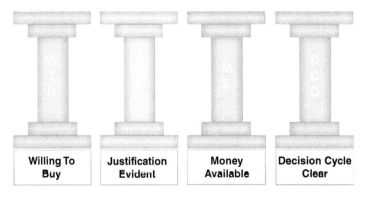

Figure 6.2 Four pillars of WTB

Pillar 1: Is the prospect Willing to Buy? (WTB)

Think of this category as the personal motivator: What's in it for anyone and everyone involved in the decision, including the key decision maker? Is the prospective buyer the ultimate decision maker? What evidence can this individual show, as a member of the group, regarding making a decision and voicing it to others within that decision group?

This particular area deals with the personal motivation of this person to see that a decision will be made. It is in addition to the tangible business justification and speaks to what is the individual benefit for this particular person. Note that in order for this to be effective, the answer to this question should be drawn from the specific words of every relevant prospect, including the decision maker, and *not* from the salesperson's perspective.

Sample questions that may be used to determine this pillar are as follows:

- Is this person (not necessarily just the decision maker) willing to make a decision?
- Why is this so, in this person's mind?
- What is the evidence that this is so – verbal assurance, impending event, upper-management insistence?
- Are there any other people who must also be WTB for this proposition to go forward?

Pillar 2: Is the justification evident? (JE)

This category is the organizational motivator: What's in it for the organization? What is the business impact that will be used to justify the organization's commitment to any proposed solution? Has this justification been articulated by your prospective buyer and/or the decision maker? What are the tangible results that the prospect organization will realize?

Some questions that need to be answered in this pillar are the following:

- Is the justification evident in this prospect's mind as well as in the decision maker's mind?
- What is that justification? (Note: Be aware that the prospect will often give you an intangible or non-qualified reason at first. It is up to the sales professional to guide the prospect as they quantify the financial impact on the business.)
- What is the time period over which savings or value will be realized?
- Is there more than just one area in which this project will save money or add value?

Pillar 3: Is the money available? (MA)

Has this acquisition or commitment been budgeted, and what is that budget? This topic explores the amount of money and resources (including people's time) available to effectively go ahead with any solution and implement it successfully. What evidence is there that funds and resources have been allocated to complete any project of this magnitude?

Some questions that need to be answered in the pillar are:

- Is there a budgeted amount for this project?
- If not, how might monies be appropriated to fund the project?
- Is the money for this project in your prospect's control or must that individual go to higher management to allocate funds for this effort?
- What is the breakdown of the projected allocation of the funds (e.g., product, services, training)?
- What is the flexibility to go for more funds if the business case warrants it?

Pillar 4: Is the decision cycle clear? (DCC)

What is the approval cycle and who specifically will be involved? This pillar is needed to clarify that the decision cycle is clear not only in the salesperson's mind, but also in the prospect's mind (even if that individual is also the ultimate decision maker). It is a critical element to gauge upfront the likelihood that after completing all the survey/discovery, demonstration (if appropriate) and proposal work, a decision will be made.

Some questions that need to be answered in this pillar are:

- What is the sign-off path through management once your prospect agrees with your recommendation?
- Are there hidden parties who may need to be sold separately?
- Is it appropriate for you to go either with your prospect or separately to the other parties to make your case? If so, what must you be prepared for?
- After what seems to be all other questions have been answered, what else could keep this project from moving forward? (Have you now considered all factors in the decision-making process?)

Addressing the whys, whos and hows

Let's revisit each pillar of the WTB questioning framework, concerning the prospect sharing deep-seated reasons for wanting to buy from you, or from anyone else for that matter.

First, salespeople must realize that this is not about them. It's about helping prospects to recall why they even embarked on the search for a solution. More often than not, by the time the prospect gets around to looking for a solution, they have gone over many times the frustrations of having to deal with their status quo and not achieving the results they were looking for. Because of this – their usual failed past attempts to solve the issues on their own – they reach a point where they just want the pain to go away. This drives them to look for relief from outside of their company environment, usually to an outside vendor to supply the solution that relieves their pain. Therefore, many initial discussions become quickly about the requirements of the solution rather than the original business problem they were trying to solve and why it has become so critical to solve it now. For the line of questioning within this particular pillar to be effective, it must be based in the reality that what we're doing for the prospect is helping them to revisit the original conditions that caused them to start to 'fix things,' what things they have tried to fix themselves, and why fixing it has become so urgent.

In following this line of questioning, the salesperson helps the prospect reflect and either reassert their intention to get an external versus internal solution or realize that it's not quite that important to resolve this issue at this time. This, then, allows the salesperson doing the questioning to assume the role of facilitator for the prospect and, at the same time, observe from the prospect's response, why they should spend their selling time working on a solution for the prospect now.

Second, the next question about 'who' is concerned with who decides the question of whether the justification is evident and who is best suited to determining this evidence (JE).

The perspective here has the same orientation as the first point, except that this is a pillar for the tangible organizational justification companies use in discussions with outside solution providers, but it falls short of the deep-seated justification that is the personal driver(s) for each person involved in resolving their current problem/issue. It is not quite to the level of influence as the first point, but it must be understood because, if a solution is possible, we can ensure it encompasses both the personal and organizational impact.

Third is the question of why the prospect would share the amount they are willing to spend (MA). This is a natural initial response, because we have all been taught to avoid talking about certain topics (money, salaries, religion, or politics). Because of this hesitance, most salespeople think that asking about budget is an intrusive move, and usually defer talking about it until they must; usually well after they have already priced and delivered their solution to the prospect. A better perspective on asking for a budget is that it is actually a respect for the prospect's as well as the salesperson's time.

In the early stages of the sales process, there is enthusiasm for the possibility of a solution on both sides of the table: pain relief for the prospect and commission for the salesperson. However, all too often the 'cold water' reality cools this early joint enthusiasm for the solution when money and budget are finally addressed. And the letdown when an unanticipated price tag is realized kills more sales than not. The reality here is that this should be one of the first pillars addressed, right after the discussion of the effect on the business. This is the best time for the prospect/salesperson team to assess whether it's worth their time to go forward or abandon the search for a solution right now and pick it up at some later time.

The fourth and final point might initially seem intrusive, but it's vital in the overall assessment of the likelihood that a decision can be made in a predictable timeframe (DCC). The reason for this is to help the salesperson assess whether the main buyer in the prospect account has the knowledge, skills, and perspective to persuade others involved in the decision-making process to make a decision in the salesperson's favor, once this main buyer is convinced that the solution is the optimal one. Many times, salespeople assume that when they have convinced the buyer of the applicability of their solution, their contacts are committed and know how to justify this solution through their own organization. This is a huge mistake that many salespeople make, not because their buyers wouldn't like to have the solution implemented, but because they lack the skills or political savvy to get the decision made in their own organization.

In summary, the WTB framework, as we have talked about it, is effective in picking which sales opportunities will close, thereby allowing salespeople to direct their focus and time to those opportunities that are most likely to close. However, the advantages and impact of the WTB framework go much further than as an aid in predicting and closing sales opportunities. Sales, for all companies, is the fuel that drives their operational and production engine, which produces their products or services. Without sales filling the gas tanks of these companies, the production engines cannot run. One problem with this company engine model is that without a predictable flow of sales fuel, the company production engine and its associated business processes cannot run efficiently. Assessing and monitoring the metrics associated with the WTB framework is critical to both selling and business success. That's the topic of our last section for this chapter.

MONITORING METRICS

Monitoring Metrics

To demonstrate the value of conducting assessments and monitoring metrics, let's examine how one company used the WTB framework not only to enhance the effectiveness of its sales team and determine the predictability of the results, but to serve as an input for resource planning, effective execution, and high-quality delivery of service to its customers.

One of the most successful implementations of the WTB framework was that of Riddleberger Brothers in Mount Crawford, Virginia. This company is a very successful regional heating, ventilation, and air conditioning company, serving many educational, governmental, and commercial companies with both construction projects and service. The president, Daniel Blosser, was facing sales opportunities that seemed to drag on, either never closing or buying from a competitor. It seemed his sales team was always working on complex quotes or bids that took a lot of time and resources to prepare, but only a small number of them resulted in business for Riddleberger. He needed to find a systematized way to categorize all the prospects his sales team was working on to gauge which might close. They could then better focus their efforts on getting good business in the door. He also claimed that because of the inaccuracy and inability of the sales team to predict which business was going to close, his technical support, construction, and service managers could not do the proper resource planning job to ensure that there were enough technicians when they were needed, and that it caused the opposite condition, when there wasn't enough of a work backlog to keep all the technicians employed. Daniel wasn't sure if the sales team members needed to be replaced, needed sales skills training, or something else.

Daniel needed a more predictable forecasting system that was based on probabilities rather than the salesperson's gut feeling. While many sales teams may run on gut feeling and think that inaccurate sales forecasts are just the nature of the beast, nothing could be further from the truth. It's just that businesspeople have not viewed forecasting as an effort in probabilities. If members of a company's upper management can be focused on a systematic and dependable way to look at the sales opportunities identified by their sales team, they can then build their product and service resources more confidently and consistently and, of course, realize more effective cost control over their production resources.

Daniel set about synchronizing the sales forecast with the production plan because he knew this would better control costs and deliver more profit. But his production/service people met his insistence on this synchronization with some skepticism. They had been with the company for some time and had experienced many assurances from the salespeople about sales that would close. Those sales never seemed to materialize, even though production had ramped up its hiring based on those assurances. Daniel took a straightforward approach to factoring the sales numbers that his sales team forecast to him. For each sales opportunity, he made his sales manager go through each pillar of the WTB framework and determine whether each pillar was known or not. Daniel developed a spreadsheet that had columns on it for each WTB pillar.

If the pillar had not been covered, the sales manager placed a 0 in that pillar's column for that opportunity. If the pillar was known, the sales manager put a 1. He listed each sales opportunity on an Excel spreadsheet and each 1 for that opportunity was given a 25 percent factor (if a given sales opportunity had two 1's and two 0's, the projected sales revenue for that opportunity was multiplied by 50% (2 x 1) x 25% = 50%). This amount was automatically calculated and put in the discounted total sales column on the spreadsheet. (Note: We will discuss sales forecasting techniques in detail later, in Chapter 12.)

It took six months to note any consistent performance improvement. But when the forecasting process that Daniel had put in place based on the WTB framework became more predictable, the downstream planning that production had to do became more consistent. Confidence quickly grew throughout the sales team and the customers benefited from Riddleberger's relaxed and competent technicians. With its new forecasting system, the company always seemed to have the right number of production resources to keep the staff consistently busy and to avoid the historic unpredictability of previous sales forecasts. This made its technical staff less stressed because they had confidence that the work would be there for them and that they would have a job for the foreseeable future. Daniel also combined this with the timeframe of the forecast projection (how many months in the future this sales opportunity was projected by the salesperson to close). The further out the closing date, the more its forecast amount was discounted internally to get a realistic view of what was likely to close. Therefore, by using WTB and this timeframe discounting strategy, the adjusted forecast led to sales results that were consistently within 10 percent of what actually closed. Once the sales team's track record was proven, the synchronization with production happened effortlessly.

In conclusion, listening to prospective buyers, asking relevant questions, understanding where they are in the buyer journey, and determining their willingness to buy by using the WTB framework, will enable salespeople to more effectively provide real value to prospects and customers, while more efficiently forecasting and allocating their time to value-creating activities for their respective organizations.

CHAPTER SUMMARY

✓ Use all forms of communication, including body language and proactive listening skills, to build understanding and create rapport.

✓ Know the types of information to present at each stage of the buyer journey.

✓ Don't accept positions at face value; use probing questions to determine underlying needs.

✓ View yourself as a sales enabler, helping the prospective buyer to solve problems.

✓ Use the Willing to Buy framework to determine the probability of each sale.

KEY TERMS

Active listening	Passive listening
Buyer journey	Proactive listening
Decision cycle clear (DCC)	Probing
Framework	Sales enablement
Influencer marketing	System
Justification evident (JE)	Willing to Buy (WTB)
Money available (MA)	

REVIEW QUESTIONS

1. What are the five categories of effective questions that can be asked during a needs analysis of a prospective buyer? Write an example question for each category.
2. Describe three common mistakes we may make that limit our ability to listen proactively.
3. Name at least four techniques that can be used to ensure you are listening actively or proactively in any conversation.
4. What is probing and why is it used in the selling process? What is the best way to respond to a prospective buyer who states information that you know is incorrect?
5. Discuss the types of information a prospective buyer is likely to be searching for at each stage in the buyer journey.
6. In what ways has the buyer journey changed over the years?
7. What is sales enablement? What are salespeople required to do differently to be effective in today's selling environment?
8. Explain the differences between a system and a framework.
9. Describe the four pillars of the WTB framework and provide one question appropriate to ask for each pillar in the framework.
10. Why is it important for salespeople to track data on successful completion of the elements of the WTB framework? How can information from tracking all prospective buyers be used by the rest of the organization?

ETHICS IN ACTION

1. Gary White is a B2B salesperson for a mid-sized company producing gloves for the hospitality industry. He has recently received multiple leads for new prospective buyers from his friend, Dean, in Marketing. While he is excited by these opportunities, he is currently managing a large number of prospects at later stages in the buying process. He is concerned about his ability to research and meet with these new prospects in a timely manner. Recent performance feedback from Ben, his sales manager, clearly indicates that he needs to close these additional sales. How should he proceed? Should he prioritize the potential new prospects over those further in the sales process, or his existing customers? What, if any, conversation should he have with Ben or Dean at this time?

2. As the sales manager, Ben has recently implemented a procedure and tracking database for all salespeople to enter their prospects and note completion of

(Continued)

the intent of each of the four pillars of the Willing to Buy framework. This information is used monthly to forecast sales and is used by the rest of the company for planning purposes. Salespeople have been told to sign off on a pillar after it has been fully completed. Salesperson Gary White has been struggling to close sales over the last nine months and is concerned about the lack of progress shown by his data. For the past three months, he has been signing off on each pillar after having an initial conversation with the prospect, instead of after a joint resolution has been reached. Is it likely that Ben will discover what Gary has been doing? What consequences may occur for Gary, Ben, and the organization due to Gary's actions?

EXERCISE

You must sell yourself, as well as the product or service, each time you meet with a prospective company or organization, so honing your conversational skills is important. For this exercise, you are tasked with visiting your campus career preparation center to set up a mock interview with a local company or organization in order to practice skills such as asking appropriate questions and listening to the speaker. After completing the mock interview, you evaluate your performance. Was it an effective needs discovery conversation? Provide details from your interview as you answer the following questions:

A. What did you say about your transferable skills and the benefits that you can offer?
B. What questions did you ask to encourage the interviewer to explain the company's *current* situation and needs?
C. Did you ask the interviewer to explain the company's *desired* situation and the timeline for making a decision?
D. How could you tell that you were truly actively listening? Who did most of the talking?
E. Did you ask permission to take notes and did you take notes?
F. What questions did you ask to show that you were actively and proactively listening?
G. How did your body language demonstrate that you were actively listening?
H. How were you able to determine and adjust to your interviewer's behavioral style?

ROLE-PLAY

Situation: You are a new sales representative with a medical equipment company that sells medical devices, including artificial hip replacement parts. You

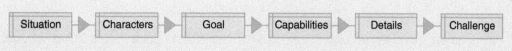

Role-play flow chart

are replacing a sales rep that was recently fired by your company. He was sub-par and unreliable and had the reputation of trashing the competition. Sales volume (or revenue) in the territory you are taking over is only 50 percent of what it should be, given the size of the territory. Your company has a bad reputation with offices locally because of this rep, and he had even been banned from a number of offices.

Characters: You are 25 years old and you have four years of sales experience out in the field representing a local manufacturing company. You joined the medical equipment company almost six months ago and have just finished your extended company training program. You are excited to be getting back out in the field with medical products. Your first call will be to the active, orthopedic practice of Drs. Abrams, Cook, and Tabb. Drs. Abrams and Cook are both in their upper 30s and Dr. Tabb is 46 years old.

Selling goal: Your goal is to obtain commitment for another meeting. You need to earn the physicians' trust in you and your company before you can even think about selling any specific products. This is not a one-shot deal, but is your first step in establishing a business relationship.

Product/service capabilities: Among its many products, your company is one of the industry leaders in developing state-of-the-art hardware for hip replacements. Your company also provides the technical expertise to work hand in hand with the physicians, not only in the operating room, but also with follow-up visits. Your company has a long history of making high-quality, long-lasting products for hip replacements.

Sales call details: After trying for four months, you have finally gotten an appointment to meet with the office manager of these three orthopedic physicians. This group kicked out your predecessor a year ago and have not used any of your products since. Dr. Tabb is clearly the final decision maker for selecting orthopedic supplies at this office.

Selling challenge: How do you handle this first call? How do you determine their willingness to buy or move forward? What can you do to build a 'win-win' selling relationship with this office? How might you suggest meeting Dr. Tabb directly?

READINGS AND RESOURCES

- Pete Caputa (2018) 'Active Listening in Sales: The ultimate guide,' https://blog.hubspot.com/sales/active-listening-guide.
- Chip Cummings (2005) *Stop Selling and Start Listening: Marketing Strategies that Create Top Producers.* Grand Rapids, MI: Northwind Publishing.
- Derek Edmond (2017) '14 Visualizations Mapping the B2B Buyer Journey,' https://komarketing.com/blog/mapping-the-b2b-buyer-journey.
- Keith Rosen (2017) *Coaching Salespeople into Sales Champions*. Hoboken, NJ: John Wiley & Sons, Inc.
- Dan Schultheis and Phil Perkins (2015) *Willing to Buy: A Questioning Framework for Effective Closing*. Bloomington, IN: AuthorHouse.

CASE STUDY: IBM AND THE COUNTY GOVERNMENT

As a branch manager for IBM, Dan Schultheis (Figure 6.3) was trying to understand from his sales team whether the County Government Director of Information Services was going to install a large mainframe computer in his facility by the end of the calendar year. However, in order for IBM to build the computer based on county government specifications, it needed a commitment six months prior to the actual installation date.

The installation was scheduled for mid-December of that year. The sales team reported that the director seemed to be 'on the fence' about installing the computer by the end of the calendar year. Dan knew the sales team wasn't getting to the crux of whether the director was *Willing to Buy* (WTB) this computer by the end of the year. Dan met with the director shortly thereafter. The director told Dan that he may install it; however, he wasn't sure. Without knowing the director's personal motivation, the risk was too great for Dan to commit IBM to building this computer.

Thus, Dan had to determine whether the director was committed and what, if anything, would be the negative impact on him for not installing the computer by the end of the year. Dan asked the director the following question: 'What would happen to the operation if you didn't install the computer this year?' The director answered that it probably wouldn't matter. Dan probed deeper with his questioning: 'Well, what if you didn't install it until next December instead of this one?' The Director replied, 'Hmm. That might be a problem.' So naturally Dan asked him the big 'WHY?' to which the director responded that the yearly county government budget begins in September. It turned out that if the director didn't install the computer before September 1 of next year, the computer purchase would need to be included in the following fiscal year's budget and there was no guarantee that the money would be there. So, Dan dug a little deeper: 'Well then, why not install it in August of the next year since it would still be within this budget year?' The director indicated that this option would also be a little risky because the closer he got to the end of the current budget year, the greater the chance the county administration would take away his unused budget.

Figure 6.3 Dan Schultheis

Dan thought they'd reached an 'aha' moment! Dan said, 'It seems that if you purchase the computer this year, it would be far enough away from the start of the new budget year that you won't risk losing the budget money.' He quickly answered, 'Yes, that's the case.' (This of course was the director's personal motivation WTB pillar.) Dan continued, 'it appears to me that we should install that computer while you still have the budget.' He enthusiastically

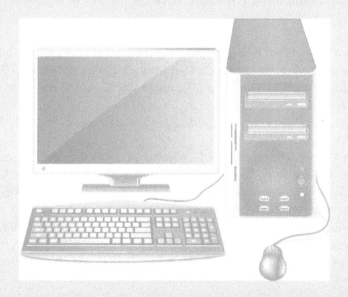

Computer image

responded: 'You are absolutely right.' Once the director made the buying decision, the deal, which was worth more than $10 million, moved on through the sales funnel.

This is a case of finding the vested interest in your prospective customer's mind to make a buying decision – which is the core of the WTB pillar. Just think, had Dan not pursued this line of questioning with the director, he would have missed the point altogether, and proceeded to try to push for a commitment, perhaps unsuccessfully, without knowing what the deal meant to the director. This is the power of using the WTB framework and the leverage it gives you in understanding whether there is sufficient motivation in your prospect's mind to make a decision happen. Dan successfully applied the WTB framework at IBM and took an under-achieving branch and increased its revenue from $60 million to $130 million in three years.

Case questions:

1. Why did Dan ask the director multiple questions about how far he was willing to delay delivery?
2. Why didn't the director accuse Dan of being too pushy?
3. What would have happened if Dan had pressured the director without finding his reason 'Why' to install?

NOTES

1. Ron Willingham (2003) *Integrity Selling for the 21st Century* (New York: Random House), pp. 25–7.
2. Ibid.
3. John Patrick Dolan, 'Discover exactly what your sales prospect wants in the negotiation process,' *American Salesman* (September 2017), 62(9), 11–15.
4. Carl Lyons (2007) *I Win You Win: The Essential Guide to Principled Negotiation* (London: A & C Black), pp. 36–46.
5. Ron Willingham (2003) *Integrity Selling for the 21st Century* (New York: Random House), p. 53.
6. John Patrick Dolan, 'Discover exactly what your sales prospect wants in the negotiation process,' *American Salesman* (September 2017), 62(9), 11–15.
7. John Boe, 'Listen while you work,' *American Salesman* (September 2019), 64(9), 29–30.
8. Keith Rosen, 'How proactive listeners sell more, coach better and win big – Part 1: Proactive listening might even bring world peace!' *HCM Sales, Marketing & Alliance Excellence Essentials* (July 2017), 17(7), 13–14.
9. Lynn Thomas, 'Listening: So what's in it for me?' *Rough Notes* (December 1998), 141(12), 63–4.
10. Ibid.
11. Sergio Román, 'Salesperson's listening in buyer–seller service relationships,' *Service Industries Journal* (July 2014), 34(7), 630–44.

12. Bill Brooks, 'The power of active listening,' *American Salesman* (December 2010), 55(12), 28–30.

13. Adapted from John Asher, 'Understand client needs better by becoming a perfect listener,' *HCM Sales, Marketing & Alliance Excellence Essentials* (November 2017), 16(11), 14.

14. Adapted from Bill Brooks, 'The power of active listening,' *American Salesman* (December 2010), 55(12), 28–30; Bill Brooks, 'Active listening,' *Advisor Today* (June 2003) 98(6), 82; and Lynn Thomas, 'Listening: So what's in it for me?' *Rough Notes* (December 1998), 141(12), 63–4.

15. Keith Rosen, 'How proactive listeners sell more, coach better and win big – Part 1: Proactive listening might even bring world peace!' *HCM Sales, Marketing & Alliance Excellence Essentials* (July 2017), 17(7), 13–14.

16. Wills Brayn, 'The ultimate guide for customer journey optimization: Do you understand the journey your customers go through before they buy from you?' *HCM Sales, Marketing & Alliance Excellence Essentials* (December 2019), 18(2), 11–17.

17. Gartner 2020, 'New B2B Buying Journey & its Implication for Sales,' www.gartner.com/en/sales/insights/b2b-buying-journey, retrieved June 2, 2020.

18. Ibid.

19. Ibid.

20. Ibid.

21. Phillip Britt, 'Sales enablement: A new role for sellers,' *CRM: Customer Relationship Management* (March 2019), Medford, 23(2), 22–5.

22. Expert Voice '4 Phases of the Consumer Buying Journey', www.expertvoice.com/resources/4-phases-of-the-consumer-buying-journey, retrieved June 2, 2020.

23. Phillip Britt, 'Sales enablement: A new role for sellers,' *CRM: Customer Relationship Management* (March 2019), Medford, 23(2), 22–5.

24. This section has been contributed by Dan Schultheis and is based on *Willing To Buy: A Questioning Framework for Effective Closing* by Dan Schultheis and Phil Perkins, https://a.co/azpAUEi, retrieved 6 July 2021.

7

PRESENTING WITH IMPACT AND COMMUNICATING VIA STORYTELLING

CHAPTER CONTENTS

PEOPLE, PRACTICES AND PERSPECTIVES FROM THE WORLD OF SALES

Greetings from the Sunshine State of Florida. My name is Marc Aldridge and I'm Managing Vice President of Sales at Gartner. I lead the sales teams selling into emerging and mid-size technology companies in the United States. I've worked in various leadership positions over my 12-year career and have found that every buyer goes through a series of mental steps each time they purchase something. *Your job as the salesperson isn't to pitch a product and hope someone buys. It is to identify the buyer's unmet needs, understand their pain, and demonstrate that your product resolves that pain. Make sure they understand the benefit of buying now and the risk of waiting until later.* Here's a quote for you: 'Sales are contingent upon the attitude of the salesman – not the attitude of the prospect' (W. Clemente Stone.)

Hello, I'm George Hackett, a sales manager with Freshworks in London, UK. I have 10 years of experience in sales and was the first sales rep hired into Europe for Freshworks. *I've found that it is important to be technical, detailed and truthful, not salesy, to know your product and topic, and to be able to add actual value, where appropriate, during the sales cycle rather than pulling in sales engineers, consultants, and other teams to help you. This will gain trust and build a lasting relationship for you to leverage post sales.* Here's a saying for you: 'Sales is a science not an art. Forget the gift of gab and read everything you can find to make you better.'

Hi, my name is Kristina Pontillo, and I'm a supply chain operations associate supervisor for Pepsi in Richmond, Virginia. Over the past two years, I've held positions in sales, sales operations, and warehouse operations, supporting both B2B and B2C customers. *I've found that no two customers are the same, so it's important to get to know each of them and build relationships. My advice is to be persistant, but not pushy, to show respect to everyone, to put your sweat and grind into it to ensure that customers realize that you want to help grow their business, and to personalize sales by remembering the little details customers have shared about themselves.* Remember that 'The customer is always right' (Source unknown.)

A good story is where genuine customer satisfaction comes from.

– Seth Godin, bestselling author

EYES ON ETHICS

Keep in mind the following ethical topics as you read through this chapter:

1. Providing potential customers with a new version of an existing product.
2. Enhancing a customer testimonial instead of capturing it verbatim.

INTRODUCTION

All salespeople must be able to create and deliver sales presentations that are informing, intriguing, and engaging in order to stimulate desire, persuade their prospects to move forward in the sales cycle, and sell. Creating dynamic sales presentations using a variety of approaches and techniques; commanding the prospect's attention and pitching with passion; and weaving storytelling into sales presentations, are the topics that we'll explore in this chapter.

CREATING DYNAMIC SALES PRESENTATIONS

According to Jon Steel, author of *Perfect Pitch: The Art of Selling Ideas and Winning New Business*, listed in the Readings and Resources section at the end of this chapter, a sales presentation is not a single event that begins the moment the salesperson stands or sits in front of their prospect and says 'Good afternoon, thanks for the opportunity to speak with you today.'[1] Steel describes the presentation as a period extending from the moment the appointment is made to the moment the buying decision is made, which may be weeks, months, or years.

Sales presentations begin with planning and preparing based on sound prospect research. Using prospect research as the foundation to crafting a presentation that addresses their needs, wants, interests, problems, and so on, is critical to creating effective sales presentations. Preparing for a sales presentation doesn't guarantee that you will obtain buyer commitment or make a sale, but it does help to build your confidence when pitching to your prospect. Proper preparation also ensures that you will know and be able to address the key points that are of concern to your prospect. In addition, salespeople must understand the various presentation approaches and be prepared to use them appropriately based on the type of prospect and selling situation. Let's begin by exploring the stages of a sales presentation and the different approaches salespeople may use.

Salesperson preparing for a sales presentation

Understanding sales presentation stages and approaches

As outlined below, there are four stages of a typical sales presentation (see Figure 7.1): the opening, body, summation, and request.[2] Let's explore each stage in greater detail.[3]

Stage 1: *Opening*. The opening is where salespeople build or strengthen their relationship and continue the needs discovery conversation (NDC) with their prospect. Salespeople should ask questions to ensure accurate understanding of the needs, wants, problems, and situation of their prospects. Asking clarifying questions at this initial stage enables salespeople to create their sales pitch to present pertinent information that provides real value to their prospects. It is critical that salespeople form a solid foundation based on customer needs and structure the sales presentation around that insight. Tailoring the presentation to what the prospect wants is the easiest way to ensure a most effective sales presentation.

The opening stage is typically less formal and requires a shorter amount of time than the other stages, unless it is the initial contact with your prospect. Salespeople should strive to build rapport with their prospects, make them feel comfortable and important, and verify the primary interests their prospects are seeking which will help to frame the next stage of the sales presentation.

Stage 2: *Body*. The body is typically the most important and the longest portion of a sales presentation. During this stage, salespeople present information about the products or services that they are offering. The average attention span is 20 minutes, so they should strive to keep their presentation succinct.[4] The body stage tends to be more formal and salespeople may use different approaches to presenting the information, as well as techniques to enhance the presentation to make it more interesting and engaging. The three most common types of sales presentations are the *prepared*, *selling formula*, and *consultative* approaches. We'll discuss these three different approaches and various presentation enhancement techniques, such as using visual aids, demonstrations, free samples, handouts, testimonials, and stories, in greater detail later in this chapter.

It is crucial for salespeople to make their sales presentations exciting and compelling, and to keep the interests and desires of their prospects at the center of their focus. Remember, the pitch is all about your prospective clients – their needs, wants, problems, and predicaments. It's not about the products or services being sold, but about how the products/services can satisfy the needs of your prospects and solve their problems. Thus, salespeople should involve their prospects in their presentations by asking them questions to ensure that they understand the benefits being offering to them in the pitch.

Stage 3: *Summation*. The summation is typically where salespeople provide a short and specific overview or summary of the main selling benefits that were presented during the body stage of the sales presentation. Salespeople should customize this summary to emphasize those key selling points that were of most interest to that particular prospect. During the summation, salespeople should invite questions from the prospect and carefully answer each one. According to Rodney van Treeck, a territory sales representative for Taylor Freezer Company, featured in the case at the end of this chapter:

> If the customer has no questions, they are not being convinced. Now would be the time to ask some accusation audit questions to get to the heart of why they are not asking you more questions. The accusation audit usually uncovers their unspoken objections. For example: 'I know you are probably thinking this equipment is too expensive.' In which case you have opened the door for them to freely discuss the financial aspect of purchasing the equipment and how Taylor can offer payment options, like a lease to own, in order to create a positive outcome for both parties.'[5]

The length of time the salespeople spend in this stage is dictated by each prospect and the number of questions being asked. Making promises to the prospect during this stage is fine as long as each promise made can be fulfilled. Ideally, the salespeople's answers to each prospect's questions should be honest, convincing, and naturally lead into the final stage.

Stage 4: *Request*. During this short stage, the salespeople wrap up their pitch and bring the presentation to an end. Salespeople may use a trial close, which is a question asked during a sales presentation to get feedback from the prospect and to build momentum toward a positive outcome.[6] A trial close question is a more focused question than merely asking if the prospect understands the material being presented. We'll discuss trial closing in greater detail in Chapter 9, but for now, you should understand

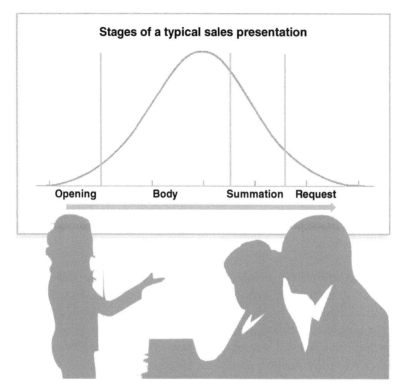

Figure 7.1   Stages of the sales presentation

that the purpose of using a trial close is twofold: first, to tell salespeople where they are in the sales process; and second, to determine when the best time to ask for the sale might be.[7] The trial close is not the same as the formal close where salespeople ask for the sale. When a trial close is used at the end of the sales presentation, salespeople are able to find out how the prospect feels about a certain element of the sale, as opposed to asking for the ultimate buying decision.[8] Here's an example:

Trial close: 'How do you feel about the variety of colors available?'

Asking for the sale: 'If I can get you this product in your preferred shade of blue, will you decide to buy?'

As revealed in the above example, a trial close is a way to engage the prospect in the conversation to explore their perspective without making them feel pressured. Savvy salespeople are not afraid to ask their prospects where they are in their decision-making process, or where they stand in relation to other competitor offers. Honest answers to these questions will help build a long-term relationship with each prospect, even if the decision to buy is prolonged.

Let's now examine the three most common approaches or types of sales presentations – prepared, selling formula, and consultative.[9]

Prepared. The prepared approach is also referred to as 'canned' as it uses a standardized method with a memorized script that is not customized to each prospect. This canned generic sales presentation type treats all prospects alike. However, a prepared

Salesperson making a sales presentation

approach may be used by inexperienced salespeople to ensure all key selling points are addressed in their pitch. Canned approaches are often used when selling low-value products or services or those that have low repeat-purchase potential, or when the salesperson is simply providing some necessary information to the prospect to quickly close the sale. Canned sales presentations rarely contribute to relationship building.

Selling formula. The selling formula approach, which is also called the 'outlined' approach, has a dual focus. While it follows a rehearsed, structured outline to ensure that all key selling points are addressed, it also encourages prospects to interact with salespeople and become active participants in the sales presentation pitch. Thus, the interaction portion of selling formula sales presentations serves as an invitation to relationship building between the salesperson and each individual prospect.

Consultative. The consultative approach, also referred to as the 'customized' or 'needs-satisfying' approach, uses a customized presentation focused on addressing the unique needs and solving the problems of each prospect. With the consultative approach, salespeople become consultants to their prospects and their presentations are based on their research and understanding of the prospect's problem and situation. Consultative selling is partnership selling where salespeople are focused on selling long-term value and creating long-term relationships with each prospect and customer, as opposed to providing products and services.[10] These salespeople typically ask questions and carefully listen to the responses from each prospect in order to adequately address each prospect's individual needs. Consultative sales presentations provide an excellent opportunity for building and strengthening relationships with prospects and customers.

As you can see, the three approaches to delivering sales presentations serve different purposes and are not of equal value in building long-term relationships with prospects and customers. However, all approaches need to incorporate techniques to enhance the presentation in order to hold the prospect's attention and get them interested. Let's explore some of the common techniques used to enhance sales presentations.

Prospects listening during a sales presentation

Using effective presentation techniques

The most common presentation techniques used to enhance sales presentations are demonstrations, free samples, handouts, testimonials, stories, and visual aids. Let's investigate each one.

Demonstrations

Showing products or services in use or operation provides prospects with proof of the functionality and resulting benefits of a product or service. Demos are used during the sales presentation to show prospects how to apply the product, service, or solution. Research shows that whenever people are engaged through their senses (sight, sound, smell, touch, and taste), they become physically and emotionally involved in whatever is being presented to them.[11] Salespeople must speak the language of their prospects when delivering a demonstration in order to encourage prospect questions and interest. Demonstrations are very effective in enhancing sales presentations.

Here's a good example of the effectiveness of demonstrations. A Canadian inventor named Gallant was meeting with a potential buyer for F.A.O. Schwarz, when Gallant unexpectedly tossed the replica of a well-known Canadian building into the air. It landed in one piece. Gallant quickly picked it up and proceeded taking the interlocking pieces apart to demonstrate that it was really an innovative three-dimensional puzzle. This clever demonstration led the buyer to immediately place an order; and six years later, Gallant's company, along with Hasbro, distributed more than 10 million three-dimensional puzzles.[12]

Free samples

Everyone loves to receive free samples! Giving away free samples is an effective technique to enhance a sales presentation and may generate a lot of sales. In some situations, free samples can boost sales by as much as 2,000 percent.[13] Free samples may be used to achieve a number of different objectives, including the following:[14]

- Introduce a product to a prospect that is unfamiliar with the company/brand.
- Foster relationships and inspire greater brand loyalty.
- Expand prospects' knowledge about the product.
- Encourage repeat sales of existing products or sales of new products.
- Generate awareness of a company or brand prior to an event, such as a trade show.

Handouts

Distributing 'leave behind' materials during sales presentations will enable salespeople to focus their prospects' attention on a particular aspect or selling point by placing physical materials in their hands. Handouts also enable prospects to examine sales materials at their own pace, in a more relaxed setting, and at any time they choose. The key to using handouts effectively during sales presentations is to ensure that they contribute to the selling message and don't distract the prospect's attention away from the salesperson's presentation. Also, salespeople must ensure that the handouts they distribute provide real value for their prospects; otherwise, the material will quickly end up in the trash. Having a solid understanding of the prospect is critical to be able to prepare and provide valuable handouts for use during the sales presentation.

Testimonials

Let's look at an example of a customer testimonial that Rodney van Treeck, a territory sales representative for Taylor Freezer Company, received from a client who is very well known in his industry. The fact that the client is well known and highly respected makes the testimonial even more valuable. Rodney has smartly posted the following testimonial on his LinkedIn page and shares it with his prospects when delivering sales presentations:

> I have been working with Rodney for 15 years. His flavor burst soft serve machines have made our company a lot of money. Rodney is always ready to be of service to his customers to help grow our businesses together. I have recommended Rodney and Taylor Freezer to many people over many years.

If you have a great product or provide outstanding service, you will likely have a potential treasure trove of valuable customer testimonials. Delighted customers will produce selling phrases that come straight from their heart, packed with emotion. The words of happy and satisfied customers are very powerful influencers when woven into a sales presentation and provide additional objective proof of the value of the product/service being presented. Sometimes salespeople may need to request input from their satisfied customers in order to obtain these valuable sales presentation enhancements. Testimonials often provide the basis for good storytelling as well, which will be addressed later in the chapter.

Stories

Stories enable salespeople to sell an unforgettable experience crafted in an exciting and dramatic manner that provides much greater emotional impact than descriptions of the product/service benefits that are normally provided in sales presentations. Research shows that prospects remember 5–10 percent of statistics and 25 percent of images, but retention increases to 60–70 percent when stories are used to present information.[15] Developing and using stories in sales presentations is so valuable and important to successful selling that an entire section will be devoted to storytelling later in this chapter.

Visual aids

Visual aids are powerful enhancers to sales presentations. People process information in the following order: images first, words second, and numbers third. The human brain processes visuals 60,000 times faster than text, and 90 percent of the information transmitted to the brain is visual.[16] Unfortunately, too often the visual aids that salespeople use are not really *visual*. Effective visual aids should have three qualities:

- *Be simple.* Apply the KISS principle, which stands for 'keep it simple stupid' as less is more when it comes to visual aids. That means presenting only one idea per slide, and limiting the number of different fonts, colors, and graphics used on each slide.
- *Be clear.* Avoid acronyms and abbreviations. Be sure to provide adequate support points so that your message is accurately understood.
- *Be concise.* Eliminate numbers, words, images, and even punctuation that are not essential to conveying the selling message.

Savvy salespeople review the visual aids they create, looking for ways to enhance and polish their visuals in order to deliver effective emotional messaging to their prospects. Anything that is not critical to the sales presentation is deleted, giving the salesperson an opportunity to provide additional information verbally. This serves to establish the salesperson's expertise and keep the prospect's attention on the person presenting. Deleting unnecessary content also provides more 'white space' (empty or blank space) on slides used for sales presentations. As Figure 7.2 shows, words can be turned into visuals by using simple clip art or images.

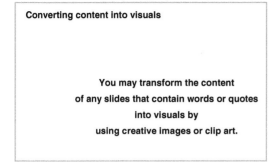
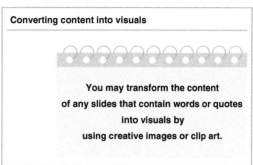

Figure 7.2 Turning words into visuals
Used with kind permission of Dan Dipiazzo.

Salespeople must often present quantitative data in their presentations. Because this data may be difficult for prospects to process quickly, salespeople find ways to make numbers more visually effective and appealing. One method is to convert a bullet-point list of numerical data into a line graph. Not only is the graph easier to understand, it can reveal patterns in the data that would otherwise be missed. Check out Figure 7.3 for four examples of how to improve numeric visual aids to provide greater presentation impact.

4ᵗʰ Quarter sales in serious decline	
YEAR	UNIT SALES (000)
2013	1,263
2014	1,196
2015	1,102
2016	1,140
2017	1,035
2018	1,044
2019	1,011
2020	889

Figure 7.3A Sales data table of numbers

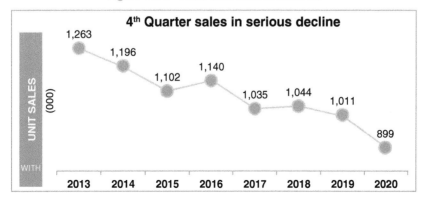

Figure 7.3B Sales data line graph

Figure 7.3

(Continued)

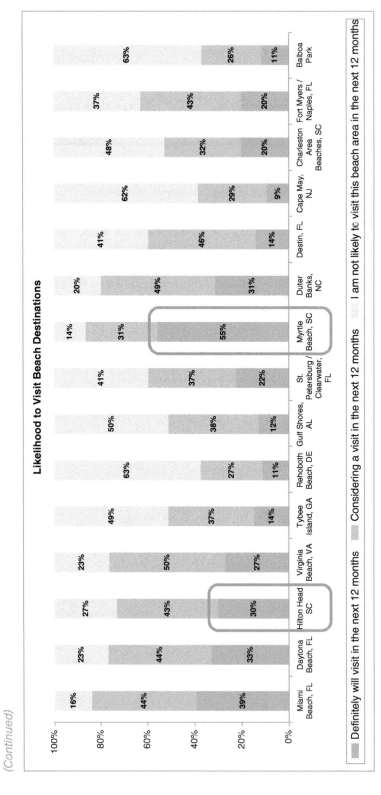

Figure 7.3C   Busy bar chart

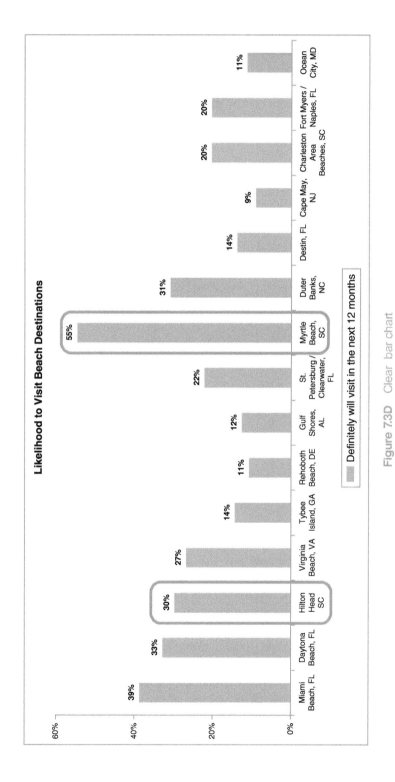

Figure 7.3D Clear bar chart

Figure 7.3 Examples of comparative slides turning numbers into visuals

Used with kind permission of Dan Diplazzo.

Adding motion to visual aids can bring images to life; however, it may also become distracting for viewers. Before adding motion, consider whether it will enhance the message or divert attention. If deciding to use motion, note that subtle animations are usually more effective than those that are fast paced. Also, be sure to stop talking during the sales presentation if the animations include sound. Mobile and digital technology has greatly affected the delivery of modern sales presentations, which is the topic of our next section.

Video-conferencing session

Employing mobile and digital technology tools

In addition to effective visual aids, salespeople may use videos and real-time broadcasting to enhance their sales presentations by showing product demonstrations, giving behind-the-scenes tours, answering questions, and otherwise engaging their prospects.[17] Mobile apps, such as Twitter's Periscope and Facebook Live, allow prospects to watch streaming videos with their smartphones and have real-time conversations with salespeople.[18] Salespeople should investigate what time works best for their prospects and broadcast on a regular basis.

Modern B2B selling involves an average of 6.8 people, thus the likelihood of getting all of the decision makers to attend a single sales presentation is slim.[19] Today's salespeople need to create a sales deck to enable their message to be digitally shared with all key decision makers. A sales deck is a slide presentation summary of the selling company and what it can do for the specific audience for whom the slides have been created.[20] Salespeople should build their sales decks around two key components: their company's story and their prospect's situation.[21] Typically, slide deck content includes the following elements:[22]

1. Title slide
2. Definition of the prospect's problem or need
3. Explanation of problem solution that the selling company can provide

4. Salesperson introduction
5. Elaboration of why this solution is optimal
6. Proof to support this solution's claims
7. Closing with a call-to-action.

Additional slides to consider including in the sales deck are: financials (profit and loss statement, sales forecast data, cash flow forecast), competitive comparative analysis, demonstration videos, and screenshots that effectively tell success stories. The title slide of your sales deck should use the voice of each prospect and should be customized to each prospect's needs. Placing a vision and value proposition on the initial slide provides a quick one-sentence overview which can be an effective attention-grabbing technique. Another is to customize the sales deck to each prospect's brand by dropping in logos and images, and using its brand colors in the overall design theme.[23] Remember, 'less is more' in terms of the number of words on a slide, with the goal of 20 words or fewer per slide for a deck to be presented, and 60 words or fewer per slide for a deck to be read.[24] Table 7.1 provides additional tips on creating effective sales decks to use in delivering presentations, both in person and online.

Table 7.1 Creating effective sales decks

Customize your slides

C-level executives: focus on overall vision; goal is to earn their respect and confidence

Budget holders: emphasize cost investment and ROI to convince them to decide

Users/practitioners: address technical aspects, provide demonstration, and show proof of the product/service benefits to encourage adoption and purchase.

Structure

Opening: use a 'wow' slide that grabs attention

Middle: showcase how you will solve the prospect's problem and sell the benefits

Closing: provide a clear call-to-action as opposed to ending with questions.

Content

Do's: show how your product/service will solve the prospect's problem; elaborate on why with a few impressive statistics; provide proof with concrete examples, testimonials, case studies, and stories; use content that's important to your prospect.

Don'ts: use bullet-point lists of product/service features; provide generic data that's already available and easily accessible to prospects; cover too many minor details; use content that's important to you.

Design

Do's: use many visuals; have a consistent look and feel throughout all presentation slides; use your prospect's brand image, colors, and tone throughout all presentation slides; leave adequate white space on slides; consider that less is more in terms of slide content.

Don'ts: show too many numbers on slides; use slides that are too wordy or slides that are all about you/your company.

(Continued)

253

Table 7.1 (Continued)

Miscellaneous

Be unique: sales decks that are unique will be remembered

Goal: the goal of the sales presentation is to persuade

Preparation: creating effective sales decks takes time; don't procrastinate; plan ahead

Time limit: know in advance the desired length of time for your presentation and factor that into the number of slides you create.

Source: Shabnam Kakar, 'How to Create a Winning Sales Deck' (June 21, 2019), www.copper.com/blog/sales-deck , retrieved September 14, 2020; and Alli McKee, 'The Sales Hacker Deck on Sales Decks: Learn how to WOW your prospects and convert!' (January 16, 2019), www.saleshacker.com/sales-deck, retrieved September 14, 2020.

There are many software tools available to enable salespeople to put together compelling slides for their sales decks. PowerPoint has been the leader in the world's presentation software for decades and continues to dominate the industry, with an estimated 90 percent market share.[25] However, many competitors are now providing innovative options. Table 7.2 provides a list of some of the most commonly recommended software programs.

Table 7.2 Sales presentation software tools

PowerPoint: Premium sales templates

- MOUVE – elegant PowerPoint template
- Property marketing sales presentation
- Sales PowerPoint
- Sales pitch PowerPoint template
- Stella PowerPoint template

Source: Sarah Joy, '25 Best Sales PowerPoint Templates (PPT Presentation Examples for 2020),' https://business.tutsplus.com/articles/best-sales-powerpoint-templates--cms-34031, retrieved September 14, 2020.

PowerPoint alternatives

Canva	Haiker Deck
Slidebean	Slides
Focusky	Prezi
Apple Keynote	OctaSales
OKVisme	KineticCast
Google Slides	Libre Office Impress
Flowvella	Slides.com
SlideDog	Zoho Show

Source: 'Best Presentation Software List of 2020: Complete Guide' (May 22, 2020), https://slidebean.com/blog/design-best-presentation-software-list-2020, retrieved September 14, 2020; and '5 Best Sales Presentation Tools for Marketers and Salesman,' http://focusky.com/learning-center/en/5-best-sales-presentation-tools-for-marketers-and-salesman, retrieved September 14, 2020.

Today, many sales presentations are delivered in a virtual format as opposed to in a face-to-face meeting. Virtual events and online sales presentations can save time and travel costs. For example, a senior sales consultant who oversees the presentations for the worldwide field sales force at Prism Solutions, Inc., claims that his company cut costs by 90 percent as he now runs many of the sales presentations for clients in Australia, Brazil, and England from his home office in the USA.[26] Salespeople should be prepared to deliver virtual sales presentations using one or more of the online platforms available.

Virtual sales presentations may be difficult to deliver effectively due to challenges associated with poor lighting or sound quality, lack of active engagement with the prospect, including too few questions and answers, pre-determined topics, and time-zone differences.[27] According to Ray Wang, author of *Disrupting Digital Business*, listed in the Readings and Resources section at the end of the chapter, salespeople can overcome these challenges by approaching virtual sales presentations with a 'live broadcast' mentality. This mentality includes making big announcements, unveiling new products and services, telling success stories about customers and partners, and incorporating physical activity into your digital service by including shared immersive experiences in the agenda, such as wine, coffee, or chocolate tasting, food preparation by celebrity chefs, or participation in activities that support charities.[28] Salespeople should incorporate ways to involve their prospects in their sales presentations so that the experience is interactive rather than just observational. Regardless of whether a sales presentation is delivered in person or in a virtual format, salespeople must pitch with passion, which is the topic of our next section.

PITCHING WITH PASSION

Pitching with passion implies that you believe in what you're selling and know that what you are offering can help your prospects to solve their business problems. Salespeople deliver effective presentations when they can form a bond with their prospects. That bond includes making eye contact with the prospect for some period of time. Typically, the length of time for eye contact varies between three and six seconds.[29] However, eye contact duration is not a perfect science, as some prospects prefer more eye contact, while others less. Passionate pitches also require the mastery of space, which we'll address in the next section.

Managing personal space

While managing personal space is the most important consideration during the sales presentation, salespeople need to consider physical and mental space as well. Let's briefly address each of these.

Physical space

Physical space pertains to the environment or venue in which the sales presentation will be delivered. Savvy salespeople always plan ahead, arrive early, and take charge of their physical space to ensure that the room is set up to maximize their presentation performance. Physical space matters include the room size, lighting, acoustics, seating arrangement, platform or podium if presenting to a group, technology and audiovisual support, and so on. When meeting one on one with a prospect, the decision to sit face to face across a desk or table may unconsciously create a barrier between the seller and the buyer, so often salespeople prefer to sit next to their prospects or utilize the corner of a conference table to sit at an angle, as shown in Figure 7.4. Eliminating unconscious barriers may improve rapport and help develop relationships between salesperson and prospect.

Figure 7.4 Corner table positioning

Personal space

Also called proxemics, personal space pertains to the amount of space between the salesperson and the prospect. How close salespeople situate themselves near their prospect may communicate friendliness or formality. Typically, as Figure 7.5 shows, there are four different zones of proximity:[30]

- Intimate – this space is up to 18 inches (45 cm) and is normally reserved for family and friends.
- Casual/friend – this space is 18 inches to four feet (45cm to 1.2 m) and is used for informal conversations with people who are familiar, including associates, colleagues, and friends.
- Social – this space is four to 12 feet (1.2 m to 3.6 m) and is appropriate for more formal communication with new acquaintances.
- Public – this space is normally 12 to 25 feet (3.6 m to 7.6 m) and is used with a public audience, such as when giving a lecture or speaking to a group.

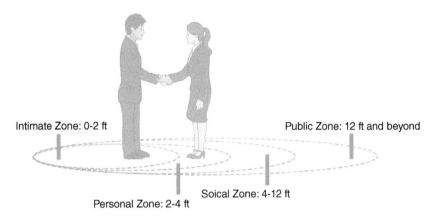

Intimate Zone: 0-2 ft

Public Zone: 12 ft and beyond

Soical Zone: 4-12 ft

Personal Zone: 2-4 ft

Figure 7.5 Zones of personal space

Personal space guidelines vary by culture, so the salespeople must know what is acceptable and expected when selling to prospects in different countries. In some countries, people are more comfortable to touch one another (such as Brazil, Mexico, and Italy), while other cultures (such as the USA, the UK, Germany, and Norway) do not typically do so.[31] In addition, it is appropriate to adjust the personal space guidelines based on your selling situation. For example, when delivering a formal sales presentation to a well-known prospect after years of a non-business relationship, a shorter distance will be more appropriate. In fact, when salespeople allow too much personal space between themselves and their prospects, they can actually negate the natural rapport of the existing personal relationship. Humans tend to be strongly territorial such that once they claim a territory, it becomes their safety zone where they can rest without worrying about someone entering into their personal space.[32] Salespeople must be aware of the ways that people claim safety zones, such as by placing a jacket over a chair or a water bottle or other personal belongings at a particular place at the conference table. These are clues to people's safety zone claims that salespeople must respect.

Given the Covid-19 pandemic that spread worldwide in 2020, personal space guidelines for face-to-face sales presentations may need to be adjusted. In some geographic locations, guidelines may require that chairs are arranged six feet apart from one another, that masks are worn by participants, and/or that hand sanitizer is available. In addition, contactless presentations with all materials provided to the prospect electronically prior to the meeting, may be required. Communicating with each prospect in advance of a face-to-face meeting to determine their comfort level with the physical meeting space, may alleviate potential distractions and help ensure an effective sales presentation.

Mental space

Mental space refers to the level of conscious nervousness that is present in your mind as you approach your sales presentation. While it is common to experience some degree of nervousness or excitement, you must possess a clear mind and be in control of your emotions in order to deliver an effective sales presentation. Take a breath. Relax. Focus on the present moment and your prospective clients and their situation. Prepare to effectively communicate by reviewing both your speaking and listening skills. The ability of salespeople to control their mental space improves their ability to hold the attention and focus of their prospects, which is the topic of our next section.

Commanding and owning the audience's attention

A common mistake that salespeople make is that they regard the purpose of presentations as imparting information, where they speak and their audience will listen, believe, and act.[33] Salespeople must earn the attention of their prospects. The secret weapon of salespeople who successfully command the attention of their prospects is their ability to present information that is of real interest to their prospects. Salespeople who are able to show they understand the situation, business drivers, and authentic problems of their prospects will not only retain the attention of their audience but will deliver effective presentations that successfully sell. Remember, selling is the ultimate goal when delivering a sales presentation. To do this, be careful not to lecture when presenting information, rather, communicate and engage with prospects using their dominant mode of communication (visual, auditory, or kinesthetic.)

Presentations that lack clear organization and flow will not command the prospect's attention for long. Like a story or a movie, presentations should have a natural beginning, middle, and ending. There are several ways to help your prospect easily follow along with your presentation, without verbally revisiting your agenda. One such way is by including a slide rule on each of your slides. As Figure 7.6 shows, a slide rule

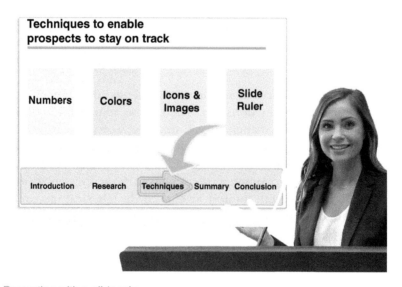

Figure 7.6 Presenting with a slide rule

included at the bottom of each slide will clearly mark the order of slides and progression in the presentation and make it easy for prospects to follow along.

Be mindful not to present too much material in a sales presentation. Most people tend to remember three pieces of information from any presentation; thus, salespeople should identify the three main points they want their prospects to take away and build their presentation around those.[34] Of course, these main points must directly align with what is most important and valuable to each of their prospects. To really connect with each prospect, customize the presentation to zero in on the key issues of most concern to each individual prospect, while delivering this content in an exciting and intriguing manner. If only it were that simple. Commanding the prospect's attention requires that salespeople project genuine passion and interest when delivering each sales pitch. Let's further explore how to pitch with passion.

Pitching passionately to the prospective customer

A winning pitch begins with the salesperson's ability to convey a winning logline. A logline is a single compelling sentence that explains the content of the presentation in a manner that hooks the prospective customer. According to science, the human brain craves meaning before detail, so that when listeners don't understand the overarching idea being presented in a pitch, they will have a hard time digesting the information.[35] To ensure that meaning is clear, the logline, using simple and plain words, should easily convey the content and value of the sales presentation for the prospect. Think of the logline as providing the vision, painting the big picture, or presenting the main unique selling proposition (USP) of the sales pitch.

To successfully convince their prospects to buy, salespeople should spend 40 percent of their time asking questions, 40 percent listening and 20 percent presenting the product or service.[36] During the short amount of time when salespeople are speaking, they must do so in a manner that resonates with the particular social and communication style of each individual prospect. As we've discussed in detail in previous chapters, salespeople must alter their communication to mirror or match that of their prospects. Thus, for the visually dominant prospect, salespeople should use many gestures while speaking, and be sure to include many images (opposed to words) on any visual aids and handouts that they provide. In addition, demonstrations that have a strong visual impact will be effective with visually dominant prospects. For auditory-dominant prospects, in-person verbal presentations are most effective when speakers are clear and concise with their messaging. If slides or other visual aids are used, salespeople should go over the items verbally, point by point, as these prospects will carefully listen to each and every word. Kinesthetic prospects value touching and holding objects, so salespeople should use hands-on demonstrations or physical samples in their sales presentations whenever possible. If visuals are required, try to make them three-dimensional or animated in order to cater to kinesthetic prospects.[37]

Presenting using props

Pitching passionately to prospects means connecting with them on an emotional level. According to screenwriting coach Robert McKee, 'Forget about PowerPoint and statistics. To involve people at the deepest level, you need stories.'[38] McKee believes that salespeople can engage their prospects on a whole new level if they learn to unite ideas with emotion. That's precisely what storytelling does and that is the topic of our next section.

STORYTELLING

Storytelling has been around for centuries, dating back to cavemen and pioneer days, long before books and movies were in existence. In sales presentations, sharing persuasive stories enable salespeople to build relationships with customers and prospects, stand out and above competitors, and effectively sell products and services.

Connecting with the prospective customer

We live in an over-communicated world where we are constantly bombarded with messages clamoring for our attention. Humans have a shorter average attention span than that of goldfish – only 8.25 seconds.[39] Unfortunately, even the most passionate sales presentations pitching numerous product benefits can sometimes result in information overload for prospective customers. The question is: how can salespeople communicate effectively in today's busy world? How can their messages break through the clutter to claim the attention of their prospects? And how can salespeople get their prospects to remember their message in order to gain commitment and build trust to establish good relationships? The answer to these questions is that salespeople need to become master storytellers. During their sales presentations, salespeople need to conquer the skill of telling attention-grabbing, persuasive stories that are intriguing and meaningful to their prospects.

Storytelling helps salespeople to effectively establish rapport, build trust, and add value. Stories are more powerful and impactful than facts and can break through distractions, disinterest, and content overload, causing the prospect to take notice, stay engaged, and remember.[40] People remember facts and figures 22 times more often when they are woven into a story.[41] Stories have the ability to hold people's attention.[42] How is this achieved? Salespeople use stories to establish rapport by emotionally getting in sync with their prospects as they relate to the story being told. When stories feature satisfied customers with testimonials, they help salespeople demonstrate the positive impact of a purchase decision and to build trust with their prospects. These genuine customer satisfaction stories add value to the sales presentation as they highlight the experiences of satisfied customers. Salespeople may connect prospects with current customers who are willing to elaborate on their stories.

Successful salespeople no longer merely talk about the features or benefits of their product (or service, event, cause, etc.). Instead, they tell a convincing and memorable story that conveys much more meaningful information to their prospects. Here's an example. Which will you remember better – the facts about L.L. Bean boots or the story of how they originated?

THE FACTS: The Maine Hunting Shoe[43]

- Is made of premium full-grain leather and high-quality rubber
- Is a waterproof rubber-bottom boot
- Ensures rugged performance
- Has a steel shank for added support
- Has a rubber chain-tread bottom for traction
- Is triple-stitched for exceptional durability
- Has L.L. Bean boot stitchers train for 26 weeks so they can master the trademark triple-stitch technique
- Is handmade in the USA
- Has a money-back satisfaction guarantee.

THE STORY: The Maine Hunting Shoe[44]

In 1911, an avid outdoorsman, Leon L. Bean, returned from a hunting trip disgruntled because his boots leaked, and his feet were damp and cold. That led him to a revolutionary idea to design a new boot by stitching lightweight leather tops to waterproof rubber bottoms. The boots worked so well that he offered them for sale via mail order and called them the Maine Hunting Shoe. Unfortunately, most of the pairs of shoes he initially sold had a stitching problem and leaked. He quickly refunded his customers' money and fixed the stitching problem. From that moment on to this very day, L.L. Bean's legendary '100 percent satisfaction' guarantee carries a lifetime promise. Your feet will be warm and dry when you purchase the Maine Hunting Shoe from L.L. Bean.

The Maine Hunting Shoe story is true and it's meaningful to you if you are interested in buying hunting boots. In addition, you are more likely to remember the story and the L.L. Bean brand much better than the facts listed about the Maine Hunting Shoe.

Stories used in selling must be factual, real, and authentic. Authenticity means that the prospect does not perceive the story to be phony, contrived, or a transparent selling effort.[45] Authenticity also implies that there is substance behind the story with details that support the story and can be confirmed. Customer testimonials are a great way to provide substance to a story. Here's another true story to help you to remember the importance of storytelling:

A few years ago, a colleague of mine told me that he tested out L.L. Bean's 100% satisfaction guarantee by returning his well-worn Maine Hunting Shoes because after nearly 40 years of wear, they developed a small hole. Despite the fact that Professor Maz's shoes were very old, the company promptly responded by sending him a brand-new pair of Maine Hunting Shoes and thanking him for his lifetime of loyalty. Professor Maz was amazed, and he's been sharing this story ever since.

Wow! Now there's a story with a substantiated testimonial woven into it. Also, this story is very persuasive in demonstrating the fact that L.L. Bean's 100 percent satisfaction guarantee is iron clad. In order to be effective, stories must inspire, evoke trust, and be persuasive to their prospects. Let's now discuss how to write a persuasive story.

Writing persuasive stories

Composing an effective, persuasive story is part art and part science. The old saying, 'It's not creative unless it sells' applies here. Stories used when delivering sales presentations must be both persuasive and believable in order to add value to the salesperson's pitch. The following seven-step process will help you to create persuasive stories.

Step 1: Do your research

Effective storytelling involves a deep understanding of human emotions, motivations, and psychology in order to truly move an audience.[46] You must understand your prospects and what their main needs and interests are with regard to whatever you are selling. Stories should be written to match your prospect's worldview. Worldview is a term that refers to the rules, values, beliefs, and biases that an individual person brings to a situation. Each prospective customer will possess a different worldview; thus, you must use your insight to better understand each individual's worldview. You cannot create a compelling story unless you can relate to your prospects, understand their unique situations, and feel their pain. Understanding your prospect's 'pain points' requires research. The more you know about your prospects, the easier it is to select relevant stories that may have an impact on their respective decision-making process.

Step 2: Set goals and objectives

You cannot create an effective story unless you know the desired goals and objectives for which the story is to be written. Once you have confirmed the prospect's needs or interests in making a buying decision, your story goal is to communicate a convincing story to entice your prospect to want to buy your particular brand of products/ services versus those of your competitors. Through your research or during your approach and greeting, you may learn of special concerns the prospect has regarding the products/services you are offering. Telling stories that address those particular concerns may help to overcome your prospects potential objections or hesitations and enable them to commit to buying. Your story must be focused on achieving your desired outcomes.

Step 3: Outline story content

You must prepare your story in advance. Salespeople who want to successfully tell stories on a regular basis will need to create a number of stories related to different topics. Thus, they will need to outline the respective content for each story to provide an overview and the gist of that story. Some storytellers use writing formulas to help them prepare outlines. For example, as we presented in Chapter 2, the copywriting formula 'A-I-D-A,' which stands for Attract **A**ttention, Arouse **I**nterest, Stimulate **D**esire, and Call for **A**ction, works to ensure a good story flow. Outlining story content is related to story structure, which we'll discuss in greater detail in the next section.

Step 4: Draft story and revise

Following the story outline that you have created, you will need to draft your story by adding relevant details. Here are a few tips to keep in mind when drafting your story:

- Be creative, but your goal is to 'sell' – convince the reader – not to merely entertain.
- Tell your story through action, not description.
- Write in the present tense and use action verbs.
- Weave in suspense and surprise, arouse curiosity, stimulate passion, and generate emotion.
- Write for the ear, not the eye. Write how you would speak and use a conversational tone.

When drafting your story, strive for empathy and provide details that are relevant to your prospect. In order to provide greater emotional impact, your story should appeal to multiple senses, in addition to sounding good. To achieve this, include details that cater to your prospect's other senses of sight, smell, taste, and touch. Once drafted, share your story with colleagues and obtain feedback in order to improve it. Keep in mind that your goal is to tell an intriguing story that captures attention and stimulates desire to buy.

Step 5: Add photos and images

Always use visual aids to fascinate prospects and make your story come alive. The old adage, *A picture is worth a thousand words*, is often true when combined with story-telling. Photographs are normally preferred over clip art; however, all photos are not equal. A photograph is basically a snapshot of a moment, but a good photograph in and of itself may tell a story. So, select your photos carefully, ensuring that they help to convey the intended message to your prospect. Compelling visual aids help your prospect both to remember and relate to your story.

Check out Figure 7.7 for some examples of inspiring photographs that have been taken and used by Paula Kosko, a realtor with RE/MAX Real Estate Group. When selling homes, Paula frames her stories around each photo. For example, Paula used a stunning sunset on a pond photo to sell a condominium that was located directly across the street. Her clever selling message was: '*You're buying this view and the condo comes with it.*' Imagine the wonderful stories she could create of relaxing hours spent by owners enjoying gorgeous sunsets from this condo. The inviting backyard pool photo easily leads anyone to envision the fun, family time, and parties that can be enjoyed at this home. Lastly, the fascinating front door image looking outside is an innovative twist to selling a home where most realtors use photos that show the reverse direction. Stories may be readily created about the beautiful yard that is apparent beyond the front door, or the awesome neighborhood and new friends that await you when you buy this home. Keep in mind that authentic stories inspire creativity and stir emotions, thus good photographs maximize the impact of the selling message.

Step 6: Polish your story

Before sharing your story with prospects, obtain feedback from others and make final edits to improve and perfect your story. Remember to include a catchy ending to your story and a call-to-action that persuades prospects to continue the buyer journey.

Step 7: Share your story!

You should rehearse your story and be mentally prepared to weave your tale into your sales presentation at the appropriate time. Sharing your story with your prospect should appear logical and natural.

Figure 7.7A Sunset pond

Figure 7.7B Pool with slide

Figure 7.7C Interior front door

Figure 7.7 Paula Kosko's real estate photos

Used with kind permission of Paula Kosko.

Now that you understand the process for creating a story, let's delve into the components and structure of story.

Understanding key story components and story structure

There are three main components to every story: the beginning, middle, and ending. Let's examine each:

- *Beginning.* The beginning of a story should provide details about the story setting (backdrop and timing) and situation so that readers can visualize and better relate to the story. The story must have at least one main character (a hero) and include a character sketch, which is an overview description of the character, to provide some depth so that readers can identify with tthis person. The beginning of the story discloses the thesis, which is a statement of the main point or the premise of the story.
- *Middle.* The middle of the story explains the predicament, which is the problem, challenge, or opportunity that the main character is facing. This component of the story also provides a narrative, which is an explanation of the events happening in the story. The plot thickens during this component of the story. The story is building interest and arousing curiosity, while it creates tension or progression of the main idea until it reaches a climax, which is the most intense or exciting point in the story. The middle of the story must arouse enough curiosity to move readers forward and keep them wanting more.

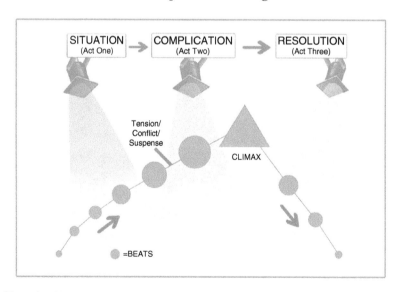

Figure 7.8   Story structure

Adapted from Laurence Vincent (2002) *Legendary Brands: Unleashing the Power of Storytelling to Create a Winning Market Strategy.* Chicago, IL: Dearborn Trade Publishing.

- *Ending*. The ending provides an explanation of the resolution of the main character's predicament. What happens? Hopefully, the hero wins! The conclusion should be written in an exciting and inspiring manner so that the story is a 'success story,' as opposed to a drama or historical lesson.

As Laurence Vincent explains in his book, *Legendary Brands: Unleashing the Power of Storytelling to Create a Winning Market Strategy*, listed in the recommended Readings and Resources at the end of this chapter, the three components come together to form the story structure, where the story is a succession of acts – Act 1, Act 2 and Act 3 (see below).[47] Stories used in sales presentations are planned persuasion that is structured around a narrative arc where the beginning introduces the topic; the middle creates tension, progression, and excitement; and the ending reveals the resolution.[48] Stories are told by a series of beats, where a beat is the smallest part of a story that still retains the essence of the story itself. A beat is the foundation of every story, which may be an event, phrase, episode, scene, anecdote, statement, and so on. A beat demonstrates a cause-and-effect relationship.[49] To elaborate, let's consider what happens in each component of the story:[50]

- **Act 1** – a dramatic question/situation is posed and tension is introduced for the main character. The beats begin and slowly grow.
- **Act 2** – a series of beats occur that raise the tension and complicate the dramatic question that the main character faces in Act 1. The beats increase more rapidly until the story reaches its climax.
- **Act 3** – all dramatic questions are answered and tensions are relieved where the main character comes to rest in a new, changed state (usually the opposite of the state in Act 1). The beats fade out as the story ends.

All beats are not of equal value in terms of their contribution to the story. The most effective beats *transform* the main character by dramatizing polarity and by impacting the emotional state of the reader. For example, a character that begins in poverty ends up with massive wealth; one that is very lonely ends up having an abundance of friends; a character perceived as being guilty of something ends up an innocent victim; a character moves from failure to success, insecurity to confidence, hopelessness to happiness, and so on. Stories that capture polar opposites are more effective as the transformation is clear and compelling. When structuring your story, remember to combine facts with emotions in a persuasive manner that matches your prospect's worldview.

Let's look at an example. Suppose you are selling ABC Communication Systems, and your research reveals that your prospective customer has a need for a new communication system. The story structure might be:

- **Beginning (Act 1):** The situation is your prospect's communication system is old and not secure, making it vulnerable to outside privacy invasions.
- **Middle (Act 2):** The complication is that your prospect's communication system has been hacked by a former disgruntled associate who distributed thousands of emails containing derogatory information in an effort to destroy your prospect's brand image. This is the story climax.

- **Ending (Act 3):** The resolution is your prospect purchasing the new ABC Communication System which safeguards the privacy of its records and prohibits potential hackers from being able to access the system. The customer is delighted because business communication problems are successfully solved.

There are other story structure formulas which it may be helpful to use when composing stories to use in sales presentations. One is the 'STAR' method, where S-T-A-R stands for:

- **S**ituation: Sets the scene; explains the characters, setting, backdrop, timing, etc.
- **T**ask: what were the character(s) challenged to do?
- **A**ctivity: what were the activities the character(s) carried out?
- **R**esults: How did the story end? What happened in the story?

Another story structure formula used by one of the greatest storytellers of all time, movie giant Pixar, is 'The Story Spine' formula. This formula, which was created by professional playwright and improviser Kenn Adams, enables storytellers to simply fill in the blanks in the following passage:[51]

Once upon a time there was ____ [blank].

Every day, ____ [blank].

One day ____ [blank].

Because of that, ____ [blank].

Because of that, ____ [blank].

Until finally ____ [blank].

Regardless of the formula used to structure your story, keep in mind that all successful stories are those that promise to fulfill the wishes of your prospect's worldview.[52] These story promises will vary based on the story goals and objectives, as well as the selling situation. They may offer a problem solution, a shortcut, resource savings, success, power, pleasure, prestige, and so on. For example, Rachael Judy, who sells medical devices for Boston Scientific, claims that patient success stories effectively turn a sales pitch into a real-life story with incredible clinical results. Doctors value clinical results much more than just seeing another medical device sales rep visiting their office and providing free lunch. These patient success stories fit their worldview (enhancing the health and well-being of their patients) and the stories are very well received.

Successful stories also utilize multi-media devices to maximize the story message since, as discussed earlier in the chapter, people process images much faster than they do words. Salespeople may use well-crafted video clips to provide engaging and entertaining content that adds value to their stories. Table 7.3 provides some additional tips to help you create and share persuasive stories.

Table 7.3 Storytelling techniques

- Take some aspect of life that caused you to feel a certain way and get others to have those same feelings.
- Determine the ultimate purpose the story will serve.
- Keep your audience in mind at all times.
- Determine what your main character is good at and throw the unexpected at this person.
- Create your ending before you flush out the middle details.
- Give your characters a personality and opinions to make them come alive.
- Most people admire characters for their efforts in trying more than for their successes.
- Convert your ideas into a story draft – write, write, write!
  - Write the big picture – the gist of the story – and polish later.
  - Write for a particular audience as it's better to customize than to generalize.

Characteristics of great stories

Great stories:

- are true, authentic, and believable
- stir our emotions – anger, disgust, fear, happiness, sadness, and surprise
- are those which people can understand and identify with
- have a main character to whom we can relate
- have an underdog to root for
- arouse curiosity because they are surprising and unexpected
- make a promise that's bold and audacious
- are simple, focused, and happen quickly.

Source: Adapted from Seth Godin (2005) *All Marketers Are Liars: The Power of Telling Authentic Stories in a Low-Trust World* (New York: Penguin Books), p. 8; Brian Peters (March 21, 2018), https://medium.com/@Brian_G_Peters/6-rules-of-great-storytelling-as-told-by-pixar-fcc6ae225f50, retrieved October 24, 2020; and Emma Coats, 'Pixar's 22 Rules of Storytelling' (December 27, 2012), https://lcoonline.wordpress.com/2012/12/27/pixars-22-rules-of-storytelling, retrieved October 21, 2020.

In conclusion, stories are powerful communication tools that enable salespeople to provide value and emotionally connect and engage with prospects. Both the value of stories and the effectiveness of sales presentations may be quantitatively assessed and measured. That's the topic of our next section.

MONITORING METRICS

The effectiveness of sales presentations and the impact of storytelling can be both qualitatively and quantitatively assessed. While the relevant metrics will likely vary by each company and selling situation, here are some examples of metrics that salespeople may gather and track:

- Number of prospects attending the sales presentation.
- Number of sales presentations delivered before the prospect committed to purchasing.

- Average length of a sales presentation.
- Number of prospect questions during a sales presentation.
- Number and percentage of times trial closing is successful.
- Number and percentage of times that a prospect agrees to move to a future meeting.
- Average number of stories shared in a sales presentation.
- Level of confidence in delivering a sales presentation.

The effectiveness of sales presentations may also be evaluated by inviting prospects to provide post-presentation comments and suggestions for improvement. Following up with prospects and requesting their feedback also demonstrate that you truly care about them and want to satisfy their needs. This type of feedback may identify distinct areas for sales presentation improvement and/or may garner valuable testimonials and story content for use in future presentations.

Posting stories on social media before you deliver your sales presentation enables you to show them during your sales presentation or invite your prospects to view them afterward. If you invite later visits, you may track and measure views, click-throughs, likes, shares, comments, and so on. The impact of stories may also prompt other customers to share their own testimonials or success stories. For example, the following testimonial demonstrates the impact of storytelling for one nonprofit organization:

> Since I began sharing emotional stories about why people participate in the Relay or who they Relay for, the number of people my posts have been shared with on Facebook has grown from an average of 50 people to 1500, peaking at 6200, and the page's previews have increased by 300 percent.

Delivering sales presentations and crafting stories is as much an art as it is a science. Since no two prospects are alike, creating effective and convincing presentations and stories requires salespeople to be flexible and creative. In our dynamic, digitally driven world, salespeople need to deliver passionate sales pitches as well as stories that sell. Though this may pose a challenge for salespeople, it may also prove to be an enjoyable activity for them.

CHAPTER SUMMARY

✓ Always remain aware of what stage you are at when delivering a sales presentation.

✓ Select sales presentation techniques that will resonate best with prospective customers.

✓ Create simple, clear, and concise visual aids to enhance your sales presentation.

✓ Include a compelling testimonial or story and a call to action in your sales pitch.

✓ Monitor metrics for your sales presentations and ask for feedback from your prospects; not just for your own improvement, but also to show you care about their needs.

KEY TERMS

Authenticity	Personal space
Beat	Physical space
Character sketch	Predicament
Climax	Proxemics
Consultative selling	Sales deck
Logline	Thesis
Mental space	Trial close
Narrative	Worldview

REVIEW QUESTIONS

1. Name and describe the four stages of a typical sales presentation.
2. What is a trial close, and how does it differ from a formal close?
3. Name and describe the three most common types of sales presentations. Which do you prefer?
4. Name and describe three of the most common presentation techniques used to enhance sales presentations.
5. What are the three qualities of effective visual aids?

(Continued)

6. What is a sales deck and what information does it contain?
7. What are the four zones of personal space, and what factors affect their rules of use?
8. What are the seven steps in the process of writing persuasive stories?
9. Describe two different methods for structuring the writing of a story?
10. List four metrics that are appropriate to use for sales presentations.

ETHICS IN ACTION

1. Karen McKay is a sales manager for a mid-sized company that produces snack food items which are distributed primarily through vending machines across the country. Her territory is a target market for new products as they are released by the company. As their current potato chips haven't been selling well, the company has improved the formulation and provided Karen with samples to test in her district. The packaging has remained the same, but a stamped-on statement indicates 'New and improved' in small print. Karen distributed the product to all her salespeople, but failed to provide the date that the new product will be available in vending machines. She didn't include the date because she knows from previous experience that dates promised never materialize. Two weeks after the samples were offered, she receives a call from her most productive salesperson stating that he has gotten multiple complaints that the product just purchased did not taste like the free sample. Does Karen need to take action at this time? If so, what should she do? Is it a reasonable defense to say that the labeling on the bag differentiates the old and new versions of the product? Why or why not?

2. Andy Adamson is a salesperson for a small, locally owned pet supply company that sells replicas of name brand toys at discounted prices. He has just received a testimonial on one of its newest products, a device that holds dog treats. This device will open in proportion to the diameter of the dog's mouth. Thus, the same product can be used from the puppy through the adult phase of a medium-sized dog's life. The customer stated: 'I've finally found one product that can entertain and keep my dogs' attention at all stages of their lives.' Andy knows that this statement may be true for medium-sized canines, but not for the smallest and largest breeds. He also knows that the company is planning to produce additional sizes if the initial offering sells well. Should Andy use this customer testimonial verbatim? If so, does he need to provide additional messaging with it? If not, what can he do instead to share this customer's feedback with other potential customers?

EXERCISE

It's storytelling time! Select a non-profit organization event or activity (hereafter referred to as 'story subject') that you feel represents a success story worth sharing. Research that story subject and write a 1–2-page *engaging* story documenting how and why the subject is both important and represents a success. Your story should document the 'impact' that the subject has had on various constituents throughout your community and follow the appropriate story structure discussed earlier in this chapter. The story must be authentic (real), not make-believe. Your story should be persuading, as if it were to be used in a sales pitch for the nonprofit organization to obtain future donor and/or volunteer support.

The story should have the following:

- a captivating title
- at least one testimonial and/or quote woven into the story
- two relevant and *powerful* photographs to accompany it
- evidence that background research was obtained
- a human-interest angle or emphasis
- a main character
- three story components (beginning, middle, and ending)
- a story structure with a logical progression from beginning to middle and ending.

ROLE-PLAY

Role-play flowchart

Situation: You work for a regional company that sells delicatessen products, packaged lunch meats, and hot dogs. You have been working in your sales territory for three years and you have a respectable market share. However, it is difficult to compete for refrigerated shelf space and advertising with the big national name brands. Your top customer is a regional food chain that does decent business with your company and you are calling on the business owner.

Characters: You are Sam Stevens, a 25-year-old college graduate who majored in marketing and completed a sales internship with Dog Deli corporate office.

(Continued)

You were offered a full-time sales position upon graduation. Your customer, Doug Downs, owns a chain of 'Dog Deli' stores throughout the eastern United States.

Selling goal: Your company's goal is to have advertisements for this premium hot dog in all the top grocery chains for the Memorial Day holiday. Your goal is to successfully pitch your company's new hot dog products to your client.

Product/service capabilities: Your company is introducing a brand new, high-end premium hot dog with cheese just before the Memorial Day weekend. Your company will be committing more money to advertising and food demonstrations than ever before. Your company provides an advertising allowance to back up the sale and can offer as many food demonstrations within stores as they would like. In-store food demonstrations can increase sales during those days tenfold.

Sales call details: By volume, your company is number three in hot dog sales with the Dog Deli chain behind Oscar Meyer and Smithfield Foods. In addition, this is a saturated market and most business owners are slow to add any new products because of limited shelf space.

Selling challenge: How do you deliver a sales presentation with impact to Doug Downs to gain his commitment for introducing a new brand of hot dog with substantial marketing impact on one of the year's busiest weekends for hot dog sales?

READINGS AND RESOURCES

- David Aaker (2018) *Creating Signature Stories: Strategic Messaging That Persuades, Energizes and Inspires.* New York: Morgan James Publishing.
- Seth Godin (2005) *All Marketers Are Liars: The Power of Telling Authentic Stories in a Low-trust World.* New York: Penguin Books.
- Andy Maslen (2015) *Persuasive Copywriting: Using Psychology to Influence, Engage and Sell.* London: Kogan Page.
- Jon Steel (2007) *Perfect Pitch: The Art of Selling Ideas and Winning New Business.* Hoboken, NJ: John Wiley & Sons, Inc.
- Laurence Vincent (2002) *Legendary Brands: Unleashing the Power of Storytelling to Create a Winning Market Strategy.* Chicago, IL: Dearborn Trade Publishing.
- Ray Wang (2015) *Disrupting Digital Business: Create an Authentic Experience in the Peer-to-Peer Economy.* Boston, MA: Harvard Business Review Press.

CASE STUDY: TAYLOR FREEZER SALES COMPANY

Preparing and delivering creative sales presentations is what Rodney van Treeck (Figure 7.9) does on a daily basis. Rodney is a territory sales representative for Taylor Freezer Sales

Company (hereafter referred to as 'Taylor'), an exclusive distributor for The Taylor Company, an international manufacturer of specialty restaurant equipment. Taylor's product line includes:

- soft serve machines
- batch ice cream machines
- frozen carbonated machines
- two-sided grills
- direct draw milkshake/smoothie machines
- frozen slush/margarita/cocktail machines.

Rodney manages a 54-county sales territory that spans two states. At any given time, Rodney has an active pipeline of 40–50 sales prospects, which typically transition into 5–10 sales and service customers. As a consultative sales representative, his main mission is to meet with business owners, understand their needs, wants and pain points, and discuss if/how Taylor's product line can solve a particular problem in its food service operation.

Figure 7.9 Rodney van Treeck of Taylor Freeze Company
Used with kind permission of Rodney van Treeck

Rodney uses a face-to-face consultative approach when he delivers his sales presentations to his prospects. Once Rodney has determined that the Taylor equipment line would be useful and valuable to the prospect, he then creates a sales presentation to demonstrate the effectiveness and profitability of the equipment for the prospect's specific situation. Normal sales presentations include a profit analysis supporting the viability of a purchase, both short term and long term. The typical return on investment on an equipment purchase from Taylor Freezer Company is within 24 months and many times under 12 months. This analysis might also include the benefits the equipment provides that could solve other issues such as high labor costs, inconsistent cooking methods, and ineffective time management in the cooking cycle. Rodney's sales presentation is complete with photos of the food product, specification sheets for the equipment, and marketable reasons why prospects should consider Taylor Freezer Sales Company as their food service partner.

If sufficient interest is generated during the face-to-face meetings, but the prospect needs a 'seeing is believing' moment, Taylor Freezer Company has a demo truck that Rodney utilizes to perform on-site demonstrations of the equipment. This innovative strategy gives the prospect a hands-on approach as well as a chance to actually have its customers taste the product and give their input and feedback.

One of Rodney's success stories is the time he was selling to a chain of high-end convenience stores nestled in the Blue Ridge Mountains. The customer initially purchased a frozen carbonated beverage machine (like 7-Eleven slurpee machines) in order to replace the 'bubble top' slush machines in the stores. Shortly thereafter, Rodney created and delivered a sales presentation on Taylor's FlavorBurst 9-Flavor Soft-Serve machines to this client, complete with a profit analysis and videos of the machine in action. During Rodney's presentation, he shared his own personal stories of the equipment that he used when he owned his business. Storytelling allowed Rodney to relate to the customer with firsthand knowledge. When Rodney presented the 9-Flavor Soft-Serve machine, the fact that he had actually owned this piece of equipment in a store that he successfully operated for 18 years was very helpful and created tremendous credibility. Rodney had also amassed and shared several referrals on LinkedIn, along with his employment history, so his prospects could further explore his credentials. In order to 'seal the deal,' Rodney conducted a demonstration. Taylor's demo truck is equipped with some of its main lines of equipment, so Rodney was able to conduct demonstrations at the prospect's location. In this particular case, the prospect was having a Coat Drive to support a local charity and had invited several vendors to set up in the parking lot to offer 'giveaways.' This was perfect timing! Rodney rolled in with the demo truck and distributed hundreds of servings of ice cream in this mountain city, in the dead of winter, while it was actually snowing! Needless to say, Rodney's sales presentation was a huge success, and Taylor received equipment orders for four stores, exceeding six figures.

Case questions:

1. How does Rodney attempt to customize his sales presentation to the needs of his prospects?
2. What techniques does Rodney utilize to enhance the effectiveness of his sales presentation?
3. If you were the sales representative for Taylor, what else might you do to create and deliver effective sales presentations to prospective customers?

NOTES

1. John Steel (2007), *Perfect Pitch: The Art of Selling Ideas and Winning New Business* (Hoboken, NJ: John Wiley & Sons), p. 9.
2. Mark Skipworth, 'The view from the other side: What buyers think of sales pitches,' *American Salesman* (November 2017), 62(11), 20–4.
3. Ibid.
4. Des King and Steve Jordan, 'Pitching to win,' *Printweek*, London (September 22, 2005), pp. 30–1.
5. Rodney van Treeck, personal communication, October 17, 2020.
6. Tim Plaehn, 'Preparing a Sales Pitch for a Trial Closing,' https://smallbusiness.chron.com/preparing-sales-pitch-trial-closing-61011.html, retrieved October 27, 2020.
7. Neal Lappe, 'Trial Closings: The key to a 100% close rate,' www.webstrategiesinc.com/blog/trial-closings-the-key-to-a-100-close-rate, retrieved October 27, 2020.
8. Ibid.
9. Adapted from Lewis Hershey, 'The role of sales presentations in developing customer relationships,' *Services Marketing Quarterly* (2005), 26(3), 41–54.
10. Susan Croft (2002) *Win New Business: The Desktop Guide* (London: Thorogood Publishing), p. 89.
11. 'How Product Demonstrations Impact Sales' (February 4, 2015), www.smartcircle.com/product-demonstrations-impact-sales, retrieved October 21, 2020.
12. Joel Saltzman, 'Be a whiz at sales presentations,' *American Salesman* (November 2019), 64(11), 28–9.
13. Kali Hawlk, 'The Science of Free Samples: How freebies can keep customers coming back for more' (June 21, 2017), www.shopify.com/retail/the-science-of-product-samples-how-free-samples-can-hook-customers-on-your-products, retrieved October 21, 2020.
14. Ibid.
15. Alli McKee, 'The Sales Hacker Deck On Sales Decks: Learn how to WOW your prospects and convert!' (January 16, 2019), www.saleshacker.com/sales-deck, retrieved September 14, 2020.
16. Tom Power, 'Like an Argument? Say stories don't belong in content marketing,' https://blog.jacobsclevenger.com/author/tom-power, retrieved October 24, 2020.
17. Dennis Nishi, 'Small Business (A Special Report): Managing technology – Live! From your company! It's a new way to market! Streaming video in real time is often more personal and more compelling than prerecorded messages,' *Wall Street Journal*, Eastern edition (May 2016), p. R4.
18. Ibid.
19. Shabnam Kakar, 'How to Create a Winning Sales Deck' (June 21, 2019), www.copper.com/blog/sales-deck, retrieved September 14, 2020.
20. Ibid.
21. Ibid.

22. Ibid.
23. Alli McKee, 'The Sales Hacker Deck On Sales Decks: Learn how to WOW your prospects and convert!' (January 16, 2019), www.saleshacker.com/sales-deck, retrieved September 14, 2020.
24. Ibid.
25. 'The Best Presentation Software of 2020: Free and paid alternatives,' https://slidedog.com/blog/best-presentation-software, retrieved September 14, 2020.
26. Chad Kaydo, 'Making online sales presentations,' *Sales and Marketing Management* (September 1998), 150(10), 16.
27. Ray Wang, 'Virtual Events Stink: Here's how to improve them' (September 30, 2020), www.destinationcrm.com/Articles/Columns-Departments/Customer-Experience/Virtual-Events-Stink.-Heres-How-to-Improve-Them-143104.aspx, retrieved October 21, 2020.
28. Ibid.
29. Sheri Jeavons, 'The number one secret for giving a great presentation,' *American Salesman* (December 2015), 60(12), 23–7.
30. Adapted from Diane Diresta, '4 Presentation Tips to Manage Space to Control the Room and Influence Results' (June 30, 2017), https://c-suitenetwork.com/advisors/4-presentation-tips-manage-space-control-room-influence-results, retrieved October 21, 2020.
31. Skills Converged, 'A Comprehensive Guide to Body Language,' www.skillsconverged.com/FreeTrainingMaterials/BodyLanguage/PersonalSpaceTerritoryandPhysicalContact.aspx, retrieved October 21, 2020.
32. Ibid.
33. Jon Steel (2007) *Perfect Pitch: The Art of Selling Ideas and Winning New Business* (Hoboken, NJ: John Wiley & Sons), p. 14.
34. 'Enhance dry presentations with stories,' *Communication Briefings* (December 2015), 34(12), 2.
35. Carmine Gallo, 'The art of the elevator pitch,' *Harvard Business Review* (Digital Articles) (October 3, 2018), pp. 21–5.
36. Dave Gleason, 'How you ask is just as important as what you ask,' *Snips*, Troy (October 2003), 72(10), 56.
37. Bryan Reiss, 'Using your clients' learning style to close sales,' *Kitchen & Bath Design News* (February 2012), 30(2), 20.
38. 'Storytelling that moves people: A conversation with screenwriting coach Robert McKee,' *Harvard Business Review*, http://web.mit.edu/tibbetts/Public/Storytelling%20That%20Moves%20People.pdf, retrieved October 24, 2020.
39. Jennifer Smoldt, 'Six Essentials for Good Storytelling – and Great Content Marketing,' *MarketingProfs* (August 18, 2016), www.marketingprofs.com/articles/2016/30493/six-essentials-for-good-storytelling-and-great-content-marketing, retrieved August 25, 2016.
40. David Aaker, '14 reasons your brand needs signature stories,' *Marketing News* (January, 2018), pp. 18–19.

41. Mike Shultz, 'The Power of Storytelling in Sales,' www.rainsalestraining.com/blog/the-power-of-storytelling-in-sales, retrieved October 21, 2020.

42. Jake Athey, 'Storytelling: Out of the campfire and into your marketing campaign' (April 13, 2016), www.marketingprofs.com/articles/2016/29729/storytelling-out-of-the-campfire-and-into-your-marketing-campaign, retrieved August 25, 2016.

43. L.L. Bean, 'Handmade in the USA,' www.llbean.com/llb/shop/516565?page=small-batch-bean-boot-lander&nav=CT0t516565-506697, retrieved October 21, 2020.

44. 50 Campfires, 'Story of L.L. Bean and the Maine Hunting Shoe,' https://50campfires.com/story-l-l-bean-maine-hunting-shoe, retrieved October 21, 2020.

45. David Aaker (2018) *Creating Signature Stories* (New York: Morgan James Publishing), p. 11.

46. Brian Peters, '6 Rules of Great Storytelling (As Told by Pixar)' (March 21, 2018), https://medium.com/@Brian_G_Peters/6-rules-of-great-storytelling-as-told-by-pixar-fcc6ae225f50, retrieved October 24, 2020.

47. Adapted from Laurence Vincent (2002) *Legendary Brands: Unleashing the Power of Storytelling to Create a Winning Market Strategy* (Chicago: Dearborn Trade Publishing), p. 55.

48. Jake Athey, 'Storytelling: Out of the campfire and into your marketing campaign' (April 13, 2016), www.marketingprofs.com/articles/2016/29729/storytelling-out-of-the-campfire-and-into-your-marketing-campaign, retrieved August 25, 2016.

49. Laurence Vincent (2002) *Legendary Brands: Unleashing the Power of Storytelling to Create a Winning Market Strategy* (Chicago: Dearborn Trade Publishing), p. 52.

50. Ibid., p. 55.

51. Brian Peters, '6 Rules of Great Storytelling (As Told by Pixar)' (March 21, 2018), https://medium.com/@Brian_G_Peters/6-rules-of-great-storytelling-as-told-by-pixar-fcc6ae225f50, retrieved October 24, 2020.

52. Seth Godin (2005) *All Marketers Are Liars: The Power of Telling Authentic Stories in a Low-Trust World* (New York: Penguin Books), p. 121.

8

MANAGING CONFLICT AND NEGOTIATING WITH FINESSE

Lisa Spiller and Linda Ficht

CHAPTER CONTENTS

PEOPLE, PRACTICES AND PERSPECTIVES FROM THE WORLD OF SALES

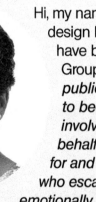

Hello, my name is Richard Jamieson and I'm Senior Director of Partnerships with New Statesman Media Group. While I'm based in London, UK, my sales territory includes the UK, Europe, and North America. My goal is to ensure that my territories hit sales and revenue targets. I have 19 years of experience with increasing levels of responsibility from sales executive to sales manager to sales director. *In my experience, the ability to articulate an argument and persuade someone to your point of view is the number one skill you need. This is closely followed by having thick skin, self motivatation, and well-honed communication skills.* 'Our greatest weakness lies in giving up. The most certain way to succeed is always to try just one more time' (Thomas Edison.)

Hi, my name is Paula Kosko. I'm a former graphic design business owner and for the past 16 years, have been a realtor with RE/MAX Real Estate Group in Erie, Pennsylvania. *If you work with the public as I do, an important skill to develop is to become a calm negotiator. Almost every sale involves negotiation – either for yourself or on behalf of your client. Knowing how to calmly ask for and get the desired outcome is key. Those who escalate and inflame a negotiation by getting emotionally charged rarely succeed. My advice to you as you interact with prospective customers is this: Be a calming influence and be their friend. Gain their trust by telling them something helpful that other salespeople would not share with them. That's what I call* **great** *customer service!*

Hello, I'm Robert Wagner, vice president and equity owner of Beskin-Divers Insurance Group located in Virginia Beach, Virginia. I am responsible for new business in commercial services nationally, but with a specific focus on the mid-Atlantic region (North Carolina, Virginia, and Maryland). With seven years of experience in the sales field, *I've learned that there will always be certain objections you cannot forecast, so continually practicing how you'll respond to objections will allow you to be sharp and composed. I've found that the better response to an objection is often less about the subject content and more about making the prospect feel confident in your ability to solve a problem.*

The customer is always right!

EYES ON ETHICS

Keep in mind the following ethical topics as you read through this chapter:

1. Determining what information to share verbally and what information the buyer can read about in the contract.
2. Determining what to do when you identify that a buyer lacks the ability to make a sound decision, due either to lack of experience or information.

INTRODUCTION

All salespeople encounter both questions and objections from the customer or prospect at some point throughout the stages of the sales process. Likewise, conflict or disagreement will likely occur during the selling conversation, along with the need to negotiate or bargain to arrive at a satisfactory sales outcome. Like it or not, conflict and negotiation are both normal and integral parts of the selling process, and they are the topic of this chapter. Objections will be explored further in Chapter 9.

Learning techniques and skills to address objections, manage conflict, and engage in productive negotiations will take the fear out of these critical aspects of selling. In all cases and situations, the most important rule for salespeople to follow is: Never argue with a customer. The customer is always right. Period. If you argue and put the customer on the defensive, you may win the argument, but you will never make the sale. Thus, you will fail to create a customer. Keep in mind that the goal in modern selling is to create a customer. Successful selling is all about building, strengthening, and retaining relationships with customers. Be sure to view the material presented here through the lens that providing *value* to customers and solving their problems are the main objectives of selling. Value is the relative worth, utility, or importance of something compared to its cost of acquisition. Sharing your knowledge and expertise with customers adds value beyond that of the actual product you may be selling. Selling isn't always easy, and this chapter explores that stage of the sales process where deals are often made or lost.

In order to make progress toward a sale, salespeople should always try to get customers focused on solutions as opposed to the problem itself. Salespeople should involve customers in the problem-solving process by constantly seeking out their opinions on options to solve their problems. By getting customers to focus on finding solutions together, salespeople can often avoid conflict. However, proactively avoiding conflict is not always possible. In fact, conflict often does occur, and can actually lead to positive outcomes, as we'll discuss in the next section of this chapter.

MANAGING CONFLICT

Conflict has been defined as the behaviors or feelings that one or both parties have when the other party has the potential to or actually obstructs, interferes with, or makes less effective a party's behaviors associated with reaching their goals in a relationship.[1] Common synonyms of the word 'conflict' include battle, fight, struggle, and skirmish. Note that these words imply a negative event or activity. However, that is an unproductive way to view conflict in selling situations. A few of the common myths regarding conflict are the beliefs that conflict is always avoidable, causes polarization, and creates inappropriate reactions.[2] In fact, conflict is not always avoidable, nor does it have to cause polarization or inappropriate reactions.

Conflicted customer

Encountering and understanding conflict

Conflict may be characterized as either constructive, which yields positive outcomes, or destructive, which results in negative experiences. Constructive conflict, also referred to as 'productive conflict,' enables salespeople to address disagreement and resolve the conflicts that arise during the selling process, so that the salespeople and their respective buyers can work together in a mutually satisfying manner. Constructive conflict can encourage creativity, open you up to new points of view, clear the air, and lead to better decision making, whereas destructive conflict can damage relationships, create barriers that weren't there before, increase expenses, and lead to poor business decisions.[3] Of course, salespeople striving to build or strengthen relationships with their customers should always work to make conflict constructive.

There are three types of conflict that salespeople need to understand – inner, interpersonal, and group.[4] Each type of conflict evolves from different root causes, such as differences in individuals' values, perceptions, beliefs, and facts. Inner conflict is brought on by challenges to your own ethics, your integrity, and what you personally value. Interpersonal conflict is conflict that occurs between two or more people due to differences in personalities, values, cultures, and so on, or due to communication breakdown. Lastly, group conflict occurs when there are differences between groups, such as different goals, roles, ideologies, resources, and so on, or due to communication breakdown. The most common type of conflict that emerges throughout the selling process is interpersonal conflict, or conflict between the salesperson and the buyer. Let's now explore each type of conflict in greater detail.

Inner conflict

All of us have this to some degree or another. It shows up usually as nervousness, anxiety, and self-talk that says things such as: 'Who am I to think I can convince the prospect to buy my product/service?' or 'I don't have the skills to answer all the questions or handle the objections the prospect might have,' or 'The prospect may try to bully or manipulate me and make me give concessions on price or content of my solution that later I'll regret.'

This inner anxiety may be diluted by first recognizing it as butterflies in our stomach, heavy breathing, or even shaky hands. Once recognized, you must regain control. How? By reviewing the messages that your inner voice is saying and then telling yourself that this isn't a 'tug of war' but a chance to engage in simple communication with another person. In fact, the other person may also be experiencing inner conflict as well. Thus, you may strive to reduce both their and your unsettling emotions. An effective way to do this is by being upfront and stating at the beginning of the conflict resolution interaction that, 'I'm a bit unsettled about the upcoming sales discussion because of the emotion that might show up. So, can we please agree to remind each other to get back to the facts and/or issues around the sales proposition in case either of us senses things getting more emotional than what we intend?' This usually has the effect of causing the conversation to become more of a project to be worked on by both parties. This 'team' effort usually makes the discussions much more reasonable and reduces the inner stress that salespeople often feel when dealing with potential customers.[5]

Interpersonal conflict

In a sales situation, this can be addressed by 'listening with your eyes.' This means that we all aware of and notice body language, or the tone or tempo of a voice that indicates discomfort, anger, or confusion. A universal way to reduce this is to 'assume' in your communications with your prospect that you are the cause of their discomfort. When you sense this, it may be effective to say, 'It looks like something I said may have made you uncomfortable (or upset, confused, angry, etc.). Am I right about that?'

This clarifying approach gives prospects the space to say 'yes' or tell what might be on their mind. This approach doesn't always cause prospects to open up, but it will come across to them that you are sensitive to their reactions and willing to assume responsibility. What this does is actually enhance the relationship and encourage the prospect to be more open with you in the future; which always helps the ultimate resolution, whether a future sale or not.[6]

Group conflict

The critical action in managing conflict among a group is to assume control of the gathering by setting the agenda of the meeting and the guidelines of how individuals within the group will interact with each other. Then, the salesperson can become the facilitator of the discussion and overseer of the mode of communications in the group within the meeting. Here's an example:

> *Salesperson*: 'Thanks for being here and these are the items (topics) that we are planning to cover today. While I realize everyone likely has a position on these discussion topics, it is important that everyone be heard. Therefore, I will attempt to remind those who want to speak to allow another who is talking to complete their point. I will also ask speakers who may, in their enthusiasm, dominate the conversation to complete their thought so that others may weigh in.'

Setting just these two expectations from above will allow the salesperson to appear professional and be a welcome resource for a more productive discussion.[7]

All conflict comes with serious outcomes or consequences for salespeople. These outcomes can be classified into three different categories: lose-lose, win-lose, or win-win.[8] Lose-lose conflict is where salespeople avoid conflict altogether by smoothing over things without ever getting the root problem or issue out into the open to be resolved. Often, lose-lose situations lead to future conflict and don't serve anyone's interests in the long run. The second possible outcome of conflict is a win-lose scenario. This is where only one party gets what they really want. While this situation may work in the short term, the losing party may not be able to live with the resolution in the long term, thus conflict is likely to reoccur in the future and affect potential sales. Lastly, a win-win conflict outcome is the best possible scenario. In win-win situations, problem-solving techniques are used to enable both parties to worth through their differences and arrive at a mutually satisfying solution. Win-win conflict leads to the most positive outcome possible, thus salespeople should strive for win-win scenarios when dealing with conflict. Let's now investigate some additional techniques that salespeople may use when dealing with conflict.

Conflict in selling

Dealing with conflict

Both salespeople and prospective buyers may generate different ideas and approaches to solving a given problem – which often creates conflict. Thus, salespeople must master conflict management techniques and practice them regularly. Conflict management refers to the diagnostic processes, interpersonal styles, and negotiation strategies that are designed to avoid unnecessary conflict and to reduce or resolve excessive conflict.[9] In every selling situation, there will be some form of conflict; at times, it will be subtle and at other times, more volatile. A way to handle these inevitable conflicts will be to use one of the two following questioning approaches:[10]

1. 'Thank you for bringing that point up, (insert person's name). Would you mind sharing what made you make that statement now?'
2. 'I can see the point you're bringing up is important to you. Could you share with me why you felt it important to bring it up now?'

Both approaches seek to determine the 'why behind the what' of the conflict. These two types of gentle questions allow prospects to have space to reflect on why getting an answer to a particular question is important now. This ultimately helps prospects feel you are interested in having them expand on their position, which enhances their trust of the salesperson and helps to reduce the volatility of future conflicts.

In selling, conflict should be seen as a moment of opportunity. Why? Because buyers are communicating their dissatisfaction or dislike with something related to the selling situation which gives you, the salesperson, a chance to resolve whatever is causing the conflict, which will lead to buyer satisfaction and problem solution. Conflict is unlike 'silent complainers': customers who never share their dissatisfaction with a company, but instead spread negative word-of-mouth communication about it. Silent complainers don't give salespeople the chance to address their conflict, which is harmful both to the current selling situation and to future business. All salespeople should welcome open conflict and hope that their customers do not hide or disguise the conflict, so that salespeople are given the opportunity to work with the customer to change the situation in a positive manner for all. Remember, relationships are the key to successful selling.

As a salesperson, you must never lose sight of your end-goal, which is serving your customers by adding value, solving their problems, and enhancing long-term relationships with them. Customers who trust you and feel a real connection with you will be more loyal and may stay with you for a lifetime. Research shows that conflict, when effectively managed, can have a positive effect on relationships and relationship outcomes. Of course, the impact of conflict in selling depends on how you, the salesperson, react to your customer's conflict. Dana Caspersen, author of the book, *Changing the Conversation*, one of the recommended Readings and Resources identified at the end of this chapter, correctly states that 'You can't change how other people act in a conflict, and often you can't change your situation. But you can change what you do.'[11]

The best way to face conflict head on is by arming yourself with information about your buyer's motives and interests. You must use all of the data that you have gathered about your customers during the previous stages of the selling process to really understand their needs, wants, fears, and so on. Perhaps it is worth repeating that 'The Customer is Always Right!' This means that salespeople always need to view conflict through the lens of their customers' eyes.

If you need to conduct additional research to fact-find a certain aspect that is generating the conflict, then do so swiftly and sufficiently. Ask your customers for feedback. Don't assume you have all of the facts. A sincere inquiry about your customer's

Salesperson actively listening to buyer

level of satisfaction can produce valuable insight. Your customers will listen to you if you listen to them first. So, be quick to seek out new information on a regular basis, especially whenever a conflict arises. Ask your customer to explain what is going on and investigate the root source of the conflict. Explore what the conflict encompasses. Seek out authentic stories from your customer to better reveal the depth of the conflict, the situation, and the people involved. Use the insight you gather to begin imagining potential resolutions to the conflict. Resolving conflict is imperative to successful selling, which is the topic of our next section.

Resolving conflict

As previously mentioned, seeking input by asking questions of your customers and actively listening to their answers and explanations is the best way to begin managing and resolving conflict. When actively listening to your customers, listen for something unique and remarkable in every conversation.[12] This unique and remarkable information should be recorded and remembered so that you may use it in subsequent conversations with that customer to drive deeper relationships. Of course, acting upon the information you obtain in your conversations with your customer is critical to successful conflict resolution.

Dana Caspersen offers 17 principles for conflict resolution which are categorized along three ordered stages: 1. Facilitate listening and speaking; 2. Change the conversation; and 3. Look for ways forward.[13] Caspersen's principles provide practical tools for salespeople to embrace and demonstrate how conflict negatively impacts a relationship, yet conflict resolution paves the way for relationship building and successful selling.

Salespeople may use different strategies when attempting to manage and resolve buyer conflict. Many different conflict management approaches and taxonomies have been proposed over the decades. The most widely recognized conflict handling style model in human resource management today is the Thomas-Kilmann Conflict Mode Instrument, which is based on the conflict management approaches originally developed by Kenneth Thomas.[14] As Figure 8.1 shows, Thomas proposed a taxonomy of five conflict management approaches – avoidance, accommodation, confrontation, compromise, and collaboration – which are arrayed along the two dimensions of level of assertiveness and cooperation.[15] Assertiveness indicates the level of concern for one's own outcomes, while cooperation indicates the level of concern for the other party's outcomes. Let's briefly explore each approach.

- *Avoidance.* This approach is where the salesperson and/or the buyer ignore or fail to consider the conflict that exists between the two parties. This approach is characterized by low assertiveness and low cooperation.
- *Accommodation.* This approach is where the salesperson recognizes conflict and simply gives in to the concerns or viewpoints of the buyer. This approach is characterized by low assertiveness and high cooperation.

- *Confrontation.* This approach is where salespeople emphasize their own perspectives and exclude their buyer's perspective. This approach is characterized by high assertiveness and low cooperation.
- *Compromise.* This approach is where the salesperson and the buyer reach an agreement by making concessions to one another. This approach is characterized by medium assertiveness and medium cooperation.
- *Collaboration.* This approach is where the salesperson and the buyer reach an agreement by exchanging information and working together to explore integrative solutions. This approach is characterized by high assertiveness and high cooperation.

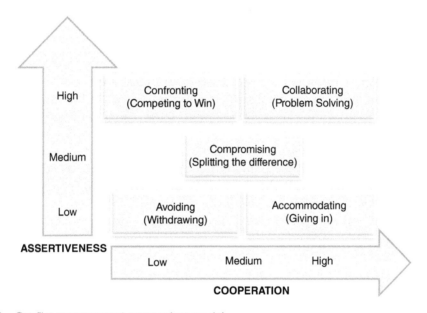

Figure 8.1 Conflict management approaches model

Adapted from Thomas, Kenneth, (1979). "Conflict and Conflict Management." In Handbook of Industrial and Organizational Psychology. Ed. Marvin Dunnette. Palo Alto, CA: Consulting Psychologists Press, 889-935; Hellriegel, D., Slocum, J. W., (2011). Organizational Behavior, (13th ed.). Mason, OH: South-Western Cengage Learning.

As revealed in Figure 8.1, while each of the five approaches vary in the level of assertiveness and cooperation, only two of the five approaches, compromising and collaborating, incorporate concern for both self and other. The compromising approach will include discussions about how to *split* the pie – which is often considered a 'win-lose' situation, while the collaborating approach investigates opportunities to *expand* the pie – which is considered a 'win-win' scenario. The collaborating approach is the most effective approach for resolving conflict in selling as it leads to productive long-term relationships being continued between salespeople and their customers.

It is important to note that there is an appropriate time in which you may use each of the five different styles. For example, confronting is a very heavy-handed, aggressive approach that would not be effective in many circumstances, but it is very effective during a crisis when decisions must be made quickly. Thus, it would be incorrect to surmise that you have one particular style that you will always use when dealing with conflict. You will want to understand all five conflict styles so you know when to use the correct style for the situation you face. However, it is equally important to identify the one style you tend to use on a regular basis. This style is typically based on your personality.

How do you handle conflict? Your effectiveness as a salesperson in handling and resolving conflict has much to do with your own personality style and comfort zone. The next section is intended to help you discover your conflict style through self-assessment and to identify areas for improvement.

Assessing your personal style

In order to determine the conflict style that you predominately use, it is critical that you be honest with yourself as you consider the attributes of each style. Based on your responses after completing the Thomas-Kilmann Conflict Mode Instrument exam, you will be categorized according to your preferences for managing conflict. There is no shame in having any particular style; in fact, you should own your style! Once you understand your style then you will be able to use this knowledge to more effectively negotiate with others. In addition, as you get to know your prospective buyers, you can predict what conflict styles they are likely to use with you in negotiations. This can be a significant advantage for you given that your assessment is accurate. There are also more general personality self-assessment tests you can order online, such as the *Myers-Briggs Type Indicator* (www.mbtionline.com), where your results identify which character and temperament type you have. Most of the questions on these tests evaluate your attitudes, behaviors, and actions when working with other people. Again, there is no right or wrong associated with being any type; type simply reflects your tendency to behave in various ways. Table 8.1 provides a sample of some of the assessment questions.

Table 8.1 Conflict management self-assessment – sample questions

The response options for the following 10 questions are:

Very Unlikely   Unlikely   Likely   Very Likely

1. I am usually firm in pursuing my goals.
2. I try to win my position.
3. I give up on some points in exchange for others.
4. I try to be considerate of other people's wishes.
5. I try to show the logic and benefits of my position.
6. I always lean toward a direct discussion of the problem.
7. I try to avoid creating unpleasantness for myself.
8. I attempt to get all concerns and issues immediately out in the open.
9. I sometimes avoid taking a position that would create controversy.
10. I try not to hurt other people's feelings.

Select either (A) or (B) to respond to the following questions:

---

1. The goal is: (A) Agreement *or* (B) Victory
2. The other party are: (A) Friends *or* (B) Adversaries
3. Regarding concessions: (A) Make concessions to cultivate the friendship, *or*
   (B) Demand concessions as a condition of the relationship
4. Regarding style: (A) Be soft on both the people and the problem, *or*
   (B) Be hard on both the problem and the people
5. Regarding trust: (A) Trust others, *or* (B) Distrust others
6. Regarding positions: (A) Change your position easily, *or* (B) Be reluctant to change your position
7. Regarding agreement: (A) Insist on agreement, *or* (B) Insist on your position
8. Regarding pressure: (A) Yield to pressure, *or* (B) Apply pressure

---

Source: Adapted from Carl Lyons (2007) *I Win You Win: The Essential Guide to Principled Negotiation* (London: A & C Black); and Helene Malmsio (2014) *Workplace Solutions: Exploring Conflict Resolution and Dealing with Difficult People* (Scotts Valley, CA: CreateSpace).

Now let's use the Thomas model (Figure 8.1), which we've discussed in the previous section, to enable you to determine where in the five interpersonal conflict-handling styles you typically fall. First, we must consider the model's two dimensions, which are concern for self and concern for others. Do you have a high level of concern for yourself or others? When you interact with people, do you find yourself being assertive, telling others what you want or need? Are you comfortable asking for what you want? If the answer to these questions is yes, then you are HIGH on concern for self (assertive). However, if you are reticent to ask for what you need, or if you find yourself replacing your own needs with the needs of others, you are LOW on concern for self (unassertive).

Now, let's consider your concern for others. Do you find yourself thinking of the needs of others, wondering how you can help other people, desiring to make life easier for others? If the answer to these questions is yes, you are HIGH on concern for others (cooperative). However, if you do not concern yourself with the needs of others, you are LOW on concern for others (uncooperative).

Now, we put the two dimensions together to see which quadrant you fall into, according to Thomas's model (Figure 8.1). If you have a high level of concern for yourself and a low level of concern for others, you are in the *competing to win* or *defeating* quadrant. Competing-to-win style is often known as the 'I Win You Lose' model. Salespeople using this conflict resolution style are trying to meet their own needs and are not concerned about the needs of their buyers. In a negotiation, these salespeople are negotiating for the best deal they can get and do not care if it is a bad deal for their buyers. This type of deal making in business is only good in the short run. As discussed elsewhere in this chapter, typically when we negotiate in business, we must consider that we will be dealing with this party many times in the future. Using a defeating style of negotiation will create a winner and a loser. Today, you may be the winner in this negotiation but the next time you may be the loser. This style relies on power to achieve its results. If you are in a position of power, you are able to use the defeating style. This may be positional power, such as you being the owner of the business, or it may be power derived from the negotiation itself, such as you needing the deal less than the buyer. If you have more bargaining power, you will have more ability to use a defeating style. However, use this style with caution. Salespeople who tend to use the defeating style are not well liked, tend to receive lower evaluations from others, and are considered coercive. The competing-to-win style may lead to you developing a difficult reputation and other prospective buyers may not be willing to deal with you in the future. In addition, prospective buyers will not trust you as they know you only care about yourself. The defeating style often ignores other options or makes prospective buyers fearful of bringing up alternative solutions. As mentioned previously, there are times when defeating style is a useful conflict style. This is primarily when we are in a crisis situation or need to break an impasse quickly.

If you have a high level of concern for yourself and a high level of concern for others, you are in the *collaborating* quadrant. The collaborating style is the style salespeople should typically strive for in today's business world. It creates 'win-win' solutions and maximizes the potential of the negotiation; and it builds trust and candor, which lead to long-term business relationships. When everyone is satisfied with the deal, it is far more likely that there will be buy-in and commitment to the deal being completed as expected. This will lead to less conflict after the negotiation. This conflict style takes more planning, work, and emotional commitment than all the other styles because you are trying to meet a variety of needs in one deal. You must remain open and honest throughout the process. When using this style, it is important that all parties are committed to the style. If you, the salesperson, attempt to use this style with a prospective buyer that insists on a defeating style, you will be exploited by the other party. This conflict style works best with both parties, the salesperson and the prospective buyer, having power parity.

If you have a low level of concern for yourself and a high level of concern for others, you are in the *accommodating* quadrant. The accommodating style represents a selfless person, who puts the relationship before everything else. This type of style is best used when you (or your company) have made a serious mistake and need to rectify it to maintain or repair the customer relationship. It is almost always a bad idea to use the accommodating style with highly competitive-style negotiators because they will take advantage of you. They will see you as weak instead of generous. Accommodating-style salespeople get high praise from others and tend to be well liked; however, they are not highly respected by buyers because they are viewed as being weak and submissive.

If you have a low level of concern for yourself and a low level of concern for others, then you are in the *avoiding* quadrant. The avoiding-style person is someone who does not like conflict. If you find yourself trying to get out of disagreements, trying to stay neutral, trying to avoid confrontation with others, then you have an avoiding conflict style. The avoiding style is definitely useful when there are low-stakes conflicts at play.

You realize that it is not worth arguing over this very minor issue, whereas those with other conflict styles will engage in a conflict on this issue. However, generally speaking, avoiding conflict is very bad for business. Ignoring conflicts will allow problems to fester and become worse. Problems do not typically go away on their own. They must be dealt with. Conflict should not be considered a negative aspect of life or business; however, it is often perceived as such. Rather than thinking about conflict as a negative, think of conflict as an opportunity for growth. It is through the conflict that we learn new or better ways of dealing with issues and problems. Thus, conflict should be embraced and not avoided. If you are a conflict avoider, try to see how the conflict might help you learn something new or grow in a new skill. Find the positive in the conflict and it will be far less stressful to encounter.

The midrange of having concern for yourself and others is called *compromising*. Interestingly, this is where most people believe that negotiations should sit; however, that is generally incorrect. In a compromise, neither the buyers, nor the salespeople, get what they truly want. Each party must give up something valuable to reach the deal. This form of conflict style is considered wasteful because it does not maximize the potential of the negotiation.

To illustrate the point about compromise, let's visit the well-known story of two daughters and an orange. One day, a mother came upon her daughters arguing over who should have the last orange. The mother took the orange from the girls, cut it in half and gave half each to the girls. This seems to be a pretty good resolution since they both got to enjoy half of what they wanted. However, if the mother had taken the time to ask each girl *why* she wanted the orange, the mother could have come up with a better solution that maximized the potential use of the orange. For example, if the mother had asked the older daughter why she wanted the orange, the daughter would have said that she wanted to eat the fruit. If the mother had asked the younger daughter why she wanted the orange, she would have found out that she wanted the orange peel for a recipe. Had the mother taken the time to speak to both daughters and understand their respective needs and interests, she would have found a more ideal solution that met the needs of both daughters, without wasting the orange. After communicating with both daughters, the mother could have suggested that the orange peel go to the younger daughter and the fruit to the older. This is why compromise is not an ideal solution. Compromise should only be engaged in AFTER enough communication has taken place to determine that there is *not* a better way to maximize the potential agreement.

Now that you know what conflict is, recognize the importance placed on understanding conflict from the perspective of your customer, know how to both manage and resolve conflict, and hopefully have an inclination of your own personal conflict style, let's tackle negotiating. It's not enough to comprehend that conflict exists and be able to identify the source and situation, you must negotiate to rectify the situation and resolve the conflict in order to successfully move forward in the selling process.

Resolving conflict with buyer

NEGOTIATING

Negotiation is defined as a process whereby two parties seek to find a mutually accept-able solution or outcome to a complex conflict.[16] This definition implies a 'win-win' situation in resolving conflict, which aligns with cooperation, compromise, and conciliation, which are common synonyms of negotiating. Negotiating is a process of give-and-take for everyone involved. Looking for common ground is critical in effective negotiating. However, research shows that four out of five people don't look for common ground in negotiations and instead look to grow value for themselves.[17] Being a good negotiator means being a good communicator, as well as being an ethical and empathetic leader.

Understanding the nature of negotiations

According to John Patrick Dolan, author of *Negotiate Like the Pros*, negotiation is one of the most commonly practiced functions of communication; however, it is often the least understood. Sadly, many salespeople have an incorrect view of what negotiating entails. Dolan claims that there are seven myths about negotiation that hinder salespeople from enjoying the negotiating experience.[18] Let's examine these and dispel the myths:

- *Myth 1: In order to be a successful negotiator, you must be a cutthroat.* This statement in completely false. Salespeople should view negotiation as an opportunity for both parties to benefit from the derived outcome.
- *Myth 2: Negotiating is synonymous with fighting.* Not true. Fights may break out when people cannot negotiate, so by mastering the strategies of negotiation, conflicts will be settled and fights will be avoided.
- *Myth 3:* Negotiating is a talent reserved for shrewd businesspeople, experienced diplomats and precocious children. Incorrect. Anyone can learn to negotiate effectively without being a genius, or manipulative.

- *Myth 4: When you sit down at the bargaining table, you must abandon all ethics to get what you want.* This statement is just plain wrong. Ethical negotiation is the only form of negotiating that should take place in today's modern world of sales. Besides, by understanding negotiation, you can prevent being conned into things you don't want to do, or getting less than you deserve.
- *Myth 5: You must have the upper hand to negotiate effectively.* Not true. If you perceive negotiation as involving one party trying to beat the other one out of a good deal, then you have an inaccurate perception of most negotiation processes that take place in selling.
- *Myth 6: Negotiating is a time-wasting activity that only clogs the wheels of progress.* In fact, the opposite is true. Negotiation is a timesaver because it makes everyone work together to find solutions.
- *Myth 7: Negotiating is always a formal process with clearly defined parameters and procedures.* In reality, negotiating may take many different forms and most people engage in informal negotiating frequently, often without even realizing it.

Negotiation is a fact of life and it is an important part of the selling process. Although every negotiation situation is different, the basic elements of negotiating don't change. Thus, in order for salespeople to become effective negotiators, they must correctly understand the practices and process associated with negotiation, which begins with understanding the differences between the various methods used to negotiate.

Many salespeople believe that there are two extreme ways or methods to negotiate with their prospective buyers: hard versus soft. Soft negotiators want to avoid conflict, so they easily make concessions to please their customer. Often, these concessions leave some salespeople feeling frustrated and dissatisfied with the transaction. On the other hand, hard negotiators take an extreme position and see the situation as a contest of wills in which the side that holds out longest basically wins.[19] Often, salespeople using hard negotiating end up damaging their relationships with their customers, which is a fatal mistake in selling. All other methods used in negotiating tend to fall somewhere in between hard and soft, but these methods normally require a trade-off to occur between getting what is really desired versus preserving the relationship between the two parties.

For example, in a distributive negotiation, also known as *competitive bargaining*, two negotiating parties will use strategies and tactics to attain their respective goals and to maximize their share of the outcome to the detriment of the other party. In a distributive negotiation situation, the goals of one party are usually in fundamental and direct conflict with the goals of the other party. Resources are normally fixed and limited, and both parties want to maximize their share.[20] This represents a 'win-lose' situation in selling, where either the buyer or salesperson will not be satisfied, thus the overall relationship will be injured as a result of the distributive negotiation process.

However, there is another way to negotiate which is *neither* hard nor soft, but rather *both* hard and soft. This method is called principled negotiation, which was developed at the Harvard Negotiation Project. Principled negotiation, also called *consultative negotiation*, can be defined as deciding issues on their merits rather than through a haggling process focused on what each side says it will and won't do. Using the principled negotiation method requires salespeople to consider all of the issues and look for mutual gains whenever possible.[21] And, if/when conflict arises between the two parties, the solution should be based on some fair standards independent of the will of either party. The basic premise of principled negotiation is to protect the legitimate interests of both parties. This method strives to safeguard the relationship between salespeople and their respective customers at all times, and instills fairness in the process of negotiating so that both parties are satisfied with the final outcome. Thus, principled negotiations lead to 'win-win' outcomes and are normally the preferred way to negotiate in most selling situations.

Negotiation in selling can be a challenging process when salespeople don't know the true needs and wants of their prospective customers. Information is power. The more information salespeople gather about their customers, the more effective and successful the negotiation process will be for both parties. Examining all of the information gathered about the prospective buyer and identifying what additional information is needed, are critical to successful negotiation. Discovering what the customer wants in the negotiation process will lead to greater negotiation success.

Salespeople must dig deep to unearth valuable customer information beyond the obvious product or service specifications, in order to fuel successful negotiation in selling. Get personal. Find out something personal about your prospective buyers and their lives, not just about their businesses. Find out what motivates them, what annoys them, what they value in life, hobbies, interests, and so on. You'll be surprised at how well you can leverage personal information when negotiating. Research shows that the top factor that separates top-performing salespeople from the rest is understanding the power and leverage held by each side in negotiations.[22]

Salesperson preparing to negotiate

Of course, this personal information includes knowing both the social style (Talker, Doer, Controller, or Supporter), and the dominant mode of language communication (Visual, Auditory, or Kinesthetic) of each prospective buyer, as previously discussed in Chapter 5. Knowing the buyer's social style and dominant mode of language communication will enable you to more effectively prepare to engage in more meaningful conversation with your prospective buyer. Remember, you must alter your communication to match or mirror that of your prospective buyer.

In addition to gathering information, proper planning and preparation are also needed to ensure successful negotiation. Let's discuss how salespeople should plan and prepare for negotiations.

Planning and preparing for negotiations

The keys to successful negotiation are preparation, experience, and confidence. You cannot just study negotiation techniques and become a master negotiator. You master negotiation skills by negotiating. It is only over time that salespeople may become skillful negotiators. Let's discuss each.

Preparation

Salespeople cannot just show up to a negotiation and begin stating terms and conditions. In order to have a successful negotiation, they must engage in a great deal of research. First, they must determine what their needs and interests are in this negotiation. What are the basic issues that they must address? They must determine how badly they need this deal, what other alternatives exist, and what are the necessary aspects of the deal. Then, they need to research the other party, the prospective buyer. They need to figure out what the buyer's needs and interests are so they can devise a negotiation plan that meets everyone's needs and interests. People often underestimate the amount of time it takes to prepare for a negotiation. Remember this: If you are underprepared, it will be readily apparent to the other side and you will be unable to maximize your negotiation outcome. In addition, people often make the mistake of not trying to understand what the other party needs in a negotiation. Rather, people focus on the stated position that the other party is making, rather than looking through that to determine the need that underlies the position. By focusing on the need rather than the position, savvy salespeople are able to directly address what the party is after, even if the party does not realize it themselves. All effective negotiations begin long before you actually sit down at the bargaining table with your prospective buyer. Planning and preparing for a negotiation are necessary and can make the difference between the success or failure of the negotiation process. Completing a negotiation preparation worksheet, such as that shown in the example in Figure 8.2, will help the salesperson to prepare for and articulate the details of the negotiation.

Today's date:		Date of negotiation:	
Parties in the negotiation:	Key decision makers:	Potential influencers:	
Background and perceptions			
Ours:		The other party:	
Objectives			
Ours:		The other party:	
Negotiable issues			
Ours:		The other party:	
Challenges, obstacles, areas of potential conflict			
Ours:		The other party:	
Methods to manage and resolve potential conflicts			
Apparent conflicts:		Real conflicts:	
Information to be exchanged			
Information you need:		Information they need:	
First meeting planning notes			
(Negotiation timeline, physical location, draft agenda, question sequence, etc.)			

Figure 8.2 Negotiation planning worksheet

Although the issues to address when planning for a negotiation may vary by company and situation, they typically include some of the following:[23]

- identifying the parties directly involved
- identifying buyer influencers
- understanding the legitimate interests of each party
- clarifying the information that is needed to protect the interests of both parties
- setting guidelines to ensure that both parties operate under the same standards
- drafting the agenda for each negotiation
- preparing the sequence of questions to be asked
- examining the potential hindrances on each side to reaching a solution
- agreeing on the negotiation timeline
- determining the physical location where the negotiations will take place
- determining with the other party what would constitute a win-win conclusion to the negotiation
- understanding the differences between the other party's position and their interests
- always starting by articulating your perception of the other's interest and verifying with them that you are correct.

As part of their preparation for negotiation, salespeople may obtain formal training to hone their negotiation capabilities and increase their confidence in negotiating. Research shows that top-performing salespeople are 9.3 times more likely to receive extremely effective negotiation training than the rest of the salespeople. In addition, buyers are 1.5 times more likely than sellers to have received extremely effective negotiation training.[24] These statistics support the notion that obtaining effective negotiation training is highly desirable to master the art and science of negotiation.

Experience

Of course, the more practice you have negotiating, the better the negotiator you will become. Many people seem afraid to negotiate initially. They worry about looking bad, being embarrassed, or being told 'no.' Research suggests that many women in particular are afraid to engage in negotiation. Preparing for negotiation will help you feel more comfortable engaging in it. As you engage in more negotiations, you will have less apprehension. You should put yourself in a position to negotiate as often as possible to help you quickly hone your skills. A great way to do this is in a low-stakes environment, such as a farmer's market, flea market, or garage sale. This will allow you the ability to engage with someone who is wishing to make a sale and to practice your negotiation skills to negotiate the terms of an agreement. The skill used in these instances is distributive bargaining, which will be covered later in this chapter. Whenever you have the opportunity to engage in a negotiation, you should take it.

Negotiating success

Confidence

If you conduct good research and negotiate as often as possible, you will gain a great deal of confidence in yourself while negotiating. Confidence is a very strong signal to the other party that you are a highly trained professional. Acting confident, even when you are nervous, is an important skill to develop, as it will help you improve your negotiation outcomes. Another way to improve your confidence is to engage a negotiation mentor. A negotiation mentor is an experienced negotiator in your field that you can learn from and interact with as you develop your negotiation skills. As you enter your chosen profession, take some time to look around and see who the people are that seem to be doing the types of deals you would like to do in the future. Find a way to get to know them and ask if they would be willing to mentor you in negotiating skills. A negotiation mentor will assist your skill development and give you an important opportunity to network within your profession.

Successful negotiators are confident in their abilities. They trust their preparation. They understand the needs and interests of all parties and use their experience and preparation to come up with creative negotiations that will leave everyone satisfied with the deal. Both training and practice can also help to increase both the skill in and comfort level of negotiating for salespeople. Negotiating is much like the game of chess where each decision or move counts in the ultimate outcome of the game. However, unlike the game of chess, one party does not have to 'win' while the other loses. Remember, in selling situations, the objective is a 'win-win' scenario for both salespeople and their customers. One way to avoid making the wrong move when negotiating is to be aware of what to avoid. Here are 10 common mistakes to avoid when negotiating in selling:[25]

1. *Lacking preparation.* Preparation will ensure that you are aptly equipped to assert mutually desirable terms, anticipate objections, and discern the motivators or 'hot buttons' that will resonate with your prospective buyer.
2. *Lacking confidence.* Projecting confidence is important as it shows compassion, which is an endearing and attractive quality. Confidence can lead to your prospective buyer feeling more amenable to whatever you are offering. Of course, backing up your confidence with sincerity and well-researched information will lead to success.
3. *Thinking something is non-negotiable.* The mindset you need to have in negotiating is that *everything* is negotiable. Nearly everything may be modified if you propose an ethical, viable, and mutually beneficial alternative solution.
4. *Not building relationships first.* This is probably one of the biggest mistakes that salespeople make with regard to negotiation. Salespeople need to make real connections with other people, especially those who may become a prospective buyer. Much useful information can be obtained during casual conversation.
5. *Not employing fair, objective criteria.* The perception of fairness is important in selling negotiations as it helps prospective buyers to independently and objectively determine the value that you, the salesperson, provide. Salespeople should liberally use fair, objective criteria, such as market value, efficiency, costs, or expert opinion when negotiating with prospective buyers.
6. *Not asking for what you want.* People naturally fear rejection or were taught not to be 'greedy' as children, so most salespeople instinctively refrain from asking for what they want. In selling, rejection is not personal, but rather is a reflection of the

fact that you, the salesperson, did not present a viable argument substantiating why your prospective buyer should agree to purchase what you are selling.

7. *Talking too much*. Salespeople need to learn how and when to stop talking, as well as how to become comfortable with the awkwardness of silence. Never underestimate the power of silence. Talking too much can be a sure-fire way to lose a sale and alienate a prospective customer. Salespeople should avoid using phrases that thwart idea generation (see the tips on this in Table 8.2).

8. *Not controlling the agenda*. Salespeople need to learn how to effectively manage the negotiation process, which includes knowing when to use deadlines and how to get the prospective buyer to perceive the value in spending time having a conversation with you.

9. *Not documenting things*. Placing the terms of the customer's agreement in writing documents the commitment they have made with you. Written documents eliminate potential perception and/or memory problems whereby each side 'thinks' this is what the other side said and/or intended. Documenting the final agreement protects the interest of all parties involved.

10. *Signing without reading*. Fully and completely reading every document or contract before you sign on the dotted line is imperative. Most salespeople are excellent at multi-tasking and can complete many different activities at the same time. However, taking time to carefully read documents before signing is just plain old good business practice.

Table 8.2 Killer phrases to avoid when negotiating

❖ Yeah, but …

❖ We've tried that before

❖ That's irrelevant

❖ Clearly, you haven't read my request

❖ Don't bother wasting time thinking about it

❖ It will never fly

❖ Don't be ridiculous

❖ It seems like more trouble than it's worth

❖ You can't teach an old dog new tricks

❖ Let's just stick with what works

❖ You've got to be kidding me

❖ Don't you realize how much paperwork it will create?

Source: Adapted from C. Thompson (1992) *What a Great Idea: The Four Key Steps Creative People Take* (Harper Perennial).

In summary, knowing what mistakes to avoid will enable salespeople to be more effective and successful in their negotiations, as will in obtaining relevant information, completing negotiation training, and practicing their negotiation skills. Now let's examine the process that effective negotiators usually follow.

Examining the negotiation process

Remember that the negotiation process really began back with planning and preparing for the actual negotiation. Without proper planning, salespeople will not likely be successful in any negotiation process. However, proper preparation enables salespeople to plan for the following five-step negotiation process.

Step 1: Validating buyer motives and interests

The first step of the process requires salespeople to review all the research that they have gathered about their prospective buyers and to validate it to be sure that changes have not occurred since the data was first collected. Salespeople should widely review all relevant buyer information, which includes, but is not limited to, the following: buyer motives, interests, needs, wants, hopes, fears, concerns, values, goals, influencers, environment, and situation. Understanding your prospective buyer from both a business perspective, with knowledge about their business, goals, stressors, trends, and competitors, and in terms of personal information, will not only increase your negotiation effectiveness, but also enhance your opportunity to form a solid relationship with that customer. Posing questions and relying on your active listening skills to really comprehend what your prospective buyer needs and wants, are the key to successful validation. Put yourself in your prospective buyer's shoes and approach negotiation from their perspective as well as your own.

Step 2: Generating options in search of a solution

Salespeople should work with their prospective buyers in generating options that may solve their respective problems and meet their needs and wants. There's an old saying: 'People will support that which they help to create.' This saying implies that if salespeople involve their prospective buyers in the process of generating ideas, they are more likely to support those ideas. Keep in mind that salespeople aren't limited to involving just the prospective buyer, but rather, anyone who may have an interest or role in the decision-making process may be included. By involving others in the search for solutions, salespeople will be able not only to generate more options, but also to strengthen the relationship with their prospective buyers and customers.

Brainstorming is an excellent strategy to use in generating options. Negotiation should be viewed as a collaborative, problem-solving process, ideally an open book.[26] Part of the brainstorming process is to offer suggestions just to see where the idea might lead. So, phrases such as *'Let's think of a few possibilities'* may be used effectively to begin the brainstorming process. During the brainstorming session, salespeople may ask 'what if' questions for exploration to help generate options. Questions such as *'What if you were to give us X, what would you need from us in return?'* or perhaps, *'What if we were to give you Y, what could you give us in return?'* may work to throw ideas out to be explored.[27] Effective questioning, as discussed in Chapter 6, allows salespeople to collect even more information from prospective customers. Of course, salespeople must use active listening when brainstorming with prospective buyers.

Step 3: Applying objective standards when bargaining

If you are seeking a mutually beneficial solution, then both parties, salespeople and their prospective buyers, must play the negotiation game according to the same set of rules. These rules must be objective, which means they must be impartial, neutral, and unbiased. When the standards or rules are mutually agreed upon in advance of negotiating or bargaining, then the negotiation process runs more smoothly as both parties are operating under the same set of standards or rules. Once the terms have been settled, salespeople should recap all of the important details and make sure that everyone's perceptions match. Whenever possible, salespeople may introduce standards that they have adopted from external sources, such as by governmental law. Of course, laws are always changing, so the standards used must be kept current in order to be relevant and meaningful.

Step 4: Obtaining commitment and establishing implementation procedures

Too often, agreements made during negotiations between salespeople and their prospective buyers start to unravel once the two parties leave the negotiation table. That is because there is a difference between 'agreement' and 'commitment.' An agreement implies an arrangement, treaty, or pact, while a commitment refers to a promise, pledge, vow, or obligation. Salespeople need to ensure that agreements made during the negotiation have buyer commitment. When people commit to a decision, they normally feel a strong sense of duty to uphold it.

Once the salesperson has reached a mutually satisfying agreement with the prospective buyer, it is imperative for the salesperson to recap the terms to which both parties have agreed. Salespeople must confirm that the perceptions of what has been agreed upon between both parties are identical. Placing the terms of the agreement in writing, such as in a contract, for everyone to review, is one sure way to avoid confusion, flush out any areas of uncertainty or difference, and guarantee that the two parties have a homogeneous understanding of the commitment being made. The salesperson can earn trust by carrying out a successful negotiation process which maximizes value for both parties involved. Agreeing on the terms of the sales contract should naturally signal the end of the negotiations and the beginning of the next stage of the selling process, which is closing the sale and obtaining buyer commitment. Keep in mind that the end goal of the negotiation process is not an agreement or a commitment, but rather a long-term relationship with that customer.

Step 5: Understanding when you need to walk away

All salespeople need to be able to recognize the point when the agreement is not likely to be made in good faith that serves the interest of both the seller and the buyer. Salespeople who are not emotionally able to say *'That's OK, I don't think we can find something that is agreeable to both of us at this time'* and walk away, will end up making a commitment that they will regret in the long run, and maybe even sooner. Put it this way: if you, the salesperson, are not able to know when to walk away, then you will likely end up conceding too much and giving everything away.[28]

If you've tried everything you can to create a collaborative agreement with your prospective buyers, but they are being very difficult and not willing to budge from their position, then you need to be willing to walk away. You need to remain in control of your behavior and not become hostile in response to an aggressive prospective buyer. Keep in mind the long-term goal of building the relationship and if you decide to walk away, be sure to leave options open for future discussions at some point. In other words, don't 'burn bridges' because people and situations may change over time. But remember, walk away *before* you accept a sub-optimal outcome.

At any time, if the negotiation process reaches a sticky point or stalls out, there are methods salespeople can use to get the negotiation back on track. For example, to help move the conversation in a desirable direction, Simon Horton, author of *The Leader's Guide to Negotiation*, suggests salespeople use the following five phrases:[29]

1. 'So, let's think of a few possibilities'
2. 'What if …'
3. 'I really like your idea that …'
4. 'So, let's get back to the bigger picture'
5. 'I'm prepared to continue talking in good faith.'

The objective here is to keep the negotiation conversation positive and moving forward. Negotiating often entails bargaining in order to reach an agreement between two parties. Let's now investigate bargaining in greater detail.

Making agreement

Developing bargaining skills

Bargaining refers to back-and-forth communication to arrive at the terms of a purchase, agreement, or contract. Bargaining deals with competitive, win-lose situations such as haggling over the price of a product.[30] Common synonyms of the word bargaining include bartering, trading, and brokering. While some people view bargaining as meaning the same as negotiating, we will separate the two terms. You might think of it this way – negotiating implies a *win-win* selling situation and is used in principled negotiations, while bargaining implies a *win-lose* selling situation and is used in distributive negotiations. In distributive negotiations, also called distributive bargaining, the goals of one party are in direct conflict with the goals of the other party, and resources are fixed and limited.[31] Thus, the bargaining goal is for each party to maximize their share of a specified fixed or limited quantity.

There are typically four prices that represent the points of analysis in distributive bargaining situations: target point, resistance point, asking price, and initial offer. Let's define each:[32]

- *Target point*. The optimal goal or the point at which a negotiator would like to conclude negotiations. This is also considered a negotiator's aspirational goal.
- *Resistance point*. A negotiator's bottom line. For buyers, it's the most they are willing to pay or the price beyond which they will not buy. For sellers, it's the smallest amount for which they will settle.
- *Asking price*. The initial price set by the seller.
- *Initial offer*. The first price figure the buyer will offer to the seller.

The fundamental process of distributive bargaining is to reach a settlement within a positive bargaining range where both parties obtain as much of the bargaining range as possible.[33] So, both parties know that they will have to settle for less than their target point or what they really want, which is typically not the goal of negotiations in most selling situations. However, bargaining skills do serve a purpose and can add value to selling negotiations in enabling effective communications to commence. Most salespeople at some time will encounter negotiation situations that are distributive; thus, in order to negotiate well, they need to understand distributive bargaining.

Regardless of whether you are engaged in distributive bargaining or in a principled negotiation process, there are times when emotions may begin to take control. To be an effective negotiator, you must be very cognizant of your emotions and the emotions of a prospective buyer. When you see yourself or the buyer becoming emotional, that is when you should press the *pause button* to help re-set the negotiation. Pressing the pause button is an extension of what we've discussed in earlier chapters regarding emotional intelligence skills and the need to recognize and control your emotions.

Let's first discuss how you press the pause button with yourself. It is very important that you understand yourself well. This may seem like a strange request as you may be thinking: Well, surely, I know myself! However, many people are not self-aware and do not truly understand what causes their emotions. That is why input from completing the Myers-Briggs Type Indicator test can be so helpful. Also, taking the time to do self-reflection on a regular basis is so important. You need to think about what triggers your emotions. Why does something trigger you? What should you do once you are triggered? Once you understand how you react to various situations, you can better manage your reactions in the future.

For example, maybe you react very poorly when people are dismissive of your ideas. By reviewing past scenarios where you became angry, you may be able to see this pattern emerge. When you get angry and lash out at people because they are being dismissive of your ideas, that only pushes them further away from your ideas. They are less likely to want to adopt or agree to anything you are suggesting because now you may be acting aggressively toward them. By using self-reflection techniques, you might determine that you were triggered by the dismissive behavior of others, and modify your reaction to it the next time it occurs.

The most effective way to do this is to be aware of the trigger and when you feel yourself getting upset, press the pause button. This essentially means that you realize a situation is occurring that has typically caused you to become emotional. In that moment, you must make the purposeful decision to react differently than you normally would. To do this, take a pause, a deep breath, and find a way to break away momentarily from the tense situation. This usually means saying something to the buyer such as, 'I think we need to take a short break and come back in 10 minutes to continue this discussion.' During the break, you need to gather your thoughts and consider how you are going to redirect your comments to the buyer without getting emotional. In other words, pressing the pause button enables salespeople to change the conversation so they can move forward and effectively continue the negotiation.

If salespeople continue their conversation after they have become upset, their emotion will overtake the dialogue. Salespeople cannot allow emotion to control their negotiation. Doing so will lead to poor communication skills and weaken their influence. Moreover, when you are upset, it is much harder to listen to and effectively read the buyer. An effective negotiator learns how to be creative. If you are approaching a negotiation from an emotional perspective, you are not thinking with reason and creativity. During an impasse, if you can remain focused on the underlying goals and ask good questions, you will reach a better agreement for the parties than if you approach the conflict from a position of emotion.

Moreover, when pressing the pause button, make sure you are clear in how long the negotiation will be paused. For example, you might say, 'Let's take a break from the negotiation today and resume tomorrow at 1:00 p.m. This sends a strong message to the buyer that you are wanting to pause, not end, the negotiation. If you were to say, 'Let's take a break from the negotiation' and then leave, the buyer may believe that the negotiation has failed and move on to other alternatives.

Sometimes the buyer, not the salesperson, is the one who is emotional. When you see that the buyer is getting upset, you should press the pause button for that person. As discussed above, when someone is upset, they are not engaged with their brain, but with their emotions. Thus, the negotiation will suffer. It is in your best interest to press the pause button and say, 'Why don't we take a break and come back in 15 minutes to further discuss this point?' During the break, you should consider what was causing the other party to get upset. There is something about the conversation that was a trigger for them. If you can correctly identify the issue here, you might creatively come up with a way to address their concern and move the negotiation forward.

Now, you may be wondering to yourself, 'Why would I press the pause button when I have the other side upset and not thinking clearly?' Or, 'Isn't it better for me to get a great deal right now while they are off their game?' It is important to understand that business relationships fare better when you focus on the long run rather than the short term. Yes, you could use the fact that the other side is emotional and negotiate a better deal for yourself today. However, what we really need to do is get the best deal that meets the needs of all parties because that is how you solidify your reputation in the industry and grow a solid business in the long run. Remember, you will not always be in a position of having the upper hand. One day, it might be you on the other side needing that pause button pressed. If you have treated others fairly, they will treat you fairly when you need it as well. Pressing the pause button will give you a very import-ant tool to step out of a negotiation – at least momentarily – to allow emotions to be reconciled, which will allow the negotiation to continue on track. If the pause button is not pressed, the emotions present in the negotiation will often derail what could have been a beneficial deal for both parties.

Successful transaction
© Ben Leistensnider/Christopher Newport University.

In summary, when bargaining, you need to understand the conflict between the par-ties. You have certain needs and interests that must be met in the negotiation. So does the other side. Emotions in a negotiation will only confuse these needs and interests.

When we begin to focus on the emotions (being afraid, upset, angry, rude, etc.) rather than what the party really needs, we will not negotiate the best deal. The best deal is found in meeting the interests and needs of both parties. When both parties can walk away feeling that they negotiated a good deal, you are creating a good business relationship. Since parties work together repeatedly, it is imperative that you are able to negotiate in a manner that preserves this business relationship, while achieving bargaining and negotiating success. What constitutes success in bargaining and negotiating? Let's now consider how to evaluate negotiation activities and monitor the metrics associated with negotiating.

MONITORING METRICS

Monitoring Metrics

Salespeople must document each and every negotiation in which they participate in order to provide information updates for each client's account plan, as presented earlier in Chapter 3. Documenting more than just the final agreement and commitment is important as well. Salespeople should record the various techniques they tried and how they worked out for each prospective buyer. Keep in mind that a technique with one type of buyer may not work but may very well work with a different type of buyer.

Remember, information is power. Throughout the negotiation process, salespeople will obtain valuable information about a prospective buyer. This information will be valuable for future engagement with the customer. Of course, salespeople must ensure that the terms of the commitment are honored, and that implementation or follow-through is provided as agreed upon. However, in addition to documenting actionable information, recording data on what techniques worked and what didn't work will also be valuable, especially for future negotiations. Lastly, assessment data regarding each and every negotiation should be recorded and stored in the company's client or prospect databases.

Salespeople should gather a variety of assessment metrics regarding each negotiation in which they participate. Over time, this data will provide valuable insight via data analytics. In addition, the data will help salespeople to assess the level of their negotiation success, as well as aid in identifying which negotiation techniques were productive and which were not. This data will also help salespeople to hone their skills for future negotiations. While the relevant negotiation metrics will likely vary by each company and selling situation, here are some examples of metrics that salespeople may gather and track:

- percentage of times commitment occurred
- percentage of times agreement to move to the 'next step' occurred
- percentage of times agreement was not met but placed 'on hold' for a future timeline
- percentage of times no agreement was made and both parties mutually agreed to walk away
- percentage of times no agreement was made and the salesperson opted to walk away
- percentage of times no agreement was made and the buyer opted to walk away
- percentage of times the potential buyer went 'silent' or 'dark' with no response about the solution
- percentage of times the prospect committed to your solution but then changed their mind.
- percentage of times your main contact said yes but couldn't get it approved at a higher level
- level of confidence in participating in the negotiation
- number of people involved in the negotiation process
- percentage of times the desired target outcome was reached
- percentage of times the pricing target was reached
- percentage of times various concessions were made.

While each of the above metrics provides quantitative assessment data regarding various negotiation activities, achieving these metrics alone will not guarantee successful selling. As we discussed in Chapter 3 with regard to account planning, negotiation activities are only significant if they help salespeople to reach their stated sales goals. Salespeople will be most productive and successful in negotiating when they sincerely believe in the product/service that they are offering and honestly view selling as creating value for people. When salespeople possess this value-creating role, they will be more highly motivated to achieve each of these negotiation metrics in order to help as many prospective customers as possible.

In conclusion, assessing the successes and failures of negotiation is an important task that salespeople must complete in order to both assess their performance and improve their negotiation skills. Of course, the most valuable use of the data is to continue to serve their current and future customers, as relationships are at the heart of all negotiations in selling.

CHAPTER SUMMARY

✓ Understand that conflict can be constructive or destructive, depending on how you manage it.

✓ Know your preferred style of conflict management and practice being collaborative.

✓ Plan and prepare for each stage of the negotiation process (complete the preparation sheet in this chapter).

✓ Follow the steps in the negotiating process; practice applying the four price points used in bargaining situations.

✓ Collect data on the success of your negotiations; evaluate it and work to continuously improve your skills.

KEY TERMS

Bargaining
Conflict
Conflict management
Distributive bargaining
Distributive negotiation

Negotiation
Negotiation mentor
Principled negotiation
Value

REVIEW QUESTIONS

1. Compare and contrast constructive and destructive conflict.
2. What are the five conflict management approaches proposed by Kenneth Thomas and included in the Thomas-Kilmann Conflict Mode Instrument? Which of these approaches is most effective for resolving conflict in selling? Why?
3. List three of the seven myths about negotiation that hinder salespeople from enjoying the negotiating experience.
4. Compare and contrast distributive negotiation and principled negotiation.
5. What are some of the issues that should be addressed when planning for a negotiation?
6. What are the five steps in the negotiating process?

7. List three of the ten common mistakes to avoid when negotiating in selling.
8. List and define the four prices that represent the points of analysis in distributive bargaining.
9. What does it mean to 'press the pause button' during a negotiation? How might this be helpful?
10. Discuss the importance of tracking and evaluating data from each negotiation process. List four metrics that may be used.

ETHICS IN ACTION

1. You are the sales manager for a home appliance store that offers a new extended warranty on select products. Sales commissions for you and your team are much higher if the warranty is sold at the time of purchase. The bullet points on the warranty brochure cover are very comprehensive, but the details in three pages of 'fine print' greatly reduce its actual value. This has been previously noted by a number of customers. How do you recommend your sales team describe the warranty to potential customers?

2. As the long-term salesperson for the Jones Brothers, Inc. account, you have a good relationship with and a solid understanding of the personality of the regular buyer for that account, Mark Goodwin. As the company's business has expanded, Mark is now responsible for purchasing supplies for an entirely different product line. He continues to unilaterally make purchase decisions, even though he has no experience or knowledge of the new manufacturing process. You have prior experience in selling supplies for this type of product and feel certain the buyer's selection won't provide the intended and desired results. What do you say to Mark when you receive the purchase order?

EXERCISE

It's time to shop! Visit a local farmer's market, thrift store, consignment shop, or some type of market where you may practice your negotiation skills to negotiate the sale price of a given product or item. Then, after your negotiation is completed, document the details of your experience. The negotiation details should include:

A. A description of the subject of the negotiation – the product/item.
B. Your needs/interests in purchasing the item.
C. What you believed the needs/interests of the seller were.

(Continued)

D. The opening offer.
E. The counter offer, if any.
F. A list of any others involved in the negotiation.
G. The negotiation outcome.
H. Your self-reflection about the experience.

ROLE-PLAY

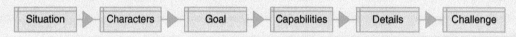

Role-play flowchart

Situation: You are a sales representative for Print and Digital Marketing Solutions. You regularly call on small businesses and creative boutiques that use external companies for printing, digital, and/or design services. You are preparing to meet with the leaders of a trade association that represents a group of local small enterprises. These leaders represent different companies; however, they act as a singular client in that they are seeking to contract a business partner to provide services to all of the businesses in the trade association. This is a challenging selling environment, however it is a potentially lucrative one.

Characters: You are Jaime Briggs and your sales manager, Bobbie Hill, is coaching you to prepare for your sales meeting with the leaders of the County Trade Association. You know that two of the leaders (Dan and Mitch) are very vocal individuals with strong opinions. The other two leaders (Sam and Luke) will pretty much follow along with whatever Dan and Mitch think.

Selling goal: Successfully negotiate a 'win-win' deal for all parties in order to move the client through the sales funnel to obtain buying commitment.

Product/service capabilities: Your company offers expert customized print and digital design services, as well as additional sales analytics if/as needed. Your company has a large, well-qualified staff to provide quick turnaround services on both print and digital projects.

Sales call details: Since County Trade Association represents many different types of businesses, it will be difficult to showcase your company's successful work on any one type of account. You will need to be prepared to address many different forms of conflict, including pricing, timeliness of product delivery, creativity, and quality. You have conducted research on LinkedIn and determined that you and Mitch both have a love of the local symphony orchestra. Mitch is on its board of directors. You have spoken to some friends who pitched to Dan a few years ago. They told you that Dan can be impatient and tends to interrupt others. You could not find any social media information on Luke, but you did find a Facebook page for Sam that highlighted his family. Sam's daughter is an accomplished horse rider.

In addition, you suspect that County Trade Association has concerns that your firm cannot meet all the needs of its various enterprises. The concern lies in whether your organization is flexible enough to pivot to each enterprise and deliver custom printing that can produce unique products for each type of account. Moreover, your research indicates that some enterprises have clear ideas of what they are looking for, while others do not.

Selling challenge: To support Bobbie by preparing to effectively deal with different types of conflict that may arise at your upcoming sales meeting with County Trade Association.

READINGS AND RESOURCES

- Dana Caspersen (2014) *Changing the Conversation: The 17 Principles of Conflict Resolution.* New York: Penguin Books.
- Stuart Diamond (2012) *Getting More: How You Can Negotiate to Succeed in Work and Life.* New York: Three Rivers Press.
- Roger Fisher, William Ury and Bruce Patton, Harvard Negotiation Project (2011) *Getting to Yes: Negotiating Agreement without Giving In*. New York: Penguin Books.
- Simon Horton (2016) *The Leader's Guide to Negotiation: How to Use Soft Skills to Get Hard Results.* Harlow, England: Pearson Education.
- Helene Malmsio (2014) *Workplace Solutions: Exploring Conflict Resolution and Dealing with Difficult People.* USA: US Office of Strategic Services.
- Chris Voss and Tahl Raz (2016) *Never Split the Difference: Negotiating as if Your Life Depended on It.* New York: Harper Business.

CASE STUDY: THE QUARRY TRUCKER NEGOTIATION

Note: The names and locations used in this case have been disguised for confidentiality purposes.

Many stone quarries rely on independent truckers to deliver the purchased stone to job sites. These truckers are not employees but are independent contractors who represent themselves and sell their own delivery services. These truckers secure contracts with buyers who are in need of their services. They operate under an agreement to be paid a certain dollar amount based on the size of load, distance travelled to the job site and back, and sometimes the time of day of the delivery. These truckers agree to these contractual

Dump truck

agreements based on the hope of acquiring an estimated number of loads they can deliver per day and per week.

The truckers who haul stone for the Jones Stone Quarry (JSQ) were having a meeting with Jay Fries, the transportation manager of JSQ, and they were complaining about the rate that had been used to calculate the fees paid to them. These independent truckers have not had any significant increase in the per-ton rate for the rock deliveries they've hauled for several years now. Because of this, a group of these independent truckers have joined together and threatened Jay that they might take their trucking business to another competitive quarry only five miles away. This action would severely impact the JSQ business, and, if not resolved, could threaten the future survival of the company.

The truckers are asking for a 50 cents per-ton rate of rock delivered. However, Jay knows he can only allow a 25 cents per-ton rate without eliminating the JCQ margin. The 50-cent demand and the 25-cent response are negotiating positions. Positional bargaining is like a tug of war where it's only resolved when one side or another gives up – which is a 'win-lose' outcome.

The only way for Jay to resolve this situation is to find the common interests that both sides possess. Jay entered into a negotiation with the group of truckers where he began by stating the common interest that both sides have – to earn more weekly income/revenue. In order to obtain this common interest, the following two factors are necessary:

1. The maximum truckload deliveries per day/week possible.
2. The optimum revenue for each of those truckloads.

The truckers agreed with Jay about their mutual interests. With that, Jay suggested to them that these are the 'whys' behind the 'what' – of obtaining more pay per load. Once that was agreed upon by the group of truckers, it became a straightforward calculation of the truckers' weekly income (revenue of each truckload multiplied by the number of loads delivered each week). Jay then showed the group of truckers their history of the quantity of loads per day/week provided by the JSQ. The truckers soon realized that other competitive quarries could not meet the combination of load pay and number of loads to be delivered per week that the JSQ provided. Once analyzed and discussed, the 25-cent pay increase on the per-ton rate seemed fair to the truckers. They quickly realized that the bottom line was they would earn more money per week by continuing to contract with JSQ versus seeking other contracts; thus, leading to a 'win-win' resolution to the negotiation.

The essence of a 'win-win' negotiation is to always recognize the positional demands of each party and seek to determine the common interests between the two parties. Then, resolution becomes a more productive process of discussing options to mutually satisfy the interests of both sides.

Case questions:

1. What initial approach would have increased the tension between the two sides and made a 'win-win' resolution more difficult to achieve?
2. Why is the 'tug of war' approach to negotiations so non-productive?
3. What are the challenges for Jay when negotiating with a group rather than with an individual?

NOTES

1. Barton Weitz and Kevin Bradford, 'Personal selling and sales management: A relationship marketing perspective,' *Journal of the Academy of Marketing Science* (Spring 1999), 27(2), 241–54.
2. Helene Malmsio (2014) *Workplace Solutions: Exploring Conflict Resolution and Dealing with Difficult People* (self-published), pp. 3–4.
3. Ibid., p. 5.
4. Ibid., p. 9.
5. Dan Schultheis, personal communication, September 15, 2020.
6. Ibid.
7. Ibid.
8. Helene Malmsio (2014) *Workplace Solutions: Exploring Conflict Resolution and Dealing with Difficult People* (self-published), pp. 41–3.
9. Don Hellriegel and Jon W. Slocum (2011) *Organizational Behavior*, 13th edn (Mason, OH: South-Western Cengage Learning), p. 384.
10. Dan Schultheis, personal communication, September 15, 2020.
11. Dana Caspersen (2014) *Changing the Conversation: The 17 Principles of Conflict Resolution* (New York: Penguin Books), p. xiii.
12. Maribeth Kuzmeski, 'Connecting through conflict: 5 ways great connectors turn angry clients into happy ones,' *Life Insurance Selling* (December 2009), 84(12), 54–7.
13. Dana Caspersen (2014) *Changing the Conversation: The 17 Principles of Conflict Resolution* (New York: Penguin Books), p. xiii.
14. Kenneth Thomas (1976) 'Conflict and conflict management,' in Marvin Dunnette (ed.) *Handbook of Industrial and Organizational Psychology* (Palo Alto, CA: Consulting Psychologists Press), pp. 889–935.

15. Barton Weitz and Kevin Bradford, 'Personal selling and sales management: A relationship marketing perspective,' *Journal of the Academy of Marketing Science* (Spring 1999), 27(2), 245.

16. Roy Lewicki, Bruce Barry and David Saunders (2016) *Essentials of Negotiation* (New York: McGraw Hill), p. 3.

17. Mike Miazga, 'We have a deal,' *Supply House Times* (July 2013), 56(5), 64.

18. John Patrick Dolan, 'Discover exactly what your sales prospect wants in the negotiation process,' *American Salesman* (September 2017), 62(9), 11–15.

19. Roger Fisher, William Ury and Bruce Patton (2011) *Getting to Yes* (New York: Penguin Books), p. 13.

20. Roy Lewicki, Bruce Barry and David Saunders (2016) *Essentials of Negotiation* (New York: McGraw Hill), p. 28.

21. Roger Fisher, William Ury and Bruce Patton (2011) *Getting to Yes* (New York: Penguin Books), p. 12.

22. Phillip Britt, 'Aggressive negotiations are still key to sales success: Sales leaders who dictate the terms of deals have a better chance of closing them,' *CRM Magazine* (April 2020), 24(3), 18.

23. Adapted from Christine Filip, 'Negotiating more profitable sales,' *Small Business Reports* (May 1994), 19(5), 14; and Dan Schultheis, personal communication, September 15, 2020.

24. Phillip Britt, 'Aggressive negotiations are still key to sales success: Sales leaders who dictate the terms of deals have a better chance of closing them,' *CRM Magazine* (April 2020), 24(3), 18.

25. Adapted from Eldonna Lewis-Fernandez, '7 negotiating mistakes,' *Sales & Service Excellence Essentials* (July 2014) 13(7), 5; and Marty Latz, 'The golden rules of negotiation for sales professionals,' *Agency Sales* (December 2004), 34(12), 50–2.

26. Simon Horton, '5 Killer Phrases That All Negotiators Should Know' (2016), www.bytestart.co.uk/5-killer-phrases-negotiators-should-know.html, retrieved June 16, 2020.

27. Ibid.

28. Bill Brooks, 'Negotiation: A fundamental skill for sale survival,' *American Salesman* (August 2001), 46(8), 16.

29. Simon Horton, '5 Killer Phrases That All Negotiators Should Know' (2016) www.bytestart.co.uk/5-killer-phrases-negotiators-should-know.html, retrieved June 16, 2020.

30. Roy Lewicki, Bruce Barry and David Saunders (2016) *Essentials of Negotiation* (New York: McGraw Hill), p. 3.

31. Ibid., pp. 28–9.

32. Ibid., p. 29.

33. Ibid., p. 33.

9
OVERCOMING OBJECTIONS AND CLOSING THE SALE WITH SATISFACTION

CHAPTER CONTENTS

PEOPLE, PRACTICES AND PERSPECTIVES FROM THE WORLD OF SALES

Hello, I'm Larry Blamer. I am currently the Managing Director of STIHL Australia. I started my career in a family business in outdoor power equipment. I quickly learned that what customers wanted was specialist advice and solutions to their problems. This has been true throughout my career, which has included positions as a North American service manager for a major manufacturer, a sales territory manager, a sales manager, a sales and marketing manager, and a director branch operations manager. *In every position, I encouraged my team to focus on solutions, not products or problems. People want the result and they want it made easy. They are willing to pay a premium price when they are given premium service.*

Hi, I'm Robert Davis, sales representative for Ferguson Enterprise LLC in Richmond, Virginia. I work with branch management, outside sales associates and customers to provide top-notch service, update client contracts, send direct quotes, and coordinate deliveries with warehouse associates. I also perform daily cold calls to generate new business as well as provide service and customer care for current partners. *With more than six years of experience in sales, I've found that my goals are the same as those learned from my coach when I played college football: to make a positive impact, put the team first, win (sales), and graduate (become promoted.)*

Greetings, my name is Rodney van Treeck, and I have been a professional B2B salesman for 15 years with Taylor Freezer Sales Company. We sell specialty restaurant equipment that helps food service operators increase sales and/or become more efficient and save costs. I sell bottom-line profit, as that is how a business survives and grows. *My long-term success is based on a simple strategy: believe in your product. When you believe in what you are selling, the objection paradigm shifts to an emphasis on the success of your prospect. There is no doubt you will get objections; however, embrace them as they give you more opportunities to make your prospect a believer.*

People buy from people they trust.

EYES ON ETHICS

Keep in mind the following ethical topics as you read through this chapter:

1. Using influencer marketing when changes occur in the influencer's view of the product/service.
2. Dealing with hesitations and objections during the closing conversation.

INTRODUCTION

This chapter addresses the point in the selling process where a prospect decides whether or not to commit to buying the product/service. Obviously, this is a crucial stage in the selling process. Years ago, salespeople were trained to view *closing the sale* as the chief objective of the selling process. While obtaining buyer commitment and closing the sale are certainly important for salespeople, they are not the only objective. As mentioned in earlier chapters, but worth repeating here, the focus of today's modern selling is relationship building. Thus, the chief objective of a salesperson is to create a customer, not just to make a sale. With that philosophy in mind, in this chapter we'll explore how salespeople can overcome buyer hesitation, understand buying signals, use various closing techniques, obtain buyer commitment, utilize up-selling, cross-selling, and continuity selling strategies, effectively ask for the sale, and build relationships after the buying decision. We'll begin by continuing the discussion from Chapter 8 regarding how to negotiate effectively and overcome buyer objections in order to move into the closing stage of the selling process.

HANDLING OBJECTIONS

Some prospective customers will ask questions during the sales presentation stage, while other buyers may raise questions after salespeople conclude their presentations. Often, buyers raise questions while negotiating with the salesperson. The best salespeople will welcome buyer questions, if not proactively seek them out. Of course, salespeople must anticipate and be prepared for common questions. They should have responses to common questions prepared in advance and know how they will respond with specific content when an issue is raised. However, often questions from the prospective customer will be in the form of an objection, hesitation, or reason why they may not be interested in buying. For example, a valid customer question might be: *What different sizes does this product come in?* Meanwhile, an objection may be phrased as: *I think that size is too large.* Do you see the difference? Both the question and the objection pertain to the size of the product; however, the objection is definitely a negative statement about the product being offered. That's the precise moment when savvy and successful salespeople have the opportunity to really sell. Let's discuss buyer objections and explore the various types and the strategies that can be used to handle them.

Buyer questioning

Understanding buyer hesitation

A buyer objection is any hesitation or reluctance that may block successful selling. When buyers raise objections, they are communicating to the salesperson that they do not believe, for one reason or another, that whatever the salesperson is offering will satisfy their needs, wants, desires, motives, and so on. They are communicating that they may not be interested in continuing the sales conversation. At that very moment, the salesperson is faced with a challenge. The best salespeople are not caught off-guard; they expect buyer objections and are ready to work through them to solve the customer's problems. The old saying, 'When the going gets tough, the tough get going' rings true here. Check out Table 9.1 which reveals some common reasons why prospects raise objections to salespeople.

Table 9.1   Common reasons for prospects raising objections

1. Due to a natural force of habit.
2. In order to get rid of the salesperson.
3. Because there is no recognized need for the product/service.
4. Because of the need for additional information.
5. Due to a resistance to change.
6. Because there are not enough apparent benefits being offered.
7. Due to the lack of funds.
8. Because the product/service is not needed.
9. Due to a lack of authority to make the buying decision.

Source: Adapted from Bill Palmroth, 'Techniques for handling objections', *The American Salesman* (1991), 36(5).

Effective salespeople welcome objections, just as quickly as they invite questions. While welcoming objections may not come easily to many people, with training and practice it soon resides within the comfort zone of most salespeople. Besides, practice makes perfect, so the more you invite and encounter objections, the better you will become at addressing them. Keep in mind that your genuine attempt to understand customers' concerns will strengthen rapport and will send a signal that you desire to serve them in a value-added way. Addressing buyer hesitation can even build trust. So, embrace this moment and rise to the challenge. Let's now talk about how you should begin to address buyer objections.

Salespeople should begin to explore customer hesitation by asking their buyers specific questions designed to uncover their hidden motives. These should be simple, specific questions, such as:

* What additional information can I provide you with at this time?
* What concerns, if any, do you have?
* What other things do you need to consider before making a decision?
* What else do we need to discuss to help you decide if XYZ product satisfies your needs?

The key to effective questioning lies in salespeople engaging in active listening, which was covered in detail earlier, in Chapter 6. Salespeople must completely and genuinely listen to and try to understand their customers' concerns and hesitations. Successful salespeople treat each prospective buyer's objection as a request for additional information. You need to put yourself in your customer's shoes and really comprehend what they are feeling. Customers often express a number of different hesitations, so salespeople must be prepared to isolate the real concerns of their buyers and deal with each of them. Let's investigate some common types of buyer hesitation.

Every sales situation is different and leads to different types of buyer hesitation. See Table 9.2 for a list of common sales objections that you may receive from prospective buyers.[1] However, once you have been selling a given product or service over a period of time, you'll be able to identify the most commonly raised objections. Those are the ones that you'll need to be prepared to address. Some of the most common types of buyer hesitation include those based on customer needs, product/service characteristics, product quality, price, company/organization, competition, personal reasons, and time.

Table 9.2 Common sales objections

Lack of budget

Examples:

* It's too expensive.
* There's no money.
* We don't have any budget left.
* We need to allocate funds elsewhere.
* We will incur less cost by purchasing it elsewhere.

Lack of trust

Examples:

- I've never heard of your company.
- We're already working with another vendor.
- I'm locked into a contract with another vendor.
- I'm satisfied with the services of your competitor.
- Competitor X says (*false statement*) about your product.

Lack of need

Examples:

- I don't see how this can help me.
- I don't see how this would benefit my company.
- I don't see what your product could do for me.
- We don't have the capacity to implement what you're offering.
- Your product doesn't have the (*specific*) feature that we need.

Lack of urgency

Examples:

- That isn't important for me right now.
- There's too much going on right now to focus on this.
- We're doing great in this area right now.
- I'm too busy right now.
- Perhaps you can contact me again next quarter.

Miscellaneous

Examples:

- I'm not interested.
- Just send me some information.
- How did you get my contact information?
- Click.

Source: Adapted from Leslie Ye, 'The Ultimate Guide to Objection Handling: 40 common sales objections and how to respond, 2020', https://blog.hubspot.com/sales/handling-common-sales-objections; and Brian Gonzalez, 'The 7 Most Common Sales Objections by Prospects and How to Overcome Them, 2020', https://blog.hubspot.com/sales/the-5-most-common-objections-during-prospecting-and-how-to-overcome-them.

As discussed in Chapter 5, each buyer's behavior style will likely affect the types of concerns or hesitations they will raise during the selling process. So, when preparing for possible objections that prospective buyers might raise, salespeople might keep in mind the following guidelines provided by Ron Willingham, in his book *Integrity Selling*:[2]

- *Talkers* like to buy from people they like and often cannot make that decision when they like multiple salespeople. Talkers normally have to obtain financial approval from others when making the buying decision and fear disapproval in making decisions. Talkers want to make sure that others are happy and will be pleased with their decisions. Talker objections might include phrases such as: *'I'll have to see how my coworkers feel about this'* or *'I'm going to need more time to run this idea past my boss.'*

- *Doers* typically don't have problems making decisions as they are more concerned with getting results. They are achievement-oriented and seek to meet the stated objectives. Unlike Talkers, social disapproval is not a big issue for Doers and they typically make decisions without input from others. Doers might object by saying: *'I'm not completely convinced that this will work'* or *'I'll need an earlier delivery date than what you are suggesting'* or *'I think I'll be able to obtain a better price than what you are currently offering.'*
- *Controllers* need enough facts and proof that what you are selling will truly meet their needs and wants. Their concerns normally arise when they don't feel they have the facts, figures, and supporting data they need to make their decision. Controllers need adequate data to satisfy their logical decision-making process and to enable them to determine that what they are buying will provide them with their desired return on investment. Controller objections may include: *'I'm not sure you've provided me with enough accurate data to make a decision at this time'* or *'I'm not convinced that you can guarantee quality control in the long term'* or *'I'd prefer not to buy until I obtain reviews from some of your current clients.'*
- *Supporters* are similar to Controllers in that they need plenty of details and facts on what you are offering as well as adequate time to make a buying decision. Supporters are curious and seek knowledge for knowledge's sake, unlike Controllers who seek knowledge to make a logical decision to ensure future performance and satisfaction.

Understanding the buyer's behavior style helps salespeople frame their responses with words that work to address each buyer's feelings and motivations. Regardless of the type of buyer objection raised, salespeople must be prepared to overcome buyer objections. The next section reveals the skills that successful salespeople use to do just that.

Overcoming buyer objections

Each buyer/customer and selling situation represents a unique circumstance which will likely require a different method to overcome buying objections. Thus, while the following methods may not always work, they are some of the most commonly used ones to address hesitation: agree and counter, boomerang, interrogation, and direct denial.

Agree and counter

This method is where you, the salesperson, first agree with your prospective buyer's objection, which shows that you understand the objection and appreciate the buyer's point of view. However, you then provide information that opposes and refutes the objection; thus, you basically affirm that the objection is not really a valid one. This method is also called the 'Yes, but' method as often those are the exact words you use when you agree and counter.

Example –*Objection*:	This computer screen is too thin and narrow.
Answer:	Yes, I see what you mean. This computer screen does appear to be narrow, but based on its measured dimensions, it's the same in thickness as most other competitor screens and is actually two inches wider than most competitor screens, which gives you a greater viewing area.

Boomerang

This method is where you, the salesperson, turn the objection around so it actually becomes a reason to agree to buy the product. This method should not be used too often during a selling situation as it may put the prospective buyer on the defensive. Also, this method may make the buyer think that the salesperson is trying to twist around every objection that is raised. However, used sparingly and appropriately, it may be effective.

Example – *Objection*:	This computer screen is too thin.
Answer:	A thin screen is precisely what you should want for your home computer as it will be lighter to lift and easier to carry, while maintaining the same impact resistance as screens twice as thick.

Interrogation

This method is where you, the salesperson, ask a series of well-framed questions to your prospective buyer to show that the objection is not completely valid or accurate. The salesperson asks a question that will get the buyer to talk and then uses the buyer's answers to disprove the objection itself. Often, the answers provided to the questions will serve to overcome the objection.

Example – *Objection*:	This computer screen is too thin.
Answer:	
Salesperson:	Do you know the size of your current computer screen?
Buyer:	Not exactly, but it's likely larger than the one that you are now showing me.
Salesperson:	Have you ever had to move your computer screen?
Buyer:	Yes.
Salesperson:	Was it heavy to transport?
Buyer:	Yes.
Salesperson:	Would you have appreciated a lighter computer screen when you had to move it?
Buyer:	Yes, I guess I would have.
Salesperson:	That's why we've designed our computer screens to be thin so that they are lighter in weight. Our screens are much easier to transport when the time comes for you to have to move them, although the screen quality is much higher than that of our competitors.

Direct denial

This method is where you, the salesperson, tactfully point out that the objection is incorrect. When you deny the objection, you must be prepared to provide factual evidence to support your claim. This method is used when an objection is so obviously incorrect that valid information must be provided to correct the facts held by the prospective buyer. This should be used when you cannot use the agree and counter method because the objection is so false that you cannot agree to it.

Example – *Objection*:   This computer screen is too thin as it is only a half-inch wide.
Answer: On the contrary, you may be surprised to learn that this computer screen measures more than an inch in width. So, it's not as thin as it actually appears.

Do you want to learn more methods for handling prospective buyer objections? If so, check out the Readings and Resources section at the end of this chapter for Leslie Ye's *Ultimate Guide to Objection Handling*. Regardless of the method(s) used to address buyer hesitation, there is an ordered process – which may be thought of as the '4 C's' – that salespeople may follow to successfully handle most objections. The '4 C's' requires salespeople to first *clarify* the objection, next *categorize* the objection, then *capitalize* on the objection, and finally use the objection to further *connect* with the prospective customer to build or strengthen the buyer–seller relationship. Here's how salespeople may use each of the 4 C's when handling objections:

1. *Clarify*. Restate the objection to be certain that you have heard and understand the cause of the prospective customer's hesitation. When restating, be sure to mirror or match the prospect's dominant mode of communication, as explained in Chapter 5, for maximum communication effectiveness.
2. *Categorize*. Relate the objection to a specific category of objections, such as price, product details, quality level, delivery time, etc. This will enable you to mentally access the predetermined selling points that you have amassed for each specific category.
3. *Capitalize*. Turn the objection into a reason to buy whatever you are selling by introducing additional information. As mentioned in the previous chapter, authentic storytelling works well to help change minds by providing specific success stories.
4. *Connect*. Put yourself in your buyer's shoes and focus on building or strengthening relationships and forging a partnership with your prospective customer. Use the objection to engage with your prospect by showing your sincerity to help solve your buyer's problem. Focusing on the solution will likely help to reduce the prospect's perceived risk in making the decision to buy.

Overcoming buyer objections is a form of problem solving. Salespeople must be prepared to help their prospects to successfully deal with their uncertainty by satisfying all of their buying hesitations. In doing so, salespeople can help their prospects realize the value of the products/services being offered and move positively toward committing to buy. Let's now discuss strategies that salespeople use when attempting to obtain buyer commitment and close sales.

Trusting relationship

EXAMINING CLOSING STRATEGIES

Closing is the act of obtaining commitments.[3] These commitments include decisions to advance the sale and open the relationship. Successful closing is relationship building – storytelling builds trust, knowing your customer on a personal level builds trust, and integrity builds trust. TRUST is the foundation for every successful business relationship. Thus, the strategies used in closing a sale are based on the relationship that you form with your prospects, which begin the moment you meet them. Everything you do either 'adds to' or 'subtracts from' the buyer's perception of the value you personally bring to the table.[4] Earning your buyer's trust is crucial to obtaining buyer commitment. In selling, obtaining commitment refers to a strategy to continually move your prospect closer to buying, which is typically achieved in progressive steps throughout the sales cycle.[5] Trust is the most effective strategic tool to successfully obtaining commitment and closing sales. Check out Table 9.3 for tips on some effective closing strategies. Let's examine the activities involved in implementing such strategies.

Table 9.3   Effective closing strategies

- Find out everything you can about your prospect.
- Plan your conversation from the prospect's point of view.
- Focus on benefits, not features.
- Be certain that your prospect understands what you are saying.
- Always use trial closing questions to explore what your prospect is thinking.
- Carefully and fully address each of your prospect's questions.
- Be completely honest when you answer questions.
- Handle every objection and confirm with a trial closing question.
- Never overpromise.
- Project confident assurance that what you are offering is the best solution for your prospect.
- Always be in closing mode.
- Know when to ask for the order and stop talking once you've asked.
- Once you have the order, finalize the details and move on.

Source: Adapted from Thomas Metcalf, 'Your Complete Guide to Closing the Sale (with Examples),' http://crosswork consulting.com/your-complete-guide-to-closing-the-sale-with-examples, retrieved October 27, 2020; and 'Top 10 Sales Closing Techniques: Learn how to seal the deal,' https://smallbusiness.chron.com/top-10-sales-closing-techniques-learn-seal-deal-70629.html, retrieved October 27, 2020.

Understanding the buyer situation

Understanding the buyer's problems based on solid research is needed in order for any closing strategies to be used successfully. Research shows that when the prospect's most important needs are uncovered, a sale occurs 86 percent of the time.[6] Thus, research is key! Salespeople must first confirm their understanding of the problems, needs, and situation of their prospects, and provide reassurance that the product/service will solve their problems. If this reassurance doesn't occur, then there is a greater chance that the prospect will later feel buyer's remorse or dissatisfaction with the buying decision.[7]

Understanding each buyer's unique problem and situation will help salespeople to intuitively know which particular closing strategies and techniques might be more effective to use and when to use them. Every buyer and every selling situation is different. Buyers may be indecisive, egotistical, or hostile; they may be known as 'experts' with preconceived notions of the product or service; they may be insistent on the best deal possible; or they may be friends of yours.[8] You need to prepare for all different types of buyers as you will inevitably meet them in selling.

Too often, salespeople attempt to close sales using techniques with which they feel the most comfortable. That tends to result in treating all prospective buyers the same. The problem is that we are all different. The salesperson must present problem solutions the way that each buyer wants to receive them.[9] Therefore, it's not enough to merely understand the buyer's problems, but the salesperson must effectively understand and appeal to each buyer's unique communication preferences and behavior style.

As detailed in Chapter 5, salespeople should adapt their mode of communication to the style preference of each of their buyers. This requires understanding and mirroring their buyer's dominant mode of communication – visual, auditory, or kinesthetic. For visual buyers, you may show slides, videos, or printed materials during your attempt to close the sale and use visual words when speaking. For auditory buyers, you should verbally present closing information, including testimonials or short stories, using the same language and tone to match that of each of your buyers. Lastly, for kinesthetic buyers, words alone may not be sufficient. Instead, you should include materials for your buyers to examine by touching and feeling.

All people are not the same. Depending on their behavior style, some people are more risk aversive, resistant to change, or reluctant to make decisions.[10] Thus, the buying decision of some prospective customers may have less to do with their perception of the product/service or their evaluation of the value/cost equation; instead, it's based on their individual behavior style. Some buyers will naturally be more apprehensive about making decisions than others. As discussed in previous chapters, salespeople must try to assess the behavior style of each of their prospects and then adjust their communication to effectively engage with each unique buyer. Let's examine the potential influence of behavior style on buyer decision making by revisiting each of the four behavior styles:[11]

- *Driver (Doer/Dominant)*. Drivers make decisions easily and will be most influenced by the benefits associated with the product/service that enable them to achieve results. Drivers may also be influenced by other customers who have purchased from you, so use testimonials when closing the sale. Drivers like to be in control, so allow them to be in charge of the buying decision and they will tell you what benefits are most valuable. If they don't tell you directly, you may ask questions to encourage them to reveal their perspectives, which will become your key closing points.
- *Analytical (Controller/Conscientious)*. Analytical buyers may interrupt you to question the accuracy of your statements as they will need proof and documentation that what you are offering will solve their problems and achieve the results that you are claiming. Since these buyers make decision based on logic, they will want to see evidence that eliminates risk before making a buying decision. Analytical buyers are rational decision makers who won't be swayed by a passionate closing pitch unless it's substantiated with details.
- *Expressive (Talker/Influence)*. Talkers are more concerned about what other people think of them, so they are reluctant to make buying decisions without reassurance that others will approve of their decisions. These buyers dislike making decisions. These buyers want to please other people, including you. Thus, often their reluctance to say 'no' to what you are offering is due to the fact that they don't want to hurt your feelings. You may need to help these buyers to make decisions in order to obtain a commitment to buy or not.
- *Amiable (Supporter/Steadiness)*. Amiable buyers avoid risk; thus, they are typically slow decision makers who will seek validation that is both well established and conservative. Amiable buyers seek security and like to please other people. When closing with amiable buyers, salespeople must clearly understand their perceptions of the risks associated with the purchase, attempt to eliminate those risks, and give them ample time to make their buying decisions.

Buyer decision making

Reading buyer signals

Salespeople must carefully read their buyers to determine their unique communication and behavior styles and adjust their closing strategies accordingly. Keep in mind that if you only use the closing style that works best for you, then you will likely be successful in closing sales with only those buyers who are just like you. Salespeople should also pay close attention to the buying signals that their prospects provide to understand what the buyer is thinking, which will aid in determining the appropriate closing techniques to use. Understanding buyer signals includes closely reading the body language of your prospect. As discussed in Chapter 5, there are many different non-verbal cues that will help salespeople to understand what their buyers are thinking long before any words are spoken. The most common positive cues are when buyers are smiling, leaning forward, and nodding their head in agreement. Negative body language cues may be more difficult to read in prospects and include the following:[12]

- rolling their eyes
- failing to maintain eye contact
- blinking rapidly
- rubbing their forehead back and forth
- crossing their arms
- folding their hands with palms facing upward
- scratching their head
- looking bewildered
- nodding their head side to side
- squinting their eyes.

As we've discussed earlier in the chapter, buyer questions and objections are obvious buyer signals. Salespeople must address each buyer question or objection fully and competently. Some verbal buying signals tend to signify that the buyer is convinced that your product/service solves their problems, thus they may be ready to make the buying decision.[13] For example, questions such as 'How much does it cost?' or 'When might it be installed?' or 'When can I take delivery?' may signal that the buyer is ready to make a buying decision. Buyers who seek the opinions of other people may indicate that they are seeking confirmation of their buying decision. Typically, a buyer who carefully examines a product with great concentration is normally in the final decision-making stage. Buyers who begin examining a contract or purchase order usually indicates that they are interested in making a buying decision. Salespeople may ask their buyers questions to expose buying signals via their answers. For example, the salesperson might ask a buyer: 'What are the first steps you'll take in implementing this solution?' Properly reading buyer signals will assist you in knowing when to use closing techniques to try to advance the sale. Let's now examine some common closing methods that salespeople use.

Buyer signaling buying interest

Examining closing techniques

There are no magic words or techniques that guarantee successful closing. If your customer doesn't like you, trust you, and feel comfortable with you, it doesn't matter what closing technique you use, you will not be successful in obtaining buyer commitment.[14] Building rapport and relationships is critical to successful closing. While it isn't necessary to become good friends with each of your prospects, you must establish some kind of bond in order to successfully ask for a commitment and close a sale. Also, as mentioned earlier, salespeople should factor in the situation and type of buyer when selecting which closing techniques to use. Think of it this way – you may have many tools in your toolbox, but only the 'right ones' will get the job done. So, select wisely. Assuming you have established rapport with your buyer, the following commonly used closing techniques may be used to obtain buyer commitments:[15]

- *Assumptive close.* This closing technique is where salespeople take the sale for granted as if its occurrence is a forgone conclusion. So, salespeople just assume that the buyer will say 'yes' to what they are offering. An example is the salesperson stating, *'I can have it delivered by next Monday in order to work with your operating schedule.'* In this example, the buyer hasn't explicitly stated agreement to buy, but the salesperson is moving ahead with delivery details. This technique works well when you have established relationships with your buyers, and they respect your judgement.[16]

- *Alternative option close.* This technique asks the buyer to choose between two options, with both of those options leading to a purchase. There is no option for these prospects to forgo the purchase; rather they must decide between two alternatives. For example, the salesperson might ask, *'Which model would you like to buy?'* As with the assumptive close, this technique also assumes the prospect will buy the product/service and works well when you have a good relationship with your buyer.

- *Balance sheet or 'T-account' close.* This technique is where the salesperson reviews both the pros and cons of the purchase decision for the prospect. The salesperson typically will accentuate the pros and briefly skim over the cons. Some types of buyers will want the salesperson to address the risks associated with the purchase, not just the benefits. If there are one or two selling points that the prospect has mentioned to the salesperson earlier in their conversation, the salesperson may spend additional time addressing those aspects. This technique is effective to use when selling to an indecisive buyer who needs a more thorough review and analysis in order to make a buying decision.

- *Compliment close.* Just as the name suggests, this technique entails offering your buyer a compliment. This technique works well for those buyers who are egotistical, consider themselves experts, or are concerned with what people think about them. Offering a compliment may help the salesperson to build rapport as it tends to cause buyers to respond with genuine appreciation and positive feeling.

- *Urgency 'time limit' close.* This technique uses an impending event or timetable to entice buyers to take action now. It is also referred to as the 'SRO' close, which means 'standing room only.' For example, *'Supplies are limited of this model, so order now'* or *'This special offer will not be available after the trade show ends.'* While this 'now or never' closing technique may be effective, it will only work if there is complete honesty and integrity in what is being claimed about the need for urgency. This technique works well when buyers have all of the details that they need in order to make the buying decision.

- *Summary of the benefits close.* This technique uses a combination of strategies to achieve buying agreement. First, salespeople will summarize the benefits presented during the sales presentation, then they confirm understanding with a trial close question, and lastly, ask for the order. This method tends to work well when the salesperson has identified the key selling points and benefits that are of most interest to the buyer. Those are the ones that will be emphasized in the summary. This technique generally works well for those buyers who need reassurance in their purchase decision as the salesperson is helping the buyers to understand the value they will be getting out of the deal.

- *Continuous 'yes' close.* This technique is similar to the summary of benefits close; however instead of summarizing benefits, the salesperson asks a series of trial close questions to which the obvious answer will be 'yes,' and ends with a quick summary of key benefits. This technique, also referred to as the 'question close,' asks questions that merely confirm the information that the salesperson already knows to be correct, but wants the buyer to explicitly agree to each fact. Here's an example of some of the questions a salesperson might pose to a prospect: *'Do you agree that increasing market penetration is important to your company?' 'And, generating greater control over the distribution of your product is one of your goals for next year, correct?' 'You said that your current sales team is overworked due to your inadequate computer system, is that correct?' 'In your opinion, does the computer system that I'm offering solve your problem?'* In this example, salespeople have used a series of questions that review the main problems that the buyer is facing in order to set up the close, whereby salespeople present how their product/service will solve all of the problems. Building a series of acceptances makes the buying decision much less formidable. As with the benefits summary method, this technique works well for those buyers who need details about and reassurance in their purchase decision.
- *Probability close.* This technique asks buyers to state a probability that they will make a buying commitment and then asks them to describe the issues that are in the remaining percentage that is holding them back from making the purchase decision. For example, if the buyer replies: *'I'll give it a 50 percent chance at this time,'* that response implies that the buyer is not convinced and has a number of objections that the salesperson needs to flush out and handle. If the buyer says: *'I'm 90 percent sure I'll buy this system,'* then the salesperson can more easily get the buyer to reveal what issue is holding the prospect back from buying. This technique works well for buyers who state that they need more time to think it over before making the buying decision. It also works well for buyers with whom the salesperson does not have an established relationship or about whom they don't have solid background research.
- *Soft close.* This technique enables salespeople to offer a special benefit or concession to sweeten the closing offer. This technique is considered a 'soft close' to obtain commitment for the buyer to want to continue the conversation and move forward in the buying decision. An example is: *'If I could reduce the maintenance fees by 25 percent, would that align with your company goals?'* or *'If I could increase the plan coverage by six months, would you be interested in learning more?'* This technique works well as a trial close where it doesn't ask for the purchase decision but asks for agreement to continue the conversation. It provides salespeople with more time to research and understand the buyer's needs, problems, and situation.
- *Premium or bonus close.* Offering something for nothing, such as free delivery, maintenance package, or add-ons, a special discount, extended credit terms, or an upgrade may seem gimmicky, but when properly used, may be effective in closing a sale. The added inducement may trigger the 'yes' in the buying decision-making process. The rule with offering an extra is to never promise what you cannot deliver. In addition, be careful not to include too many extras or else the buyer will assume that the original

deal was insufficient, or the product/service is inferior and needs extras in order to provide adequate value. This method works well when you have a relationship with the buyer and know that the buyer is in the final stage of the buying decision process.

- *Secondary close.* This approach uses a secondary decision which, if answered positively, signals that the prospect is probably going to make the bigger decision of buying your solution. An example of this is: *'Ms. Jones, where in your office will you set up this copier to ensure your employees will use it more?'* If she describes where it will be placed, that is a strong indicator that she's about to make a decision to buy your copier as it solves her employee usage problem.
- *Direct close.* As the name implies, this closing technique is where the salesperson asks the buyer for the order. The biggest advantages of using the direct close is that it is concise and offers excellent clarity. This technique may be used effectively with buyers who make up their minds quickly and confidently. Typically, this technique entails a bit of risk and should be used when salespeople are fairly confident that their buyer's response will be positive. This technique is most effectively used as the final method in a series of closing techniques as it is difficult to continue on in the conversation to try to obtain buying commitment if the buyer replies 'no' to the direct question.

Research shows that the average sale includes three rejections and objections.[17] Thus, salespeople must be able to effectively read their buyers and be prepared to ask for their buying commitment a number of times using different techniques. Research also reveals that approximately 64 percent of salespeople don't ask for the order.[18] Regardless of the technique used, salespeople must ask for the sale. Salespeople must be persistent, though not pushy, in continuing the closing conversation after the initial objection or rejection is made. Effectively asking for buyer commitment includes selecting and using the appropriate words and proper order of closing techniques, based on the unique buyer type and situation. *How* a salesperson asks the buyer for commitments is just as important as the actual act of asking. Let's now explore the topic of asking for commitments.

Commitment – shaking hands

ASKING FOR COMMITMENTS

The prospect will make many decisions and various types of commitments throughout the selling process. Some commitments will occur early, others midway, while others occur toward the end of the selling process. Following are some buyer actions that indicate commitment at different points in the selling process.[19]

Early commitments:

- responding to an email that asks if the prospect is experiencing a certain problem/issue
- agreeing to speak with a salesperson on the phone
- agreeing to meet with a salesperson in person
- assisting the salesperson in gathering information.

Midway commitments:

- explaining current problems, plans, priorities, and company goals
- explaining what solution evaluation process will be used
- offering suggestions to the salesperson regarding how to make the recommended solution more attractive to prospects
- contacting the salesperson's current customers for a reference
- agreeing that the salesperson's solution or proposal will satisfy their needs.

Final commitments:

- requesting an implementation plan with dates and objectives as part of the solution proposal
- buying the product/service being offered by the salesperson
- writing a testimonial for the salesperson
- recommending the salesperson and the salesperson's company to others.

Seeking buying commitment

Some salespeople who possess strong convictions or beliefs that their product/service is the best solution for their buyers, will have a more natural tendency to quickly focus on closing the sale. These salespeople follow the common 'ABC' rule of 'Always be closing.' Trial closing may be appropriately used throughout the entire selling process. The trial close, as defined in Chapter 7, is a question asked during a sales presentation to get feedback from the prospect and to build momentum toward a positive outcome.[20] A salesperson typically uses multiple trial closes to gauge the buying interest of their prospect. A trial close is no different than any other technique to close a sale; however, it is generally used earlier in the selling process. If a trial close is successful, it becomes the final close. If it is unsuccessful, the salesperson will continue trying different closing techniques to obtain a buying commitment.

One common way to use a trial close is to add the phrase 'in your opinion' to any question that you pose to your buyer. This phrase will work to reveal the buyer's feelings and potential objections, which will enable you to either address this person's concerns or use this buyer insight and opinion in your closing pitch.[21] Here's an example: *'In your opinion, is the variety of colors available adequate?'* If the buyer replies *'Yes,'* the salesperson knows the choice of colors is adequate and may be used as one of the selling points when closing the sale. If the buyer replies *'No, it doesn't come in blue,'* the salesperson may respond by asking: *'Would you be interested in it if I can find one in blue?'* Asking for the buyer's opinion enables additional relevant questions to follow which may move the buyer closer to making a buying commitment.

Check out Table 9.4 for some questions that you may use in trial closes. Most trial closing questions tend to be open-ended. They are designed to get your prospect talking so you can learn more about their opinions and determine when the right time to ask for the sale might be.

Table 9.4 Examples of trial closing questions

* How do you feel about what we have discussed so far?
* What do you think about the solution I've shared with you?
* How does what we've talked about sound to you?
* Based on what you've heard so far, what are your questions?
* What do you think about [product 'X'] so far?
* If you had your way, what changes would you make to the proposal?
* What do you think of the proposal?
* Does this product/solution make sense to you?
* What do you see as the next step in the process?
* When might be a good time to send you the paperwork?

Source: Adapted from Rhys Metler, 'The 8 Best Sales Trial Closing Questions to Guarantee the Deal,' www.salesforcesearch.com/blog/8-best-sales-trial-closing-questions-guarantee-deal, retrieved October 27, 2020; and Neal Lappe, 'Trial Closings: The key to a 100% close rate,' www.webstrategiesinc.com/blog/trial-closings-the-key-to-a-100-close-rate, retrieved October 27, 2020.

Trial closing questions may be a salesperson's most valuable diagnostic tool to assess how the prospect feels about the product/service. Typically, buyer responses to trial questions will enable salespeople to place their buyer into one of three categories: *Cold-as-ice*, *Warm-I'm-feeling-it*, or *Hot-Ready-to-roll*.[22] Understanding where you stand with your prospects and the stages at which they are in the decision-making process, is crucial to being able to respond appropriately with follow-up questions to try to obtain buying commitments and close sales.

How do salespeople know when it's time to close the sale and ask for a buying commitment? Of course, the correct answer is, whenever the buyer is ready! However, as mentioned earlier, all buyers and all selling situations are different, thus there is no precise timing that works best to close the sale. All salespeople must diagnose each of their unique buyers and selling situations and close when they think each buyer is 'ready' to buy. Salespeople must also know when they've completed the closing stage of the selling process. Some indicators are when:[23]

- all of the buyer's concerns have been successfully addressed
- the buyer understands that the benefits of purchasing the product/service outweigh the costs incurred
- the buyer expressly wants what you are offering.

Ideally, the closing stage ends when the buyer commits to buying the product/service. However, salespeople may also incorporate some additional follow-up strategies to build and strengthen relationships with their buyers after the buying decision has been made, which is the topic of our next section.

Discussing and meeting

Building relationships after the buying decision

The buyer–seller relationship doesn't end when a buying commitment is achieved; it simply then transforms into a customer relationship. There are additional selling opportunities that salespeople may utilize during the final point of the closing stage of the selling process when the buyer becomes a customer. Examples are up-selling, cross-selling, continuity selling, and subscription offers. Let's briefly examine each.

Up-selling

Up-selling is the suggestion of more expensive products/services over the product/service originally discussed or purchased. You might think of up-selling as suggestive selling, since the salesperson is suggesting a more expensive product/service as opposed to the initial one the buyer selected. For example, with the purchaser of a computer system, customers might be offered software package upgrades, a lifetime service protection plan, additional computer accessories, or an improved wide-screen monitor.

Cross-selling

Cross-selling refers to offering new products/services that may be related or unrelated to those the customers are already buying. For example, the purchaser of a computer system might be offered a communication system, security system, other digital products, an insurance policy, a home power tool, or a vacation package to a tropical resort. Remember, the product/service does not need to be related to the purchased item. The most important element of successful cross-selling is the manner in which the buyer views the reputation, reliability, and overall image of the salesperson and the salesperson's company. Trust is crucial to successful cross-selling.

Continuity selling

Continuity selling describes offers that are continued on a regular basis, whether weekly, monthly, quarterly, or annually. These offers are also called 'club offers' and are a hallmark of salespeople and companies who want to acquire customers who will remain active for an extended period of time. In continuity selling, customers buy related products/services as a series of small purchases, rather than all at a single time. Common examples are book clubs and wine clubs.

Subscription offers

A subscription offer, also referred to as a subscription model, is where consumers must pay an up-front subscription price in order to receive regular delivery or access to certain products/services for a specified period of time. Examples are Amazon, Netflix, Spotify, and Ring. Subscription models are different from typical pay-per-service models. Subscription models offer consumers extra conveniences, such as free and/or timely delivery, easy access to services, and up-front knowledge of the cost of the products/services to which they subscribe. Basically, a subscription model simplifies the business process for both buyers and sellers. Subscription models also enable salespeople to focus on customer retention and the lifetime value of customers, which will be discussed in Chapter 13. Subscription models are geared to buyers' needs and wants and typically offer various options or levels. For example, Netflix, an international provider of on-demand Internet streaming media, offers three streaming plans to meet consumer needs. The plan selected determines the number of devices consumers can stream Netflix on at the same time. Regardless of which plan is selected, consumers can install the Netflix app on as many devices as they want, and enjoy as many television shows and movies as they want, anytime, anywhere.[24]

Amazon also offers an extremely popular subscription model, Amazon Prime. More than 100 million Amazon Prime customers worldwide receive 31 distinct benefits, among which are exclusive shopping deals and selection, streaming of movies, TV shows and music, free fast shipping for eligible purchases, and many others.[25] In addition, Amazon, like many other companies using subscription offers, extends multiple offers to consumers. For example, Amazon offers a free 30-day trial period of Amazon Prime, and for students, a 50 percent discount.[26]

Subscription models are not limited to final consumers, as B2B subscription offers are quite effective as well. For example, creative software manufacturer, Adobe, offers two subscription-based services – Creative Cloud for business (ideal for small to mid-size businesses) and Creative Cloud for enterprise (ideal for large businesses and institutions), both with different service features that are designed for each type of client.[27] Business customers pay a monthly subscription fee to access Adobe's customized products.[28]

Fulfillment

Beyond investigating additional selling opportunities with your buyer, it is important to finalize all of the fulfillment details associated with the current sale, such as delivery, payment terms, installation, training, customer service, and so on. Fulfillment is the act of carrying out a customer's expectations. Strictly defined, fulfillment means sending the product to the customer or delivering the service agreed on. Loosely defined, it includes the entire dialogue (all interactions with the customer), as well as delivery functions. Salespeople view fulfillment as a part of the 'extended product,' or the intangible parts of selling the product. Fulfillment is often referred to as the 'back end' of the selling process, which may include product fulfillment, call center, and customer service operations.

Customer service (after the sale)

Fulfillment entails anything and everything that happens *after* the buying commitment. When customers place an order, they expect delivery of the ordered item by the time promised by the salesperson. Many experts contend that back-end functions alone cannot make a sale, but certainly can break one. More importantly, the lack of efficient fulfillment operations and good customer service can injure the relationship the salespeople have built with their customers, and ultimately lead to the loss of that customer. Thus, the salesperson should strive to achieve a call-back, which is a future appointment to meet with the customer to ensure their satisfaction with the purchase, delivery, and post-purchase matters. A call-back allows salespeople to provide additional value to their new customer and to strengthen the relationship. Salespeople may need to provide multiple call-backs spanning several years if the purchased item was of high-value, highly technical, or capital goods, such as machinery or equipment. As mentioned in previous chapters, but worth repeating here, the end goal of selling is to earn a customer, not make a sale, so long-term relationship building is critical to successful selling.

Keeping the door open

However, if the buyer does not commit to the purchase and does not become a customer at that particular time, savvy salespeople will follow up with that buyer and maintain a good relationship. Salespeople should never take a rejection personally, as not all buyers will be convinced that the products/services being offered will solve their problems. In dealing with rejection, salespeople may explore why the buyer did not commit to the purchase to learn more about the buyer's situation. Did the buyer not value the product/service? Was the selection or variety of models, colors, features, and so on, not adequate? Was the cost or price too high? Obtaining a clear understanding of why the customer didn't buy is important to future selling success.

Salespeople are wise to always keep the door open and look for future selling opportunities with their prospects. Offering valuable information, expert advice, or connections with other companies or service providers will demonstrate your willingness to be of assistance to your buyers, regardless of buying commitment. Perhaps your assistance will be rewarded by obtaining a buying commitment in the future. If not, keep in mind that word-of-mouth communication and referrals are vital to the image and reputation of salespeople. Thus, closing the sale is never the absolute end of the selling process, as building relationships can lead to future success. Success in selling can be evaluated and measured in many different ways, which is the topic of our last section.

MONITORING METRICS

Performance metrics, which are measures of a business' or employees' tasks and activities, are often quantifiable and can be tracked.[29] Key performance indicators (KPIs), which are used when assessing and measuring closing activities, should be established based on the

Monitoring Metrics

desired outcome relevant to each action. To encourage optimal salesperson performance, KPIs should be set based on revenue goals and profitability by agreeing on a minimum margin that factors in the costs of delivering the salesperson's services.[30] Ideally, KPI targets should be established to set salespeople up for accountability and success.[31]

Assessment metrics can be tracked to analyze trends in closing strategies and to enable salespeople to focus on the most productive sales opportunities. Metrics should be evaluated for a particular period of time and comparisons made between various time periods, such as monthly, quarterly, or annually. While the relevant closing metrics will likely vary by each salesperson, company, and selling situation, here are some examples of metrics that salespeople may gather and track:[32]

- average number of buyer objections raised during the selling process
- percentage of times salesperson successfully overcame buyer objections
- number of open opportunities or accounts each salesperson (or sales team) is working at any given time
- number of closed opportunities or accounts each salesperson (or team) has made during a given period of time
- average number of sales calls made to a buyer to achieve buying commitment
- average duration or time (typically in days) it takes a salesperson to obtain buying commitment
- average conversion rate or win rate
- average deal size or average sales price of the salesperson's (or team's) closed deals
- actual sales revenue generated by each salesperson (or team) during a given period of time
- percentage of prospects who made a commitment to move to the next step
- percentage of prospects who made a commitment to buy
- percentage of prospects who placed their buying decision 'on hold' for a future time
- percentage of prospects who did not commit to purchase and had no future discussion planned (also called sales funnel leakage)
- average number of people involved in the closing process
- percentage of prospects for whom the desired target outcome was reached
- percentage of times up-selling was successful out of the number of times up-selling was attempted

- percentage of times cross-selling was successful out of the number of times cross-selling was attempted
- percentage of times continuity selling was successful out of the number of times continuity selling was attempted
- percentage of times subscription selling was successful out of the number of times subscription selling was attempted
- percentage of existing customers renewing or extending their contract
- percentage of prospects for whom the pricing target was reached
- percentage of sales closed where various concessions needed to be made in order to close the sale
- percentage of customers receiving call-backs.

While each of the above metrics provides a quantitative assessment of the success of various closing activities, achieving these metrics alone will not guarantee successful selling. Establishing trust, overcoming hesitation, solving buyer problems, and providing value are the foundation to successful closing and selling. There's no magic closing pill that will ensure that each and every prospect will commit to buying. In fact, successful selling requires salespeople to deliver high-quality service from the initial contact with the prospect through perpetuity. At all times, strong relationships are the heart of closing and of all successful selling activities.

CHAPTER SUMMARY

- ✓ Prepare to address potential buyer questions and objections.
- ✓ Identify and address the behavior styles of your buyers.
- ✓ Always observe prospects closely for non-verbal cues and body language.
- ✓ Present additional selling opportunities once the buyer commits to the purchase.
- ✓ Measure the success of closing activities at both the salesperson and sales team levels.

KEY TERMS

Buyer objection	Fulfillment
Call-back	Performance metrics
Closing	Subscription offer/model
Commitment	Trial close
Continuity selling	Up-selling
Cross-selling	

REVIEW QUESTIONS

1. What is the difference between a common customer question and an objection?
2. In his book, *Integrity Selling*, Ron Willingham describes four buyer behavior styles that affect concerns they will raise during the selling process. List them and give two characteristics of each.
3. What are the four most commonly used methods to address hesitations or objections? Which of these can you see yourself using most often?
4. Describe the four steps (4 C's) in the process that salespeople may follow to successfully handle objections.
5. List three examples of positive non-verbal cues and three examples of negative body language that salespeople must watch for in their prospects when preparing to close.
6. Name and describe the two closing techniques in which salespeople take for granted that prospects will buy, even though no affirmative statement has been made yet by those prospects. Will these techniques work with all prospects?
7. What are two closing techniques that work well for indecisive prospects who have all the facts, but need reassurance that making the purchase is the right decision?
8. Describe each of the four additional selling opportunities that salespeople may use at closing, once the buyer becomes a customer.
9. What is a call-back and why is it important?
10. List at least four key performance indicators that might be used when assessing the successs of closing activities.

ETHICS IN ACTION

1. Dan Johnson is a salesperson for a large pharmaceutical company. He has been working diligently with a large health care system in the southeast to close the sale of the first drug in a new class of medications for chronic migraine. He knows that the prospect has been largely influenced by an early report of the success of this treatment by the highly influential neurologist, Dr. James Streng. As Dan prepares for the closing meeting with this prospect, he learns through the VP of Sales and Marketing that a follow-up study just completed by Dr. Streng contradicts the results of the initial study, and that Dr. Streng will be publishing this work in the next month or two. What do you suggest Dan do with this new information? Should he make his prospect aware of this news at the closing meeting? Why or why not?

2. Fred Hently is a salesperson for a timeshare resort in Daytona Beach, Florida, which is part of a larger network of properties, with connections to international holdings. He completed his training program two years ago. Training was long and intensive due to the complexity in the terms of the contract buyers must sign to become

(Continued)

timeshare owners. He recognizes the complexity of the contract and always simplifies the language in his presentations to make it more understandable to all. One day, during the closing discussion with a couple from Indiana, Fred was surprised by the number of hesitations and objections they had about the verbiage in the contract. Some questions were so complicated that Fred wasn't able to answer them with specific details. He did assure them verbally of the intent of the contract and reassured them when they pressed him about apparent differences between what he was saying and the language in the contract. He appeased them by stressing that they had five days to have the contract reviewed by their lawyer. Though they indicated that doing that would be difficult since they'd still be traveling, he complimented them on their cautious nature and was able to close the purchase. If Fred were to place a call-back to them one month later, what do you think he might learn? What things could Fred have done differently or additionally during the closing to ensure these customers would be satisfied?

EXERCISE

It's time for *Shark Tank* or *Dragon's Den*. You are an entrepreneur preparing to present your product or service in the tank/den. Think of an innovative product or service (real or fictitious) and get ready to close the deal. The goal of your pitch is to convince or persuade the Sharks/Dragons (your fellow classmates) to buy or commit to whatever action you are seeking. Students should form small groups to carry out this exercise, where each one takes a turn being the salesperson, while the rest assume the role of the established entrepreneurs (Sharks/Dragons).

Each pitch should be incredibly concise (a maximum of five minutes in length) and should be passionate, persuasive, and memorable. The Sharks should time each pitch and are asked to cut you off if you run past the five-minute limit. You may use any closing techniques you feel are appropriate to entice commitment. Sharks are encouraged to interrupt and ask questions, so be prepared to engage in a lively conversation.

Your pitch should use the following format:

Opening: *'My name is _____ and I'm seeking _____ (your desired commitment.)'*

Body: Sell the three main benefits and value of your innovative product/service.

Close: Ask for the Sharks' commitment.

This is a friendly competition. So, after all of the students in the group have taken their turn trying to persuade the Sharks, each student will submit in writing which pitch was most effective in obtaining their commitment, and explain why. Your professor or a designated group leader will tabulate and announce the winners of each 'Shark Tank' student group. Good luck, entrepreneurs!

ROLE-PLAY

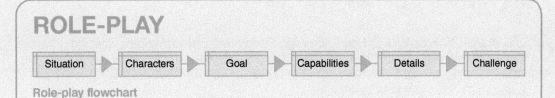

Role-play flowchart

Situation: You work as a manufacturer sales representative for a snack foods distributor that represents a variety of well-known global snack brands. You've spent the past few months trying to acquire a new large account. You just received an email invitation for another meeting scheduled early next week with the buyer who works for a conglomerate of retail convenience stores in 73 countries. You are guardedly excited because your two previous meetings went well.

Characters: You are Mel Webb and you're 34 years old. You first started working at Snacks Unlimited shortly after you graduated from college 12 years ago. Your prospect is Jess Baxter, the buyer representing Stop and Shop Variety stores. Jess is about 50 years old and has a great deal of experience as a buyer. While Jess is friendly, she is very astute and is clearly seeking the very best deal for her company.

Selling goal: It's time to land this account as you know the snack brands would generate excellent profits for the retail chain, as well as for your company.

Product/service capabilities: You represent leading snack foods that have outstanding brand recognition and affinity with consumers. Your company provides its clients with a digital inventory reporting system that can easily integrate with any analytical software and database system. Your company also provides its clients with point-of-sale retail displays, merchandising assistance, and a global network of customer service associates.

Sales call details: Jess had a number of specific questions, which were essentially buying objections, during your second meeting with her and you thought that you successfully addressed each of them. One pricing/profit margin question required you to check with your district sales manager; however, you provided that additional information to Jess a few days ago. So, with all of her buying hesitations addressed, you are hopeful for a successful sales call.

Selling challenge: How should you prepare for this third meeting with Jess? What additional objections might Jess have? What else might you be ready to do in order to obtain her buying commitment?

READINGS AND RESOURCES

- Jeb Blount (2017) *Sales EQ: How Ultra High Performers Leverage Sales-Specific Emotional Intelligence to Close the Complex Deal.* Hoboken, NJ: John Wiley & Sons, Inc.
- Steli Efti, '18 Essential Sales KPIs: What to measure and how to track everything,' https://blog.close.com/sales-kpis-metrics.
- Neil Rackham (1988) *Spin Selling.* New York: McGraw-Hill.
- Brian Tracy (2004) *The Psychology of Selling: How to Sell More, Easier, and Faster than You Ever Thought Possible.* Nashville, TN: Thomas Nelson.
- Leslie Ye (2020) 'The Ultimate Guide to Objection Handling: 40 common sales objections & how to respond,' https://blog.hubspot.com/sales/handling-common-sales-objections.

CASE STUDY: BROKER SELLING TO SWEET SHOPPE INTERNATIONAL

Note: The names and locations used in this case study have been disguised for confidentiality purposes.

'TRUST is the most essential ingredient to closing a sale,' according to Elizabeth Wood, national account manager of Delta Global Products, a worldwide service organization that brokers more than 225 different product items encompassing beverage, food, non-food, snack, confection, health and beauty, prestige brands, sporting, softlines (clothing), technology, auto and hardware product lines. Elizabeth represents the confection/seasonal product line of Delta Global Products, and her prospective customers are various buyers who purchase confection products on behalf of their respective retail businesses. The average number of active prospective buyers and customers that Elizabeth interacts with at any given time is 35. Elizabeth works hard to close sales; however, she works even harder to nurture good relationships with her network of buyers as her success is measured by her ability to continuously sell confections to her buyers, beyond obtaining their initial commitment.

She is 'Liz' to her prospective buyers and has effectively established rapport with each of them. Liz strives to become their 'go-to' person, working as a strategic advisor to help grow and develop their business. Liz cultivates personal relationships and trust by offering her prospective buyers extraordinary customer service, problem solving and negotiating based on her decades of sales experience. She spends time planning and preparing customized sales presentations to close sales and obtain buyer commitment by communicating effectively, creating a connection with the manufacturer, buyers, and co-workers, and understanding the elements of her buyers' businesses. In addition, Liz is familiar with personal aspects of each of her buyers and always speaks directly to their needs.

For example, last week Liz met with Katlyn Tabor, the buyer for Sweet Shoppe International, a global conglomerate of retail stores headquartered in Sydney, Australia. Liz was selling Katlyn a variety of confection brands, including Hershey, Godiva, Ghirardelli, Jelly Belly, and Tootsie Roll for global distribution through Sweet Shoppe International's 276 retail stores. Liz collaborated with colleagues, manufacturers, and buying teams to develop the best proposal that would produce successful results for Sweet Shoppe International.

Sweet Shoppe International logo

Based on her research and multiple interactions with Katlyn, Liz customized her sales deck, gathered samples of new products, and prepared her overview of the promotional support using advertisements, temporary price reductions, and in-store displays during key merchandising periods to be provided to Sweet Shoppe International upon buyer commitment. She carefully reviewed with Katlyn the product category and key consumer trends, innovations, and 'how- to' strategies to drive growth within each brand category. Liz used fact-based selling, effectively converting features-to-advantages-to-benefits (FAB) and was mindful to accentuate the positive and downplay any negative aspects of the sale.

Liz was aware of the fact that Katlyn was very concerned about merchandising the new confection lines, and sure enough, during the trial close, she raised several questions (objections) about that precise subject. Liz was prepared. With a few clicks on her keyboard, sample planograms, created to show proportion based on the shelf space that Sweet Shoppe International stores can accommodate, appeared on the screen. Liz carefully walked Katlyn through the planograms (see Figure 9.1) to answer all of her questions. Liz also explained Delta's new mobile app that Katlyn would be able to download to receive real-time business analytics associated with Sweet Shoppe International's planograms once she committed to the sale and displays were set. These meaningful analytics include inventory assessments, display integrity, and out-of-stock item analysis. At that point, Katlyn actually felt the merchandising support of Delta Global Products was another reason to commit to the deal.

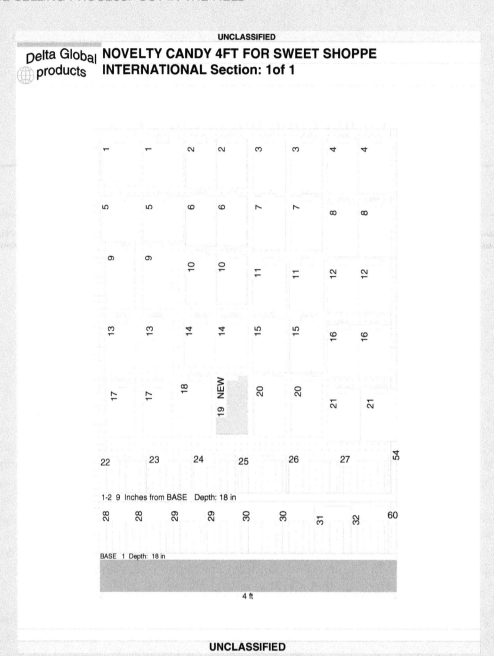

Figure 9.1A   Planogram A

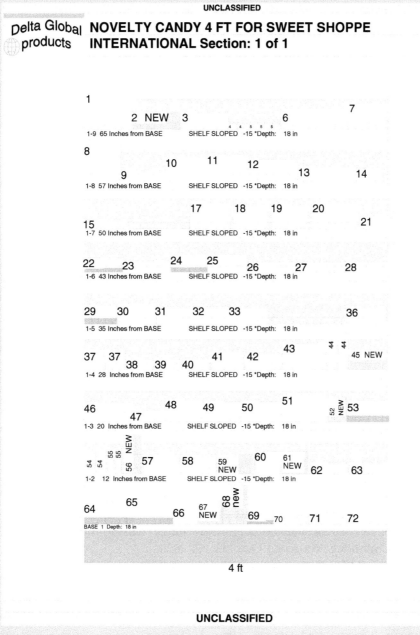

Figure 9.1B   Planogram B

Figure 9.1   Sample planograms

Liz continued her presentation, using closing questions such as:

- How does that sound?
- How do you feel about what we discussed?
- When will you finalize your review cycle?
- What date will you go live for the in-store planogram set?

Lastly, Liz was so passionate about selling Delta Global Products that her enthusiasm was contagious. Her passion became an effective closing tool because Liz believed in what she was selling, was completely focused on Katlyn's needs, and effectively used benefit statements to create belief in the confection brands she was selling. Katlyn trusted Liz and placed her faith in her ability to deliver on the promises that she made. Successful closing has never been so sweet!

Case questions:

1. Why is building trust imperative to successfully closing sales and obtaining buyer commitment?
2. What techniques did Liz use in order to attempt to obtain Katlyn's commitment to buy?
3. Based on all of the different closing techniques that Liz used, which do you think had the greatest impact in successful closing of the sale?

NOTES

1. Leslie Ye (2020) 'The Ultimate Guide to Objection Handling: 40 common sales objections and how to respond,' https://blog.hubspot.com/sales/handling-common-sales-objections, retrieved June 16, 2020.
2. Ron Willingham (2003) *Integrity Selling for the 21st Century* (New York: Random House), pp. 160–3.
3. Anthony Iannarino, 'Closing: The ability to ask for and obtain commitments' (February 7, 2010), https://thesalesblog.com/2010/02/07/closing-the-ability-to-ask-for-and-obtain-commitments, retrieved October 27, 2020.
4. Mark Holmes, 'Gain the Buyer's Commitment at Each Step in Your Sales Process,' www.salesrevenuecoach.com/blog/gain-the-buyers-commitment-at-each-step-in-your-sales-process, retrieved October 27, 2020.
5. Ibid.
6. Kerry Johnson, 'Closing techniques – Part 1,' *Senior Market Advisor* (November 2012), 13(11), 74.
7. Ibid.
8. Crosswork Consulting, 'Your Complete Guide to Closing the Sale (with Examples),' http://crossworkconsulting.com/your-complete-guide-to-closing-the-sale-with-examples, retrieved October 27, 2020.
9. Kerry Johnson, 'Closing techniques of peak performers,' *Senior Market Advisor* (June 2013), 14(6), 24.

10. Ron Willingham (2003) *Integrity Selling for the 21st Century* (New York: Random House), p. 126.

11. Adapted from Ben Janse (2019) *'Merrill Social Styles Model,'* www.toolshero.com/communication-skills/merrill-social-styles-model, retrieved October 11, 2020; and Ron Willingham (2003) *Integrity Selling for the 21st Century* (New York: Random House), pp. 127–8.

12. Adapted from Dan Marinucci, 'Don't underestimate body language,' *Tire Business*, (February 2018), 35(24), 7; 'Closing techniques,' *Sell!ng* (December 2005), p. 14; and Kerry Johnson, 'Closing techniques of peak performers,' *Senior Market Advisor* (June 2013), 14(6), 24.

13. 'Your Complete Guide to Closing the Sale (with Examples),' http://crosswork consulting.com/your-complete-guide-to-closing-the-sale-with-examples, retrieved October, 27, 2020.

14. 'Closing techniques,' *Sell!ng* (December 2005), p. 14.

15. Adapted from Adam Wiggins, 'How to Close a Sale: 7 closing techniques and why they work,' https://blog.hubspot.com/sales/sales-closing-techniques-and-why-they-work, retrieved October 27, 2020; Crosswork Consulting, 'Your Complete Guide to Closing the Sale (with Examples),' http://crossworkconsulting.com/your-complete-guide-to-closing-the-sale-with-examples, retrieved October 27, 2020; and Thomas Metcalf, 'Top 10 Sales Closing Techniques: Learn how to seal the deal' (January 28, 2019), https://smallbusiness.chron.com/top-10-sales-closing-techniques-learn-seal-deal-70629.html, retrieved October 27, 2020.

16. Ibid.

17. Kerry Johnson, 'Closing techniques of peak performers,' *Senior Market Advisor* (June 2013), 14(6), 24.

18. 'Your Complete Guide to Closing the Sale (with Examples),' http://crosswork consulting.com/your-complete-guide-to-closing-the-sale-with-examples, retrieved October, 27, 2020.

19. Adapted from Jack Cullen and Len D'Innocenzo, 'Gain Commitment in Sales: Corporate sales coaches,' www.corporatesalescoaches.com/wp-content/uploads/2015/10/Gain_Commitments_in_Sales.pdf, retrieved October 27, 2020.

20. Tim Plaehn, 'Preparing a Sales Pitch for a Trial Closing,' https://smallbusiness.chron.com/preparing-sales-pitch-trial-closing-61011.html, retrieved October 27, 2020.

21. Thomas Metcalf, 'Top 10 Sales Closing Techniques: Learn how to seal the deal' (January 28, 2019), https://smallbusiness.chron.com/top-10-sales-closing-techniques-learn-seal-deal-70629.html, retrieved October 27, 2020.

22. Jacob Geiger, 'Sales Strategies: Trial closings (Part 2)' (Nov. 22, 2012, updated Sep. 18, 2019), https://richmond.com/business/learning-center/sales-strategies-trial-closings-part/article_84a34e08-b126-52d3-bcb7-e79680b47b82.html, retrieved October 27, 2020.

23. Ron Willingham (2003) *Integrity Selling for the 21st Century* (New York: Random House), p. 197.

24. Netflix, 'Plans and Pricing,' https://help.netflix.com/en/node/24926, retrieved May 26, 2019.

25. Insider, '25 Amazon Prime Member Benefits that go Beyond Free 2-day Shipping — and How to Make the Most of Them,' www.businessinsider.com/amazon-prime-benefits-what-is-included, retrieved May 26, 2019.

26. Ibid.

27. Adobe, 'Creative Cloud for Teams,' www.adobe.com/creativecloud/business.html, retrieved May 26, 2019.

28. Mashable, 'Adobe Goes All-In on Subscription Pricing Model', https://mashable.com/2013/05/06/adobe-subscription-pricing-only, retrieved May 26, 2019.

29. Aja Frost, 'The 5 Most Important Sales Performance Metrics Every Rep and Manager Should Track,' https://blog.hubspot.com/sales/sales-performance-metrics, retrieved October 27, 2020.

30. Marisa Fong and Galia Barhava-Monteith, 'You get what you measure,' *NZ Business + Management* (August 2017), 31(7), 42–3.

31. Ibid.

32. Adapted from Aja Frost, 'The 5 Most Important Sales Performance Metrics Every Rep and Manager Should Track,' https://blog.hubspot.com/sales/sales-performance-metrics, retrieved October 27, 2020; and '5 Key Sales Metrics and KPIs You Should Know,' www.insightsquared.com/blog/the-5-key-sales-metrics-sales-vps-must-use-to-analyze-performance-and-results, retrieved October 27, 2020.

10

FOLLOWING UP TO CULTIVATE AND MANAGE CUSTOMER RELATIONSHIPS

CHAPTER CONTENTS

PEOPLE, PRACTICES AND PERSPECTIVES FROM THE WORLD OF SALES

Hello, my name is Carol Davanay and I'm a realtor with Liz Moore & Associates. I assist clients and customers in the buying and selling of residential real estate in the Hampton Roads region of Virginia. Throughout my 15-year career in sales, I've found that although being a realtor can be stressful in the extreme, there is something wonderful and fulfilling about helping people realize their dreams. *My advice is to be honest and truthful. When you don't know the answer to a question, don't guess, instead verify the answer to the best of your ability. Your clients and customers will not only thank you for it, but they will admire you.* 'Mean what you say and say what you mean!' (Source unknown.)

Hi, I'm Anne Perry, a national account manager for OSCWEBco. My responsibilities include building and nurturing loyal, long-lasting relationships with clients, building TRUST, and providing a consistent, reliable client experience. As a strategic advisor with 40 years of sales experience, my goal is to grow and develop the business. *I've found that selling is relationship building, and that storytelling and relating on a personal level build trust, as do integrity and effective communication. Leaders accomplish goals and objectives through effective communication.* 'There is never a good sale unless it's a good buy for the customer' (Herbert Marcus.)

Hello, my name is Dave Warren. I am president of STIHL Limited in Canada. I've been with the organization for 27 years across both Canada and the USA. My journey has taken me from humble beginnings as a warehouse worker, to a territory manager, sales and marketing manager, director, and president. Our customers range from family-owned one-store businesses, to larger multi-location organizations; however, all have one thing in common – they are independently owned and support their local communities. *If I could share one point that helped shape my career, it is to treat people with dignity and respect, focusing on what is important to them. My customers or direct reports didn't always agree with me over the years, but in more cases than not, we were able to find solutions through honest dialogue.*

It's always better to under-promise and over-deliver.

EYES ON ETHICS

Keep in mind the following ethical topics as you read through this chapter:

1. Closing sales to meet quotas.
2. Providing personalized service after the sale is closed.

INTRODUCTION

Congratulations! You've successfully made the sale. All of your hard work for weeks, months, or maybe even longer, along with all of the meetings, emails, and/or telephone calls have finally paid off. You've spent much time and effort understanding your prospective customer, planning and preparing your sales presentation, earning your buyer's trust, and ultimately obtaining this person's commitment to buy. Now what? Should you celebrate your successful sale? Sure! However, right after your short celebration you should get back to work on ensuring your new customer's satisfaction and strengthening your relationship with your customer. When you obtain a new customer account, your selling activities do not end, but rather, they begin in the form of fulfillment, customer service, and customer relationship management (CRM). That's what we'll address in this chapter, so let's get started.

Good relationships
© Ben Leistensnider/Christopher Newport University.

FOLLOWING UP AFTER THE SALE

Your relationships with your customers formally begin when they buy their first product or service from you. Prior to that point, you were building and strengthening your relationship with your 'prospective customers' or prospects. Remember, as we've addressed in earlier chapters, the buying journey encompasses all of the stages in the selling process – including lead generating and prospecting – however the customer journey begins when the decision to buy first occurs. In this chapter, we'll briefly review all of the stages in the buying journey, but we'll delve more deeply into the 'back-end' stages or those activities that should occur after a sale is made. This chapter may be considered the back-end of the selling process, as without it, your new customers are not likely to buy from you again. Thus, customer service or 'back end' selling is critical to ensure future success and repeat business for your company.

Performing post-sales activities

There's an old saying of unknown source: 'the back-end can't make a sale, but it sure can break a sale,' and that saying applies to engaging in appropriate post-sales activities. Post-sales activities are defined as the collection of sales, marketing, and operations processes that occur after closing a sale with a customer.[1] The following are common elements of the post-sales process:[2]

- Order fulfillment – ensuring the delivery of ordered products and/or the activation of services.
- Billing and collections – invoicing the customer for orders and collecting sales revenue.
- Cancellation and order revisions – handling canceled orders or alterations from the initial order as invoiced.
- Returns – processing requests for returns and refunds.
- Complaints – receiving customer complaints and appropriately resolving them.
- Additional support – providing supplementary assistance or information to ensure the customer the greatest possible success with the product/service purchased.
- Incident management – investigating and resolving issues with a purchased product or service.
- Relationship management – building, strengthening, and sustaining relationships with customers.
- Feedback – surveying customers to obtain feedback on their level of satisfaction with the buying experience and the product/service purchased.
- Upselling and cross-selling – convincing customers to upgrade or purchase additional related or unrelated products or services.
- Customer referrals – encouraging satisfied customers to refer future business opportunities to you/your company.
- Maintenance and supplies – delivery of maintenance services and providing needed materials associated with the product or service purchased.
- End-of-support services to aid customers in dealing with end-of-life for a product or service.

Salespeople should conduct post-sales activities in a timely manner, with a customer retention focus to strengthen customer relationships and drive future business opportunities. Two post-sales activities that should be carried out immediately after the sale is closed, include thanking the customer and delivering on any promises made to the customer during the selling process. Let's talk a bit about each of these important follow-up activities:

- *Thanking the customer.* As mentioned in Chapter 5, a *handwritten* personal note expressing your appreciation for the customer's business demonstrates your extra care and makes a greater impression than a typed one or an email message. The thank you note may be brief, but should be customized and personalized to each new customer. A well-written thank you note conveys your sincere gratitude for the purchase and also reassures the customer that you are available to them if/as needed now and in the future. The brief note should communicate that your relationship with the customer is highly valued and that you intend to continue it into the future. See Figure 10.1 for a sample thank you note.

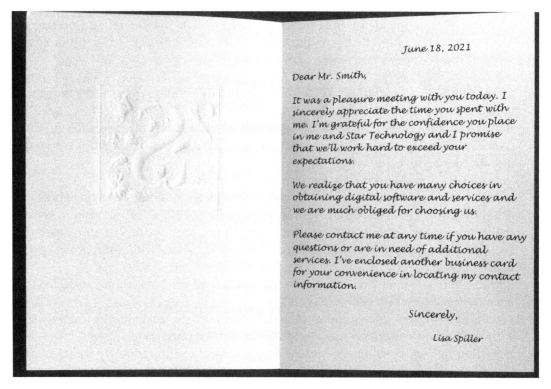

Figure 10.1   Thank you note sample

- *Delivering on promises.* A lethal mistake when selling is to over-promise the features, benefits, or value of a product/service when you are selling. Why? It's simple. Because whenever you build the expectations of customers to be really high, you are likely to have a hard time meeting them, which typically leads to customer dissatisfaction. Think of it this way: whenever customers spend money to purchase a given product/service, those customers expect to receive some amount of value that they believe is equal or worth the amount of money paid. Whenever you give your customers precisely what they expected, you are creating customer satisfaction. Satisfied customers are great, but an even better strategy is to under-promise so that you can more readily deliver a product/service that exceeds customer expectations, which typically leads to delighted customers. As you'd expect, this strategy only works well when your under-promise meets the customer's needs.

Most customers spread word-of-mouth communication only when they are either dissatisfied or delighted. Thus, post-sales activities that add value and ensure that customers are delighted are important strategies. In addition, those salespeople who follow up to ensure the satisfaction and delight of their customers, will strengthen customer loyalty and be seen as 'referral worthy,' which is a highly desirable quality to possess. Research reports that 90 percent of customers are more likely to make further purchases if a company provided excellent customer service.[3] Fulfilling promises made to customers and providing excellent customer service require effective communication, both with the customer and throughout the company. That's the topic of our next section.

Word of mouth communication

Providing customer service

Unfortunately, many companies are lacking in their customer service as they prioritize more resources on the selling process to acquire new customers than on serving these customers after the sale. This is a critical error for a company, as evidenced by a Mattersight study of consumers which revealed that just one bad customer experience caused 70 percent of consumers to not buy again from that company.[4] In fact, research by the Dunvegan Group found that 20 percent of customers who feel 'satisfied' with their purchase will switch to a competitor in the future. So, not only do poor customer experiences lead to customer deflection, but even typical ones will result in a portion of your customers seeking out products/services from your competitors.[5] We'll address the metrics associated with customer retention a bit later in the chapter, but for now, let's focus on how to deliver excellent customer service.

Your number one priority with customer service is to do everything you can to make sure your customers are happy. Sounds simple? Well, maybe in theory, but in practice it may be more challenging. First, communication is the key. Throughout the sales funnel stages, your prospective customer has likely articulated a number of desires, questions, preferences, and so on. Excellent customer service begins with a comprehensive review of all of the issues raised by the prospect leading up to closing the sale. This is facilitated by creating a check-list of those items at each stage, so you can be sure to address each one. In other words, you must understand the customer and create the post-sales lifecycle from the customer's perspective in order to address all of the elements that are truly important to the customer.[6]

Effective communication among associates or departments throughout the company to confirm that everyone is both on the same page and aligned with the customer's needs and wants, will provide a smooth transition from pre-sales to post-sales activities. The transition period between the sales cycle and the 'becoming a customer' portion of the client relationship is referred to as the sales hand-off, and it often sets the tone for how the rest of the customer service will evolve. Thus, salespeople must ensure they transfer all relevant customer information, such as key contact, challenges, goals, values, desired outcomes, and any promises made to the customer to the customer service managers or account managers, in order to ensure success. We'll explore the role of account managers in greater detail later in the chapter. What's important is a smooth sales hand-off with adequate data transfer to enable excellent customer service to be provided.

The sales hand-off should include the manner in which customer service value will be delivered and measured to ensure success. Specific goals should be established to ensure the new customer account is set up properly and that valuable service is provided to the customer. Salespeople should check in with new customers early and often to find out if the product/service is living up to their expectations, and to inquire if there is any additional assistance that they may desire. Sometimes, new customers feel unsure about who to reach out to if they have a question. Thus, a proactive team approach is needed where salespeople work with their company's customer service providers to ensure excellent customer service is being provided, customized to each customer. After all, serving the customer is everyone's job!

Serving the customer
© Ben Leistensnider/Christopher Newport University.

Salespeople can contribute to delivering excellent customer service even before the sale is made by practicing ethical selling behavior and being blatantly honest with prospective customers about whether or not a product/service will truly serve their long-term needs. Thus, salespeople must resist the urge to close deals that are likely to churn in a short period of time. Instead, salespeople should seek successful long-term relationships with customers and consider the pre-sales and post-sales cycles as the singular lifecycle of the customer.[7] When salespeople focus only on the customer's short-term needs, customer dissatisfaction and/or customer complaints are likely to arise in the future.

Invariably, some customers will have a complaint and they should be met with the same team approach, as well as due diligence, to ensure their complete satisfaction. Handling customer complaints includes the following strategies, and they are most effectively carried out in order:[8]

1. **Listen** – always actively listen to your customers and allow ample time for them to vent before attempting to find a way to resolve the problem.
2. **Empathize** – try to understand your customers – put yourself in their shoes – in order to truly see the situation from the customer's perspective.
3. **Apologize** – offer a sincere apology to your customers when something has gone wrong as owning up to a problem and seeking their understanding and forgiveness can be very effective techniques if they are genuine.
4. **Solve** – to determine an adequate resolution to the problem, ask for the customer's input and offer your own ideas in order to find the best possible solution to the problem.

The best practice is to anticipate customer complaints in advance through effective and ongoing communication with customers in order to rectify any potential situation that may lead to a complaint. In other words, excellent customer service can deflect complaints *before* they have a chance to be formed. That's why successful sales hand-offs to account managers require great attention to detail in order to effectively manage customer relationships. Let's now examine what is involved in customer relationship management.

MANAGING CUSTOMER RELATIONSHIPS

Successful long-term business is based on good relationship management with customers. Most companies achieve successful operations by using a 'hunter-farmer' model where the salespeople (the hunters) are responsible for capturing new business by sourcing leads, prospecting, qualifying, delivering sales presentations, handling objections, negotiating, and ultimately, closing sales. Once the commitment has been achieved and the sale is closed, the customer is handed over to an account management team (the farmers) who grow the relationship by providing post-sales activities.[9]

Managing accounts and territories (and CRM tools)

Account management is a post-sales role that focuses on nurturing client relationships. So, sales activities tend to be more transactional, while account management activities are more relational.[10] That's not to say that salespeople should not focus on relationship selling; however, the primary role of salespeople revolves around transactions. Account managers are the employees in charge of overseeing client accounts once a salesperson has closed the business deal.[11] Account managers serve as the day-to-day point of contact for customers or clients, and have two primary objectives: retaining the client's business and growing the account value. Thus, they focus on performing post-sales activities to ensure client satisfaction and delight, which include providing customer service, managing relationships, up-selling and cross-selling, renewing contracts, and so on.[12] Effective account management entails a team approach to gaining the trust of customers, which directly impacts customer retention and company profitability. Table 10.1 provides some tips to ensure effective account management.

Table 10.1 Effective account management techniques

➢ Nurture client relationships by becoming a strategic partner with clients.

➢ Understand the needs of clients to determine client contact method preferences.

➢ Be proactive in contacting clients for input on a consistent basis.

➢ Perform regular performance evaluations and share the results with clients.

➢ Provide new client onboarding to discuss workflow and service expectations.

➢ Become a consultant to clients and provide professional recommendations.

➢ Keep clients abreast of the latest developments in the company and industry.

➢ Upsell and cross-sell only when it aligns with the client's goals.

➢ Use CRM software tools to track all client information.

➢ Always follow through in a timely manner.

➢ Collaborate with other departments and oversee all service delivery.

➢ Hire and train competent account management staff to enable duty delegation.

➢ Always be transparent and accessible.

➢ Never stop learning and stay informed.

➢ Be accountable to clients and help them achieve their goals.

Source: Adapted from Julian Hooks, '6 Account Management Tips for Sales Success,' www.tenfold.com/lead-management/6-account-management-tips-sales-success, retrieved December 3, 2020; Robert Izquierdo, 'How Account Management Can Impact Your Business,' www.fool.com/the-blueprint/account-management, retrieved December 3, 2020; and 'The 6 Golden Rules of Account Management,' https://yesler.com/blog/customer-engagement/the-6-golden-rules-of-account-management, retrieved December 3, 2020.

Sales managers are also responsible for defining and managing sales territories which are developed primarily based on data about their current clients. Traditionally, a sales territory referred to a geographical area assigned to an individual salesperson or team; however, the modern definition, reflecting changes due to digital connectivity, is much broader.[13] A sales territory is the regional, industry, or account type assigned to a specific salesperson or sales team.[14] Characteristics used to determine sales territories include sales potential, industry segment, product or service, customer type, purchase history, referral source, verticals (pipeline sales paths), number of customer accounts, and other relevant factors.[15] Thus, not all sales territories require an in-person presence, and many salespeople work remotely to service clients via telephone, email, and video sales calls.[16] In fact, the type of service required by the client may be a way to organize clients and determine sales territories. Another way to organize client accounts offered by Mason Minor, is based on the K.A.R.E. framework, which categorizes current accounts according to the following:[17]

- *Keep*: existing accounts with which you have solid relationships, acceptable profit margins, and minimal investment.
- *Attain*: target accounts that match the profile of existing high-profit-potential customers.
- *Recapture*: previous accounts that have been lost but would offer acceptable profit margins.
- *Expand*: on existing accounts that have the potential for growth and development.

Establishing and managing sales territories requires constant evaluation of three main areas: current active client accounts, the territories themselves, and salespeople.[18] Planning and structuring sales territories require careful deliberation because it is important for sales managers to effectively assign sales territories appropriately the first time as constant changes are harmful to the productivity and morale of salespeople, as well as to client relationships.[19] As salespeople and account managers work to develop and nurture trusting relationships with their clients over time, changes in the salesperson and/or account manager assigned to a client's account are disruptive.

Sales managers create sales territories for the following three main reasons:[20]

1. **For customers** – territories enable increased market coverage and good customer service to be delivered.
2. **For salespeople** – territories can lead to more motivated and enthusiastic salespeople and sales teams, as well as greater team cohesion.
3. **For sales managers** – territories offer enhanced control of promotion coordination and allocation of costs per territory.

Sales managers are responsible for sales territory management, which is the process of creating, managing, and optimizing sales territories and the salespeople that are responsible for them.[21] Sales territory management includes strategically defining and evaluating territories, setting goals, and providing sales teams with the tools needed to achieve success. Central to successful sales territory management is proper cadence management, which is the process of prioritizing, structuring, timing, and conducting account interactions. Thoughtful and strategic sales territory management aligns salespeople with the most appropriate customers based on their strengths, weaknesses, and levels of expertise. Salespeople should keep thorough and up-to-date records of each and every client engagement. In addition, they should enter both client and meeting notes on a regular basis into the CRM system. Synchronous data updates should be used to allow salespeople to update and access customer data in real time.[22] By integrating sales territory management with your company's CRM system, you can identify opportunities to help your sales team decide where to dedicate their time and resources.

Southern Territory
Eastern Territory
Central Territory
Northern Territory
Western Territory

Sales territories

Managing sales territories and client accounts are important activities for sales managers and account managers. Given the dynamic and often complex business conditions and competitive situation, sales managers and account managers must determine how to most effectively allocate their time and limited resources in managing relationships with their clients. Sales managers and account managers prioritize clients and focus on those key accounts, also referred to as 'strategic accounts,' that are more likely to result in a long-term relationship that will produce significant returns for many years. Let's now explore key accounts in greater detail.

Conducting key account management

All customers are not of equal value; however, they may be categorized according to the strength of their relationship with a company or an organization. As Figure 10.2 reveals, prospects and customers can be placed in a hierarchy with the least valuable at the bottom and the most valuable at the top. As described in earlier chapters, *suspects* are those prospective consumers that you think may have a need or want for your company's product or service. *Prospects* are 'hand-raisers' who have identified themselves as having an interest in your company or organization. Prospects may have visited your website or have become a qualified lead. *Customers* have placed an order with your company. They could be called 'single buyers' as you do not know if they will return for a repeat purchase. *Clients* are multi-buyers. These are repeat customers with whom you have an established relationship. At the top of the customer hierarchy are *advocates* – these are your most valuable customers.

Highly satisfied customers tend to be loyal ones, and loyal customers generate greater profits for an organization over their lifetime of patronage. This is for the following four reasons:

1. Loyal customers tend to increase their spending over time. These customers are better to have and more profitable than other customers.
2. Loyal customers cost less to serve than new customers. Repeat customers have greater familiarity with an organization's processes and procedures, and therefore are more quickly and easily served.
3. Loyal customers are normally happy customers who tell others about the organization, commonly referred to as word-of-mouth advertising, which in turn generates additional business.
4. Loyal customers are less price sensitive than are new customers. They see value in their relationship with the organization and may spend more freely because of their high level of satisfaction with the company.

In addition, according to Frederick Reichheld, author of *The Loyalty Effect*, a five-percentage-point increase in customer retention in a typical company will increase profits by more than 25 percent.[23]

Key account management is the process of building long-term relationships with your company's most valuable client accounts. These clients represent the majority of your company's business. According to the well-known 80/20 principle, approximately 80 percent of a company's business is generated by 20 percent of its customers. Thus, it is critical to analyze your customer database to determine who your best customers are and to spend more effort (and budget) in retaining and growing these client accounts. Key account management starts with understanding who the company's best customers are and how they want to be served. Check out Table 10.2 for some tips on executing a key account management strategy.

Figure 10.2 Customer value hierarchy

Table 10.2 Key account management strategies

- Limit the number of 'key' accounts to a manageable number based on total number of clients to be managed.
- Carefully define the criteria for key account designation.
- Apply the specified key account criteria consistently when selecting key accounts.
- Ensure a high level of service is provided to all key accounts.
- Routinely measure key account performance to ensure the client continues to qualify.
- Regularly review all client accounts to identify new key account candidates.
- Prioritize communication and service delivery to key accounts.
- Build a dedicated KAM team to consistently serve key accounts.
- Orchestrate and oversee service delivery with key accounts.
- Use CRM tools to track communication with key accounts and coordinate with the KAM team.
- Identify ways to grow the relationships and partnerships with key account clients.

Source: Adapted from Aja Frost, 'Key Account Management: The ultimate guide,' https://blog.hubspot.com/sales/key-account-management, retrieved December 3, 2020; and Robert Izquierdo, 'How Account Management Can Impact Your Business,' www.fool.com/the-blueprint/account-management, retrieved December 3, 2020.

A **key account manager** (KAM) is responsible for turning a company's most valuable clients into business partners via dedicated resources, unique offers, and periodic meetings. The specific goals of a KAM are:[24]

➤ collaborating with the client on mutually beneficial projects
➤ helping the client meet target objectives
➤ making sure the client is receiving the necessary support.

Many companies have started key account management programs as they realized that key accounts spend 33 percent more on average than do other clients.[25] In addition, according to the *Harvard Business Review*, customer satisfaction increases 20 percent within a few years of starting a key account management program.[26] But, how do you determine which of your client accounts should be designated as key accounts? The criteria to use when choosing key accounts should be broadly based and will typically vary by company and selling situation. Here are some selection criteria that you may factor into your decision:[27]

✓ product fit between the client and your company
✓ solvency and reputation of the client company
✓ existing relationships with the key people at the client company
✓ potential for a long-term collaborative relationship
✓ possibility of becoming a channel partner with your company
✓ cultural fit between the client and your company
✓ geographic location alignment and/or desirability
✓ business potential for a broad network of customer contacts
✓ purchasing processes in place at the client company
✓ sales revenue potential.

Selecting accounts solely based on revenue is not the best strategy, although customer value is one significant criterion. Let's now explore how to determine the value of your customers.

Quantifying customer value and customer relationships

Quantifying customer value can help sales managers and salespeople in strategic account planning by determining those customers that should be designated as key accounts. It is important to note that customer retention strategies normally generate greater profitability for companies than do new customer acquisition strategies. This is partially due to the value of the established relationship that current customers have with a given company. Remember, strong customer relationships are directly correlated to strong customer loyalty; and loyal customers are more profitable.

Many companies attest to the claim that it costs at least five times more to acquire a customer than it does to retain a current customer. This can be easily calculated mathematically. For example, let's say it costs $5 to keep a customer happy and loyal to your firm (a customer retention strategy) and it costs $25 (five times $5) to obtain a new customer (a new customer acquisition strategy). Let's perform the math given a budget of $175. Table 10.3 shows that if we allocate the majority of our budget to acquiring new customers, we net 11 customers. However, if we allocate the majority of our budget to retaining current customers, we net 23 customers. Given the same budget, the mathematical difference is significant.

Table 10.3 Acquisition versus customer retention

Customer Acquisition Focus:	Customer Retention Focus:
$150 to acquire customers = 6	$75 to acquire customers = 3
$25 to retain customers = 5	$100 to retain customers = 20

Understanding the value of each customer or account is an important metric for sales managers and salespeople to explore via their CRM system. CRM tools should be employed to track all of the outbound touchpoints from a company, including email, direct mail, SMS text messaging, banner ad marketing, direct response television advertisements (DRTV), and traditional channels such as radio, newspaper, and magazine ads. Sales managers, key account managers, and salespeople need to tap into this valuable customer data to better understand both how customers make purchase decisions and what needs they may have at the post-sales stage. CRM provides a variety of sales, marketing, and service functions that allow interaction with customers across the organization and multiple media channels. The main benefit is that all information – from prospect communication, through commitment to buy, to service history – is tracked, analyzed, and used to manage engagement with that customer and future prospects based on patterns that emerge with analytics.

By focusing on CRM at the initial point of contact, sales managers, key account managers, and salespeople have a far better chance of nurturing long-term relationships that generate satisfaction for their customers and revenue or value for their company. Understanding the value of loyal customers is a necessary element in the development of effective customer engagement activities. Customer engagement is a measure of a company's interaction with its customers across all touchpoints throughout its lifecycle. Conducting research to better understand customers is the first and most important step in the CRM and customer engagement process. Let's now discuss how sales managers, key account managers, and salespeople can analyze and track the metrics associated with customer value and customer relationships.

As we have previously discussed, all consumers are not alike. They can be grouped into market segments based on similar needs and wants using insight from research and data stored in company databases. This data includes information about the actions taken by consumers, which is critical insight for everyone in the company. However, while all forms of customer data are very important, the most valuable information is that which comes after the first sale. This includes the products and services purchased, the amount or value of the sale, the date the sale occurred, the people involved in the buying decision process, and so on. These pieces of data can be aggregated from multiple customers to reveal the similarities among them.

Data analytics

Researching, gathering, and organizing customer transaction data in a customer database or CRM system enables a company to determine the value of each customer. How does a database help you quantify customer value? How do you measure and calculate customer value? How do you use transactional data to determine customer value? Those are the questions we'll address in this section. While there are a number of different methods for calculating customer value, we'll explore the following two: recency/frequency/monetary (RFM) assessment and customer value equation.

Recency/frequency/monetary (RFM) assessment

Specific transaction data may include the products each customer has purchased, how recently (recency), how often (frequency), and how much the customer spends (monetary). This information provides an avenue to analyze each customer through some variation of the recency/frequency/monetary (RFM) assessment. By recording the date and volume of purchases in the customer database or CRM system over a period of time, salespeople can assess the transaction record of each customer in a given period, which helps determine the future potential of that customer.

The exact RFM formulation naturally varies by company according to the importance given to each of the variables in relation to each other. For some selling situations, the company might need to manipulate its calculations by weighting one of the factors, so that, for example, the results will show those customers who have purchased most recently. More sophisticated data analysis uses multivariate statistical techniques to mathematically determine the RFM weights for stronger predictive value.

Table 10.4 shows how to evaluate customers in a database according to the combined RFM values of their transactions over time. For the purposes of this example, the following weights are assigned to the variables: recency (× 5), frequency (× 3), and monetary (× 2). In the example, three customers (identified as A, B, and C) have a purchase history calculated over a 24-month period. Rating scales were created in

Table 10.4 RFM values

ASSUMPTIONS:

Recency of transaction: 20 points if within past 3 months
10 points if within past 6 months
5 points if within past 9 months
3 points if within past 12 months
1 point if within past 24 months

Frequency of transaction: Number of purchases within 24 months x 4 points each (Maximum: 20 points)
Monetary value of transaction: Gross dollar volume of purchases within 24 months x 10% (Maximum: 20 points)

Example: Cust.	Purchase#	Recency	Assigned Points (x5)	Wght. Points	Frequency	Assigned Points	(x3) Wght. Points	Monetary	Assigned Points	(x2) Wght. Points	Total Wght. Points	Cum. Points
A	#1	3 mths	20	100	1	4	12	$30	3	6	118	118
A	#2	9 mths	5	25	1	4	12	$100	10	20	57	175
A	#3	24 mths	1	5	1	4	12	$50	5	10	27	202
B	#1	12 mths	3	15	2	8	24	$500	20	40	79	79
C	#1	3 mths	20	100	1	4	12	$100	10	20	132	132
C	#2	6 mths	10	50	1	4	12	$60	6	12	74	206
C	#3	12 mths	3	15	2	8	24	$70	7	14	53	259
C	#4	24 mths	1	5	1	4	12	$20	2	4	21	280

Weighing assumption: Recency = 5; Frequency = 3; Monetary = 2.

order to score the recency, frequency, and monetary factors for each customer. Using the same scales allows multiple customers to be compared to one another directly. RFM scores for each customer were then calculated, according to the RFM formula, with appropriate weights applied to recency, frequency, and monetary factors. The resulting cumulative point calculations – 202 for A, 79 for B, and 280 for C – indicate a potential preference for customer C. Customer C's RFM history, and perhaps A's as well, justify spending more effort in retaining these customers. Customer B is likely to be a less-profitable investment of time for the company's sales team.

Customer value equation

To quantitatively calculate average customer value, you should follow this five-step process:

1. Take a random sample of customers (active and inactive) who first bought from you about three years ago. (Note that the sample size should be large enough to represent all customer segments.)
2. For each customer, add up the dollar amounts for all purchases within three years of the date of their first purchase.
3. For ALL customers in your sample, add up the three-year total dollar amounts.
4. Divide the grand total by the number of customers in your sample.
5. Multiply the result by the percentage that represents your average profit margin.

For example, let's pretend you now own a company that sells household gifts. You are in your fourth year in business and want to calculate the average value of your customers. What do you do? You use the following three easy steps of A, B, and C:

A. You randomly select 1,000 customers who have been purchasing with your company for a minimum of three years and obtain a computer printout of their buying history. You see that these customers have placed a total of 1,775 orders during this period, with a total value of $89,300.
B. You calculate your average profit margin on your household gift lines and determine it to be 20 percent.
C. Now let's do the math. Dividing total sales by customers ($89,300 by 1,000) results in average sales of $89.30 per customer. Then, by multiplying that figure by the average profit margin percentage (20 percent), you determine that the average customer value is $17.86.

The figure represents what the average customer you acquired three years ago was worth to you in terms of future profits. The real benefit of calculating customer value is that it can be calculated on a segment or cluster basis, or on an individual basis. The process for calculating individual or segment customer values is basically the same, however you would not select a 'random' sample of customers; rather, you would select *only* from the segment or cluster of interest. On the basis of these customer value calculations, you can determine which customers or customer segments are generating the most profitability for your company and concentrate on retaining those customers. You would also seek out new prospects that closely resemble those customers who are most valuable.

Why should you calculate the value of your customers? Three reasons are offered here:

1. It determines how much each customer is worth to your organization, so you may designate those most valuable as key accounts and prioritize them.
2. It guides you in terms of how much money you can afford to spend to acquire a new customer like your current customers.
3. It helps you to identify your best customers in order to seek out new prospective customers who match the customer profiles of your best customers.

Customer relationships translate into customer retention, which usually means repeat customer purchases or transactions over time. When a customer is retained, it is not only the revenue generated in a one-month or one-year period that constitutes the value of that customer, it is the present value of the future stream of revenue that must be taken into consideration. This may also include the opportunity for servicing contracts to be obtained in the future, as some products, such as computers, equipment and machinery, require service after a sale is made.

Assessing and measuring the impact of customer engagement programs is critical to identifying those post-sales strategies and practices that are effective and those that may need to be altered or discontinued. That's the topic of our last section in this chapter.

MONITORING METRICS

Monitoring Metrics

Analyzing the data acquired from your customer encounters helps to determine what customer engagement activities work for each customer segment and sales territory. While there are no precise formulas to measure the value of follow-up activities, several specific metrics may be good indicators of customer sentiment and customer satisfaction level. According to V. Kumar, author of *Profitable Customer Engagement: Concept, Metrics and Strategies*, one of the suggested Readings and Resources provided at the end of this chapter, customer engagement value may be evaluated and measured. Customer engagement value, which is the set of metrics that describe customers who value the brand and contribute to the firm through purchase activities, referrals, positive influence on other customers, and feedback to the company, may be tracked and measured. Let's examine some of the data associated with customer engagement value:[28]

- ✓ **Customer lifetime value (CLTV)** – net present value of future cash flows from a customer over the lifetime of their patronage with the company.
- ✓ **Customer referral value (CRV)** – monetary value associated with future profits generated by each referred prospect.
- ✓ **Customer influence value (CIV)** – monetary value of customer's impact on other acquired customers and prospects.
- ✓ **Customer knowledge value (CKV)** – monetary value a customer contributes to the firm through their feedback.

Customer engagement value may either directly or indirectly effect the profitability of a company. Each of these metrics is determined by the effectiveness of post-sales activities. Thus, assessing the impact of follow-up activities provided after a sale is possible. Additional positive post-sales indicators that may be tracked and analyzed, include the following quantitative metrics:[29]

- increase in customer retention rates – repeat purchases or renewal rates
- reduction of churn rates
- increase in cross-selling and up-selling success rates
- increase in number of subscribers
- shorter purchase cycle lengths
- increase in the number of brand evangelists
- enhanced customer service ratings
- increased customer satisfaction scores
- increased number of customer referrals
- increased number of repeat visits to a company's website and/or physical store.

In addition, you may assess sales volume and other related outcomes of sales territories to optimize territory division. Items to monitor with regard to sales territories include:[30]

- increased or decreased sales in a specific territory
- disparities between sales in different territories

- associated costs with each territory
- salespeople and/or sales teams' meeting quotas
- salespeople and/or sales teams' inability to follow up on sales leads
- underserved regions that may be in need of additional coverage.

When sales managers monitor and react to these metrics, they are better able to maintain even territory division among salespeople, which leads to increased post-sales service, customer satisfaction, and customer engagement. This culminates in improved long-term customer relationships and greater profitability for the company.

CHAPTER SUMMARY

✓ A negative post-sales experience undermines a good relationship built during the buyer journey.

✓ Always remember to provide a personal thank you to a customer once a sale is finalized.

✓ Customer complaints must be addressed well to ensure ongoing customer satisfaction.

✓ Calculate the value for each customer in order to understand and prioritize accounts.

✓ Identify a key account manager to focus on each customer designated as a key account.

KEY TERMS

Account management
Account managers
Cadence management
Customer engagement
Customer engagement value
Key account management
Key account manager

Post-sales activities
Recency/frequency/monetary (RFM) assessment
Sales hand-off
Sales territory
Sales territory management

REVIEW QUESTIONS

1. Discuss four common elements of the post-sales process.
2. Name three methods of expressing your appreciation for the customer's business. Which is considered the most effective method?
3. Explain the four strategies for handling customer complaints in the order in which they should be applied.
4. What is the difference between how sales territories have been traditionally defined and how they may be defined in the current age of digital connectivity?
5. Once sales territories have been carefully established, what impact does making constant changes to them have on salespeople and clients?
6. Identify four reasons why highly satisfied, loyal customers generate greater profits for an organization over their lifetime of patronage.
7. Name three specific goals of a key account manager and explain why each goal is important.
8. Identify and explain four criteria that can be used when selecting key accounts.
9. Describe two reasons why you should calculate the value of your customers.
10. Identify and briefly explain three metrics that are associated with measuring customer engagement value. Which do you think is the most important of these?

ETHICS IN ACTION

1. John Carter is a sales representative at a local car dealership. He has struggled to meet his quota for the past two months. He is currently working to close a deal with a prospective customer who states the need for a mid-sized vehicle for her family, but can't afford her selected model. John shows her a similarly equipped, compact car and forcefully sells her on the improved gas mileage and clever seat configurations that enable more storage space. Though she is still hesitant about the size of the car, he wins her business after offering a special incentive to purchase this model. He is relieved to have made the sale the day the month ends. Has John done the best he could for his customer? What might the customer experience as she and her family use this vehicle on a daily basis?

2. Sally Newsome is the sales representative for a local electronics store. She has been increasing her sales of laptop computers steadily over the last three months. While the sales manager asks all of the salespeople to make a follow-up call to customers after the sale, Sally has been so busy with new customers that she has failed to do this. On her shift one day, Sally receives a telephone call from a recent customer, complaining about the service he received post-sale. Feeling that she doesn't have time to deal with this, she apologizes to the customer and promptly transfers the call back to the customer service department. How is the customer likely to react to this? Why did the customer call Sally directly that day? How likely is the customer to buy from this store in the future?

EXERCISE

Congratulations! You've just been hired as the inaugural key account manager (KAM) for a financial services company. Your initial responsibility is to prepare a proposal to determine which clients should be designated as key accounts for the company, and the process you plan to use in making those determinations. In addition, the proposal should address the specific services and activities that you and your KAM team will use in strengthening the relationship with and growing the value of each of the designated key account clients. Your boss wants to see your KAM proposal on her desk in one week. She has asked that you include the following elements in your proposal:

A. Criteria you will use in designating key account clients.
B. Specific activities and/or services that each key account client will receive.
C. Methods you and your KAM team will use to increase the value of each key account.
D. The reporting time periods and specific metrics you will use to assess the effectiveness of your KAM activities.

ROLE-PLAY

Role-play flowchart

Situation: You are an account management representative working for Payroll Systems Solutions and you're meeting for the first time with associates at Berkley Corporation. Berkley is one of your company's key accounts and you've recently taken over servicing this account for Marsha Newberry who retired from the company so she could spend more time with her grandkids. You've been informed that the new payroll software installed last week is proving more challenging to the accounting staff at Berkley than was anticipated.

Characters: You are 28-year-old Aubrey Jones, a friendly and talkative individual with outstanding knowledge about the new software programs offered by your company. You are eager to help your clients benefit from all of the features that the new payroll software provides. You are meeting with Jean Van Tripp, Vice President of Berkley. She oversees the business operations and human resources offices and has been with Berkley for 30 years. You've been told that Jean tends to be a no-nonsense, very direct individual. Plus, she's a power-player at Berkley. Jean had a good working relationship with Marsha, as they'd worked together for more than two decades.

Selling goal: To determine an adequate resolution to the problem and ensure customer delight.

Product/service capabilities: Payroll Systems Solutions (PSS) has been in business for nearly 50 years, and started as a small, family-owned company. Over the years, it has grown into a global enterprise serving companies and organizations in 28 different countries. Its brand reputation is stellar and its software systems are perceived as being state of the art. In order to remain on the cutting edge, PSS is constantly producing upgraded systems that often require training in order to reap the full benefits of their payroll services. PSS offers training for all new software programs, as well as additional online training webinars on a periodic basis. Its software systems are competitively priced, but are usually on the higher end of the spectrum.

Sales call details: Jean is extremely busy, but carved out time for a meeting with you because she's not pleased that the new software program isn't providing all of the benefits that were expected. She didn't provide much context other than that complaint.

Selling challenge: How should you prepare for this first meeting with Jean? What specific complaints might Jean have? What will you need to do in order to turn this dissatisfied client into a delighted one?

READINGS AND RESOURCES

- Roderick J. Brodie, Linda D. Hollebeek and Jodie Conduit (eds) (2016) *Customer Engagement: Contemporary Issues and Challenges*. Abingdon, UK: Routledge.
- Mark Donnolo (2017) *Essential Account Planning: 5 Keys for Helping Your Sales Team Drive Revenue*. Alexandria, VA: ATD Press.
- Max Fatouretchi (2019) *The Art of CRM: Proven Strategies for Modern Customer Relationship Management*. Birmingham, UK: Packt Publishing.
- V. Kumar (2013) *Profitable Customer Engagement: Concept, Metrics and Strategies*. New Delhi: SAGE.
- Shil Niyogi (2016) *Lean Customer Engagement*. New Delhi: SAGE.
- Customer Engagement (website) – https://vwo.com/customer-engagement.

CASE STUDY: BOSTON SCIENTIFIC

Figure 10.3 Boston Scientific logo
Used with kind permission of Boston Scientific.

Maintaining excellent relationships to preserve and strengthen trust between the salesperson and the client after a sale is made is critical. Following up with clients is something that Rachael Judy knows very well as she works for Boston Scientific, a medical device manufacturer represented in 120 countries. Boston Scientific is dedicated to transforming lives through innovative medical solutions that improve the health of patients around the world. Rachael works in the Neuromodulation Division and is responsible for selling a spinal cord stimulator device. She works in the field to ensure that stellar customer service is provided directly to her physician accounts, as well as patients, after implantation (see Figure 10.4).

Figure 10.4 Rachael Judy in the field
Used with kind permission of Rachael Judy.

Rachael is a member of the customer service team for any local patients who are implanted with the Boston Scientific spinal cord device. On a regular basis, Rachael services approximately 20 active accounts of pain management physicians, spine surgeons, and neurosurgeons. In addition, she calls on multiple medical offices each month that could potentially provide referrals to the physicians who perform spinal cord procedures with Boston Scientific devices. While the physicians are the decision makers, their medical practice staff is equally important for Rachael to service as the office managers, referral coordinators, and nurse supervisors are the gatekeepers.

It is important to have regular contact with clients to assess patient and physician needs. Rachael varies her follow-up techniques in order to connect with each individual customer on a personal level. She visits each of her clients weekly to update them and provide them with valuable clinical information, patient education ideas, and ways to continue to educate the community. During each client visit, Rachael specifically asks if there is anything that her team can do better. Rachael never takes business relationships for granted. Even when she thinks she has very loyal clients, she realizes her competition is *always* knocking at their door.

Rachael is a firm believer in using patient success stories as a method to educate the community. In Rachael's words: 'There is absolutely no better way in my mind to promote spinal cord stimulation as a therapy option locally than the patient success story. I have seen tremendous success with this concept.'

At Boston Scientific, a patient success story takes place when one of its very happy patients who was implanted with the spinal cord stimulator and is receiving tremendous results in pain relief, allows Rachael to share the patient's success story with the patient's primary care physician. The implanted patient signs an authorization form, allowing Boston Scientific to share this information. Next, Rachael creates a folder of information on the patient, including the procedure, the results, the physician who performed the procedure as well as information on spinal cord stimulation. Then Rachael schedules a meeting between the primary care physician and the interventional pain provider at a neutral location to discuss the patient update. This continuum of patient care is of great value to both physicians.

These follow-up meetings educate the medical community on spinal cord stimulation as a therapy option, share real-life patient success, and enable Rachael to build a strategic relationship with her physician network. Dr. Smith sees Rachael as an asset to his practice, helping to educate the local community on some of the therapies he provides. Patient success stories offer an effective way to highlight the benefits of Boston Scientific devices to patients and to encourage brand preference through positive patient outcomes. Following up is important and, thus, Rachael is always on the lookout for the next patient success story to serve her client accounts.

Case questions:

1. How does Rachael prioritize the needs of her clients when providing service after the sale?
2. Why are Boston Scientific patient success stories an effective technique to use when providing follow-up service?
3. Who benefits from providing follow-up service after the sale?

NOTES

1. John Spacey, '13 Examples of Post-Sales' (April 11, 2019), https://simplicable.com/new/post-sales, retrieved December 3, 2020.

2. Adapted from John Spacey, '13 Examples of Post-Sales' (April 11, 2019), https://simplicable.com/new/post-sales, retrieved December 3, 2020; and Adam Honig, 'You Closed the Deal, Now What? 6 things to do after the sale' (June 21, 2018), https://customerthink.com/you-closed-the-deal-now-what-6-things-to-do-after-the-sale, retrieved December 3, 2020.

3. Lou Orfanos, 'Don't Care What Happens After the Sale? That's your first mistake,' https://blog.hubspot.com/sales/hard-truth-about-sales, retrieved December 3, 2020.

4. '7 Ways to Gain Lifelong Customers after Making a Sale' (November 13, 2015), www.quicksprout.com/7-ways-to-gain-lifelong-customers-after-making-a-sale, retrieved December 3, 2020.

5. Ibid.

6. '5 Customer Success Post-Sales Pitfalls' (July 5, 2017), www.clientsuccess.com/blog/5-customer-success-post-sales-pitfalls, retrieved December 3, 2020.

7. Lou Orfanos, 'Don't Care What Happens After the Sale? That's your first mistake,' https://blog.hubspot.com/sales/hard-truth-about-sales, retrieved December 3, 2020.

8. Adapted from '7 Ways to Gain Lifelong Customers after Making a Sale' (November 13, 2015), www.quicksprout.com/7-ways-to-gain-lifelong-customers-after-making-a-sale, retrieved December 3, 2020.

9. Robert Izquierdo, 'How Account Management Can Impact Your Business,' www.fool.com/the-blueprint/account-management, retrieved December 3, 2020.

10. Lucid Chart, 'Why Account Management is Key to Business Success,' www.lucidchart.com/blog/what-is-account-management, retrieved December 3, 2020.

11. Leslie Ye, 'Account Management vs. Sales: What's the difference?' https://blog.hubspot.com/sales/account-management-vs-sales, retrieved December 3, 2020.

12. Lucid Chart, 'Why Account Management is Key to Business Success,' www.lucidchart.com/blog/what-is-account-management, retrieved December 3, 2020.

13. Emily Bauer, 'The 5-Step Guide to Creating a Balanced Sales Territory Plan for Your Team' (January 4, 2018), www.propellercrm.com/blog/sales-territory-plan, retrieved December 3, 2020.

14. Richard April, 'Sales Territory Planning and Management: What you need to know,' https://blog.hubspot.com/sales/how-to-strategically-divide-your-sales-territories, retrieved December 3, 2020.

15. Adapted from Emily Bauer, 'The 5-Step Guide to Creating a Balanced Sales Territory Plan for Your Team' (January 4, 2018), www.propellercrm.com/blog/sales-territory-plan, retrieved December 3, 2020; and Peter Thompson, '6 Best Practices to Help You Ace Sales Territory Management,' www.repsly.com/blog/sales-territory-management-best-practices, retrieved December 3, 2020.

16. Richard April, 'Sales Territory Planning and Management: What you need to know,' https://blog.hubspot.com/sales/how-to-strategically-divide-your-sales-territories, retrieved December 3, 2020.

17. Mason Minor, 'The Definitive Guide to Sales Territory Management' (March 27, 2018), https://medium.com/@Mason_MMC/the-definitive-guide-to-sales-territory-management-772580a6ea44, retrieved December 3, 2020.

18. Mary Clare Novak, 'Stop Winging Your Sales Territory Management: Make a plan' (April 8, 2020), https://learn.g2.com/sales-territory-management, retrieved December 3, 2020.

19. Adapted from Emily Bauer, 'The 5-Step Guide to Creating a Balanced Sales Territory Plan for Your Team' (January 4, 2018), www.propellercrm.com/blog/sales-territory-plan, retrieved December 3, 2020.

20. Onsight, 'Sales Territory Management: Why it is important,' www.onsightapp.com/blog/sales-territory-management-important, retrieved December 3, 2020.

21. Mary Clare Novak, 'Stop Winging Your Sales Territory Management: Make a plan' (April 8, 2020), https://learn.g2.com/sales-territory-management, retrieved December 3, 2020.

22. Spotio, 'Best Sales Territory Management: A thorough guide for reps and managers' (November 11, 2020), https://spotio.com/blog/sales-territory-management, retrieved December 3, 2002.

23. Frederick F. Reichheld (1996) *The Loyalty Effect: The Hidden Force behind Growth, Profits and Lasting Value* (Cambridge, MA: Harvard Business School Press).

24. Aja Frost, 'Key Account Management: The ultimate guide,' https://blog.hubspot.com/sales/key-account-management, retrieved December 3, 2020.

25. Ibid.

26. Ibid.

27. Adapted from Aja Frost, 'Key Account Management: The ultimate guide,' https://blog.hubspot.com/sales/key-account-management, retrieved December 3, 2020; and Joseph DiMisa, 'Strategic account management,' *Sales & Service Excellence Essentials* (March 2015), 14(3), 9–10.

28. Adapted from V. Kumar (2013), 'Profitable Customer Engagement: Concept, metrics and strategies' (ebook), SAGE Publications.

29. Adapted from VWO, 'Customer Engagement,' https://vwo.com/customer-engagement, retrieved December 3, 2020; and V. Kumar (2013), 'Profitable Customer Engagement: Concept, metrics and strategies' (ebook), SAGE Publications.

30. Emily Bauer, 'The 5-Step Guide to Creating a Balanced Sales Territory Plan for Your Team' (January 4, 2018), www.propellercrm.com/blog/sales-territory-plan, retrieved December 3, 2020; Kent Holland, 'How to Create a Sales Territory Plan: A step-by-step guide' (November 18, 2020), www.copper.com/blog/sales-territory-plan, retrieved December 3, 2020.

SECTION 3

Evaluation and Sales Management – 'Back in the Office'

11

RECRUITING, TRAINING, AND LEADING SALESPEOPLE

Lisa Spiller and Dan Schultheis

CHAPTER CONTENTS

PEOPLE, PRACTICES AND PERSPECTIVES FROM THE WORLD OF SALES

Greetings from Chile. I am Jorge Bullemore, an adjunt professor at Universidad del Desarrollo in Santiago. My responsibilites include teaching, researching, and delivering executive education in Chile, Perú, and Bolivia. My work is focused on organizational consumers. *My advice is to always remember the importance of sales, marketing and human resources alignment.* A quote for you to consider: 'Stay hungry. Stay foolish' (Steve Jobs speech at Stanford University.)

Hi, my name is Rick Pallen. I'm a self-motivated Canadian national with more than 30 years of international sales, marketing and business development experience in the supplier, manufacturing, high tech, and physical security and service industry. *I'm tenacious in acquiring new business, enhancing customer loyalty, and forging strong relationships with external, as well as internal, business partners. I've mentored and coached more than 20 sales teams in 12 countries. I've also coached Canadian football and hockey, and US youth hockey teams for more than 20 years. I'm a firm believer in team leadership and my advice to you is to gain coaching experience wherever you can as it will be invaluable to you in leading sales teams one day.*

Hello, I'm Dimitri Sakellarides, a sales executive in Market Development for FedEx Services to customers in the Alexandria and Arlington, Virginia areas. My responsibilities include generating incremental growth and the management of 100+ customer accounts (B2C, B2B and e-commerce), and prospecting to bring on new business from the competition or company start-ups in the area. *My advice is to always be willing to take on responsibilities because you will learn new things every day that will help you grow personally, professionally, and mentally. Your personal growth/learning is made up of: 70% experiences, 20% relationships, and 10% education.* 'Don't watch the clock; do what it does. Keep going' (Sam Levenson.)

Treat others as you want to be treated.

– The Golden Rule

EYES ON ETHICS

1. Onboarding practices when recruiting top candidates is difficult or impossible.
2. Goal setting given unrealistic corporate expectations.

INTRODUCTION

This chapter addresses the different roles of sales managers in guiding their sales teams to be successful in the selling process. Sales managers' performance of the various tasks associated with recruiting, training, and leading salespeople have a direct impact on the behavior of their salespeople. Topics to be explored in this chapter also include salesforce structure and evaluating sales management effectiveness. We'll begin by overviewing salesforce structure before we delve more deeply into the many hats that most sales managers must wear.

SALESFORCE STRUCTURE

The function of sales management, whether as a full-time role or a part-time function of the owner/entrepreneur, is exciting but also may be wearying because of the multiple roles a sales manager has to play and swap between during any given business day. These multiple roles require a degree of structure and consistency to create an environment where salespeople can serve prospects and customers, close business deals, and improve their skills for handling future business relationships.

Examining the multiple roles of sales managers

What many people don't realize about the sales management role is that it actually encompasses four functions: supervising, training, coaching, and mentoring. We'll discuss these roles in greater depth later in the chapter, but for now, let's briefly overview each of these sales management functions according to the order in which they are typically implemented by sales managers.

Sales manager
Used with kind permission of George Jones.

Trainer

This function is necessary to teach the skills needed for salespeople to execute the sales process and adequately represent the company as well as the products/services provided. These skills are usually provided in a written or verbal format to salespeople, either in an on-boarding process or over the course of their early employment with a company.

The training function starts with an assessment of the skills and information each salesperson needs, both internally and externally, to adequately do their job. This can be done by testing, by observation, or even by assumption. A basic training program is then put in place for everyone to build their skills and knowledge of the product and customers. Then, subsequent individualized training can be done as needed for each salesperson, based on the level of skills, knowledge, and retention of the initial training. This training function has highest priority, of course, when on-boarding or restructuring the sales team to better serve the goals of the company. Training becomes less frequent as the salespeople begin to operate in their territory. However, ongoing competency assessments by the sales manager must be done to determine if and when any additional training/reinforcement is required.

Supervisor

This function is about overseeing the sales force, measuring the capability of salespeople to complete pre-defined tasks, holding them accountable, and taking corrective actions as needed when tasks are not performed adequately. As such, it has to do with reporting certain levels of activity and results, as well as reviewing those levels to ensure compliance with established guidelines.

With awareness of the skills and knowledge needed by salespeople, the sales manager must define the behaviors, activities, and results, both qualitatively and quantitatively, that salespeople must perform. This is the process in which the 'metrics' most likely to produce sales are identified and implemented. It's not unlike developing players for a football team. You can tell the players that they need to have tackling, running, throwing, or blocking skills, but it is only with practice and input from coaches that they produce consistent results, improve their stats, and contribute to a winning team.

Coach

This function is what sales managers should do as they observe salespeople executing their defined tasks. Coaching takes into account the different styles and skill levels, as well as experience, of each of the salespeople reporting to the sales manager. This means that extra effort must be taken to coach individual salespeople to apply the skills and information taught in training classes. Coaching is the activity that is most readily discontinued due to the time crunch required for getting business 'in the door.' Unfortunately, it is even scarcer when sales management is a part-time function of a senior executive or owner.

Coaching is actually the most developmentally important function of a sales management role. Unless each salesperson is observed and coached individually, the quality and effectiveness of their activities does not dramatically improve over time. Instead, their skill level tends to remain the same, with progress much slower than it could have been, or it may even regress. So once training and supervision are in place, the sales manager creates a schedule of periodic, formal coaching sessions. Informal sessions are also important, but without the structure of a formal schedule, coaching and skill development cannot be assured.

Mentor

This function is a bit more informal and involves showing new salespeople 'the ropes,' how things actually work in the company, and when working with customers. Mentoring is not meant to undermine any of the other functions, rather it acknowledges that there is some variance from the written rules when salespeople actually engage with prospects or customers, or support people. Sales managers typically spend a minimal amount of time in this role as their other duties take up most of their time and attention.

Mentoring by sales managers adds the finishing touch to a salesperson's or a sales team's development. This is where the sales manager teaches salespeople 'how it really works in the field.' Mentoring usually happens when the sales manager assumes the role as a sales partner with the salesperson and makes sales calls. This is an opportunity for managers to give guidance on the best ways to handle customer complaints and internal support conflict. The wise advice offered by sales managers can make things go more smoothly for salespeople and help them understand the structure within which they must operate.

Mentor relationship
© Ben Leistensnider/Christopher Newport University.

Though these four functions may seem reasonable and logical, what typically happens at some companies with a high-transaction volume is that whoever is responsible for the sales management role only has adequate time to focus on the supervisory function. Thus, the other functions are often not performed on a regular basis. However, it is critical that sales mangers prioritize their time to adequately perform each function. As we shall discuss a little later, while supervision is needed, it alone cannot develop a successful, professional sales team.

Unfortunately, when all four of the functions are not carried out, it creates an environment in which the sales manager is likely to:

- require salespeople to continually meet a certain quantitative level of activity
- focus only on the results of sales and/or quotas
- direct the salespeople who are below their expected sales transaction volume to work harder to either 'prospect more' or 'close more business'
- dole out penalties by reducing sales territories or threatening to fire salespeople if their sales transaction results don't improve.

This, of course, leads to a more stressful working environment. No one in a sales management role wants or intends for the environment to feel that way. Thus, effective time management on behalf of sales managers is needed in order to adequately perform or delegate all four managerial functions on a regular basis.

We will talk more about the steps required to put in place a sound sales manager job structure that includes supervisory, training, coaching, and mentoring roles. Although setting up this approach may seem daunting at first, even small steps toward structuring these sales management roles will provide enormous benefits. Good sales management begins with recruiting qualified sales talent, which is the topic of our next section.

Recruiting/meeting new employees

RECRUITING SALES PROFESSIONALS

Recruiting good salespeople is critically important and requires more strategic focus than most other hiring decisions because salespeople directly affect the profit or loss of a company.[1]

In addition, there are many activities associated with recruiting and hiring salespeople, such as onboarding, orienting, and training, each with related costs. Thus, attracting high-quality sales talent is an important sales management task that must be performed well.

Attracting sales talent

The key to attracting sales professionals is to always be looking for talent regardless of whether or not there is a current opening on the sales team. Even top sports teams have scouts who are continuously looking for future talent to replace underperforming, injured, or retiring players in order to maintain the consistency, strength, and growth of overall team performance. It's the same with sales teams. There are four steps that should be applied continually in order to successfully attract sales talent. These steps are:

Step 1: Determine the personal skills/attributes of the ideal sales candidate. These include strong interpersonal skills, experience in selling the types of products/services your company supplies, certain educational background, etc.

Step 2: Define the key performance indicators (KPIs) that a candidate must or should have. This includes indicators such as a defined personal sales territory strategy (who to target, how to contact them, etc.), a track record of exceeding the sales objectives they were given, and a personal organization/filing routine that ensures consistent follow-up with prospects/customers.

Step 3: Create a list of recruiting website/social media entities. This list includes platforms such as LinkedIn, Indeed, Google Ads, etc., and also continual solicitation of current sales team members for candidates they might recommend.

Step 4: Assign responsibility to a member of your company's management team. Regardless of whether that person is the owner in a small company or a sales executive/manager in a large organization, recruiting must be an ongoing process for the person assigned to the task. It is imperative to continually search, using the above three steps, for this final step to be productive.

Once you have successfully recruited potential sales professionals, the next step is to screen them to determine whether they are qualified. We'll tackle that topic in the next section.

Screening and hiring sales candidates

Busy sales managers should not 'cut corners' or skim over the screening and selection tasks when hiring salespeople. If they do, they will likely pay the price of making a poor hiring decision, which ultimately leads to a costly and time-consuming rehiring process. Some tasks they should be sure to pay attention to include:[2]

- Creating and applying checklists for required and preferred screening criteria to ensure the candidate meets the standards established for the position.
- Conducting a background check to validate, reinforce, and obtain professional opinions about the candidate.
- Positioning reference calls with open-ended questions that reveal the character of the candidate.
- Performing a social media review to detect any indicators of behavior that demonstrate the candidate's poor judgement or an inconsistency with the values of your company.
- Adjusting their expectations of the candidate to reflect reality.
- One important factor in screening candidates is to establish a consistent, objective method for comparing candidates for the sales position. This helps mitigate, to some degree, the inclination of most interviewers to make an emotional decision about a given candidate using subjective judgement, which usually leads

to an ineffective vetting process to find an optimal fit for a sales position. One method that may be used to inject objectivity into an interview process is referred to by the acronym SEARCH, which stands for skills, experience, attitude, results, cognitive, and habits. As Table 11.1 demonstrates, you may apply the SEARCH screening method to objectively evaluate each candidate and to plan interview questions that may be posed to those candidates that are selected for an interview. This method may be applied even when using separate interviewers to determine a candidate's fit.

Table 11.1 SEARCH screening method

Candidate attributes	Proof that attribute exists	Probing questions to verify skill level	Rating (1–5) (low to high)
Skills: – Common sense	Demonstrating problem solving	Tell me about a difficult problem that you solved.	
– Communication skills	Demonstrating the ability to express oneself clearly	Tell me about an event in your life that has made you who you are today.	
Experience: – Related experience	Describing relevant examples	Describe a situation where you provided _____ services.	
Attitude: – Desire to excel – People-oriented – Self-motivation – Integrity, dependability, loyalty, commitment	Describing past situations that show commitment, self-motivation, improvement, and leadership qualities Revealing personal values	What is success in your mind? How do you personally demonstrate leadership? What hobbies do you have and what do they entail? Give an example that demonstrates your loyalty, dependability, and commitment.	
Results: – 1–3-year goals – Prior accomplishments	Communicating career and/or personal goals Expressing pride in past accomplishments	What are your goals? Please share with me some of the accomplishments that you are most proud of.	
Cognitive: – Sales knowledge – Intelligence level	Answering questions correctly Demonstrating good verbal and nonverbal skills	Describe a sales principle that you know very well. What was the last book you read and what did you think of it?	
Habits: – Multi-tasking	Showing an ability to do more than one thing at a time	Tell me about how you manage your time when you have multiple tasks to complete in a short timeframe.	

Source: Dan Schultheis, 2020. Used with kind permission.

Unfortunately, research shows interviews to be practically worthless in predicting how well the candidate will perform in the future.[3] During an interview, a salesperson is doing what they do best – sell. However, most companies typically require formal interviews as part of the hiring process. Regarding what to look for in a candidate for a sales position, the best way to predict future performance of a candidate is past performance. Thus, work samples, job knowledge tests, peer reviews, and ratings of past performance may be better indicators.[4] Research also shows that industry experience alone isn't always a good basis for making a hiring decision. Instead, sales managers should consider hiring candidates who have the potential in terms of skills and traits to become top-performing salespeople with adequate training.[5] When interviewing qualified candidates, sales managers should use the techniques provided in Table 11.2 to increase the potential value of candidate interviews.

Table 11.2 Interview technique tips

- Be objective and keep an open mind during the interview.
- Be kind, courteous, respectful, and welcoming to the candidate.
- Include multiple company associates in the interview process.
- Have the same people attend all interviews to ensure equal treatment.
- Ask the same interview questions to all candidates being evaluated.
- Ask the candidate for permission to take notes, and then take notes.
- Ask questions relevant to the position qualifications and duties.
- Do not ask personal questions, such as those about spouse, children, etc.
- Ask open-ended, opposed to 'yes/no,' questions to obtain more insight.
- Ask thought-provoking questions to challenge the candidate's thinking. For example:
    a. Tell us about a challenging sale you recently won that you believe followed the perfect process.
    b. Tell us about a sales opportunity that you could not close. What went wrong? What was the specific objection you could not overcome?
    c. In your professional opinion, what are the three traits that the 'best' salesperson in the world possesses?
- Notice how clearly the candidate articulates their answers to questions.
- Observe the candidate's body language and take note of 'cues.'
- Listen carefully and fully to each answer the candidate provides.
- Spend more time listening than you do speaking to the candidate.
- Explain the process and timeline for making hiring decisions.
- Invite the candidate's questions and completely answer each one.
- Always represent the company well and create a positive impression.

Source: Adapted from Carter McNamara, 'How To Interview Job Candidates,' https://managementhelp.org/staffing/screening.htm, retrieved November 16, 2020; John Dano, 'A Really Tough Screening Process That No Salesperson Can Bluff,' https://business.linkedin.com/talent-solutions/blog/recruiting-tips/2017/a-really-tough-screening-process-that-no-salesperson-can-bluff, retrieved November 3, 2020.

When making hiring decisions, sales managers should rely on rational, as opposed to emotional, thought processes. People hire people, so before you extend a position offer to a prospective salesperson, you should try to get to know the candidate. Inviting candidates to interact with your salespeople will allow you to determine how well they will fit in with your current sales team. Also, if you take candidates out for a meal, you will be able to assess how they interact with others, such as the hostess, waitress, and general public. Examining the interpersonal skills of candidates is imperative when hiring salespeople since they will spend much of their time out in the field engaging with prospects and customers. Exceptional personality-related (soft) skills, such as communication, professional etiquette, emotional intelligence, and others discussed in Chapter 2, are the hallmarks of a candidate who will become a successful salesperson and trusted advisor.[6] Seek out those traits when searching for candidates for sales positions.

Interviewing a candidate

Knowing what character traits to avoid is equally important when screening candidates. Research has revealed some 'red flags' that sales managers should look out for when hiring prospective salespeople, such as if the candidate is arrogant, self-centered, motivated by money, fails to listen, or possesses low energy.[7] In addition, sales managers should avoid hiring job hoppers because business development takes time and requires serious focus and commitment.[8] All new hires require a substantial investment in training and development, so longevity with a company is an important factor. Training is the topic of our next section.

TRAINING SALESPEOPLE

Now that you've successfully recruited your new salesperson, you'll need to train that person to ensure both employment and sales performance success. In sales positions, these two objectives are typically intertwined. Just think of superstar athletes who are constantly training to stay in top-notch physical shape in order to perform optimally on the court or in the arena, rink, or stadium. For athletes, their game performance dictates their career success. It's much the same with selling, where ongoing training should be provided to help salespeople be successful both out in the sales field and in their careers. However, newly hired salespeople require specific types of training, referred to as onboarding, indoctrinating, and orienting. Let's explore these training topics.

Onboarding and indoctrinating salespeople

Onboarding is the strategic management process used to empower new employees with the necessary knowledge, skills, tools, and behaviors in order to become effective organizational members and insiders.[9] Onboarding is also called organizational socialization, as the process entails integrating new employees into an organization and familiarizing them with the company's culture and products/services. Applied to sales management, indoctrinating is the process of teaching a new employee certain ideas, attitudes, cognitive strategies, or professional methodologies. In essence, onboarding and indoctrinating salespeople involve instilling them with the values, initiatives, beliefs, and acceptable behaviors in accordance with the company's culture and mission. These programs should be customized and designed to meet the needs of individual salespeople, since the professional development needs of new salespeople differ from those of established salespeople.

Training meeting
© Ben Leistensnider/Christopher Newport University.

Unfortunately, at many companies onboarding/indoctrinating (O&I) is one of the areas that receives the least amount of attention from sales managers once hiring is completed. This creates a less than optimal environment for the success of new salespeople. It takes new hires 8–12 months to gain proficiency comparable to that of their established sales team members, with lost productivity incurring costs ranging from 1 to 2.5

percent of total business revenues.[10] In the USA and the UK alone, an estimated $37 billion is spent annually to retrain unproductive employees who do not fully understand their job responsibilities.[11] Research shows that only 6 percent of newly hired salespeople exceed their employers' expectations, while 48 percent fail.[12] The good news is that these statistics can be turned around with proper onboarding activities. Organizations with a standard onboarding process experience 54 percent greater new hire productivity. In addition, 77 percent of new hires who hit their first performance milestone have had formal onboarding training.[13]

Though the comprehensive nature of onboarding and indoctrinating may vary by the size and availability of resources in the company, it is still essential for a formal process to be executed. At its most basic level, the process for O&I should include the following:

1. A 'manual' of critical information the new salesperson will need to start their training and development (e.g. product/service detailed descriptions, territory definitions, company organization charts with titles/responsibilities, etc.).
2. An outline of all the topics to be covered in the O&I.
3. A schedule for the O&I period, including checkpoints and reviews with management along the way.
4. A list of the criteria management will use to assess the readiness of the salesperson to take on an active sales territory.
5. An assigned 'mentor' who will act as a guide for actual sales team operations (to include customer/prospect visits with experienced salespeople, an exposure to the sales process, such as prospecting, proposal writing, presentation skills, etc.)
6. An overall coach responsible for reinforcing or correcting skills/behaviors noticed during the O&I period.
7. Basic sales training to equip them with the knowledge and skill needed to be successful in selling.

While in smaller organizations there may not be enough people to assign the above roles and tasks to different individuals, it is essential that the functions described above be handled even if this effort falls to one individual or the business owner. Without implementing this oversight process, management will be relying on the chance that the new salesperson already has a readiness to sell. Unfortunately, this only happens in a minimal number of cases. This is a major reason for the high turnover rate in the sales profession. Some of the turnover may be due to accepting more challenging or better paying sales positions elsewhere; however, more often the turnover is a result of an inadequate O&I process which leads to low sales performance. For this reason, an effective onboarding program is often considered the first step to successfully retaining sales employees.

In today's digital world, technology enables sales managers to establish onboarding programs and schedules that are customized to meet the needs of each new salesperson, following a disciplined approach that avoids data-dumping and information overload. Tech tools are quickly becoming the go-to solution for onboarding new employees.

Most organizations have innovative onboarding and training tools, such as online play-books, peer-based videos, and mobile training solutions, for every stage of the sales cycle. Many sales managers are using multiple digital options to get new sales hires up to speed. The most popular design and delivery modes include company-wide intranet, e-learning, web-based portals, videos, webinars, and survey tools.[14] These tools must be used repeatedly to maximize their benefits and improve employee retention rates.

Onboarding should not be confused with orientation. They are different activities, and orientation is actually one part of the onboarding process. Table 11.3 presents a comparison of orientation and onboarding. Successful onboarding programs integrate and align sales coaching activities with sales training activities.[15] A synergy is created when all of the different training activities are woven into an onboarding program. We'll discuss coaching a little later in the chapter, but for now let's examine orientation in greater detail.

Table 11.3 Orientation versus onboarding comparison

Orientation	Onboarding
A business operations activity	A strategic process
An event	A program
Short duration – typically lasts one day or a few days	Long duration – typically lasts several months to a year
Requires new-hire paperwork to be completed during the event	Requires new-hire paperwork to be completed prior to beginning the program
Primary purpose is to supply company information to new employees	Primary purpose is to provide new employees with knowledge, skills, and tools
Formal introductions and socialization	Informal socialization and interactions
Standard and universal for all employees	Customized specifically to each individual employee
Reviews and follows procedures in employee handbook	Models company culture and uses strategic plan for direction
Provides a rapid start to selling	Delivers a smooth transition to selling
Salesperson will begin selling immediately upon completion	Salesperson will shadow a senior team member immediately upon completion
Relatively inexpensive to implement	Requires an investment to implement
Typically leads to a high turnover of salespeople	Typically enables a high retention of salespeople

Source: Adapted from Andy Miller, 'Onboarding Salespeople vs. Orientation,' https://bigswiftkick.com/onboarding-salespeople-vs-orientation, retrieved November 3, 2020.

Orienting salespeople

From a sales management perspective, orientation is an operationally driven process whereby new employees are introduced and welcomed to a company, given informa-tion about its history, acquainted with its culture, and asked to complete employment paperwork. Most often, orientations are one-time events which typically last for a specified time period, such as a day or a week, as opposed to onboarding and training which happen on an ongoing basis. Most orientations will occur on the new salesperson's very first day of employment. Typically, new salespeople experience the following orientation activities. They are:

- assigned a 'guide' to escort them around the physical premises and orient them to the functional areas of the physical space that they will occupy, including the location of their desk/office
- provided with explanations of the company organizational chart along with the titles and responsibilities of each of the individuals they will typically come in contact with in performing their duties
- given a benefits and compensation presentation and discussion. If there is a Human Resources (HR) administrator or department in the company, that office normally describes in detail the various components of the benefits and compensation plan, which usually includes vacation, sick days, healthcare, etc. If no one has this specific HR role, then the salesperson's direct manager should present this part of the orientation. Benefits discussion should include at least the following: daily work hours, paid holidays, vacation days, sick days, allowable reimbursable expenses, healthcare, and any 401(k) or profit sharing. We'll discuss compensation in detail later in the chapter
- offered a detailed discussion with the salesperson's manager. In this discussion, the manager typically addresses the:
  - requirements for the position as itemized in the position description
  - pay and compensation structure, along with potential commission earnings
  - salesperson's territorial and/or account responsibilities and expectations for performance or sales results
  - progress review process and schedule whereby the sales manager formally evaluates the development of the salesperson over defined periods of time.

In addition, orientation is normally the time to review an outline regarding the training content new salespeople will receive and the sequence of events that will occur to prepare them for their respective positions. This should include, but not be limited to, the following:

- the top executive of the company and/or the highest-level executive that the salesperson will have access to providing information and encouraging discussion about the history and growth of and future plans for the company
- company product and/or services description and detailed information on capabilities
- definition of the role of the salesperson in their territories/accounts, description of the major activities and responsibilities expected of the salesperson in that role, and examples of how to go about executing them
- specific performance metrics associated with the expectations of salespeople

- industry and competitor knowledge that includes the types of products and services that are in competition with the company's own products and services
- success stories provided by an existing salesperson who has experience producing the desired results with this company
- the company's culture, as it applies to the sales process, customer service, and relationship-building procedures
- self-management activities
- a robust question-and-answer period.

As discussed at the beginning of the chapter, training new salespeople is just one of the many important roles that sales managers assume within their respective companies. One of the most important elements of an effective sales training program is designing the program content in a logical, progressive, step-by-step sequence.[16] Let's now continue to explore the other roles, beginning with the leadership role they must possess in order to direct and supervise their salespeople.

Sales leadership and follower

© Ben Leistensnider/Christopher Newport University.

LEADING SALESPEOPLE

Sales leadership is defined as activities undertaken by those in a sales organization that motivate others to pursue common goals for the collective good of the organization.[17] Sales managers are primarily responsible for creating and managing organizational culture, which is the shared set of assumptions, values, and beliefs that employees hold.[18] Sales managers can directly and indirectly affect the performance of salespeople since they are tasked with helping to create a positive work environment.[19] When employees are happier with their jobs, they become more committed to their company, gain greater confidence in their capabilities, and become more motivated to work harder and smarter.[20] Effective sales managers can drive changes that have positive outcomes on the company and its employees. However, sales managers may use different leadership styles in producing transformation and creating a positive organizational culture, which is the topic of our next section.

Using different leadership styles

There are three basic leadership styles that focus on followers – considerate, transformational, and servant leadership. Let's examine these different leadership styles.

Considerate leadership

Considerate leaders listen and respond to employee feedback, use this feedback in decision making, and provide appropriate resources to enable their followers to accomplish organizational duties and tasks.[21] Sales managers adopting this leadership style often partner with followers to create an environment of psychological support and friendliness.[22] The leadership approach of considerate leaders is participative and supportive of their salespeople, who respond well to the sales-leader influence.[23] Considerate leadership has led to improvements in salesperson morale and satisfaction; however, it has also been associated with decreased sales performance as it is focused on achieving organizational objectives as opposed to salesperson objectives.[24]

Transformational leadership

Transformational leaders influence the behavior of their followers by articulating a vision, modeling appropriate behavior, promoting the acceptance of group goals, and supporting individuals.[25] Sales managers who adopt a transformational leadership style will stimulate their salespeople intellectually and communicate high sales performance expectations.[26]

Transformational leadership is associated with transactional leadership, which entails sales managers informing their salespeople about their responsibilities, instructing them on how to perform their associated tasks, and attaining their compliance by using rewards or punishment.[27]

Thus, transformational leadership is likely to add to transactional leadership in motivating salespeople to put forth greater effort to achieve better sales performance with greater satisfaction.[28]

Servant leadership

The primary focus of servant leaders is on meeting the needs of their followers and helping them to achieve success. The priority of servant leaders is ethically serving the needs of their followers as opposed to achieving organizational objectives.[29] Thus, servant leadership is a different approach to the typical leader–follower relationship of both considerate and transformational leaders, and tends to be very well suited to modern selling where the focus is on building and nurturing relationships. Let's delve more deeply into this valuable approach to sales leadership.

Max Cates, author of *Serve, Lead, Succeed! How Servant Leaders Are Reaching Breakthrough Sales*, featured in the Readings and Resources section at the end of this chapter, claims: 'Servant leadership is not a strategy or management technique. It is an attitude. It is the selfless spirit of supporting, encouraging, coaching and defending your salespeople.' Servant leaders embrace a 'we did it' attitude, not an 'I' focus. Thus, the best servant leaders are there to support and guide when needed, but otherwise, their existence is barely known. The benefits of servant leadership for employees include the following:[30]

- ✓ provides a positive and productive work environment
- ✓ encourages initiative and challenge
- ✓ shares desired direction, guidance, and priorities
- ✓ offers a team approach to work toward a common goal
- ✓ fosters the feelings of appreciation and importance
- ✓ encourages the desired motivation.

Research shows that salespeople who view their managers as servant leaders demonstrate higher levels of customer orientation and are more likely to use adaptive selling techniques and to perform extra customer-focused activities.[31] In addition, research reveals that servant leadership generates feelings of empowerment, which in turn stimulate innovative behavior, commitment, and trust.[32] Sales managers who employ servant leadership attest to its effectiveness. For example, Keith Costello, senior vice president of sales for Building Materials & Construction Solutions (BMC), a leading provider of diversified building products and services in the residential housing market, notes that sales have increased 12.4 percent over the previous year at his company. He believes the improvement was due to servant leadership. He oversees some 500 sales professionals at BMC, where leadership philosophy holds that the executives exist to serve the associates and the associates exist to serve the customers.[33]

Adopting a servant leadership style may produce very positive outcomes for leaders, including that it:[34]

- promotes effective leadership by allowing leaders to mentor and coach in a more empathetic manner
- fosters open, honest communication, allowing leaders to be proactive in quickly solving problems
- affords the opportunity to frequently express sincere and deserving appreciation that leads to inspired and motivated sales personnel
- builds a team approach and positive work environment that transcends the company and assists in attracting, recruiting, and hiring top sales personnel and talent
- makes the employee performance review process open, honest, and constructive, and ensures that table-to-document and mapped-out goal setting, improvement needs/areas, and desired career advancement and paths are agreed upon and documented.

Most importantly, customers benefit because salespeople working with effective servant leaders observe and learn proactive listening, which leads to improved communication when interacting with clients. This builds strong relationships, in which clients feel that everyone at the company is there to solve problems and make their jobs easier and more efficient. As care and empathy are demonstrated, customers view the company as a trusted supplier with whom they desire to build a business relationship.[35] Research shows that the impact of servant leadership on customer relationships is greater for less experienced salespeople.[36] This may be because sales managers who are servant leaders typically possess the critical ability to adapt to the different personality styles of their salespeople. While the overall servant leadership objectives and strategies are the same, the tactics may differ when working with seasoned long-tenured salespeople versus newly hired field or inside salespeople. In all cases, servant leader sales managers are always expressing confidence in their salespeople. Table 11.4 presents some techniques sales managers can use, and other techniques that are best avoided when adopting a servant leadership style.

Table 11.4   Servant leadership techniques

Effective techniques:

- Giving credit to the salesperson for accomplishments and 'wins'
- Listening and empathizing
- Taking action to assist salespeople where warranted
- Asking for input and opinions from salespeople
- Exuding optimism – reassuring salespeople that things will work out well
- Asking probing questions to encourage salespeople to open up and communicate fully
- Telling salespeople what they've done well and why it was important

---

Ineffective techniques:

- Critiquing performance too frequently
- Maintaining a negative verbal tone
- Stating ultimatums
- Injecting fear
- Behaving in an overly commanding or manipulative manner
- Taking too much personal credit for success instead of recognizing the team

---

Source: Steven W. Spiller, personal communication, November 2, 2020.

Over the past few decades, the roles of sales managers have changed, and they will continue to do so due to technology, automation, empowerment, team selling, and relationship selling.[37] Servant leadership may represent yet another approach to drive even more radical change in the sales manager's role. Next, we'll explore the important roles of coaching and mentoring for sales managers.

Coaching and mentoring
© Ben Leistensnider/Christopher Newport University.

Coaching and mentoring salespeople

Coaching and mentoring are not the same, yet they go hand in hand, and both are important resources that enable salespeople to grow and develop professionally. Coaching and mentoring have become the management model for sales managers in today's relationship-selling world. As applied to sales management, coaching may be defined as a process of empowering sales employees to exceed established performance standards by identifying areas for improvement and praising what they have done well.[38] Quality coaching has an extremely positive impact on salesperson performance. Research reveals that effective coaching can improve salesperson retention rate by 40 percent, increase win rates of forecasted deals by 8.2 percent, and augment overall revenue attainment by 5.2 percent.[39] In addition, it has been shown that a great coach can increases the sales team's emotional commitment to the company by 52 percent.[40] Check out Table 11.5 for some tips on effective sales coaching.

Effective sales coaching should be part of salespeople's daily or weekly routine, individualized, designed to reinforce or correct behavior, and focused on skills and techniques rather than numbers.[41] Sales coaching may be used for many different purposes, including the following:[42]

- navigating company resources and procedures
- reviewing a sales call with a salesperson to identify strengths and weaknesses
- offering inside sales training and techniques
- identifying key experts to add to the salesperson's network
- holding weekly reviews with salespeople to discuss those areas in which they lack confidence
- listening to a salesperson's telephone call or observing a meeting with a prospect.

Table 11.5 Techniques for effective sales coaching

- Prepare and plan in advance for a variety of different coaching scenarios with salespeople of differing skills, knowledge, and abilities.
- Target coaching salespeople who are 'average' performers as opposed to the 'top' or 'bottom' performers, to make the biggest impact.
- Share both the company and sales manager vision with salespeople and seek to obtain buy-in and commitment.
- Hold one-on-one goal-setting meetings customized to each salesperson.
- Have salespeople articulate their goals and objectives.
- Discover the motivations driving the behavior of each salesperson.
- Periodically hold team meetings to share and compare overall sales team progress toward meeting goals and objectives.
- Offer both monetary and non-monetary incentives associated with improved performance.
- Hold sales contests with prizes for achievement.
- Provide recognition and rewards for accomplishments.
- Experiment with innovative coaching styles and techniques.
- Shadow the salesperson to spend more time observing selling activities out in the field.
- Obtain salesperson input on the effectiveness of coaching activities and techniques.
- Have salespeople formally evaluate their sales coach.
- Take action on all viable suggestions for improving coaching activities.

Source: Adapted from Aja Frost, 'Sales Coaching: The ultimate guide,' https://blog.hubspot.com/sales/sales-coaching, retrieved November 3, 2020.

During coaching sessions, the sales manager may offer advice to salespeople regarding how to implement and fine tune what they have been taught during the company training program. It is also the time to discuss certain legitimate workarounds for processes needed in the company that may not be documented. The best way to understand coaching is to examine a role-play between a sales manager and one of the manager's salespersons. See Table 11.6 for a sample coaching session. Note the guidance the sales manager provides during a coaching session to help the salesperson grow and develop. Sales managers should realize that the best coaching tool is the time they spend with their salespeople on a one-to-one basis.

Table 11.6 Sample formal coaching session

Manager: Jane, I wanted to have this session with you to talk about your performance in three areas: first, your activities in your sales territory; second, your customer satisfaction level and how you can improve it; and third, results and how to ensure that you achieve them. Do you have anything other than these three areas that you'd like to talk about during this session?

Jane (salesperson): No, I think those are the areas I'd like covered also.

Manager: Well then, let's move to the first point and that is your activities in your sales territory. I've watched you performing activities, made calls with you, and reviewed your reports to me.

From your time-recording sheets and from listening to you on the phone, I see that you are very good at getting into conversations with potential customers. I like the way you introduce yourself and the company and the friendliness in your voice as you speak. A suggestion for improvement in the future is to try to be more succinct, so the calls will be a bit shorter without seeming abrupt. I sense a tendency for you to engage in discussions that last longer than needed. While I can see that people respond well to you, lengthy conversations have the potential to turn off prospective clients. I have actually seen in the past where prospects no longer accept phone calls from other salespeople who've done this. Making your calls brief will ensure this won't happen to you. What questions do you have about this?

Jane: Do you have a number of calls that you think I should make a day to use as a target?

Manager: I would suggest targeting an average of five conversations a day. This means that some days you may only have three, while other days you may hit seven. I think shooting for that average will make you more sensitive to the need to compress your interactions on each call.

Manager: I have made three face-to-face calls with you and an existing customer. I want to complement you on your conversational style with customers and how you clearly put every one of them at ease with you. That is a real strength for you and will serve you well in the future! As the conversation proceeds, one area of opportunity for you is in your transition to talking about what other services or products they might need. I noticed that you tend to switch too quickly from a general dialogue mode to a selling mode. This may seem a little abrupt to some customers. I suggest preparing a few sentences that make a smooth transition and practicing them ahead of time until they come naturally to you. With that minor modification, I believe that most of your existing customer calls will be A+.

Jane: Thank you for those comments. I do believe that I have a strong ability to connect with people and I am comfortable talking with all types of customers. Your suggestion that I prepare and practice a smooth and natural transition between conversational and selling modes is a great idea and I will do that.

Manager: The third topic is your understanding of the standard reports you submit to show your sales results in your territory. I'm talking about both the week-to-week and monthly reports. These reports are important to understand as they hold the clues for how to adjust your territory behaviors to improve your results. I'm concerned that you aren't using these as well as you could be. I say this because when I ask you about your results on a weekly basis, you seem to struggle with that knowledge. I suggest you meet with your sales administrator to discuss how to pull the reports and interpret the data so that you can clearly describe your results. Most importantly, learning to look for patterns in the data will help you to identify ways to improve your future sales performance.

Jane: I agree with you that I need to hone in on this more, and I will make that a priority before our next formal coaching session. Thank you so much for your advice.

Manager: Jane, you've become a valuable member of our team in a short amount of time. Your ability to build rapport with our sales team members, prospects, and customers is well recognized. I look forward to our next meeting and to seeing how your overall sales results improve as you continue to learn, grow, and use your performance data well.

Mentoring is defined as an interpersonal exchange between a senior level or experienced person and a less experienced person in which the mentor provides support, direction, and feedback regarding career plans and personal development.[43] Mentoring typically involves frequent interactions between the mentor and the protégé to enhance the salesperson's competencies and assist in that person's career development. Thus, where training focuses on a salesperson's knowledge and skills, mentoring concentrates on the salesperson's overall career trajectory.[44] Mentoring enables wisdom and experience to be shared on a one-to-one basis with the goal of accelerating the sales development of the protégé. Often, the teaching, advising, and consulting activities of mentors may become more personal, as opposed to strictly professional.

Mentoring programs typically provide measurable results for their companies. Research on the performance of salespeople with a formal mentor shows that they cut their ramp time in half, were three times more likely to meet sales quotas, and achieved nearly 300 percent improvement in deals closed when compared with counterparts without an assigned mentor.[45] Certain components should be included in a mentor program to ensure its success. These components include:[46]

- establishing clearly defined roles and responsibilities for the mentor and mentee
- hosting a kick-off meeting to launch the program and enable structured face-to-face conversations between mentors and mentees

- developing mutually agreed-upon expectations and milestones for mentor relationships
- holding group meetings to share best practices and express appreciation to the mentors
- providing opportunities for program evaluation and feedback.

Mentoring
© Ben Leistensnider/Christopher Newport University.

Both coaching and mentoring sessions may be formal as well as informal. The informal may occur on a day-to-day or transaction-by-transaction basis where the sales manager advises the salesperson on ways to interact with potential or existing customers more effectively. However, it is important to have formal scheduled coaching sessions, especially during the first year of the salesperson's employment. These coaching sessions may be held on a weekly basis for the first 60 days, biweekly for the next 30 days, monthly for the next quarter, and then quarterly until the end of the new salesperson's first 12 months. Then, after the one-year period, formal sessions may be scheduled on an as-needed basis. Formal coaching programs tend to be more valuable for salespeople, as research shows the percentage of salespeople who were formally coached met or exceeded their sales quotas 62.3 percent of the time versus 42.9 percent of the time for those informally coached.[47] Formal coaching and mentoring programs may also lead to increased levels of job satisfaction which directly affects how well companies can retain their salespeople. That's the topic of our next section.

Compensating, rewarding, and retaining salespeople

Compensating, rewarding, and retaining salespeople are all related to one another and may determine how well sales managers can keep their salespeople motivated, productive, and happy. Let's examine each of these important sales management areas.

By definition, a sales compensation plan is the strategy that businesses use to pay salespeople and drive their performance in a way that will help the business become more profitable.[48]

Compensation plans set the standards of performance for salespeople and they should be grounded in a fair measurement system. While salespeople should be rewarded for their performance, the framework for each company's compensation plan varies. There are different compensation plans that may be implemented to serve different sales management and company goals. These include the following:[49]

- salary only: simplifies calculating sales expenses and offers consistent pay
- commission only: provides maximum selling incentives
- base salary plus commission: simplifies calculating sales expenses while offering incentives for salespeople
- base salary plus bonus: provides consistency for covering expenditures
- absolute commission: prioritizes particular company goals over others while motivating salespeople to exceed specified expectations such as 'You will get paid $___ (amount) for every ___ (product X) you sell'[50]
- relative commission: measures salespeople's success based on sales quotas or targets which may be specified monthly, quarterly, or annually, such as 'Your quarterly sales quota is $150,000 in new unit sales and your commission amount is $12,500 per quarter.'[51]

Each type of compensation plan has advantages and disadvantages, and each company must determine the one that works most effectively for its business operations. Compensation details for new sales associates include verifying starting salary plus commission range, stating whether or not a merit-based increase process for salary is in place for this position, and confirming whether or not overtime is allowed.

Compensation is not the only way to motivate salespeople to perform. Many businesses offer other forms of recognition, including awards, clubs, contests, games, and so on. Most salespeople are motivated when they see the fruits of their labor pay off.[52] To determine the most effective ways to recognize and reward successful sales performance, sales managers may ask their salespeople for suggestions. When implementing their suggestions, sales managers demonstrate that they value their salespeople and want to provide them with meaningful reward and recognition. Keep in mind the saying, 'People will support that which they help to create' when developing reward and recognition and programs. Doing so will boost salesperson morale and improve employee retention.

Receiving award
© Ben Leistensnider/Christopher Newport University.

Employee retention is a strong indicator of the organizational culture in any company. Companies that provide training, coaching, and mentoring of their salespeople have higher retention rates than those that do not. The three main reasons why employees leave a company are: compensation, conflict (behavioral or personality conflict with supervisors or coworkers), and people skills (in management).[53] Thus, sales managers need to evaluate their employees' salaries on a regular basis to ensure they are competitive, train their employees on how to adapt to different behavior styles, and sharpen their own managerial skills to effectively communicate and interact with their salespeople. Determining the underlying reasons that cause salespeople to quit their job is vital to the success of every business.

Research reveals that the average cost of replacing a salesperson is $115,000, which includes the cost of acquisition and training, as well as lost sales opportunities.[54] In addition, the average tenure of a sales representative is 14–30 months, while it takes an average of 12 months to get the productivity of a new salesperson to match that of established salespeople.[55] Thus, the longer sales managers can retain their salespeople, the higher the productivity of that sales team.

The Sales Management Association lists the following top factors for retaining salespeople:

1. Organizational culture.
2. Professional development, including training and coaching.
3. Job promotion opportunities.
4. Cash compensation.

Let's briefly discuss each of these topics in terms of how they help retain salespeople.

Organizational culture. Poor sales culture will drive salespeople away if they lose belief in the company's ability to deliver positive results to their clients.[56] Companies who value their salespeople will prioritize investing time and resources in empowering them to be productive and successful performers. The company culture and its recognition and rewards systems must reflect this employee-centered focus and be embraced throughout the entire corporate hierarchy. Moreover, program initiatives and activities must be in sync with a positive organizational culture and must operate to serve the dynamic needs of the firm's salespeople.

Professional development. By investing in the professional development of salespeople, companies will not only improve employee retention rates, but also overall company profitability as salespeople perform at optimal levels. As we've discussed earlier in this chapter, training and coaching are highly valuable professional development programs that all companies must provide on an ongoing basis. Including their salespeople in evaluating 'what works' enables sales managers to identify best practices and continue those programs that accelerate salespeople's performance and increase retention rates.

Job promotion opportunities. Limited career growth opportunities and boredom with their current position cause turnover for top salespeople across a wide range of industries. Research shows that 70 percent of sales representatives who left their organization due to the lack of promotion opportunities, were top performers.[57] Sales managers should provide new challenges, opportunities, and clear paths for the advancement of their salespeople, as well as determine ways to increase the emotional connection their salespeople have with the company in order to improve retention rates. Sales managers should also address career development during their one-on-one meetings with each salesperson. Too often, meetings only focus on sales performance and the metrics associated with evaluating it. Sales managers should also strive to build camaraderie among their salespeople since friendships among sales team members may be an effective strategy for retaining salespeople.[58] Research shows that 70 percent of employees claim that having friends at work is the most crucial element to a happy professional life.[59]

Cash compensation. Keep in mind that the expectations for salespeople's performance should always be realistic. When sales mangers establish unreasonably high sales objectives (sales quotas, target levels of customer satisfaction, etc.), it lowers the likelihood that they will be achieved, and can be detrimental to salespeople's self-esteem and job satisfaction. This is likely to result in increased employee turnover. If using a quota system, sales managers should set realistic quotas in collaboration with salespeople in order to stimulate optimal sales performance, which leads to increased employee retention.

Unfortunately, turnover in the sales force is a fact of life in business. Although sales managers can never completely eliminate turnover, they should strive to lessen the amount of it. Evaluating the effectiveness of sales management programs may reveal ways to improve the retention of salespeople. Doing this well requires the collection and analysis of pertinent data. Let's now explore the many metrics associated with assessing sales management effectiveness.

MONITORING METRICS

Monitoring Metrics

There are many types of metrics for evaluating the performance of sales managers. First, sales managers are responsible for the performance of the sales teams they lead. Thus, the key performance indicators (KPIs) that track those activities by salesperson and/or sales team may be used to assess the effectiveness of sales managers. Performance measures may be categorized as behavior, pipeline, or results metrics, and may include the following.

Behavior metrics

Behavior metrics are also called 'activity' metrics, those that demonstrate the number of critical sales activities that are in the salesperson's control. Goals for each one can be adjusted up or down in order to achieve the target for specified overall results metrics. Behavior metrics include:

- number of emails/texts sent to prospects per day/week
- number of phone dials completed per day
- number of phone conversations per week
- number of first-time sales calls (Zoom calls) with prospects per week
- number of product/service demonstrations/presentations given per week/month
- number of proposals submitted per week/month.

Pipeline metrics

These metrics are associated with the number of opportunities that the salesperson and/or sales team is currently working on and the amount of time taken to move leads through the stages of the buyer journey. Some common pipeline metrics are:

- number of new qualified leads per week
- number of referrals
- number of new meetings booked
- lead-opportunity conversion rate

- pipeline pace at which a lead moves through your sales pipeline
- average deal size or value
- reasons for losing a deal.

Accuracy in reporting the pipeline metrics is an important metric in itself, as it helps to ensure accurate forecasting. Pipeline metrics often reflect on the ability of sales managers to coach, guide, and support their salespeople to ensure positive forward movement of sales opportunities through the pipeline from proposal to closed deal.[60]

Results metrics

These metrics include revenue, profit, and won opportunities, and are important lagging indicators of sales manager performance. Results metrics are used to indicate whether an adjustment needs to be made to one or more of the behavior metrics targets. Results metrics for salespeople or sales team include:

- average number of orders per week/month
- amount of revenue per week/month
- average of revenue per new customer order
- number of weeks/months during which the assigned sales goal per quarter was achieved
- percentage of weeks/months during which assigned sales goals were achieved.

Other metrics

Sales managers may also be evaluated based on metrics associated with the performance of their various managerial roles. Such measures may include those related to recruiting, leading, and retaining salespeople. Some recruiting metrics are:

- number of candidates applying for the position
- number of candidates screened and/or interviewed
- number of candidates accepting a new sales position
- percentage of offers accepted.

Evaluating a sales manager's training and leadership effectiveness may address metrics associated with the onboarding, orientation, training, coaching, and mentoring programs that they supervise. Associated metrics may include:

- number or percentage of new salespeople successfully completing O&I programs
- number or percentage of salespeople participating in or successfully completing coaching and/or mentoring programs
- number of sessions held on training, professional development, skills development, etc.

- number of employees participating in various training sessions offered
- program evaluations of onboarding, orientation, training, coaching, and/or mentoring programs/sessions
- number of sales associates promoted in a given time period.

Sales managers may also be evaluated based on efforts to increase sales employees' retention rates. The effectiveness of any program designed to retain sales employees may be assessed and measured. Sales employee turnover rate, which measures the percentage of employees who leave a company's sales department over a given time period, should be assessed and tracked. Sales employee turnover rate is calculated by dividing the number of sales employees who leave the organization in a given time-frame by the total number of sales employees working during that same period.[61]

Summary

There are so many different ways to assess sales managers as leaders. These include sales manager self-assessment as well as reviews by peers and employees. Ultimately, since sales managers must be able to inspire their salespeople to deliver outstanding sales performance, salespeople should be asked to regularly evaluate the perceived effectiveness of their respective sales manager. Signs of employee morale, such as active attendance and participation at programs and events presented by the sales manager, also provide insight into their (the sales manager's) managerial effectiveness.

In conclusion, maximizing salesperson performance begins with quality recruiting and onboarding, effective training, and servant leadership by management. Though they fill these multiple roles, sales managers must ensure that all activities associated with managing salespeople are done in a timely and effective manner. The success of sales managers relies on the success of their salespeople. Successful sales performance and high employee morale lead to successful selling, high employee retention rates, happy customers, and more profitable businesses.

CHAPTER SUMMARY

- ✓ Seek job opportunities that include onboarding, coaching, and mentoring programs.

- ✓ Determine and learn from the various leadership styles of sales managers and executives.

- ✓ Recognize that your attitudes and behaviors contribute to company culture; always help to maintain a positive work environment.

- ✓ As a sales manager, study and employ those tactics that have been shown to increase employee retention.

- ✓ As a sales manager, ensure that all goals are created using SMART criteria.

KEY TERMS

Coaching

Indoctrinating

Key performance indicators (KPIs)

Mentoring

Onboarding

Organizational culture

Orientation

Sales compensation plan

Sales employee turnover rate

Sales leadership

REVIEW QUESTIONS

1. What are the four roles of a sales manager? Which do you think is the most important, and why?
2. List and describe the four steps that should be applied continually in order to successfully attract sales talent.
3. What does the acronym SEARCH stand for, and during what activity is it applied?
4. What are the similarities and differences between orientation and onboarding?
5. List and describe the three styles of sales leadership that focus attention on salespeople.
6. Describe sales coaching and give three examples of what it can be used for.
7. Define mentoring and explain how it differs from training.
8. According to the Sales Management Association, what are the four top factors for retaining salespeople?
9. Create a SMART goal from this statement: Increase sales revenue this year.
10. List the three categories of the performance metrics that may be used to assess the effectiveness of sales managers and give two examples of each.

ETHICS IN ACTION

1. Nathan Reston is the sales manager for a mid-sized, specialty health food company. He has been fortunate in the past to recruit salespeople who are dietitians or nutritionists. They've proven to be strong contributors to sales for the company and have exceptionally good rapport and teamwork. Due to a recent economic downturn, however, entry-level sales compensation has been decreased. Nathan has had multiple sales positions open over the last six months, but he has not successfully recruited candidates with the needed background and personal characteristics, given the

new compensation structure. Company executives have been pressuring him to hire quickly, so he extends offers to two candidates who don't have strong nutrition backgrounds but have sales experience with somewhat related food products. Did Nathan do the right thing under the circumstances? What can Nathan do during the onboarding process to help ensure these candidates will be successful new hires?

2. Nathan Reston continued to struggle with recruiting and retaining strong salespeople. Eventually, he decided to leave the company for a senior sales-person position elsewhere. Beth Cook was hired as his replacement. As she meets her salespeople, she learns that the goals Reston had set were unrealistically high and not motivational for the team. When she meets with company executives, she learns that their expectations for improvement in sales revenue are also unrealistically high. As she proposes new goals, what, if any, discussion should she have with the executives? How can she ensure that her goals will be motivational for her salespeople and encourage their retention? In addition to the goals themselves, what should her message be to the salespeople?

EXERCISE

Congratulations! You're now a new sales associate at Capital Lakes Incorporated with a promising career ahead at this very prestigious tech services firm. Part of its onboarding program is to place you with a mentor from the company. In the past, the sales managers at Capital Lakes have been very successful with their mentor program placements by seeking input from each new salesperson. You've been asked to provide input regarding the characteristics you believe your ideal mentor should possess, the types of advice and assistance you hope to secure, along with your expectations for the type of relationship you'd like to have with your mentor. The online form asks you to specify the following items regarding your ideal mentor:

A. The mentor's position within the company.
B. The mentor's years of corporate and/or sales experience.
C. The mentor's years of experience at Capital Lakes.
D. Types of advice and assistance your mentor will provide.
E. Specific skills and knowledge you hope to obtain from your mentor.
F. The frequency and location of mentor meetings.
G. Other specific criteria for your mentor.

READINGS AND RESOURCES

- David A. Brock (2016) *Sales Manager Survival Guide: Lessons from Sales' Front Lines.* New York: KCD Press.
- Max Cates (2020) *Serve, Lead, Succeed! How Servant Leaders Are Reaching Breakthrough Sales.* St. Petersburg, FL: BookLocker.com, Inc.
- Neil Rackham (2011) *The Challenger Sale: Taking Control of the Customer Conversation.* New York: Penguin Group.
- Mike Weinberg (2016) *Sales Management: Simplified.* New York: HarperCollins.
- John Whitmore (2017) *Coaching for Performance: The Principles and Practice of Coaching and Leadership,* 5th edition. London: Nicholas Brealey Publishing.

CASE STUDY: SERVANT LEADERSHIP AT AIRBORN, INC.

Figure 11.1   AirBorn logo
With kind permission of AirBorn.

There's little down time for Steven Spiller as he oversees two territory sales managers, one inside salesperson and three manufacturer representation firms in two different countries. Steven is a regional sales manager with AirBorn, Inc., an employee-owned company head-quartered in Georgetown, Texas, with eight manufacturing plants in the USA, and one in both Canada and the UK. However, AirBorn technology is distributed worldwide via a network of hundreds of distributors. AirBorn's wide range of products and services includes electronic connectors, cable assemblies, flexible circuits, battery and power supplies, and electro-mechanical assemblies. AirBorn offers standard catalog products as well as design-to-order, build-to-order and test-to-order solutions to meet the unique requirements of its clients, most of whom are original equipment manufacturers (OEM) for the military and aerospace markets or in fields such as medical technology and commercial aviation. The company also offers a variety of comprehensive value-added services.

Steven relies on his 30 years of sales experience to manage sales associates within a corporate culture of uncompromising quality and excellence with regard to its products and services. His position responsibilities include managing AirBorn salespeople and manufacturer representative firms in the Central USA and Canada. He is also responsible for recruiting, hiring, training, and coaching his sales team. Steven formally meets with sales personnel on a weekly, monthly, or bi-monthly basis, while he communicates with most of them on a daily basis via email, telephone, or video-conferencing platforms (see Figure 11.2). Larger group sessions, typically held at the manufacturing plant locations, include AirBorn product trainings, new product review introductions, and 'all hands' company updates, such as sales and profitability assessments. Also, AirBorn conducts mid-to-high-level managers' meetings to review strategic planning and management training. These are normally module based with break-out sessions on topics such as company culture, as part of the firm's critical 'servant leadership' initiative.

Figure 11.2 Steven Spiller in a meeting
Used with kind permission of Steven Spiller.

Servant leadership is the basis, foundation, and means of implementing AirBorn's desired culture. Servant leadership helps all AirBorn employees constantly strive for and maximize three critical aspects of its culture: customer intimacy, continuous improvement, and constant innovation. Steven uses servant leadership in managing his sales personnel on a regular basis. As the following success story will reveal, servant leadership has had an extremely positive impact on the performance of AirBorn's salespeople as well as on the company's success.

AirBorn received a web-based sales lead from a large military and aerospace OEM company. The AirBorn team reviewed the application that would call for high-reliability, complex electronic connector components and high-level assemblies involving cables and special circuitry. The company's end product was a high-grade aerospace communication box that would be integrated into a military aircraft. A bi-lateral non-disclosure agreement (NDA) was signed/executed. The NDA was an early positive sign of the prospect's trust and confidence in AirBorn's capabilities.

The project required highly technical resource personnel and cross-functional collaboration among three plants, with all working on the design and combining the electrical, mechanical, and manufacturability critical paths in the schedule for the AirBorn assembly. Because of the complex scope, high sales revenue potential, and expenditures involved, the project required vetting by a senior management committee within AirBorn. The committee trusted the project team's business plan and provided a strong positive directive with full encouragement to 'green light' the program.

Steven's team, with a keen desire to learn more about the prospective customer's needs, launched into a series of design review meetings with the prospect. These meetings spanned several months. The project's design went through many iterations as each side jointly challenged each other for continuous improvement to the functionality, performance, and reliability of the end product. Rapport was established, and mutual confidence and trust were built on both sides along the way.

Steven's team finished the design, and AirBorn provided full documentation, modeling and a mockup sample, followed by prototype parts and production qualification units. Later, the aircraft became officially funded by the military and released to production. AirBorn was officially selected as the full production supplier for its respective product portion that would be integrated into the communication box.

Using servant leadership, Steven was able to produce a successful 'win-win' scenario. The customer benefited greatly in that it now has a unique, newly approved supplier who can meet the mission critical – highly technical, complex electronic requirements from both product and service standpoints. AirBorn has benefited by securing a large contract which will generate $3 million in sales revenue over three years. As this case demonstrates, Steven was able to utilize many positive servant leadership practices, including teamwork, diligence, motivation, encouragement, and shear ongoing optimism.

Case questions:

1. Carefully review the case again to identify the numerous servant leadership words, phrases, and concepts. Create a list and count them. How many did you locate? In your opinion, which ones contribute the most to successful leadership? Why?
2. Had Steven used a different leadership style that focuses on followers (transformational or considerate), do you think AirBorn would have achieved the same level of selling success? Why or why not?
3. How might servant leadership impact AirBorn's future business relationships with its prospects, customers, and employees?

NOTES

1. Kevin Hallenbeck, 'How to recruit new salespeople,' *New Hampshire Business Review*, Concord (April 2018), 40(8), 11.
2. Adapted from Chris Peterson, 'Hiring the right salespeople,' *Security Systems News*, Yarmouth (October 2019), 22(10), 1, 13.
3. Brian Offenberger, 'How to hire top-performing salespeople,' *SDM: Security Distributing & Marketing* (May 2016), p. 60.
4. Ibid.
5. Troy Harrison, 'Hire with your head,' *eMPS* (March 2016), 18(3), 32–3.
6. Brian Williams, 'Sales rep crash and burn blamed on employers' failure to launch,' *PR Newswire*, New York, November 28, 2018.

7. '12 Red Flags To Look Out For When You're Screening Potential Salespeople,' December 13, 2018, www.forbes.com/sites/forbesbusinessdevelopmentcouncil/2018/12/13/12-red-flags-to-look-out-for-when-youre-screening-sales-position-hopefuls/?sh=7b2c52937d19, retrieved November 3, 2020.

8. Ibid.

9. Wikipedia, retrieved November 16, 2020.

10. Elearning Infographics, 'The Onboarding New Hire Statistics You Need to Know' (2019), https://elearninginfographics.com/onboarding-new-hire-statistics-need-know, retrieved November 16, 2020.

11. Ibid.

12. Brian Williams, 'Sales rep crash and burn blamed on employers' failure to launch,' *PR Newswire*, New York, November 28, 2018.

13. Elearning Infographics, 'The Onboarding New Hire Statistics You Need to Know' (2019), https://elearninginfographics.com/onboarding-new-hire-statistics-need-know, retrieved November 16, 2020.

14. Ibid.

15. Zahed Subhan and Scott Rader, 'Running an effective induction program for new sales recruits: Lessons from the financial services industry,' *Society for Marketing Advances Proceedings* (November 2013), 25, 227–8.

16. Ibid.

17. Thomas N. Ingram, Raymond W. LaForge, William B. Locander, Scott B. MacKenzie and Philip M. Podsakoff, 'New directions in sales leadership research,' *Journal of Personal Selling & Sales Management*, (2005) 25 (Spring), 137–54.

18. Ibid.

19. Ibid.

20. Ibid.

21. Charles H. Schwepker, Jr., 'Servant leadership, distributive justice and commitment to customer value in the salesforce,' *Journal of Business & Industrial Marketing* (2016) Santa Barbara, 31(1), 70–82.

22. Ibid.

23. Fernando Jaramillo, Douglas B. Grisaffe, Lawrence B. Chonko and James A. Roberts, 'Examining the impact of servant leadership on sales force performance,' *Journal of Personal Selling & Sales Management* (Summer 2009), 29(3), 257–75.

24. Charles H. Schwepker, Jr., 'Servant leadership, distributive justice and commitment to customer value in the salesforce,' *Journal of Business & Industrial Marketing* (2016) Santa Barbara, 31(1), 70–82.

25. Ibid.

26. Ibid.

27. Fernando Jaramillo, Douglas B. Grisaffe, Lawrence B. Chonko and James A. Roberts, 'Examining the impact of servant leadership on sales force performance,' *Journal of Personal Selling & Sales Management* (Summer 2009), 29(3), 257–75.

28. Ibid.

29. Ibid.

30. Steven W. Spiller, personal communication, November 2, 2020.

31. Fernando Jaramillo, Douglas B. Grisaffe, Lawrence B. Chonko and James A. Roberts, 'Examining the impact of servant leadership on sales force performance,' *Journal of Personal Selling & Sales Management* (Summer 2009), 29(3), 257–75.

32. Camilla Krog and Krishna Govender, 'Servant leadership and project management: Examining the effects of leadership style on project success,' *Proceedings of the European Conference on Management, Leadership & Governance* (2015), pp. 201–10.

33. 'Servant salesmanship,' *Hardware + Building Supply Dealer*, Chicago (January 2019), 45(1), 20.

34. Steven W. Spiller, personal communication, November 2, 2020.

35. Ibid.

36. Fernando Jaramillo, Douglas B. Grisaffe, Lawrence B. Chonko and James A. Roberts, 'Examining the impact of servant leadership on sales force performance,' *Journal of Personal Selling & Sales Management* (Summer 2009), 29(3), 257–75.

37. David W. Cravens, (1995) 'The changing role of the sales force,' *Marketing Management*, 4(2) (Fall), 48–57.

38. Shalonda Bradford, Brian Rutherford and Scott Friend, 'The impact of training, mentoring and coaching on personal learning in the sales environment,' *International Journal of Evidence Based Coaching & Mentoring* (February 2017), 15(1), 133–51.

39. Jack Hubbard, 'Good coaching leads to improved sales results,' *ABA Bank Marketing & Sales* (November 2014), 46(9), 12–13.

40. Ibid.

41. Aja Frost, 'Sales Coaching: The ultimate guide,' https://blog.hubspot.com/sales/sales-coaching, retrieved November 3, 2020.

42. Adapted from Jenny Dearborn, 'Sinking FAST,' *T+D* (December 2013), 67(12), 44–7; and Aja Frost, 'Sales Coaching: The ultimate guide,' https://blog.hubspot.com/sales/sales-coaching, retrieved November 3, 2020.

43. Aja Frost, 'Sales Coaching: The ultimate guide,' https://blog.hubspot.com/sales/sales-coaching, retrieved November 3, 2020.

44. Justin Zappulla, 'Sales Coaching, Mentoring and Training: What's the difference?' (February 22, 2019), https://trainingindustry.com/articles/sales/sales-coaching-mentoring-and-training-whats-the-difference, retrieved November 3, 2020.

45. Jenny Dearborn, 'Sinking FAST,' *T+D* (December 2013), 67(12), 44–7.

46. Adapted from Alex Mackenzie, '7 Steps to Establish a Successful Sales Mentorship Program,' https://blog.hubspot.com/sales/sales-mentorship-program, retrieved November 3, 2020.

47. Jack Hubbard, 'Good coaching leads to improved sales results,' *ABA Bank Marketing & Sales* (November 2014), 46(9), 12–13.

48. Mary Clare Novak, 'A Sales Compensation Plan That Will Inspire and Reward Reps' (February 6, 2020), https://learn.g2.com/sales-compensation-plan, retrieved November 3, 2020.

49. Ibid.

50. Gordon Daugherty, 'Absolute versus Relative Sales Commission Plans' (March 13, 2014), http://shockwaveinnovations.com/absolute-versus-relative-sales-commission-plans, retrieved November 29, 2020.

51. Ibid.

52. Ben Goldstein, '8 Ways to Retain Your Top Sales Reps (after they've gotten their bonuses),' www.nutshell.com/blog/8-sales-rep-retention-tips, retrieved November 3, 2020.

53. Gregg Greggory, 'Why good employees leave – and how to retain more of them,' *American Salesman* (February 2019), 64(2), 7–10.

54. Steve DeMarco, 'Research-based Advice for Improving Sales Retention and Performance,' www.salesforce.com/quotable/articles/research-improve-sales-retention, retrieved November 3, 2020.

55. Ibid.

56. Ben Goldstein, '8 Ways to Retain Your Top Sales Reps (after they've gotten their bonuses),' www.nutshell.com/blog/8-sales-rep-retention-tips, retrieved November 3, 2020.

57. Ibid.

58. Ibid.

59. Ibid.

60. Kevin Higgins, 'Simple Metrics to Accurately Measure Sales Manager Performance,' (January 18, 2018), https://trainingindustry.com/articles/measurement-and-analytics/6-simple-metrics-to-accurately-measure-sales-manager-performance, retrieved November 3, 2020.

61. A.J. Beltis, 'Sales Employee Turnover Rate: How to measure (and lower) it,' https://blog.hubspot.com/sales/employee-turnover-rate, retrieved November 3, 2020.

12
BUDGETING AND FORECASTING FUTURE SALES

CHAPTER CONTENTS

PEOPLE, PRACTICES AND PERSPECTIVES FROM THE WORLD OF SALES

Greetings from the United Kingdom. My name is Nina Abdali, I'm an academic sales consultant and my sales territory is London. I have nearly 20 years of sales experience predominately within the publishing sector, working in roles from field sales rep to senior national account manager. *I've always taken a keen interest in sales figures, budgets and sales forecasting, often working closely with business analysts to contextualise the numbers and create meaningful measures and goals. In particular, sales forecasting has enabled me to focus on the customers and deals that will have the most impact. I've always considered myself a builder of relationships rather than a seller of goods. So much of sales is about making it easy for people to do business with you, from the basics like offering genuine value for money to being authentic, reliable and working in collaboration with your customers.*

Hi, my name is Rachael Judy. I work in medical device sales for Boston Scientific's Neuromodulation Division. Prior to that, I owned a small medical marketing company, assisting local medical practices to expand their brand awareness and increase their patient population. *In all of my career roles, strategizing a plan (short and long term), forecasting, and setting future goals have been essential to success. My advice to you is to always take the time to think ahead. It is never a waste of time.* One of my favorite quotes is: 'Failing to plan is planning to fail' (Alan Lakein.)

Hello, I'm Steven Spiller, regional sales manager with AirBorn Inc. My responsibilities include the hiring, training, coaching, and recruiting of salespeople and manufacturer representatives, and the forecasting of sales territories in Central USA and Canada. *Over my 30-year career, I've found that intelligent forecasting and budgeting are critical business tools that assist senior management in making staffing decisions, evaluating capital equipment acquisitions, optimizing the operations, and planning for material expenditures. My advice to you is to focus on building rapport and relationships with your customers, as there is no finer way to experience professional enjoyment and satisfaction. Knowing that you were fully prepared to effectively deliver a product or service that delighted your customers, will make both you and your company proud.*

Good decisions start with good data.

EYES ON ETHICS

Keep in mind the following ethical topics as you read through this chapter:

1. Tendency to set sales goals with an 'under-promise and over-deliver' mentality.
2. Failure to communicate errors in forecast accuracy with executive management.

INTRODUCTION

This chapter discusses planning for a company's sales revenue and expenditures via budgeting and sales forecasting. Knowing where money is coming from and where it's going is key to operating a successful business. Budgeting is an important part of business planning for all sizes and types of companies and organizations. Without adequate resources, a business cannot operate. While both sales budgets and sales forecasts are predictions of future sales revenue amounts for a specified period of time, they are not the same.

The main difference between a sales budget and a sales forecast is that the sales budget is a quantified expectation of the total sales revenues that will be achieved during a given period of time, whereas the sales forecast specifies estimated future sales along with specific details about what products/services are to be sold during

Budgeting

a specific time period. Another difference is that the sales forecast is normally determined *after* the sales budget has been set and breaks down what exactly is forecasted to be sold during the particular time period.[1] A final difference is that sales forecasts are more often structured for shorter periods of time, such as per week or per month, whereas sales budgets will often look at the long-term, quarterly, or annual figures.[2] Sales forecasting is an important business activity which enables leaders throughout the company, especially sales managers, to make smarter decisions with regard to setting goals, budgeting, hiring, business planning, prospecting, daily operations, and other revenue-impacting factors.[3] In this chapter, we'll delve into both sales budgeting and sales forecasting topics to better understand the activities, processes, and issues involved in planning and handling the flow of monetary resources of a company. Let's begin now with budgeting.

BUDGETING

A budget is defined as a formal written plan used to allocate scarce resources and to measure and evaluate success against performance goals.[4] There are two types of budgets – financial budgets and operating budgets. Let's discuss them both.

A financial budget consists of the capital budget, the cash budget, the budgeted balance sheet, and the budgeted statement of cash flows.[5] Financial budgets reveal the impact of the planned operations on the company's overall financial position at year end and are usually prepared by the accounting staff with some collaboration from line managers.[6]

An operating budget is a financial representation of the short-term plans of the organization across all functions. Operating budgets consist of the income statement and all supporting budget schedules.[7] Typically, people from several departments actively participate in preparing the operating budget since they set short-term plans and develop detailed budgets for their own respective departments. For example, contributors include:[8]

- marketing managers, who contribute promotional information which may affect both the timing and volume of sales
- product managers, who provide information regarding new product development and release dates, as well as insight into the discontinuance of older products
- sales managers, who help to determine business strategies and define the key assumptions that the operating budget figures represent
- executive team members, who provide budget reviews and revisions based on their insight into the company's strategic planning process.

The most basic component of any operating budget is the sales budget.[9] The sales budget memorializes a business's expected sales for the coming budget period and attached expected gross revenue to the sales plan.[10] Let's now explore the sales budget in greater detail.

Examining the role of sales budgeting

The sales budget is a critical building block of the operating budget and drives the resource allocation of other areas, including manufacturing, supply chain, sales, and marketing.[11] The sales budget, as well as the process of creating it, serves as a guide to direct a company and its sales team over the rest of the month, quarter, and year.[12] Of course, the more precise and accurate a sales budget is, the more effectively the company can be managed.[13] Larger companies, with a wide variety of products, normally aggregate the sales budget into specific product categories and/or geographic regions, while smaller companies tend to create the sales budget for the entire business.[14]

The sales budget offers a number of important benefits, including:[15]

- allowing company managers to assess the resources they need and the cost of those resources in order to achieve established goals
- improving cash flow management
- guiding the production levels of products and services
- establishing specific sales goals for salespeople and sales teams to reach
- motivating salespeople and sales teams with monthly, quarterly, or annual milestones
- assisting in determining overhead costs
- contributing to appropriate pricing strategies
- communicating company plans and priorities
- serving as a reference to assess the company's performance.

The sales budget provides direction across the entire company or organization; thus, it should be based on accurate and reliable assessments and projections. Unfortunately, unethical practices, such as padding out estimates to ensure enough resources are allocated, or lowballing projections in order to obtain a higher bonus after the year-end analysis, are known to occur and result in inaccurate budgets.[16] Thus, the process for setting sales budgets must be documented and include safeguards against such unethical practices. Let's now explore the process for creating a sales budget.

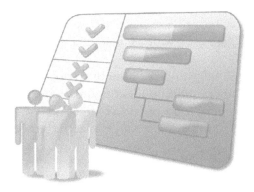

Budget direction

Creating a sales budget

Here's a step-by-step process to preparing a sales budget that is realistic, accurate, and actionable:[17]

Step 1: Select a time period for the budget. Sales budgets are typically established on an annual basis with quarterly budgets specified along with an annual total.

Step 2: Collect sales prices. This includes the current selling prices of each unit or service being offered by the company, as well as any anticipated price increases or reductions.

Step 3: Gather historical sales data. This data is normally easily obtained from past sales records, previous budgets, or CRM systems. It is important to gather last year's sales data from the same period that will be used for the current budget. This data should include the number of salespeople employed as well as sales revenue figures.

Step 4: Review industry information. Obtaining information on similar companies will provide industry sales benchmarks. Industry-wide growth estimates and other financial data about a specific industry can usually be acquired from governmental sources.

Step 5: Determine market trends. While past sales figures provide a strong baseline for future sales, they are not precise in predicting future business. Current market trends associated with consumer demand, competition, technological innovation, and so on, can affect future sales outcomes and should be investigated and factored into budget estimates.

Step 6: Consider business model changes. It is important to document changes in the company's business or sales strategy as those changes will affect sales budget estimates. These changes may include introducing new products, discontinuing current products, expanding into new sales territories, and so on.

Step 7: Obtain input. Seeking future sales projections from existing salespeople who are interacting with customers on a regular basis will provide valuable estimates, as they learn of intentions to buy directly from customers.

Step 8: Create the budget. Using the information gathered in steps 3 through 7 above, the projected sales budget may be estimated with confidence.

The sales budget should be expressed in tangible measures, such as units, pounds, billable hours, square feet, or the number of clients serviced, and then given a monetary value based on an average price per unit of measure (UM). The UM should connect the financial results directly to the bloodline of the business and address questions such as: What was sold? What was the average price? To calculate the sales budget, the estimated sales volume (expressed in a UM) is multiplied by the average sales price per unit of measure (UM). Table 12.1 provides a sales budget example for a company that has three products.

Table 12.1 Sales budget example

Description	Unit of measure (UM)	Customer demand	Price per UM ($)	Sales budget ($)*
Product A	Each	200,000	2.50	500,000
Product B	Each	110,000	8.50	935,000
Product C	Each	68,000	12.20	829,600
Total budget				**$2,264,600**

*Product A = 200,000 each x 2.50 per unit = $500,000
Product B = 110,000 each x 8.50 per unit = $935,000
Product C = 68,000 each x 12.20 per unit = $829,600

For companies with many products or customers, the 80/20 principle (20 percent of your customers generate 80 percent of your business) is typically applied. A detailed and accurate budget is calculated for the products that represent 80–90 percent of sales revenue, while the remaining percentage is estimated using simple math.

Sales budgets must be reviewed and revised on a regular basis, such as quarterly, to ensure their accuracy and value. The projected unit sales directly impact the production budget, from which the direct materials and direct labor budgets are created. In addition, the sales budget provides a general sense of the scale of operations needed for the budgeted time period, which factor into the overhead budget and the selling and administrative expenses budget.[18] Thus, the accuracy of the sales budget is critical as it directly impacts the planning and budgeting of many different areas throughout a company. Effective business planning and operations are contingent upon reliable and accurate budgeting. In today's modern world, many companies are automating their budgeting processes using the digital tools available to assist in creating the budget and improving its accuracy. Let's investigate these budgeting tools.

Computer software

Using budgeting tools

A variety of budgeting software tools are available for companies to manage their annual budgets, project sales for a specified budgeted period, estimate the direct costs of the sales, and calculate fixed costs or overheads.[19] Online budgeting tools are a valuable option for any company that wants to move its budgets out of a spreadsheet format and manage them in a streamlined and organized manner. Today's budgeting software tools are easy to use and quickly implemented. Most online providers regularly release software updates so that the tools are state of the art.[20] Examples of these tools are: Scoro, Centage, Prophix, Float, Planguru, GIDE, and Maxiplan.[21] In addition, there are a number of open-source budgeting software programs that may be downloaded at no cost. These software programs offer online support and flexibility to meet business needs. To learn more about these free budgeting tools, check out the budgeting software website listed in the Readings and Resources section at the end of this chapter.

Using budgeting software tools offers companies a number of key benefits, including:[22]

* user-friendly software
* the ability to analyze data and run reports
* self-sufficiency, without the need for consultants
* an audit trail for identifying budgeting errors
* the ability to track who made budget changes and when
* more control over operations within the company
* tracking of previous expenditures
* effective cash flow management.

Developing a sales budget entails more than forecasting marketing expenses using software tools. There must be sound, strategic reasoning based on an analysis of how to serve target customers to support the budget expenditures.[23] That's where sales forecasting can provide insight and detail. Sales forecasting is the topic of our next section.

SALES FORECASTING

Sales forecasting refers to the process of estimating future sales. Sales forecasts may be conducted for any specified period of time (monthly, quarterly, semi-annually, or annually). Confirming the timeframe of the sales forecast is critical in order to accurately predict sales. The timeframe selected may be contingent on the ability to qualify prospects' needs properly and on knowledge of prospects' buying cycles, as well as on the unique buying situation of each prospect. The main purpose of sales forecasting is to provide information to enable smart business decisions to be made, such as managing inventory levels, expenses, profits, cash flow, or planning for business growth.[24] Forecasting sales is a critical business action that serves the needs of almost everyone in a company or an organization. Let's now examine sales forecasting in greater detail.

Understanding sales forecasting

A sales forecast is basically an educated guess about the future. Since we're humans, when we attempt to predict the future, we're not always accurate or precise. However, what we can do well is to conduct detailed analysis of the sources and levels of past sales revenues, identify the factors affecting business operations and sales transactions, and plan the future by making assumptions based on market knowledge and experience. The most important activity is to review and revise sales forecasts on a regular basis to ensure that resource allocations and business decisions are being made based on current and relevant data. Making good business decisions relies on obtaining and using relevant, representative data. What data should be included in sales forecasting?

The data and information to use as the foundation for sales forecasting, include:[25]

- **Sales goals** – determining SMART sales goals for both individual salespeople and sales teams serves as targets or quotas.
- **Sales process** – documenting the actions and steps required to move a prospect through the sales funnel provides insight into the likelihood that sales will close.
- **Standardized definitions of leads, opportunities, and closes** – clarifying the precise meaning of these concepts enables clear reporting, tracking, and measuring.
- **Benchmark sales metrics** – identifying basic metrics, such as the average price of a deal, average conversion or renewal rates, or average duration of the sales process provides standards against which to measure sales performance.
- **Information on product costs, expenses, and price fluctuations** – knowing the costs of doing business is critical given the uncontrollable market conditions in which companies operate.

Analyzing data

Just like a weather forecast, a sales forecast should be viewed as information that enables you to make plans, rather than as an absolute prediction that requires absolute accuracy. Of course, basing a forecast on accurate projections results in better decisions being made. Accurate sales projections can lead to cost savings and reductions by facilitating better production and inventory planning, competitive pricing, and timely promotional planning;[26] whereas inaccurate sales estimations can prove costly and lead to inventory shortages, fulfillment problems, and dissatisfied customers.[27]

In order for sales forecasting to be effective, it must be perceived as reliable, accurate, and producing valuable benefits.[28] The benefits of sales forecasting include (but are not limited to) the following:[29]

- managing customer expectations after they place an order with the company
- encouraging salespeople to be more objective about their selling potential
- motivating salespeople to more efficiently manage their time by prioritizing their selling activities throughout the stages of the selling process
- identifying potential problems or issues in advance, so there is time to make adjustments to avoid or mitigate the issue
- revealing potential uncontrollable factors and marketplace dynamics that require changes to be made in sales territories and with client account assignments
- providing greater insight into the strengths and weaknesses of each salesperson's ability to close sales
- improving hiring and staffing strategies
- aiding in developing realistic budgets and resource allocation plans
- empowering good strategic and operational planning for the company.

The people who benefit from sales forecasting extend throughout the entire organization and stem from the various uses or applications of sales forecasts. Typically, sales managers use forecasts to estimate the deals their sales teams will close in a given period, while directors use forecasts to anticipate department sales revenues, and vice-presidents of sales use department forecasts to project company sales.[30] In addition, sales forecasts are often shared with company leadership, board members, and/or stockholders.[31] Sales forecasts don't need to be perfect in order to be a valuable aid in business decision making. However, salespeople are more likely to exceed their sales targets or quotas when they have an accurate and informative plan for how they can

Sales forecasting meeting

be achieved. Sales planning and accurate forecasting help to develop objectives into realistic actions for salespeople to follow.[32] Thus, striving for sales forecast accuracy is typically the goal of those sales managers tasked with the job of forecasting sales. Unfortunately, achieving sales forecasting accuracy is often challenging. We'll examine why this is the case in the next section.

Striving for accuracy

In today's digital world of big data, there's no lack of available data to support business decisions. However, sales managers and salespeople must be aware of the different factors that may impact the reliability of the data in forecasting sales accurately. Since sales forecasts influence sales territory alignment, sales force assignments, compensation structures, budgeting, manufacturing plans, and so on, some degree of accuracy is essential. Factors affecting accuracy in sales forecasting can come from both inside and outside of a company and may be either positive or negative. Some examples of internal and external factors are listed below.[33]

Internal factors:

- Hires and fires – opportunities gained by new sales reps or lost by terminated ones.
- Policy changes – impacts due to adjustments in sales compensation plans.
- Territory changes – sales affected by an unfamiliarity with new sales territories.
- New products/services – sales affected by new product/service introductions.
- Marketing/promotional campaigns – the effects of advertising and promotional efforts.

External factors:

- Competition – impacts due to increased or decreased direct competitors.
- Economic conditions – fluctuations in demand due to the state of the economy.
- Market changes – shifts in demand caused by changing consumer needs or wants.
- Industry shifts – changes in demand associated with complementary product sales.
- Legal regulations – new laws affecting the sales of products/services.
- Seasonality – the influence of timing on product/service demand.

When forecasting sales, it's important to clarify and document assumptions about the internal and external factors that may affect the accuracy of the forecast, as well as to comprehend what drives sales, such as advertising, web traffic, or salesperson pitches.[34] Experienced sales professionals tend to possess a greater ability to accurately forecast sales due to their years of knowledge about their customers, products/ services, industry, and so on. In addition, forecasting sales for an established business with repeat customers is easier than forecasting the sales for a new business because an established business has a baseline of past sales to analyze when predicting the future. This is not to say that history will *always* repeat itself; however, historical data is typically a good predictor of the future. A company's sales revenues from the same month of a previous year, coupled with knowledge of the internal and external impact factors, usually work well to predict the sales for a particular month in the future.[35] If a business has repeat customers, salespeople may inquire whether their purchasing levels are likely to be similar in the future, which can aid in accurately predicting sales. Often, sales managers will create a range of forecasts to aid in accurately predicting future sales, which entails creating two additional sales forecasts – one based on optimistic figures and the other based on pessimistic ones. A range of forecasts will produce a best-case scenario and a worst-case scenario, which is helpful for business planning purposes. Check out Table 12.2 which provides some tips on techniques for effective sales forecasting.

Table 12.2 Techniques for effective sales forecasting

- Be sure to use accurate or 'clean' data.
- Use clear standards to ensure consistency in record keeping.
- Consider both the quality and quantity of sales leads.
- Perform spot checks on sales records to identify potential inconsistencies and/or errors.
- Use automated sales forecasting tools to save time and increase accuracy.
- Incorporate 'what-if' analyses to explore different possibilities.
- Pair qualitative with quantitative sales forecasting methods to obtain greater forecasting insight.
- Factor in the effects of seasonality, if applicable.
- Take into account the impact of competitors.
- Encourage collaboration and make sales forecasting a team effort to obtain valuable contributions and different perspectives.
- Review and revise sales forecasts on a regular basis.
- Determine and use the sales forecasting method that is most appropriate for your company and selling situation.
- Look for trends and key drivers that may lead to future business opportunities.
- Ensure that your forecast is aligned with your company's strategic action plans.
- Hope for the best-case scenario while planning for the worst.

Source: Adapted from Tim Berry, 'How to Forecast Sales,' https://articles.bplans.com/how-to-forecast-sales, retrieved November 20, 2020; and Gregg Schwartz, '10 Simple Strategies for Creating a Better Sales Forecasting Model,' https://blog.hubspot.com/sales/accurate-sales-forecasting-model-tips, retrieved November 20, 2020.

Conducting sales forecasting on a monthly basis is normally preferred as it provides a much more realistic prediction of business performance as opposed to annual forecasts, as well as enabling sales managers and salespeople an opportunity to regularly review forecast results and revise actions if/as needed.[36] The method used for forecasting sales may also impact the accuracy of the forecast. Let's now investigate some common methods used for forecasting sales.

Examining sales forecasting methods

There are a number of methods that may be used when forecasting sales, with most companies embracing the use of several methods to ensure accuracy. These methods vary in type from simple qualitative techniques, such as expert opinion, through the quantitative analysis of linear trends from historical data, to advanced predictive modeling, such as multivariable analysis. Of course, each sales forecasting method possesses advantages and disadvantages. Some of the most common methods used for forecasting sales are as follows:[37]

1. *Survey of salespeople opinion.* This method entails sales managers polling their salespeople to determine the various stages in which their deals are currently located in the sales funnel and their expectations regarding both when their deals will likely close and their approximate value. This educated guess method is based on subjective opinions; thus, it often results in inaccurate sales forecasts due to salespeople either overestimating sales performance, or underestimating it, knowing that their sales quota will be associated with their forecast predictions.
2. *Historical data.* This method bases the forecast on a record of past performance data under similar conditions to estimate how sales will perform in the future. This method may be more accurate than educated guessing, however it may ignore those factors that have changed in the last year or forecast period, affecting the accuracy of predictions.
3. *Deal stage.* This forecasting method takes into account the various stages of the sales process that the deal is in, whereby you assign a probability of closing a deal to each stage in your sales process. Then, at any given time, you can multiply that probability by the size of a deal to generate the estimated revenue that may be expected during a given time period. The premise is that the further along a deal is in the pipeline, the more likely it is to close. Here's an example – let's say you've established the following likely-to-close percentages to your pipeline stages:

- initial call – 5%
- qualified lead – 10%
- sales presentation and product demonstration – 40%
- product trial – 60%
- contract sent – 90%
- deal closed – 100%
- deal lost – 0%

Based on this forecasting method, a $1,000 deal at the product trial stage has a 60 percent likelihood to close in a stated timeframe, thus the forecasted amount for this deal would be $600, whereas a $1,000 deal in the sales presentation and product demonstration stage has a 40 percent chance of closing, thus $400 is the forecasted amount. While this forecasting method is simple to apply, it disregards the age of the sales opportunity and treats a deal that is two weeks old the same as it would one that is two months old. As you would expect, a deal that has been stalled for a while at a stage in your pipeline doesn't likely have the same probability of closing as that of a new deal that is moving along well through your sales pipeline.

4. *Length of sales cycle.* This method uses historical data to understand how the age of individual deals in the sales pipeline compares to the time when those deals actually closed. Based on this correlation, a company can predict when any deal is likely to close given its current stage in the pipeline. This method relies on objective data; thus, it will produce a more realistic and accurate forecast. For example, say a salesperson schedules a product demonstration with a new prospect and reports the subjective opinion that the deal will close soon. The length of sales cycle method will calculate that the sale isn't likely to close soon since it is a new opportunity that hasn't been in the pipeline long enough. This method will take into account different sales cycles and adjust the calculations accordingly. For example, a normal lead may take approximately six months to buy, leads generated from trade shows usually take eight months, and a referral often takes only one month.[38]

5. *Lead value.* This forecasting method involves analyzing historical sales data from each lead source and assigning a value to each lead source to obtain a better sense of the likelihood of those leads producing sales revenue. To apply this method, the following metrics are needed:

   - leads per month for the previous time period
   - lead-to-customer conversion rate by lead source
   - average sales price by lead source.

To calculate lead value, begin by sorting the entire CRM database by lead source. Next, for each source, compute the average sales price. Then, for each type of lead source, multiply the average sales price by the average close rate. The result is the value for each type of lead source. For example, let's say, based on historical data, we know the average sales price and average conversion rate for each of a company's three main lead sources:

   - website leads close at $1,500 per customer, at a 20% conversion rate
   - trade show leads close at $2,000 per customer, at a 25% conversion rate
   - paid advertising leads close at $1,000 per customer, at a 10% conversion rate.

The value of each of these different types of leads would be $300/website lead ($1,500 x 20%), $500/trade show lead ($2,000 x 25%), and $100/paid advertising lead ($1,000 x 10%). This method relies on historical data; thus, it may ignore those factors that have changed in the last year or forecast period, which can affect the accuracy of the predictions. Adjustment of these calculations with current, relevant data would need to be done off-line.

6. *Multivariable statistical analysis.* This is the most sophisticated sales forecasting method, which tends to produce the most accurate sales forecasts. This method uses predictive sales analytics and incorporates variables such as average

sales cycle length, probability of closing based on deal type, and salesperson performance. This method requires advanced analytics, appropriate software, statistical expertise, and clean data. More sophisticated statistical sales forecasting models provide more robust techniques that can detect and extrapolate on patterns in sales data, such as seasonality, sales cycles, trends, responses to promotions, etc.[39]

Two common approaches for forecasting sales using statistical methods are time-series models and regression models. The time-series model bases the forecast solely on historical data to capture patterns in the sales data and project them into the future. However, time-series techniques are best used with short-term forecasting and when you can assume a reasonable amount of continuity between the past and the future.[40] Dynamic regression models can incorporate causal factors such as prices, promotions, and economic factors into the sales forecasts. The models combine Ordinary Least Squares (OLS) regression with the ability to use dynamic terms to capture trend, seasonality, and time-phased relationships between variables.[41] Dynamic regression models can enable sales managers to conduct 'what if' analyses, to generate alternative forecasts based on different variable scenarios, such as higher or lower prices.

The type of forecasting method selected by sales professionals may be based on convenience, personal comfort zone, the availability (or lack thereof) of data, or access to and ability to use appropriate software.[42] Of course, if your business doesn't have any or much historical data, then relying on the opinions of salespeople might be the only sales forecasting method to use, whereas if your company tends to have a busy pipeline, then deal stage or length of sales cycle forecasting methods may be feasible options. When you are seeking more detailed sales pipeline forecasting, multivariable

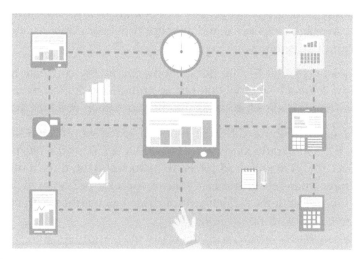

Digital integration

analysis is likely the method to use.[43] Regardless of the method selected for forecasting, it is critical to communicate your forecasting strategies with your salespeople and to integrate your forecasting practices with your customer relationship management (CRM) system. This is the topic of our next section.

Integrating CRM data and sales forecasting

One of the biggest challenges in being able to effectively and accurately conduct sales forecasting is the availability of sufficient resources, including reliable customer data. That is why a company's CRM system should be integrated with its sales planning and sales forecasting activities. As discussed in previous chapters, CRM requires efficient, integrated business systems to provide an organization-wide process to develop an image of the customer to be shared across the entire company.[44] CRM tools give salespeople a database for tracking sales opportunities, which will enable more accurate predictions of sales performance based on closed deals. Research shows that salespeople who rely on their CRM system hit their quotas 82 percent of the time versus 65 percent for non-CRM users.[45]

A potential drawback of using your CRM system for sales forecasting is that a database is only as good as the data that it captures, thus forecasting accuracy will be reliant upon the diligence of the sales team to accurately capture and update customer data in real time.[46] In addition, CRM systems do not typically offer the following features:[47]

- track history via machine learning to obtain artificial intelligence (AI) insight
- process deal signals stemming from other database systems, such as lead generation
- easy adaptation to new product line introductions or growth initiatives.

Most companies realize that CRM is essential for business operations and successful selling, however, as an analytical tool, CRM alone is limited in its predictive power. That is why many companies are combining CRM tools with sales analytics to improve the forecasting capabilities of CRM systems.[48] We'll discuss sales analytics in greater detail in the next chapter, but for now, it's important to understand the data integration needed for carrying out sales forecasting.

Integrating CRM tools with analytics and artificial intelligence (AI) which uses computer systems to perform tasks that normally require human intelligence, can help a company to avoid forecasting bias and improve both collaboration and the accuracy of sales forecasts.[49] AI can contribute to traditional sales forecasting methods to help identify and measure the internal and external variables affecting sales forecasting accuracy.[50] In addition, AI can help sales managers extract the relevant knowledge and understand the complex projections that are often associated with sales forecasting. For example, AI brings visibility to sales activity data that can show sales managers and salespeople where they have a sales pipeline risk or a sales opportunity, which aids decision making regarding allocating resources.[51] Integrating

CRM tools, sales analytics, and AI can make sales forecasting tasks easier for sales managers, as the reporting measures associated with all of them have become more user-friendly and reliable than in the past.

Accurate and reliable budgeting and sales forecasting are the business goals of all sales managers. How are budgeting and sales forecasting activities assessed for their effectiveness? That is the topic of our final chapter section.

MONITORING METRICS

Monitoring Metrics

Assessing the effectiveness of budgeting and forecasting activities encompasses justifying your sales budget and sales forecast with concrete metrics and analytics that show the accuracy of your predictions. Once the budgeted and forecasted time period is over, you should conduct variance analysis, which is comparing the actual results with the expected figures to determine how accurate the budgeting and forecasting activities were. Variance analysis can also reveal any unforeseen errors and/or uncontrollable variables that may have affected the observed differences. Some of the common errors that may be identified are:[52]

- **Type and category misalignment** – the product categories and types do not match the information obtained from accounting statements, sales reports, and other historical data documents.
- **Ignorant guessing** – educated guesswork was not applied using last year's budget (if available) as a baseline, to estimate the differences between last year and the current year.
- **Margins** – varying account margins that directly affect a product/service's selling price, such as those due to selling through retail channels, were not taken into account and led to inaccurate budget calculations.

Additional assessment activities may include utilizing several different budgeting or sales forecasting methods for a particular time period, and applying variance analysis to compare the results between each of the methods to reveal which method(s) produced the most accurate budgets and forecasts. Perhaps the most important assessment is determining whether the firm's budgeting and sales forecasting activities enabled its salespeople and sales teams to reach their personal, as well as overall company, goals. If not, it's time to investigate the reasons why and to consider readjusting them. As stated previously, budgeting and sales forecasting are activities that should be assessed regularly to ensure their accuracy and reliability. Sales managers should include input from salespeople when analyzing the strengths and weaknesses of their budgeting and forecasting techniques, and modify them if/as needed to ensure continuous improvement. Keep in mind that the value of budgeting and sales forecasting is in providing direction to salespeople as well as communication to the entire company. From a salesperson perspective, the sales budget often communicates expectations, raises or lowers motivation, and transfers inspiration.[53] Thus, budgeting and sales forecasting represent crucial steps in the sales management process.

CHAPTER SUMMARY

✓ An established sales budget communicates goals and drives resource allocation across the entire company.

✓ Historical sales data as well as industry and market trends must be factored in to establish accurate budgets.

✓ Use budgeting software tools for self-sufficiency, reporting, tracking changes, and identifying errors.

✓ Apply multivariable statistical models to improve forecast accuracy by including seasonality, sales cycles, trends, responses to promotions, and other factors.

✓ Perform variance analyses of proposed and actual budgets and forecasts to identify uncontrollable variables or errors that may have affected the accuracy of predictions.

KEY TERMS

Artificial intelligence	Sales budget
Budget	Sales forecast
Financial budgets	Sales forecasting
Operating budgets	Variance analysis

REVIEW QUESTIONS

1. Describe the information that multiple departments provide when preparing the operating budget of a company.
2. List three important benefits that companies derive from creating a sales budget.
3. List the eight steps for creating a realistic, accurate, actionable sales budget.
4. Why is it important to determine market trends when setting a sales budget?
5. Describe four of the key benefits of using budgeting software tools compared to a simple spreadsheet.
6. What pieces of data and information are used as the foundation for sales forecasting?
7. Give examples of the two types of factors that can affect the accuracy of sales forecasting.
8. Compare and contrast the forecasting methods of length of sales cycle and multivariable statistical analysis.
9. How is lead value calculated, and why is it important to determine lead value for multiple sources when forecasting?
10. List two types of errors that variance analysis of budgets and forecasts may reveal.

ETHICS IN ACTION

1. Jesse Sunder is the sales director for a mid-sized manufacturer of home décor products that are sold online all over the world, with 80 percent of sales coming from the USA. With the threat of a national recession looming, Jesse is concerned about using historical sales results to set his sales forecast for the coming year. He also knows that executive management tends to penalize those sales teams that do not reach their strategic goals. He undercuts his forecast by 15 percent. What impact will this have on the sales team? How will the decreased forecast affect the rest of the organization, as well as potentially affect end customers?

2. Angela Baxter is Vice President of Sales and Marketing for a local chain of dry-cleaning stores. She sets the budget for the coming fiscal year based on historical service data from each location. The budget is enacted by executive management. During the first month of the new year, the operations manager of the flagship store complains to Angela that her forecast is inaccurate. Angela investigates and realizes that she had not taken into account the potential new business from a housing division recently completed in that neighborhood. She hesitates to adjust the forecast (only one month into the year) and fails to admit her mistake to senior management. What impact will her behavior have on the company over the next three to six months? What is likely to happen at the flagship store? How will the customer experience change if the store's capacity for service is exceeded?

EXERCISE

You are the sales manager for York Company, a distributor of three brands of industrial machinery and power tools. York has been successfully operating for 18 years now and it has achieved profitability each year. One of your many responsibilities is to create the sales forecast for the company for the upcoming fiscal year. Select one of the sales forecasting methods presented in this chapter and explain how you would go about using that method to forecast sales for York. Be sure to address each of the following in your explanation:

A. The specific sales forecasting method selected.
B. Reasons for your selection.
C. People included in your forecasting efforts.
D. The specific sales forecasting data that will be included.

READINGS AND RESOURCES

- Mike Gale and Julian Clay (2000) *Sales Manager's Desktop Guide*. London: Thorogood Publishing.
- Lianabel Oliver (2000) *Cost Management Toolbox*. New York: AMACOM.
- Jae K. Shim, Joel G. Siegel and Allison I. Shim (2012) 'Budgeting Basics and Beyond' (ebook). Hoboken, NJ: John Wiley & Sons, Inc.
- 'Sales Forecasting Software 2020: Ultimate Guide,' www.cuspera.com/categories/sales-forecasting.
- 'The Best 7 Free and Open-Source Business Budgeting Software,' www.goodfirms.co/blog/best-free-open-source-business-budgeting-software-solutions.

CASE STUDY: AMAZON BUSINESS AND AMAZON FORECAST

What direct-selling company comes to mind first when you think about shopping with ease, speed, convenience, and great prices? If you're like most people, you'll think of Amazon. Amazon's Marketplace is an online site where it sells everything 'from A to Z.' As most people know, Amazon also offers Amazon Prime (a membership buying club that provides members with more shopping benefits, such as free shipping) and Amazon Web Services (a cloud-computing website).[54] However, what you may not *yet* know about are the services it offers to business customers. Amazon Business, which is an online platform that sells hundreds of millions of products to businesses, was launched in the USA in 2015[55] (Figure 12.1). In response to consumer demand, Amazon Business has quickly expanded internationally to the UK, Germany, Japan, India, France, Italy, and Spain, and has grown twice as fast as Amazon Marketplace in terms of annualized sales, which reached $10 billion in 2019.[56]

Figure 12.1 Business purchasing activities

Amazon Business was designed to serve B2B purchasing agents and procurement teams and provide them with the same speed, ease, and personalization that they enjoy when shopping via Amazon Marketplace. Amazon Business customers include schools, hospitals, businesses, and governmental organizations.[57] Some of the benefits of using Amazon Business when purchasing business products, are the massive choice available, excellent prices, accuracy of delivery service, reliable, instant communications, secure logins with different levels of security for different employees, and the unique opportunity for bartering among business customers.[58] Amazon Business offers customers and sellers specific features designed for trade, such as automatic value added tax (VAT) invoicing, a business analytics page to show sales or purchase histories, and an eligibility badge displayed next to the company name to reveal Amazon has vetted it.[59]

Amazon Business services can improve the time-consuming purchasing processes of most companies, which typically involve endless internal work flows for assessing needs, obtaining purchase approvals, sourcing suppliers, negotiating terms, and securing fulfillment.[60] Amazon realized that those companies selling their products on Amazon Business are just as much its customers as those who buy from the business platform. Thus, Amazon provides services to assist sellers to grow their business and achieve selling success, such as:[61]

- dedicated sales representatives who assist new sellers with initial setup and launch, account registration, catalog integration, shipping and inventory settings, advertising and brand building, quality control standards, and more
- guidance provided to sellers on budgeting for features such as business-specific pricing and quantity discounts, which buyers have come to expect.

Another valuable service offered to companies selling on Amazon is forecasting. As Figure 12.2 shows, Amazon Forecast is a fully managed service that uses machine learning based on historical time-series data and combines it with additional variables (such as price, discounts, web traffic, number of employees, product descriptions, promotions, etc.) to produce highly accurate predictions of future business revenue and opportunities.[62]

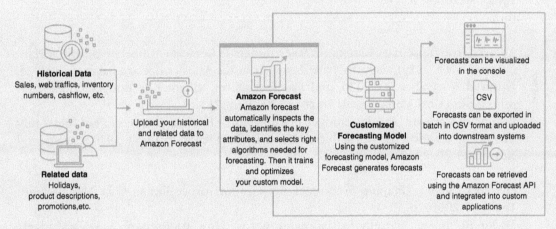

Figure 12.2 Amazon forecasting model
Used with kind permission of Amazon, Inc.

Amazon Forecast helps to predict future business outcomes, such as product demand (to ensure appropriate inventory levels), resource needs (to help plan staffing levels and raw material quantities), and/or financial performance (to predict sales revenue expenses, cash flow, etc.), with models customized to the needs of each business customer using the service.[63] By offering these complex, machine-learning analyses, Amazon Forecast provides highly accurate and timely forecasts which enhance business efficiency for those sellers on its online platforms.

Case questions:

1. Which Amazon Business services might improve a company's product procurement activities from both a business operations and a budget perspective?
2. What types of value-added services can the dedicated sales representatives of Amazon Business provide its business customers?
3. What are the benefits that Amazon Forecast services provide? What makes Amazon's machine-learning model different from other forecasting models presented in this chapter?

NOTES

1. Taylor Robinson, 'Step-by-Step Breakdown of How to Prepare a Sales Budget,' https://mapmycustomers.me/blog/how-to-prepare-a-sales-budget-with-examples, November 20, 2020.
2. Ibid.
3. Aja Frost, 'The Ultimate Guide to Sales Forecasting,' https://blog.hubspot.com/sales/sales-forecasting, retrieved November 20, 2020.
4. Jason Porter and Teresa Stephenson, 'Creating an Excel-based budget you'll really use,' *Strategic Finance*, Montvale, 91(8) (February 2010), 26, 28–33.
5. Lianabel Oliver, 'Chapter 5: Budget preparation procedures,' Cost Management Toolbox (2000), p. 71.
6. Ibid.
7. Ibid.
8. Adapted from Rosemary Carlson, 'A Sales Budget Is Central to Effective Business Planning' (July 11, 2019), www.thebalancesmb.com/the-sales-budget-an-example-393024, retrieved November 20, 2020; and Lianabel Oliver, 'Chapter 5: Budget preparation procedures,' Cost Management Toolbox (2000), p. 71.
9. Rosemary Carlson, 'A Sales Budget Is Central to Effective Business Planning' (July 11, 2019), www.thebalancesmb.com/the-sales-budget-an-example-393024, retrieved November 20, 2020.
10. Ibid.
11. Lianabel Oliver, 'Chapter 5: Budget preparation procedures,' Cost Management Toolbox (2000), p. 71.
12. Taylor Robinson, 'Step-by-Step Breakdown of How to Prepare a Sales Budget,' https://mapmycustomers.me/blog/how-to-prepare-a-sales-budget-with-examples, November 20, 2020.
13. Lianabel Oliver, 'Chapter 5: Budget preparation procedures,' Cost Management Toolbox (2000), p. 71.
14. Ibid.
15. Adapted from Sampson Quain, 'Why Is a Sales Budget Important?' (November 5, 2018), https://smallbusiness.chron.com/sales-budget-important-60445.html, retrieved November 20, 2020; and Made Dana Saputra and Made Agus Putrayasa, 'Analysis of sales budget and actual sales at CV Sumberjaya,' *Proceedings [S.l.]* (May 2018), 1(1), p. 141, http://ojs.pnb.ac.id/index.php/Proceedings/article/view/857, retrieved November 20, 2020.
16. Jason Porter and Teresa Stephenson, 'Creating an Excel-based budget you'll really use,' *Strategic Finance*, Montvale, 91(8) (February 2010), 26, 28–33.
17. Adapted from Taylor Robinson, 'Step-by-Step Breakdown of How to Prepare a Sales Budget,' https://mapmycustomers.me/blog/how-to-prepare-a-sales-budget-with-examples, retrieved November 20, 2020; and John Csiszar, 'How to Prepare a Sales Budget' (January 28, 2019), https://smallbusiness.chron.com/prepare-sales-budget-41276.html, retrieved November 20, 2020.

18. Accounting Tools, 'Sales Budget Example' (February 5, 2019), www.accounting tools.com/articles/2017/5/17/sales-budget-sales-budget-example, retrieved November 20, 2020.

19. Good Firms, 'The Best 7 Free and Open Source Business Budgeting Software', www.goodfirms.co/blog/best-free-open-source-business-budgeting-software-solutions, retrieved November 20, 2020.

20. Karola Karlson, '14 Best Business Budgeting Software and Tools,' www.scoro.com/blog/12-best-business-budgeting-software-tools, retrieved November 20, 2020.

21. Ibid.

22. Good Firms, 'The Best 7 Free and Open Source Business Budgeting Software,' www.goodfirms.co/blog/best-free-open-source-business-budgeting-software-solutions, retrieved November 20, 2020.

23. Brian Hill, 'How to Determine the Strengths and Weaknesses of a Sales Budget,' https://yourbusiness.azcentral.com/determine-strengths-weaknesses-sales-budget-27094.html, retrieved November 20, 2020.

24. Susan Ward, 'How to Create a Sales Forecast: Every business needs one' (April 8, 2020), www.thebalancesmb.com/sales-forecasting-2948317, retrieved November 20, 2020.

25. Adapted from Karri Bishop, 'Sales Forecasting 101: Definition, methods, examples, KPIs' (July 1, 2019), www.saleshacker.com/sales-forecasting-101, retrieved November 20, 2020; and Ryan Robinson, '7 Modern Sales Forecasting Strategies for Startups (and how to pick the right one for you)', https://blog.close.com/sales-forecasting-strategies, retrieved November 20, 2020.

26. Emir Zunic, Kemal Korjenic, Derim Hodzic and Dzenana Donko (2020) 'Application of Facebook's prophet algorithm for successful sales forecasting based on real-world data,' *International Journal of Computer Science & Information Technology*, 12(2), 23–36.

27. Ibid.

28. Mike Gale and Julian Clay (2000) 'Chapter 2: Sales planning', *Sales Manager's Desktop Guide* (London: Hawksmere), p. 40.

29. Adapted from Mike Gale and Julian Clay (2000) 'Chapter 2: Sales planning', *Sales Manager's Desktop Guide* (London: Hawksmere), p. 40; and Aja Frost, 'The Ultimate Guide to Sales Forecasting,' https://blog.hubspot.com/sales/sales-forecasting, retrieved November 20, 2020.

30. Aja Frost, 'The Ultimate Guide to Sales Forecasting,' https://blog.hubspot.com/sales/sales-forecasting, retrieved November 20, 2020.

31. Ibid.

32. Mike Gale and Julian Clay (2000) 'Chapter 2: Sales planning', *Sales Manager's Desktop Guide* (London: Hawksmere), p. 40.

33. Adapted from Aja Frost, 'The Ultimate Guide to Sales Forecasting,' https://blog.hubspot.com/sales/sales-forecasting, retrieved November 20, 2020; and Susan Ward, 'How to Create a Sales Forecast: Every business needs one' (April 8, 2020), www.thebalancesmb.com/sales-forecasting-2948317, retrieved November 20, 2020.

34. Tim Berry, 'How to Forecast Sales,' https://articles.bplans.com/how-to-forecast-sales, retrieved November 20, 2020.

35. Ibid.

36. Adapted from Tim Berry, 'How to Forecast Sales,' https://articles.bplans.com/how-to-forecast-sales, retrieved November 20, 2020; and Susan Ward, 'How to Create a Sales Forecast: Every business needs one,' (April 8, 2020), www.thebalancesmb.com/sales-forecasting-2948317, retrieved November 20, 2020.

37. Adapted from Aja Frost, 'The Ultimate Guide to Sales Forecasting,' https://blog.hubspot.com/sales/sales-forecasting, retrieved November 20, 2020; Karri Bishop, 'Sales Forecasting 101: Definition, methods, examples, KPIs' (July 1, 2019), www.saleshacker.com/sales-forecasting-101, retrieved November 20, 2020; Michael Pici, '3 Proven Sales Forecasting Methods for Greater Accuracy' (July 2, 2019), www.saleshacker.com/sales-forecasting-methods, retrieved November 20, 2020.

38. Aja Frost, 'The Ultimate Guide to Sales Forecasting,' https://blog.hubspot.com/sales/sales-forecasting, retrieved November 20, 2020.

39. Forecast Pro, 'How Do I Use Statistical Models to Forecast Sales?' www.forecast-pro.com/2020/07/22/how-do-you-use-statistical-models-to-forecast-sales, retrieved November 20, 2020.

40. Ibid.

41. Ibid.

42. Jeffrey Hoyle, Rebecca Dingus and J. Wilson Holton (2020) 'An exploration of sales forecasting: Sales manager and salesperson perspectives,' *Journal of Marketing Analytics*, 8(3), 127–36.

43. Aja Frost, 'The Ultimate Guide to Sales Forecasting,' https://blog.hubspot.com/sales/sales-forecasting, retrieved November 20, 2020.

44. Jeffrey Hoyle, Rebecca Dingus and J. Wilson Holton (2020) 'An exploration of sales forecasting: Sales manager and salesperson perspectives,' *Journal of Marketing Analytics*, 8(3), 127–36.

45. Ryan Robinson, '7 Modern Sales Forecasting Strategies for Startups (and how to pick the right one for you)', https://blog.close.com/sales-forecasting-strategies, retrieved November 20, 2020.

46. Michael Lowe, '12 Sales Forecasting Methods (and Which Is Right for You),' www.clari.com/blog/sales-forecasting-methods, retrieved November 20, 2020.

47. Ibid.

48. Ryan Robinson, '7 Modern Sales Forecasting Strategies for Startups (and how to pick the right one for you)', https://blog.close.com/sales-forecasting-strategies, retrieved November 20, 2020.

49. Ibid.

50. Ibid.

51. Michael Lowe, '12 Sales Forecasting Methods (and Which Is Right for You),' www.clari.com/blog/sales-forecasting-methods, retrieved November 20, 2020.

52. Tim Berry, '5 Classic Fails in Budgets and Forecasts' (July 8, 2019), www.sba.gov/blog/5-classic-fails-budgets-forecasts, retrieved November 20, 2020.

53. Steffen Strubel, 'The Effective Sales Budget: You reap what you sow' (August 28, 2020), www.linkedin.com/pulse/effective-sales-budget-you-reap-what-sow-steffen-strubel?articleId=6705076236663746560, retrieved November 20, 2020.

54. Mohammad Qasim (2018) 'Amazon's next mountain: B2B procurement,' *The Globe and Mail*, Toronto (January 2018), p. B4.

55. Lyndsey Cambridge, 'Is Amazon a threat to the wholesale sector, or does it offer an opportunity?' (September 12, 2019), *The Grocer: Web Edition Articles* (UK), https://0-infoweb-newsbank-com.read.cnu.edu/apps/news/openurl?ctx_ver=z39.88-2004&rft_id=info%3Asid/infoweb.newsbank.com&svc_dat=AWNB&req_dat=0FAC5E234F77BA39&rft_val_format=info%3Aofi/fmt%3Akev%3Amtx%3Actx&rft_dat=document_id%3Anews%252F175EE5A43A697208, retrieved December 2, 2020.

56. Ibid.

57. Spencer Soper, 'Amazon Says Business Sales on Pace for $10 Billion Annually' (September 11, 2018), www.bloomberg.com/news/articles/2018-09-11/amazon-says-business-sales-reach-10-billion-annualized-rate, retrieved December 2, 2020.

58. Lyndsey Cambridge, 'Is Amazon a threat to the wholesale sector, or does it offer an opportunity?' (September 12, 2019), *The Grocer: Web Edition Articles* (UK), https://0-infoweb-newsbank-com.read.cnu.edu/apps/news/openurl?ctx_ver=z39.88-2004&rft_id=info%3Asid/infoweb.newsbank.com&svc_dat=AWNB&req_dat=0FAC5E234F77BA39&rft_val_format=info%3Aofi/fmt%3Akev%3Amtx%3Actx&rft_dat=document_id%3Anews%252F175EE5A43A697208, retrieved December 2, 2020.

59. Ibid.

60. Mohammad Qasim (2018) 'Amazon's next mountain: B2B procurement,' *The Globe and Mail*, Toronto (January 2018), p. B4.

61. Peter Lucas, 'The Ins and Outs of Selling on Amazon Business' (April 1, 2019), www.digitalcommerce360.com/2019/04/01/the-ins-and-outs-of-selling-on-amazon-business, retrieved December 2, 2020.

62. AWS, 'Amazon Forecast,' https://aws.amazon.com/forecast, retrieved December 2, 2020.

63. Ibid.

13

PERFORMING SALES ANALYTICS AND TRACKING PRODUCTIVITY

CHAPTER CONTENTS

PEOPLE, PRACTICES AND PERSPECTIVES FROM THE WORLD OF SALES

Greetings from the Netherlands. My name is Joan de Jester and I've been an academic sales consultant for SAGE Publishers for four years now and my sales territory is Benelux. *I believe that in any sales role, it is essential to always keep track of your data. You want to know who is using your product, how many users you have in total, and what they think of the product, among other details. Tracking productivity requires you to be able to use your tools, which will usually come in the form of a CRM system. The data you input and track in these CRM systems will help you decide in which areas you need to do more work in order to obtain a customer and where more information is needed to succeed.* Here's a straightforward sales-related quote for you: 'Don't bullshit the customer.'

Hi, I'm Taylor Forte, a venue sales coordinator for Live Nation Entertainment, an American global entertainment company. I assist the director of venue sales in generating sales and coordinating the Venue Sales VIP program. This entails coordinating and managing events for our clients on event nights, maintaining our client email database, creating marketing emails, and prospecting for new clients. I believe that a great sales professional is always curious and asks their prospect or client questions. My advice to you is to keep track of your wins by recording any time that your manager recognizes your hard work or asks you to be part of a project, and so on. By recording your quantifiable outputs, you'll have examples for your resume and any future interviews or promotional opportunities.

Hello, my name is Ian McPhaden and I'm a senior marketing associate at *Highlights for Children*, an American children's magazine. I have been with *Highlights* for three years and I handle sales and marketing promotion of our digital business. *As we all know, the 'only constant is change' and that old adage holds especially true in our digital world. That's why I always make it a point to conduct competitive research and remain up to date and aware of the latest sales analytical tools related to mobile apps and social media, as well as trends in children's publishing industries.* My advice to you is this: You must have a growth mindset and always be willing to learn. You learn a lot more from failure than success.

We need more insight, not more data.

EYES ON ETHICS

Keep in mind the following ethical topics as you read through this chapter:

1. Reporting clear, non-confounded metrics that lead to proper interpretation.
2. Dealing with data inaccuracy when reporting sales analytics.

INTRODUCTION

Sales has always been a numbers-driven field; however, given the digital explosion of big data, sales analytics has become even more critical in today's modern selling world. Data collection is essential in selling for many reasons, as it can transform sales performance, maximize company profitability, and empower salespeople to better serve their customers. In this chapter, we'll explore several categories of and benefits from using sales analytics, describe types of data metrics acquired and tracked, and examine how dashboards are used to monitor sales productivity, sales enablement, and the effectiveness of the selected sales analytics.

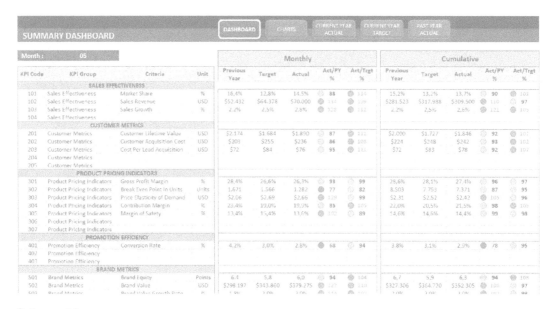

Sales metrics

SALES ANALYTICS

Sales analytics is formally defined as identifying, modeling, understanding, and predicting sales trends and outcomes, while aiding sales management in understanding where salespeople can improve.[1] Basically, performing sales analytics is the process of examining data to reveal strategic insights that enable leaders to make better business decisions. Implementing a sales analytics system improves company performance and provides clarity for sales managers and salespeople, resulting in many benefits that include:

- improving future sales performance
- understanding prospects and customers better
- selling more efficiently and effectively
- reducing sales force attrition
- forecasting future sales more accurately
- setting and revising sales goals and quotas
- providing insight for nurturing long-term relationships.

Overall, sales data has enhanced the manner by which salespeople and sales managers think and make decisions. They are no longer forced to rely on gut instinct, as enhanced computer capabilities provide ready access to a broad range of sales metrics data.

How should sales managers and salespeople approach sales analytics to ensure that the insight gleaned from the data provide the desired benefits? Here's a step-by-step process to follow for using sales analytics:[2]

Step 1: Review company and sales goals and objectives. Revisiting the company and sales teams' account plans (presented in Chapter 3) should provide you with a clear focus of the need and purposes for using sales analytics.

Step 2: Detail the specific questions that arise from the sales objectives specified in Step 1. Questions should be derived by determining what you need to know in order to make better decisions.

Step 3: Identify the sales metrics that are required to provide the insight you need at the present moment. Over time, as sales objectives change, these metrics will likely vary. Let's now examine the different types of data that may be gathered and used in sales analytics.

Examining data characteristics

Simply measuring revenue or sales volume is typically not enough to foster business growth. Companies should track as many different, meaningful metrics as possible; however, the 'right' metrics to track depend on both the company and selling situation.

In addition, data must be accurate, relevant, and properly collected in order to be trusted and valuable for decision making. The only thing worse than not having enough data is having plenty of data that you cannot trust.[3] In Chapter 3, we discussed the five criteria to use in evaluating the usefulness of data, where the most important criterion was *relevancy*. Recall that regardless of whether the information is current, accurate, and available, it will not provide meaningful and actionable insight unless it is relevant. Since all sales data are not equally relevant, sales managers and salespeople must be able to strategically extract pertinent insight from the abundance of metrics available in today's data-driven world. All sales metrics may be organized into one or more of the nine categories of sales metrics shown in Figure 13.1.

Figure 13.1 Sales metrics categories

These categories cover a plethora of sales data available. It is typical for each company to select the specific measures and set targets that are most relevant and meaningful for their success. When specifying metrics, it is wise to include at least one metric from each of the nine categories shown in Figure 13.1. Doing this will ensure that the most important elements of the sales process are being monitored within the organization. As with all metrics, the relevancy of each metric should be confirmed on a periodic basis. As priorities shift within an organization, adding or revising metrics may be required.

Though the relevance of some metrics varies by company, based on their corporate culture and selling situation, there are others that will most always be important to monitor (revenue being one example). Although metrics may vary among organizations, they may be grouped according to which element of the process they measure. Specific measures are available to monitor the following elements of the selling process: the performance of salespeople, the nature of sales deals, and the overall business operation. Let's briefly review each of these elements.[4]

Salesperson metrics are used to track salesperson performance and productivity, and to identify areas in which improvement is needed in the salesperson's respective sales pipeline. Metrics may include: [5]

- sales per activity – how many sales were made by each activity (telephone calls, email outreach, in-person meetings, etc.)
- deals per salesperson – how many sales each salesperson closed during a given time period
- lead-to-customer conversion rate – the percentage of leads that become customers
- win/loss rate – how many customer accounts are successfully closed versus lost
- sales funnel leakage – the number of sales opportunities that did not close.

Deal metrics monitor the effectiveness of the sales process itself, as it is followed by all salespeople. Metrics may include:[6]

- all salesperson metrics when they are aggregated across the entire sales force
- sales quota attainment – the number of salespeople reaching 100 percent of their quota
- average deal (or sale) size – the average amount of sales revenue generated by each sale
- sales by lead source – where sales are coming from and which lead-generation sources are productive
- total sales by time period (weekly, monthly, quarterly, etc.) – sales performance over time (monitored for increasing or declining trends)
- year-on-year growth – a comparison of the current year's sales versus last year's
- win/loss rate – the percentage of customer accounts that are successfully closed versus lost
- average customer lifetime value (CLTV) – how much revenue a customer will generate throughout a lifetime of patronage with a company.

Business metrics evaluate the overall sales strategy and its impact on the success of the whole company. These metrics include:[7]

- total revenue – the amount of revenue your sales team produces in a given time period
- revenue per sale – the amount of revenue generated by each sale
- revenue by product – how much revenue is generated by each product/service sold
- revenue by territory – how much revenue is being generated by each sales territory
- percentage of revenue by customer type – how much business is generated by new versus existing customers

- year-on-year growth – a comparison of the current year's revenue versus last year's
- cost of selling – how much a company is spending to generate sales
- referral rating – the degree to which your customers would recommend your company
- market penetration – how much your product/service is being used by customers compared to the total potential market available for the product/service.

As stated, different companies and selling situations require different types of data to be acquired and analyzed. Factors that determine what sales metrics are most relevant include the stage of growth a company is in, as well as the size of that company. Based on these factors, the available sales data may be classified as belonging to a certain stage – beginning, intermediate, and/or advanced metrics:[8]

- **Beginning metrics** – these metrics enable a better sense of the sales funnel and how it impacts revenues and profitability. Beginning metrics include salesperson lead volume (the total number of prospects that enter the sales funnel), opportunities won or sales closed, lead-to-sales ratio or conversion rate to assess how effectively prospects are moved through the sales funnel, the duration of time required to close a sale, average deal size or contract value, and so on.
- **Intermediate metrics** – as a company grows, there is a need for additional insight in order to optimize its sales processes. Intermediate metrics include lead source, buyer touchpoints required to close sales, overdue opportunities that are in the sales pipeline longer than the average length of time to close, performance per salesperson based on individual sales quotas established, product performance and demand to identify those items that are most popular with customers, actual and forecasted sales, cross-sell and up-sell rates, customer retention rates, churn rates (number of customers who decline to renew contracts or terminate agreements), and the prospect's relative company size (which often dictates the length of time in a sales cycle, as larger companies with bigger deals typically take longer than smaller companies with smaller deals).
- **Advanced metrics** – these sales metrics are associated with larger-sized companies with more sophisticated selling needs. Examples of advanced metrics that affect profit margins are the application of discounts, which are often used as negotiation tactics, and deal complexity, such as customization and special concessions offered by salespeople in order to gain commitment. Using advanced sales analytics for pricing and discounting decisions enables consistency between salespeople. When salespeople learn that others have achieved higher prices for the same deals with similar customers, they recognize the potential for improvement. Thus, advanced analytics that mine all historical sales data will enable salespeople to see where they are pursuing suboptimal pricing, and to challenge sales teams to reconsider their deal structures.[9]

Data should not be collected just to have it. A meaningful data collection plan is essential to a company's success. This plan should consider issues of ethical data management prior to the start of data collection. The plan should also document how the data will be analyzed and reacted to in a consistent manner. This requires knowledge of the different types of sales data available. That's the topic of our next section.

Computer metrics

Exploring types of sales data

Most analysts break down sales data into four distinct types in terms of what their output might indicate:[10]

1. **Descriptive**: This is the simplest and most widely used type of data. Descriptive analytical data shows what happened in the past. This data is summarized in simple charts and graphs that are easy to understand. An example is identifying an increase in the sales of a particular product category during a certain period of time or in a specific geographical area.
2. **Diagnostic**: This type of data examines the possible causes of past performance, which helps sales managers to better understand the situation and adjust their actions in the future. Diagnostic data reveals deeper insight than descriptive data in terms of data discovery, data mining, and correlations. It uncovers more about how sales teams are performing by revealing data such as pipeline metrics, salesperson activities, opportunities, and closed deals. An example is identifying where leads drop out of the sales funnel and become lost opportunities. When overlaying the performance of competition across a given timeframe, sales managers may better understand a unique situation. Thus, diagnostic analytics can enable them to determine ways to rectify such sales funnel leakages.
3. **Predictive**: Unlike descriptive and diagnostic analytics which assess past events, this type of data predicts what's likely to happen in the future. Thus, predictive

data uses past behavior obtained from descriptive and diagnostic results to forecast future results. An example is where predictive data may forecast which sales leads salespeople should focus their efforts on, based on the likelihood of successfully closing the deal.

4. **Prescriptive**: This type of data provides probable explanations for predictive analytical results. Prescriptive analytics guide sales teams in real time by determining the most likely consequence of taking various courses of action. Interpretation by the sales team of the results of these analyses can indicate the best course of action to take to reach ideal selling outcomes. Prescriptive analytics is similar to a feedback system that consistently gains intelligence by analyzing actions and their effects. Prescriptive analytics helps salespeople determine the best actions to take, while it also provides sales managers with better direction for successfully coaching them. An example is where, in advance of making sales calls, salespeople obtain talking points that tell them the aspects of the product or service that are most important to a prospective buyer so that they may emphasize those during their sales presentations.

Sales analytics can inform decisions, inspire new ideas, and reveal opportunities for growth.[11] This is accomplished by collecting and analyzing data at a detailed process level. Most advanced sales applications in today's modern selling world rely on sales analytics. Let's now explore the various uses or applications of sales analytics in all areas involved in successful selling.

Figure 13.2 Sales analytics applications

Investigating the applications of sales analytics

As Figure 13.2 shows, there are many different applications of sales analytics that add value to support, diagnose, design, or improve the processes and activities of both salespeople and sales managers. Ten common sales analytics applications are as follows:[12]

1. **Hiring the right sales professionals**. Descriptive data can reveal the skills that your sales team's top-performing salespeople have, so you can use that insight to tailor your hiring process to select those candidates who possess qualities similar to those of your best salespeople.

2. **Conducting performance assessments and developing incentive plans**. Sales analytics can help identify the key performance indicators (KPIs) that are best aligned with business priorities, and can help determine the specific metrics to drive desired outcomes.[13] For example, a US industrial services company was experiencing a high customer churn or turnover rate of 20 percent. Analytics showed that if customers stayed for six months, they would likely stay for a full year. Based on this insight, the company redesigned the incentive program for its salespeople to include a 'revenue persistency metric' which was based on their earning a share of revenue that continues for more than six months after sale.[14] Thus, sales analytics was used to redirect salespeople from a 'hunting' mode to a 'farming' one. This also improved the onboarding process and emphasized maintaining customer relationships.[15]

3. **Building an effective onboarding program**. Sales analytics can gather descriptive data about what your most productive salespeople do to nurture and close sales. These 'best practices' may be used when developing an onboarding program to help develop all salespeople.

4. **Making coaching an everyday occurrence**. Sales analytics insights will enable ongoing 1:1 coaching and feedback sessions to occur based on the real-time performance data of each salesperson.

5. **Improving value propositions and price points**. Sales analytics can help to ensure that salespeople communicate the right information, to the right prospect or customer, at the right time. Analyzing the previous success rate of various sales approaches enables salespeople to avoid the typical 'one-size-fits-all' approach to value propositions. They can consider the profile of each specific buyer and customize their offers to target each one individually. Likewise, analytics provides data on the effectiveness of different price points to enable salespeople to propose an optimal price for each prospect or customer and each unique buying situation.

6. **Eliminating or refining product offerings**. Evaluating sales data provides the capability to identify products that are under-performing overall or under-performing in a certain customer segment. This enables sales managers to investigate the reasons for the poor performance and to make decisions regarding which products to continue to produce and/or distribute in the future.

7. **Conducting accurate sales forecasting**. Sales analytics may be used to predict future sales based on historical data. Barring significant changes in the industry or economy, historical data can provide an accurate, realistic prediction of how much

the sales team should produce within a particular period of time. As discussed in Chapter 12, accurate sales forecasts are critical in order to allocate resources and manage sales teams and all other company resources efficiently and effectively.

8. **Increasing repeat purchases from existing customers**. Sales analytics can reveal those customers who are likely to repeat purchase orders in the future. This knowledge can enable salespeople to capitalize on cross-selling or up-selling opportunities. Based on the book *Marketing Metrics*, listed in the Readings and Resources section at the end of this chapter, salespeople have a much higher likelihood (60–70 percent chance) of selling to an existing customer, than they do selling to a new prospect (5–20 percent).

9. **Pipeline management**. Sales analytics enables comparison of leads to historical data on similar customers, so salespeople can segment leads in their pipeline base on how profitable they are likely to be and how engaged they are – which is an indicator of how quickly they are likely to commit. Pipeline sales analytics may also reveal weak points or bottlenecks where sales leads are either stalled or falling out of the pipeline altogether.

10. **Increasing retention rates**. Research conducted by Frederick Reichheld of Bain & Company shows that increasing customer retention rates by 5 percent increases profits by 25 to 95 percent.[16] Sales analytics reveal the company's most valuable customers, so salespeople may spend more time and energy taking care of them to ensure their satisfaction and retention. Common sense may tell a sales manager or salesperson who their largest accounts are, however the sales analytics of transactional data will provide greater clarity and reveal other accounts that are growing quickly, so that salespeople may prioritize serving these accounts as well. In addition, sales analytics can reveal the top factors that cause customers to churn. This information enables salespeople to identify and proactively reach out to at-risk accounts to address any potential concerns they may have, in an attempt to retain their patronage.

Happy customers
© Ben Leistensnider/Christopher Newport University.

It's worth repeating here that successful selling implies long-term relationships with customers. Thus, retaining customers is not only one of the applications of sales analytics, but it is a critical goal shared by everyone within a company – from the top C-suite level on down. Happy customers are more loyal and will be retained more easily. However, it is important to identify those who are dissatisfied as they tend to spread negative stories at a much faster rate than do satisfied customers. Well-established marketing metrics reveal that, on average, a happy customer tells five to seven people; while an unhappy customer complains to seven to 15 people; and too many customers (26–30) are 'silent complainers' who never complain out loud about their dissatisfaction, but will simply discontinue buying. Sales analytics on follow-up calls can be used to root out silent complainers, encourage them to interact with you, and stay engaged to give you an opportunity to address their concerns and better serve their needs. Thus, sales analytics can help sales managers track the productivity within each element of the entire sales process. That's the topic of our next section.

TRACKING PRODUCTIVITY

Sales managers, salespeople, and anyone in the company may use sales analytics to identify a particular type of customer or company, and to monitor business trends. Real-time data that tracks sales performance can lead to better business decisions. But how is the sales data reported and presented with the clarity needed to enable strategic decision making to occur? That's the purpose of sales dashboards.

Using sales dashboards

What comes to mind when you think of a dashboard? If you're like most people, you'll think of an automobile dashboard with its gauges for speed, amount of fuel, engine temperature, miles traveled, time, and so on. Similar to the dashboard in an automobile, business dashboards are used to report sales analytics to provide insight about sales performance metrics. Dashboards are created in software applications that systematically combine the available data into charts and graphs. A sales dashboard is a tool that provides a comprehensive overview of key performance indicators (KPIs) and shows how sales teams are tracking towards goals and revenue targets.[17] Basically, sales dashboards refer to the visual representation of sales data. Similar to a sales report, which is a static, historical descriptive account of sales data, dashboards may include the number of deals closed, quota attainment, average deal size, sales funnel leakage, total daily, weekly, monthly, quarterly, annual sales, and so on.[18] However, unlike a sales report, a sales dashboard is an active tool that can analyze real-time data and provide a more inclusive view of sales performance in terms of both activities and outcomes. Dashboards provide important sales performance insight at a quick glance as opposed to extracting the data in a time-consuming manner by poring over numerous sales reports.

In today's data-driven business world, using sales dashboards provides a simple and reliable way to track and assess sales performance metrics. Sales dashboards offer users several key benefits, including the following:[19]

1. Tracking the right metrics across different platforms.
2. Documenting sales performance in a timely way that promotes insight.
3. Motivating salespeople and sales teams to reach established targets.

In addition, sales dashboards serve many different purposes. Sales managers may use sales dashboards to track the progress of their salesperson and/or sales team toward specified goals, to adjust compensation, award bonuses and incentives, and identify issues before they become large problems.[20] Of course, sales dashboards may be used by salespeople, managers, and upper-level executives to make decisions, establish plans, and adjust strategies. When creating a dashboard, consideration must be given to who will be using the dashboard, how often it will be utilized, the purposes for which it is being created, the time periods to be included, and what information in terms of metrics, visualizations, and calculations will be included.[21] Sales dashboards are unique and may be customized to each company and its customers' needs. As Table 13.1 presents, there are many different types of sales dashboards, with each serving a different purpose. For example, sales managers may want to track sales team metrics, pipeline activity, or deals won.

Table 13.1   Types of sales dashboards

Dashboard type	Purpose
Sales representative	Enables individual salespeople to track their own sales performance metrics
Sales manager	Provides a macro-level view of sales performance metrics for all salespeople and sales teams
Deal performance	Reports the amount of time it takes to successfully close deals, which enables the progress of each deal to be monitored and compared to the average deal performance and sales revenue to be forecasted
Leaderboards	Displays the performance metrics of all salespeople to provide motivation and encourage healthy competition
Product/deal performance	Shows which products customers prefer and in which locations, and provides a comparative analysis of multiple products or product categories
Win/loss	Displays the number of deals won versus deal opportunities lost for each salesperson or sales team, which enables comparative analysis
Sales activities	Provides an overview of the daily activities that salespeople are performing and the methods they are using to communicate with prospects and customers
Performance overview	Shows a comprehensive summary of a wide variety of sales performance metrics, which may be customized to track and include any sales data metrics desired
Time-tracking	Reports on how salespeople are spending their time, both while in the office and out in the field

Source: Adapted from Meredith Hart, '9 Sales Dashboard Examples That'll Help You Set Up Your Own,' https://blog.hubspot.com/sales/sales-dashboard, retrieved November 12, 2020; and Matt Bullock, 'Why use a Sales Dashboard?' https://spinify.com/blog/why-use-sales-dashboard, retrieved November 12, 2020.

As shown in Figure 13.3, sales dashboards may include dials, leaderboards, bar graphs, historical trend graphs, pie charts, funnels, plotted points, and more. When determining which graphic to use on the dashboard to display sales data, keep in mind that the goal is to show sales performance in an easy-to-understand fashion. Remember, a sales dashboard should provide relevant insight at a quick glance, so select the option that most effectively and efficiently displays the data.

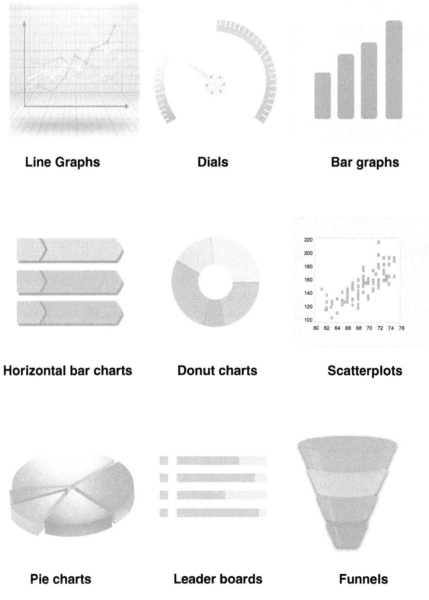

Line Graphs **Dials** **Bar graphs**

Horizontal bar charts **Donut charts** **Scatterplots**

Pie charts **Leader boards** **Funnels**

Figure 13.3 Dashboard visualization options

Some tips for creating effective sales dashboards are the following:[22]

- Use a clean layout with easy-to-read graphs and charts.
- Lay out your dashboard in a grid format to help organize the data.
- Organize your dashboard so reports are read from left to right.
- Place the most important chart in the top left-hand corner of the dashboard as it will be viewed more frequently than those on the right.
- Include calculations that provide additional context to make the metrics understandable.
- Use a consistent pattern when reporting data, such as starting each quarter in the same column.
- Use colors and size to help identify the most relevant time periods for comparison
- Use colors wisely to provide emphasis, such as bright red versus softer shades.

The dashboard should be integrated with a company's customer relationship management (CRM) system to provide accurate real-time transaction and performance data. Let's now explore the utilizing of CRM data and the enabling of salespeople, by providing them with more detailed data.

Integrating CRM data and enabling salespeople

According to research conducted by global management consulting firm McKinsey, while fast-growing organizations use sales analytics more effectively, most still struggle to synchronize sales performance data with sales models that are properly aligned with customer needs.[23] Common challenges include effectively analyzing customer needs, struggling to demonstrate value creation, and failing to secure the knowledge and tools needed to translate a product's core strengths into customer success.[24] In addition, recent business trends, such as digitization, consolidation, and commoditization have changed customer expectations and redefined customer value.[25] Uncontrollable variables associated with the dynamic marketplace and consumer needs and desires, require sales analytics to be constantly evolving in order to provide relevant insight. Sales is a dynamic field with so many different things happening at any given moment that it can be difficult to track and measure performance. That's where CRM system integration becomes invaluable.

The best analytics programs are those that are integrated with a company's CRM system which can track all prospect and customer activity and automate tasks, such as email follow-ups and contact updates.[26] As described in Chapter 10, CRM system data should include detailed information from the following five areas:[27]

- **contact information**: name, postal address, phone number, email address
- **demographic data**: age, gender, geographical region
- **behavioral data**: bounce rate, click rate, webpage views
- **transaction history**: time of purchase, sale value, payment method
- **communications**: emails, telephone calls, live chats.

A CRM system will also keep sales teams aligned and make all pertinent sales data available on a continual basis so that it may be tapped when needed. In addition, integrating sales analytics with the company's CRM system will help sales managers and sales teams to make better decisions and create an effective sales enablement program that maximizes profit. As you may recall from Chapter 6, sales enablement is the strategic, ongoing process of equipping salespeople and sales teams with the content, guidance, and training they need to effectively engage buyers.[28] Common sense tells us that when you enable salespeople with the right data, tools, and resources, they'll have a greater chance of selling more effectively and efficiently, which results in more deals and increased sales revenue for a company.[29]

Sales enablement is a vital part of maintaining successful selling operations in today's world, with its increased competition and more empowered buyers. Sales enablement saves salespeople and sales teams valuable time by keeping them aligned and in tune with sales performance.[30] Research shows that companies with sales enablement programs see measurable results, including 32 percent higher team sales quota attainment, 24 percent better salesperson quota achievement, and 23 percent higher lead-conversion rate.[31] In addition, more than 75 percent of companies are using a sales enablement tool, which is a platform or system that provides visibility across the sales content lifecycle, reporting higher sales over a one-year period, with 59 percent of them exceeding their revenue targets.[32]

There are four functions that are critical for a sales enablement program to be effective. Those functions are:[33]

1. **Content** – high-quality content must be created and made available to salespeople as they will need quick access to the right content at the right time. Marketers should produce content based on performance data to help salespeople close more deals.
2. **Training** – salespeople must be trained in multiple skill areas including selling, product, marketing, industry, business, and technology. In addition, companies should train sales managers and salespeople to increase their data literacy and provide them with the right tools to create and interpret analytical displays.
3. **Tools and technology** – salespeople must be able to use the tools and technology to leverage a single platform for all their sales enablement needs, from training to content to analytics in order to derive optimum benefits from them.
4. **Strategy and execution** – sales enablement extends to a multitude of sales management activities, such as hiring, onboarding, forecasting, budgeting, and performance reviews, as well as empowering salespeople to close deals. Sales enablement also promotes the alignment of sales and marketing on those goals, strategies, and tactics that maximize revenue.

Enabling the sales force to sell more effectively by harnessing the power of sales analytics begins with clean, prepared, and well-managed data.[34] Clean data implies that all accounts and opportunities are defined and consistently structured the same way within the CRM system so that their meanings are identical for all sales teams, regardless of what

Sales team preparing

location or country the various sales teams are in. Beyond standardized analytic definitions and processes, clean data should come from a widely adopted CRM system and should be analyzed by analytically minded sales operations staff who have knowledge of and experience in data mining. They must be able to understand the data, analyze the data properly, extract insights from their analysis, and recommend optimal courses of action for sales managers and salespeople to achieve successful outcomes.[35] Companies should be prepared to embrace an analytics platform which has the capability to connect to their CRM system and other data sources to enable advanced sales analytics. This includes hiring capable, technology and statistically savvy associates to apply sophisticated, statistical methods and communicate findings in a manner that empowers the sales teams. Check out Table 13.2 for some tips on how to ensure you have a quality data set that leads to accurate sales insights.

Table 13.2 Components of a quality data set

- Aligned with overall company goals
- Analysis provided by analytically minded operations employees
- Modern data analytics platform with user-friendly software applications
- Accurate or 'clean' data – correct, valid, and entered correctly
- Trustworthy and reliable data source(s)
- Up-to-date data reflecting current or real-time activities
- Sufficient quantity – enough data upon which to make decisions
- Integrated with a company's CRM system
- Uniform automated processes to gather data
- Consistent and streamlined data format for ease of interpretation
- Unified data storage in one place

Source: Adapted from Uzi Shmilovici, 'What makes good sales data? Here are the types of good sales data you need to make winning decisions,' Zendesk blog (January 23, 2019), www.zendesk.com/blog/good-sales-data, retrieved November 12, 2020.

Sales analytics are most effective when integrating a company's customers' specific needs, the value proposition, and the sales force's competencies.[36] By tapping into the data-driven insights produced by sales analytics, sales managers can better understand the needs of their core customers and/or targeted prospects, and adapt how and where their sales teams sell in order to maximize success. Sales analytics should enable salespeople to achieve greater success by preparing them for value-based interactions with the right set of customers or prospects at each stage of their respective buyer's or customer's journey.[37]

Beyond preparing sales teams for success out in the field, sales analytics can also enable scientific analysis to be applied to tracking sales productivity and results, such as evaluating market penetration. That's the topic of our next section.

Evaluating market penetration

As previously mentioned, research has shown that it is more cost-effective to concentrate selling efforts on customer retention and customer relationship building than it is to prioritize new customer acquisition. It is also well known that prospective customers are similar to current customers. Thus, it is important to take the time to identify and characterize your most valuable customers first. Having done that, you can determine commonalities among these customers and search for customers who possess similar characteristics. It sounds simple, right? But where do you look? How do you begin? How do you know which markets, market segments, or clusters of customers will be more likely to respond positively to your offer? One method is by conducting market penetration analysis.

Statistical modelling techniques can correlate market penetration with demographics, lifestyle research, transaction data, and buyer behavior to reveal those markets that contain the largest proportion of a company's customers. Market penetration is a measure of the extent to which a product or service is being used within a defined population or 'universe.' It defines what percentage of the total universe of potential buyers are currently your customers. Market penetration analysis may be performed on any universe, as specified by: geography (regions, states, cities, counties, ZIP code areas, etc.), product lines, customer market segments, or specific demographic categories (gender, age, education, etc.). Market penetration is calculated by dividing the number of customers in a specific category (such as a geographic county) by the total number of people in that category (or geographic county), and multiplying by 100 to express the result as a percentage of the total market. In this example of market penetration, you can conclude that a certain geographic county contains the largest proportion of customers, while another geographic county contains the smallest proportion. Thus, market penetration analysis can assist sales managers and salespeople in determining which geographic county to target for new customer acquisition efforts, including lead-generation and prospecting activities. As shown in Figure 13.4, salespeople often map their customers according to geographic market penetration in order to visually reveal those geographic areas that should be targeted for future promotions.

471

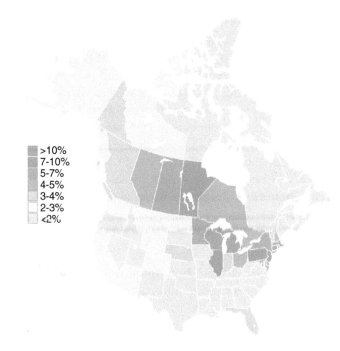

Figure 13.4 Market penetration map example

Often, salespeople make the mistake of targeting the market in which they have the least penetration in an attempt to increase the presence in that specific market segment (for example, a particular state). This is not normally a wise strategy because there is usually a reason that the consumers in that geographical market are not responding to the salesperson and/or company's offers in the first place. Perhaps these customers do not have a need or desire for the company's products or services. Therefore, a more effective strategy is to concentrate future new customer acquisition efforts on those market segments that contain larger customer penetrations.

Because there are so many different sales metrics and analytical tools, it may be difficult to determine which metrics will provide the relevant insight. The question is, how do you evaluate and measure the effectiveness of sales analytics and sales enablement programs? That's the topic of our last section.

MONITORING METRICS

The main purpose of sales analytics and sales enablement programs is to help salespeople and sales teams sell more effectively and efficiently. Thus, sales managers must hold their sales analytics methods and sales enablement programs accountable for providing relevant and actionable insight. Measuring sales performance against pre-established company goals and objectives is likely the best method to determine

Monitoring Metrics

the impact of a company's sales analytics methods and sales enablement program. How much progress has been made toward specified goals? Has the insight obtained from the sales data the company acquires and tracks for analytical purposes, helped the salespeople and sales teams? If so, how do you know? What performance measures point to the value obtained via the company's sales analytics and/or sales enablement program?

Controlled trials may be run to evaluate the effect of using various options for sales content, tactics, and/or sales strategies, to identify the variation that produces the desired results. Then, changes can be made to incorporate that variation into the sales process going forward. To ensure that trial results are reproducible, performance metrics from the revised process should be verified against specified goals. In addition, a detailed examination and analysis of successful deals can reveal those tactics that worked and those that did not. It is important to maintain records of the process changes made and outcomes achieved, so that lessons learned in the past can be applied to future improvement efforts. Of course, measuring the failures of sales efforts is also important and provides valuable insight into which data metrics or activities no longer serve sales managers and their sales teams. Having the right metrics provides actionable insight into what to expect from the investment that's being made.[38]

Continual feedback loops are needed to properly monitor the impact of the sales metrics being gathered and used, as well as a company's sales enablement program. These monitoring efforts should be an ongoing process, with sales and marketing aligning closely and sharing information frequently.[39] In addition, since salespeople are the ones interacting on a 1:1 basis with prospects and customers, they should be tapped for feedback on the value of sales analytics and sales enablement programs. Their input on possible improvements to daily selling activities should be considered along with their suggestions on how to better serve the needs of their prospects and customers. The best sales enablement programs track and enforce whether resources are being used optimally across the sales organization.[40] Validating the usage and impact of sales analytics will lead to developing strategies to continuously improve the sales data collected, analytics generated, and sales enablement programs operated to better serve salespeople, sales teams, and ultimately prospects and customers.

CHAPTER SUMMARY

✓ Sales analytics prompt the evaluation of data and the discussion and interpretation of results, which can identify improvement opportunities for individuals as well as companies.

✓ Robust sales analytics programs cover all areas involved with selling, from recruiting/onboarding salespeople through sales volume and company revenue.

✓ Proper application of data mining and statistical tools offers additional insights into the potential factors affecting the effectiveness of sales operations.

✓ Sales dashboards are used to communicate sales efforts and results across the company.

✓ Geographical markets with high penetration are good targets for future sales efforts.

KEY TERMS

Market penetration

Sales analytics

Sales dashboards

Sales enablement

Sales enablement tool

Sales report

REVIEW QUESTIONS

1. What benefits do companies experience as a result of using sales analytics?
2. Describe the three-step process to follow for using data analytics.
3. Are small, start-up companies or large, established companies more likely to use advanced sales metrics? Why?
4. Identify and describe the four distinct types of sales data.
5. Describe three of the ten most common applications of sales analytics that support, diagnose, design, or improve sales processes.
6. What are sales dashboards and what benefits do using them provide to an organization?
7. Explain three tips for creating effective sales dashboards.
8. What four functions are critical for a sales enablement program to be effective?
9. What is market penetration and how is it calculated?
10. Market penetration data shown by county clearly reveals areas of high penetration compared to areas with low penetration. Which areas are best targeted to maximize sales in the future? Why?

ETHICS IN ACTION

1. Beth Rubert is a data specialist recently hired to monitor and perform data analytics for a mid-sized company struggling to improve market share of their newest product line. She reports to Ted Bander, who is the company's chief information officer, a senior executive who also sits on the board of directors. Ted has asked her to obtain data that shows that the disappointing country-wide sales are really limited to the northwest and reflect a lack of effort by sales teams in that region. In response, Beth creates and provides him with a pie chart of total sales by territory. Ted presents this to the executive team. Is this data enough to confirm Ted's hypothesis? Why or why not? Describe any additional data that could be presented to clarify possible causes for the lack of sales in the northwest.

2. In her position as data specialist, Beth Rubert has established analytical sales dashboards that she populates monthly and sends to her manager, Ted Bander, the chief information officer. Ted reviews these and presents them monthly to the executive team, who use them for forecasting and company-wide planning purposes. On the morning of Ted's presentation, Beth realizes that an important piece of data has somehow been reported incorrectly for the last three months. She has enough time to warn Ted that the report is incorrect, but not enough time to investigate the discrepancy or reanalyze the data. What should she say to Ted about this? What should Ted report to the senior team that day?

EXERCISE

Congratulations! You've been promoted to a senior sales manager position and your primary responsibilities involve overseeing 12 field sales teams that cover wide geographical sales territories spanning five countries. In order to evaluate the performance of each of your 12 teams, you review a sales dashboard on a regular weekly basis. Using the sales metrics categories shown in Figure 13.1, illustrate what your ideal sales dashboard will contain and look like. Be sure to include the following:

A. Layout and design of the sales dashboard.
B. Methods for displaying the metrics (graphs, charts, leaderboards, etc.).
C. Reporting time periods.
D. Categories of sales metrics.
E. Specific sales data.
F. Goals displayed with data.

READINGS AND RESOURCES

- Neil Bendle, Paul Farris, Phillip Pfeifer and David Reibstein (2021) *Marketing Metrics: The Definitive Guide to Measuring Marketing Performance*, 4th edition. Upper Saddle River, NJ: Pearson Education.
- Jason Jordan with Michelle Vazzana (2012) *Cracking the Sales Management Code: The Secrets to Measuring and Managing Sales Performance.* New York: McGraw-Hill.
- Steve Wexler, Jeffrey Shaffer and Andy Cotgreave (2017) 'The Big Book of Dashboards: Visualizing your data using real-world business scenarios' (ebook). Hoboken, NJ: John Wiley & Sons, Inc.
- 'Top 13 Sales Pipeline Metrics to Track in 2020 (According to the Experts),' spotio.com (August 4, 2020), retrieved November 30, 2020.
- '18 Essential Sales KPIs: What to measure and how to track everything,' http.//blog.close.com/sales-kpis-metrics, retrieved October 27, 2020.

CASE STUDY: ANALYTICS AT ALPHA INTERNATIONAL, INC.

Note: The names and locations used in this case have been disguised for confidentiality purposes.

Obtaining key insight from sales data is a routine activity for Maxwell Waters. Max is vice president of sales and marketing at Alpha International, Inc., a worldwide snack foods organization based in London, UK. The company brokers a wide variety of snack food categories, such as chips, pretzels, popcorn, nuts, seeds, snack mix, crackers, cookies, fruit snacks, granola bars, meat sticks and jerky, to retail stores in 89 countries. Alpha International represents many leading snack food manufacturers by distributing their well-known brands, including PepsiCo's Lay's, Fritos, Doritos, Tostitos, Sun Chips and Cheetos; Betty Crocker's Fruit Gushers, Fruit Roll-ups and Fruit by the Loop; Jack Links Protein snacks; Welch's Fruit Snacks; Annie's Organic Snacks; Planters Nuts and Nut Mixes.

Max has 32 years of sales experience, with 22 years at Alpha International. He has worked his way up to his current VP position by excelling as a field sales representative and amassing years of valuable managerial sales experience in various positions. Max currently has hundreds of sales professionals working under him at Alpha International, each with different data needs. Max understands the vital role of sales analytics in strategically helping his sales associates at various levels to perform their respective tasks, including the following:

- business development managers – acquiring new manufacturer accounts
- national account managers – serving their network of manufacturers, working closely with their buyers, and growing the value of each manufacturer account
- regional sales managers – providing leadership and strategic direction to their sales teams
- field sales representatives – providing value to their prospects and customers, and successfully closing sales.

Max's primary responsibility is to work with his team of analysts to coordinate the dynamic and continuous flow and uses of sales data throughout his company to maximize positive sales results. This function requires exceptional strategic vision, solid analytical prowess, and outstanding communication skills. Of course, the company's data analytics depend on the availability, accuracy, and currency of internal and external sources of data. The main internal sources are Alpha International's sales transaction data, reports from regional sales managers on product category trends, and insight from national account managers, who directly interact with the buyers for the different manufacturers that Alpha International represents. External sources include subscribing to publicly available market research companies, such as IRI, Mintel, and Nielsen to obtain consumer, shopper, and retail market intelligence; and acquiring specific product category information via national account managers working directly with buyers from each of the manufacturers that Alpha International represents. See Figure 13.5 for the data that Max obtains to perform sales analytics and track productivity. Max also obtains cost data that is categorized in the same manner as sales transaction data.

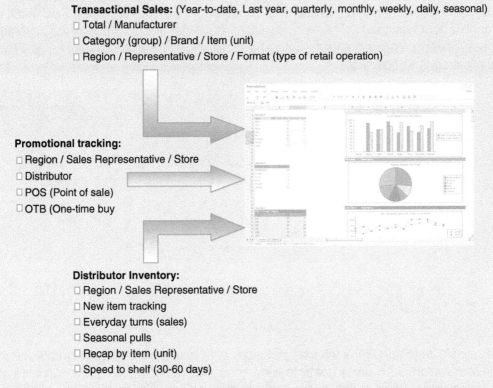

Transactional Sales: (Year-to-date, Last year, quarterly, monthly, weekly, daily, seasonal)
- ☐ Total / Manufacturer
- ☐ Category (group) / Brand / Item (unit)
- ☐ Region / Representative / Store / Format (type of retail operation)

Promotional tracking:
- ☐ Region / Sales Representative / Store
- ☐ Distributor
- ☐ POS (Point of sale)
- ☐ OTB (One-time buy

Distributor Inventory:
- ☐ Region / Sales Representative / Store
- ☐ New item tracking
- ☐ Everyday turns (sales)
- ☐ Seasonal pulls
- ☐ Recap by item (unit)
- ☐ Speed to shelf (30-60 days)

Figure 13.5 Alpha International sales analytic data

Using the gathered data, Max and his analysts run reports, compile dashboards, and distribute data intelligence on an ongoing basis. While the uses of the data are endless, the common applications carried out include:

a. Reporting sales by region, sales representative, retail store.
b. Evaluating the performance of product category, product unit, territory.
c. Rewarding or coaching the sales team.
d. Tracking the performance of sales promotions.
e. Assessing and ensuring inventory quality control standards.
f. Preparing monthly target missions for the sales team to carry out while out in the field, such as investigating seasonal products, special promotions, planograms, etc.
g. Executing monthly demonstrations, special events, couponing, required photos, etc.

Sales force automation enables Alpha International's business development and sales teams to spend more time in the field, securing new clients and servicing existing ones. Its mobile app, 'Real Track,' is designed to work with its retail store inventory planogram system to provide real-time mission audit-related data, including inventory assessments, out-of-stock conditions, and display integrity, which enable managerial assessment and performance tracking (see Figure 13.6). Max knows as a broker that his job is to ensure that the snack foods of manufacturer clients that Alpha represents are on the shelves and displayed properly at the retail stores throughout all of its global territories. Real Track is one mobile tool designed to gather meaningful data that leads to action to guarantee successful selling. Alpha's clients are also able to download Real Track to receive real-time business analytics and insight.

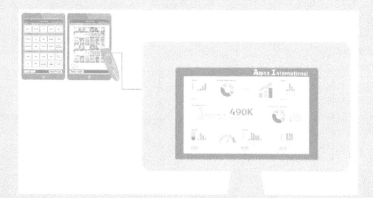

Figure 13.6 Alpha International's Real Track mobile app

Each manufacturer that Alpha International represents is unique, with varying data needs. Some manufacturers sufficiently gather their own data and do not require additional data from Alpha International; other manufacturers desire particular types of sales analytics, while others need complete analyses. While producing meaningful sales analytics is not a 'one size fits all' job, its value is crucial for successful selling in today's highly competitive and digital world.

Case questions:

1. How do sales analytics serve the manufacturers that Alpha International represents? What kind of real-time business insight might Max produce for each manufacturer?
2. How might the data obtained from Alpha International's Real Track mobile app generate relevant insight and assist Alpha's business development managers, national account managers, regional sales managers, and field sales representatives to carry out their respective tasks?
3. Based on the types of data gathered at Alpha International, what specific data might Max and his team use to analyze customer value and market penetration? How might the sales analytics be used in account planning for Alpha International?

NOTES

1. Cem Dilmegani, 'The Ultimate Guide to Sales Analytics in 2020' (November 2, 2020), https://research.aimultiple.com/sales-analytics, retrieved November 12, 2020.
2. Allie Decker, 'How Data in Sales Can Transform Your Sales Team and Performance,' https://blog.hubspot.com/sales/data-in-sales, retrieved November 12, 2020.
3. Uzi Shmilovici, 'What Makes Good Sales Data? Here are the types of good sales data you need to make winning decisions' (January 23, 2019), www.zendesk.com/blog/good-sales-data, retrieved November 12, 2020.
4. Ibid.
5. Adapted from Allie Decker, 'How Data in Sales Can Transform Your Sales Team and Performance,' https://blog.hubspot.com/sales/data-in-sales, retrieved November 12, 2020; and Whatagraph, 'Sales Dashboard (Live Reports) to Achieve More Goals' (April 6, 2020), https://whatagraph.com/blog/articles/sales-dashboard, retrieved November 12, 2020.
6. Ibid.
7. Ibid.
8. Danny Wong, 'Sales Analysis Basics for Small Businesses,' www.salesforce.com/solutions/small-business-solutions/resources/sales-analysis-basics, retrieved November 12, 2020.
9. Brian Selby, 'Power sales performance by harnessing analytics,' *Harvard Business Review* (Digital Articles) (October 30, 2018), pp. 1–4.
10. Adapted from Elise Musumano, '4 types of sales analytics,' *Sales & Service Excellence Essentials* (March 2016), 15(3), 20; Cem Dilmegani, 'The Ultimate Guide to Sales Analytics in 2020' (November 2, 2020), https://research.aimultiple.com/sales-analytics, retrieved November 12, 2020; and Danny Wong, 'Sales Analysis Basics for Small Businesses,' www.salesforce.com/solutions/small-business-solutions/resources/sales-analysis-basics, retrieved November 12, 2020.

11. Meredith Hart, '9 Sales Dashboard Examples That'll Help You Set Up Your Own,' https://blog.hubspot.com/sales/sales-dashboard, retrieved November 12, 2020.

12. Adapted from Thomas Wyatt, '5 Ways Sales Managers Can Use Data to Manage Their Team – But Probably Aren't', https://people.ai/blog/5-ways-sales-managers-can-use-data-to-manage-their-team-but-probably-arent, retrieved November 12, 2020; and Brian Schofield, '9 Ways Sales Data Analysis Can Help You Generate More Revenue' (September 22, 2019), www.business2community.com/sales-management/9-ways-sales-data-analysis-can-help-you-generate-more-revenue-02242335, retrieved November 12, 2020.

13. Doug Chung, Isabel Huber, Viany Muthy, Varun Sunkku and Marijer Weber, 'Setting better sales goals with analytics,' *Harvard Business Review* (Digital Articles) (July 9, 2019), pp. 2–5.

14. Ibid.

15. Ibid.

16. Brian Schofield, '9 Ways Sales Data Analysis Can Help You Generate More Revenue' (September 22, 2019), www.business2community.com/sales-management/9-ways-sales-data-analysis-can-help-you-generate-more-revenue-02242335, retrieved November 12, 2020.

17. Meredith Hart, '9 Sales Dashboard Examples That'll Help You Set Up Your Own,' https://blog.hubspot.com/sales/sales-dashboard, retrieved November 12, 2020.

18. Whatagraph, 'Sales Dashboard (Live Reports) to Achieve More Goals' (April 6, 2020), https://whatagraph.com/blog/articles/sales-dashboard, retrieved November 12, 2020.

19. Matt Bullock, 'Why use a Sales Dashboard?' https://spinify.com/blog/why-use-sales-dashboard, retrieved November 12, 2020.

20. Meredith Hart, '9 Sales Dashboard Examples That'll Help You Set Up Your Own,' https://blog.hubspot.com/sales/sales-dashboard, retrieved November 12, 2020.

21. Ibid.

22. Adapted from Steve Wexler, Jeffrey Shaffer and Andy Cotgreave, (2017) 'The Big Book of Dashboards: Visualizing your data using real-world business scenarios' (ebook), pp. 72–6; and Meredith Hart, '9 Sales Dashboard Examples That'll Help You Set Up Your Own,' https://blog.hubspot.com/sales/sales-dashboard, retrieved November 12, 2020.

23. Senthil Gunasekaran, 'The right data can help your sales team sell better,' *Supply House Times* (February 2020), 62(12), 44–6.

24. Ibid.

25. Ibid.

26. Allie Decker, 'How Data in Sales Can Transform Your Sales Team and Performance,' https://blog.hubspot.com/sales/data-in-sales, retrieved November 12, 2020.

27. Uzi Shmilovici, 'What Makes Good Sales Data? Here are the types of good sales data you need to make winning decisions' (January 23, 2019), www.zendesk.com/blog/good-sales-data, retrieved November 12, 2020.

28. Highspot, 'The Definitive Guide to Sales Enablement,' www.highspot.com/sales-enablement, retrieved November 20, 2020.

29. Hubspot, 'What Is Sales Enablement?' www.hubspot.com/sales-enablement, retrieved November 20, 2020.

30. Ibid.

31. Roderick Jefferson, 'Demystifying Sales Enablement: What it is, why it matters, and how to do it right' (May 29, 2019), www.saleshacker.com/what-is-sales-enablement/#s2, retrieved November 20, 2020.

32. Ibid.

33. Adapted from Pouyan Salehi, 'Sales Enablement: How to use content, training, strategy and technology to drive productivity in your sales force,' https://blog.persistiq.com/sales-enablement-to-drive-productivity, retrieved November 20, 2020; and Highspot, 'The Definitive Guide to Sales Enablement,' www.highspot.com/sales-enablement, retrieved November 20, 2020.

34. Brian Selby, 'Power sales performance by harnessing analytics,' *Harvard Business Review* (Digital Articles) (October 30, 2018), pp. 1–4.

35. Ibid.

36. Senthil Gunasekaran, 'The right data can help your sales team sell better,' *Supply House Times* (February 2020), 62(12), 44–6.

37. Ibid.

38. Tiffany Schultz, 'Prove the Value of Your Program: How to measure sales enablement success' (July 2, 2020), https://lakeonedigital.com/how-to-measure-sales-enablement-success, retrieved November 20, 2020.

39. Ibid.

40. Scott Albro, 'Sales Enablement: The who, what, how, when, and why of sales enablement,' https://blog.topohq.com/sales-enablement-who-what-how-when-why, retrieved November 20, 2020.

Appendix A
COMPREHENSIVE CASES IN THE SALES INDUSTRY

CASE A: HOME SELLING WITH RE/MAX REAL ESTATE GROUP

'Real estate is about people, not homes,' declares Paula Kosko, a realtor with RE/MAX, a global real estate company operating in 110 different countries throughout the world (Figure A-1.) Paula has been serving residential real estate clients for 16 years and is passionate about providing outstanding personalized service. Her services vary depending on whether her client is a home seller or a home buyer; however she builds and nurtures professional relationships with them all. For Paula, just like millions of real estate agents, successful selling is all about relationships.

Figure A-1   RE/MAX logo
Used with kind permission of RE/MAX Real Estate Group.

How do these relationships begin? Do her clients find her or does she find them? According to Paula, that too varies, and there's no 'right' way for relationships to originate in real estate selling. Some of these ways are:

- referrals – word-of-mouth from previous clients and people who know her
- networking – family, relatives, friends, neighbors, alumni, etc.
- neighbors of properties she has listed
- open houses where potential home buyers visit her currently listed properties
- formal prospecting methods, such as targeted direct mail where Paula sends post-cards to neighbors to inform them of houses recently sold in their neighborhood or properties that are actively on the market. She also sends emails periodically to connect with her clients and offer tips and articles of interest to homeowners.

Paula often asks her new clients how they first heard of her so she knows what methods work well to generate new prospective clients. Her favorite method for meeting new clients is through referrals, since old-fashioned word-of-mouth communication is still highly effective. Of course, Paula must maintain her stellar reputation and brand image in providing 'personal service always,' as these directly impact the decision-making process of prospective clients when selecting their sales agent. Real estate selling is a highly competitive industry, with thousands of different real estate companies and agents vying for residential client relationships (Figure A-2.) Beyond creating a brand image for themselves, most real estate agents establish 'niche' specialty areas based on geography, a chosen market segment, or an area of specialty (such as working with first-time home buyers, downsizers, or buyers of luxury homes or condos), to distinguish themselves from other agents. One of the value-added services that most real estate salespeople provide is that of knowing their local market – the parks, entertainment, shopping areas, and so on – which helps prospective clients to be successful in obtaining their desired real estate sales outcomes.

Figure A-2 For Sale by Paula sign
Used with kind permission of Paula Kosko.

Clients are unique, with varying personalities, social styles, life experiences, present living situations, and desired outcomes with respect to buying or selling real estate. Thus, Paula regularly practices adaptive selling techniques to meet the individual needs of each of her clients. In addition, her client interactions or touchpoints are often guided by whether the client is a home buyer or a home seller. However, Paula's 'all about you' perspective carries through each of her client's selling/buying experience. Regardless of the unique situation, Paula strives to enhance and provide value to both the home selling and buying experience.

When Paula is contracted as the buyer agent, she'll help her client locate the home that best meets their needs and wants, which typically entails four groups of activities:

- **Pre-sale** – educating home buyers on the real estate sales process and providing information on amenities, home values, and expected appreciation rates.

- **Home shopping** – scheduling house visits, and visiting and evaluating properties with clients.
- **Contract/closing** – preparing an attractive offer, negotiating the best terms for her client, negotiating home inspection findings and assessment details, and helping the client to prepare for their move.
- **Post-closing** – checking on new homeowners to ensure their satisfaction.

Ultimately, Paula's goal is to see each of her clients happy in their new home, such as the family shown in Figure A-3.

Figure A-3   New home, happy family
Used with kind permission of Paula Kosko.

When Paula is contracted to sell a client's home, her interactions normally include the following four groups of activities:

- **Pre-listing** – educating home sellers on the real estate sales process; providing information and guidance on how to prepare their homes for sale, including removing clutter, cleaning, completing needed repairs, and staging, either by adding props or simply paring down what's already there; and educating them on appropriate price ranges and the effects of over- and underpricing strategies. In addition, Paula is a firm believer in the concept that 'a picture is worth a thousand words' and she is well versed in taking and editing photos to portray the home and property in the best possible manner. Check out Figure A-4 to see the improvement that editing provides when using an owner-supplied photo. First impressions of a house for sale are usually made via a photograph posted online, so the image needs to be a compelling one. For this reason, Paula takes the real estate photographs herself whenever possible.

- **Listing/marketing** – securing accurate placement in a Multiple Listing System (MLS) database and obtaining proper market exposure enables prospective buyers to locate the house digitally. Compelling photography and optimal pricing ensure that the right buyers can view the property online and respond quickly to the listing.
- **Contract/closing** – explaining offers and how they differ; negotiating the best price and terms for her client; and preparing the seller for the inspections and appraisal.
- **Post-closing** – checking in with new homeowners to ensure their satisfaction.

Figure A-4A   Before editing house photo

Figure A-4B   After editing house photo

Figure A-4   Before-and-after house photos

Used with kind permission of Paula Kosko.

The goal of residential real estate sales is to help clients solve their problems related to housing. Successful real estate agents must maneuver around a number of obstacles in order to close sales and ensure that clients are highly satisfied. Some reasons why a sale might not occur in a timely manner include issues with the property:

- it is incorrectly priced too high
- its condition is not up to par
- its location is less than ideal
- doesn't have much curb appeal
- was not staged to show its best features.

Additional reasons why a house may not sell are related to the real estate sales agent:

- failed to adequately promote the house on online platforms
- used incorrect data when listing the house
- failed to make the house look appealing in photos
- did not successfully negotiate the offer that was received.

Home sellers and buyers place their trust in the real estate agent they select to represent them. This means the clients believe in their integrity and selling prowess. The main reason that Paula entered residential real estate sales was because she experienced first-hand how some agents put their own needs ahead of their client's. Paula vowed to do better. She's honest, sincerely helpful, and completely client-focused. Regardless of whether her client is a home seller or a home buyer, Paula embraces the challenge of achieving success for her clients.

Figure A-5   Sold by Paula sign
Used with kind permission of Paula Kosko.

For example, Paula received an email asking for help in locating a home for a buyer couple relocating from two different countries (Germany and Iraq). They could not be present in person until the day before the closing. This was a challenging adventure, since it occurred a decade before live video conferencing became available. Being in three different time zones required many emails, videos back and forth, and conversations at odd hours.

Buying a house in an unfamiliar area that the couple had not actually seen in person held enormous potential for disaster. Paula's fears? Several! First, the couple would arrive and not like the house. Second, they wouldn't arrive when expected, or arrive at all. Third, maybe only one of them arrives and the loan has to be reworked, causing delays and a scramble to locate temporary housing. These were only a few of the possible scenarios that disrupted Paula's sleep, keeping her awake and questioning if anything was overlooked. The outcome? Fortunately, the couple arrived as scheduled and loved the house! Happy clients and successful sale closed. *Paula's advice to anyone going into sales: Give personal service and put your client first. Always.*

Case questions:

1. If you were the real estate agent in this case, how would you approach selling real estate? Would you envision any differences between how you would sell versus Paula's style?
2. Summarize the different real estate selling activities that are needed when representing a home buyer versus a home seller. Which type of real estate selling would you prefer most? Why?
3. Review the different social styles described in Chapter 5, to assist you in describing what you would do to adapt to each of your real estate clients if they possessed a driver, analytical, expressive, or amiable social style.

CASE B: STIHL'S SUCCESSFUL B2B SALES STRATEGY[1]

Innovative product manufacturer. Global network of devoted dealers. Passionate and knowledgeable customer service delivery. Dramatically different from competitors. Sustainable business operations. These are some of the qualities that are associated with STIHL. STIHL (pronounced *steel*) has become a manufacturing powerhouse of the world's number one selling brand of gasoline chain saws by strategically opting to sell its products exclusively through independent dealers around the world. STIHL dared to be different by positioning itself against two of the most powerful forces in commerce – the big box mass retailing stores (such as Lowe's and The Home Depot) and the Internet (selling directly and digitally to final consumers) – and it has paid off magically. But make no mistake: STIHL's sales success didn't happen by accident – it

Figure B-1 STIHL logo
Used with kind permission of STIHL.

was ingeniously ushered in by an entrepreneurial vision and family-operated company culture dedicated to serving the needs of its people – employees, distributors, retail partners, and end-use customers. Let's start this story from the beginning.

In 1926, Andreas Stihl, a Swiss-born engineer, opened his engineering office in Stuttgart, Germany, with the vision to 'make it easier for people to work in and with nature.' He accomplished that by inventing his first electric chain saw. That initial vision, which still drives the company today, has made STIHL the world's top-selling chainsaw brand since 1971. As demand increased, STIHL opened production companies in Brazil, Switzerland, and the United States. The company became a global conglomerate but retained its family-owned structure with Andreas Stihl's children, Eva and Hans Peter, taking over business operations after his death in 1973. Eva and Hans Peter Stihl soon expanded the international production facilities, developed a robust sales organization, and retained a focus on quality first. The Stihl family believed that its company's responsibility was to offer customers the best product through innovative designs, solid engineering, highest-grade materials, and precision manufacturing. STIHL products grew from individual saws to elaborate machine tools, including hedge trimmers, handheld and backpack blowers, wet/dry vacuums, pressure washers, hand tools, pole pruners, concrete cutters, drills, and more.

Figure B-2 STIHL products
Used with kind permission of STIHL

The privately owned and operated company has grown from a one-man operation to a massive international manufacturer of chainsaws and power tools, with more than 17,000 employees. Stihl family values, such as treating employees with the utmost respect, permeate throughout the company. This culture has continued to spread throughout its distribution network and has been adopted by STIHL's distributors and retail partners, which provide end-use customers with the best buyer experience possible. The buyer experience includes first-class showrooms, highly trained technicians and sales staff, detailed product demonstrations, sufficient availability of replacement parts, and committed management throughout the entire distribution channel. STIHL's well-trained worldwide distributor and dealer network is crucial to the company's successful business model and to its selling activities in more than 160 countries.

Figure B-3 STIHL map
Used with kind permission of STIHL

STIHL uses a two-step distribution system in distributing its products worldwide. The company sells its products through more than 53,000 independent retail dealers throughout the world. These dealers, including hardware stores such as Ace Hardware, Do It Best, and True Value, are supported by a large network of wholesale distributors. STIHL invests in its channel partners by providing them with financial, marketing, and administrative support to enable them to build, renovate, and/or remodel their operations and showrooms. For example, years ago STIHL analyzed more than 10 million historical customer records to reveal sales trends and provide insight that helped their independent dealers compete more effectively with the powerful mass merchant retailers. In addition, the company insists on periodic training for dealers in the correct application, operation, and maintenance of each of the STIHL products they sell. Another benefit for retail dealers is the opportunity to display a big orange STIHL sign, which promotes the store's reputation as an authorized retailer of premium, world-class STIHL products.

Unlike purchasing from mass retailers, end-user customers cannot simply buy STIHL products online and have them shipped to their homes. The company doesn't believe machinery should be sold in a box without interaction with customers to ensure their satisfaction and familiarity with the product's operation. The company's selling philosophy is centered on building relationships with its customers through its dealers. However, STIHL in the USA offers an online shopping program called STIHL Express, where customers may purchase a STIHL product online and then pick it up at the dealer. When the customer visits the dealer, they will pick up a fully assembled product and receive expert training and advice if/as needed. Dealers can also offer

Figure B-4 STIHL retail display
Used with kind permission of STIHL

future, knowledgeable service and maintenance support for the purchased machinery. This value-added selling is part of what puts STIHL in a class above its competitors.

STIHL believes its independent dealers are the lifeblood of the company, and uses a personal approach to taking care of them. For example, groups of dealers from all over the world are regularly invited to the head office for a tour, training, and conversations with STIHL executives to ensure they understand the vital role they have in the firm's operating and selling success. During these meetings, photo sessions are held with top STIHL executives, and the company provides these dealers with their photo which typically becomes proudly displayed in dealer showrooms all over the world. Trusting relationships matter at STIHL and are the basis for successful value-added selling.

Years ago, STIHL publicly professed its decision to avoid the big box retailers by placing a series of full-page advertisements in *The Wall Street Journal* and other well-known publications and trade periodicals that serve dealers. The headlines of these ads made bold statements regarding STIHL's sales strategy, such as: 'Why is the world's number one selling brand of chain saw not sold at Lowe's or Home Depot?' (see Figure B-5). This was STIHL's innovative and effective approach to demonstrating its strong commitment to its dealers.

Selling outdoor power tools has had its challenges and STIHL has weathered the various uncontrollable storms (slowing global economic growth, trade wars, global weather

Figure B-5 STIHL's 'Why is' advertisement
Used with kind permission of STIHL.

conditions, etc.) by sticking to its P³ formula for success – people, processes, and products. Its commitment to people, innovative processes, and state-of-the-art products with top quality has served the company well as it posted 3.9 billion euros in revenue across the STIHL Group for 2019, an increase of 4 percent over the previous year. STIHL continues to be committed to embracing technological ingenuity in developing new products that both 'make life in the outdoors easier' and are sustainable in the future.

The company recognizes that the outdoor power tool industry is interwoven with the worldwide growth and development of the agricultural sector, that's why STIHL is focusing its efforts on more than just selling existing products. STIHL is investing in outreach to potential new customers with the hope that they realize the added value that their support of machinery and mechanical tools can provide. For example, in India, STIHL provides training for sales partners and dealers throughout the country, using a roadshow specifically designed to reach and impact additional geographical areas. 'Parivartan Yatra' (Journey of Transformation) involves STIHL dealers visiting remote areas with videos that explain product applications onsite, holding machine demonstrations in the field, and seeking out direct dialog with farmers. STIHL is working with various agricultural cooperatives to try to bring about a mechanical revolution. In addition, STIHL is collaborating with farmers in India to gather information regarding their specific needs and concerns. With this insight, STIHL will develop a range of products that meet the needs and requirements of customers in emerging markets. This international STIHL production alliance is another reason why STIHL is in a class above the rest when it comes to successful value-added selling that serves its customers.

Case questions:

1. Do you think STIHL's exclusive focus and reliance on B2B selling has been a successful strategy? How has it positioned the STIHL brand?
2. How might STIHL continue its strong relationships with its retail dealers while effectively serving the changing needs and demographics of outdoor power tool customers?
3. What uncontrollable factors may affect STIHL's global business model? What impact might they have on STIHL's selling strategies in the future?

NOTE

1. Sources used include: www.stihlusa.com; STIHL Annual Report 2019; Andrew R. Thomas and Timothy J. Wilkinson (2015) *The Customer Trap: How to Avoid the Biggest Mistake in Business*, Chapter 6: The STIHL Story, pp. 75–90; Stephanie Overby (2014) 'Tilling data to grow sales,' *CIO*, 28(2), 18–20; Kyle Stock (2014) 'Big-box cutter,' *Bloomberg Businessweek* (April 28, 2014), Issue 4376, pp. 60–61; and Richard E. Wilson, 'Stihl Incorporated: Go-to-market strategy for next-generation consumers,' http://streamer.gulfcoast.edu/TECH/kallan/MAN3503/SWOT%20Project/Stihl%20Inc.%20Case.pdf, retrieved December 3, 2020.

Appendix B
CAREERS IN SELLING

Thinking about pursuing a career in selling? If so, reflect on the type of work environment that is most appealing to you and explore the many career options available. Keep in mind that types of selling responsibilities vary greatly between 'inside' versus 'outside' sales positions, with the responsibilities of 'direct' sales positions often being a combination of the two. Let's briefly review some of the potential differences between sales positions but remember, selling responsibilities will vary by company as well.

TYPES OF SELLING

Inside sales positions

In these positions, you'll work almost exclusively in an office setting with a more structured schedule, limited travel requirements, and a more casual dress code. If you like predictability in terms of your schedule and income, then inside sales positions may be right for you. Depending on the specific position, you may spend much of your time working on the telephone or computer to follow up on sales leads, schedule appointments, arrange demonstrations, gather data, compile reports, and so on. You'll need good technical skills as you'll likely be working with a company's CRM system to track and analyze data. Some inside sales positions will require you to have 'thick skin' as you'll face many rejections if your duties include prospecting and generating leads. Remember, it often takes a bunch of 'no' responses to get to a 'yes' in selling. Good listening skills are needed for inside sales positions.

Outside sales positions

In outside sales positions, you'll spend most of your time out in the field, calling on prospects and customers. You'll manage your own schedule and be your own daily supervisor. Your workplace changes daily, often due to weather, traffic delays, or other people's schedules. Your appearance is very important as you must always look professional and be ready to interact with prospects and customers. If you want to work in outside sales, you'll need to be highly self-motivated, and possess excellent organizational, time-management, and multitasking skills. Above all, you'll need to have excellent communication and interpersonal skills as you'll engage in face-to-face conversations and deliver sales presentations on a regular basis. In addition, you will likely be constantly networking and using your keen listening skills and emotional intelligence. So, if you are ambitious, outgoing, thrive on tackling new challenges each day, and enjoy meeting new people and building relationships, then outside sales may be the right career for you.

Table B-1 Sales career position titles

Sales representative:	Sales management:	Executive-level management:
Account representative	Account manager	Director of inside sales
Advertising sales representative	Area sales manager	Director of national sales
Automotive sales representative	Business development manager	Director of sales
Customer care representative	Direct sales manager	Executive vice president of sales
Direct salesperson	District sales manager	
Distribution sales representative	Franchise development manager	**Account executives and advisors:**
Enterprise sales representative	Group sales manager	Account executive
Equipment sales representative	Inside sales manager	Channel partner sales executive
Equipment sales specialist	Manager, business development	Corporate sales account executive
Healthcare sales representative	Market development manager	Financial advisor/financial planner
Industrial sales representative	Marketing manager	Group and events sales coordinator
Inside salesperson	National sales manager	Key account manager
Insurance sales representative	Regional manager	Major accounts manager
Medical sales representative	Regional sales manager	National accounts sales general manager
National accounts sales representative	Retail store manager	Regional sales account manager
Outside sales representative	Sales and community marketing manager	Regional sales executive
Retail sales representative	Sales manager	Sales account executive
Route sales representative	Territory manager	Strategic account manager
Sales assistant	Territory sales manager	Territory business manager
Sales associate	Wholesale sales manager	Wealth management advisor
Sales representative		
Sales trainee		**Administrative positions related to sales:**
Salesperson		Business development representative
Specialty sales representative		Enterprise resources planning representative
Territory sales representative		Financial sales assistant
		Fixed income specialist
		Industry representative
		Investments representative
		National accounts sales analyst
		Regional dealer recruiter
		Sales coordinator
		Sales operation coordinator
		Sales representative – territory lead

Source: Adapted from Alison Doyle, 'Sales Careers: Options, job titles, and descriptions' (updated August 4, 2019), www.thebalancecareers.com/sales-job-titles-2061545, retrieved December 8, 2020.

CAREER PREPARATION

The level of education, years and type of experience, and skills required for a career in sales typically vary by company or organization, industry, geographic location, and type of sales position. Many require a bachelor degree, while for others, a high-school diploma is adequate. In fact, some sales positions, such as retail sales, require no formal education. Most sales positions will provide extensive sales training, on-the-job training, and onboarding programs. Review Chapter 11 to recall the value and type of onboarding activities that salespeople may experience.

As Table B-1 reveals, sales career position titles are numerous. A career in sales involves creating and undertaking strategies to sell a product or service, as well as understanding the consumer buying process and the needs and wants of targeted prospective buyers and customers. However, in today's business world, the roles of sales and marketing tend to overlap, with more and more companies creating dual-role positions, such as 'Director of Marketing and Sales.' This convergence is enhancing the effectiveness of serving prospects and customers and will likely continue well into the future.

COMMON SALES POSITION TITLES AND DESCRIPTIONS

Here are some common career positions and descriptions that may be helpful to you in determining whether a sales career might be a good fit for you:[1]

- **Sales assistants** support sales teams by maintaining databases, updating contact records and invoice data, communicating promotions and pricing changes, preparing sales tracking reports, placing product orders, arranging shipments, resolving inventory issues, and performing administrative duties.
- **Business development representatives** assist in finding new business opportunities, conduct background research on sales leads to determine whether the sales team should pursue them, and help to build relationships with prospects and customers to increase the potential for future sales.
- **Account executives** typically work for advertising agencies, marketing, or media companies and serve as the liaison between the company and its clients in managing day-to-day communication, compiling performance and progress reports, providing suggestions for improving service delivery, and may be responsible for selling additional services.
- **Pharmaceutical sales representatives** often specialize in representing specific drug manufacturers in meeting with physicians and pharmacists to educate and update them on products and treatments, in order to assist them in prescribing appropriate pharmaceutical products for their patients.
- **Sales managers** are responsible for developing and implementing strategic sales plans to generate sales revenue for a company and for overseeing (hiring, training,

coaching, and supervising) sales staff, which typically includes both sales representatives and account managers.

- **Territory salespeople** are responsible for all sales activity within a defined geographic sales territory, including identifying potential new business opportunities, meeting face to face with prospects and customers, educating and training customers on product or service usage, and maintaining good client relationships.

- **Car sales executives** work for an automotive dealership in assisting customers to locate and purchase new and used vehicles by providing information on different model types and features, showing and demonstrating vehicles, discussing warranties and financing options, and negotiating pricing.

- **Medical sales executives** represent medical device manufacturers to provide education and advice on a variety of medical products such as stethoscopes, thermometers, medical implants, and prosthetics, as well as distribute free samples, provide assistance in placing orders, and maintain good relationships with physicians and other decision makers at healthcare organizations.

- **Real estate agents** assist people or business entities in buying or selling properties by providing information and property tours, answering questions, serving as the liaison between buyers and sellers, discussing sale conditions, negotiating pricing on behalf of clients, scheduling property inspections, preparing contracts, and maintaining close relationships to encourage referral business.

- **Sales engineers** provide technical product or service expertise/knowledge by translating it into easy-to-understand product presentations, participating in prospect and customer meetings, answering questions, offering suggestions to improve results from product or service usage, and representing their company at trade shows, conferences, and corporate events if requested.

- **Sales directors** typically work for larger companies and are responsible for overseeing all sales efforts, including motivating sales teams, assisting with the introduction of new processes, procedures, and new product or service launches, ensuring the sales department adheres to company policy, and supervising sales managers or directly managing all sales staff if required.

- **Sales and marketing managers** are responsible for the research and development aspects of marketing and the implementation of sales strategies, including new product or service introductions, the promotion of current offerings, the assessment of progress on projected sales goals, and budget allocations.

- **Sales representatives** seek to understand the needs, wants, and problems of prospective and existing customers to help them find products or services that satisfy their needs and wants or solve their problems, provide customer service, negotiate prices, close transactions, complete sales reports, and work to generate sales volume for the company and meet sales goals.

- **Insurance agents** sell various forms of insurance such as health, life, auto, and homeowner policies, assist with insurance claims, perform inspections on properties and vehicles, and provide information to their clients.

- **Retail sales associates** perform a variety of duties to serve customers, including stocking shelves, assisting store customers, cashiering, implementing price changes, switching out promotions and merchandise, and working in returns and exchanges as needed.

- **Telemarketers** work primarily over the telephone to deliver sales pitches and encourage prospective customers to make a purchase, and/or existing customers to renew a subscription or to repeat purchase.
- **Manufacturing sales representatives** represent manufacturers and sell their products to businesses, governmental organizations, or other organizations by contacting prospective customers, explaining the features and benefits of products/services, answering questions, providing samples (if applicable), negotiating prices, and assisting in placing orders.

Sales positions range from entry-level ones, such as retail sales associate, to those that require more education and/or experience, such as sales manager. Careers in selling are diverse and always evolving due to digital transformation. To keep abreast of the career trends in sales, along with sales position opportunities and associated salaries, visit the following websites:

- www.bls/gov/ooh/sales/home.htm
- www.indeed.com
- www.monster.com

Best wishes for a successful future career in sales!

NOTE

1. Adapted from '14 Common Careers in Marketing and Sales' (March 12, 2020), www.indeed.com/career-advice/finding-a-job/careers-in-marketing-and-sales, retrieved December 8, 2020; and '14 Sales Jobs That Pay Well' (November 25, 2020), www.indeed.com/career-advice/finding-a-job/sales-jobs-that-pay-well, retrieved December 8, 2020.

Appendix C
SELF-SELLING

WHAT IS SELF-SELLING?

Self-selling is a process whereby individuals sell themselves or their services, talents, abilities, leadership skills, or any need-satisfying offering that they possess to serve the needs/wants of prospective customers. The term 'customer' is broadly used to represent *any* target audience. This means that the customer may be a potential employer, client, patient, donor, volunteer, student, constituent, citizen, and so on. This process is also referred to as 'selling yourself' and the purpose or objective of any personal self-selling effort is to obtain a measurable response from your target audience.

For example, when you send a resume with a cover letter or complete an application form for an internship or career position, your initial objective is to be invited for an interview, and your end goal is to be offered that internship or career position. When you complete a scholarship application, your goal is to be awarded the scholarship. If you are a political candidate, you are promoting yourself with the hope of gaining volunteers to join your campaign team, supporters to provide monetary donations, and ultimately citizens' votes on Election Day. You will be more likely to succeed if you set objectives and measure your effectiveness for each step you take toward reaching any of these goals.

Here's an example. If you're a photographer and you want to earn your living photographing weddings, then your target market will include brides-to-be and their parents, since parents often pay for the wedding expenses. Your objective is not just to have brides-to-be and their parents learn about you and your services, but to have them contract you to photograph their wedding. Let's say you decide to go to a wedding expo one weekend and you spend six hours interacting with prospective brides, showing your portfolio of photography work and distributing your brochures and business cards. After the exposition ends, you surely hope to have many of these brides-to-be contact you to hire you to photograph their wedding, right? So self-selling is as simple as that – you are promoting yourself in order to entice people to hire you for your photography services.

All selling, regardless of whether you are selling a product, a service, an event, an activity, a person, or a place must begin with understanding the needs, wants, and desires of the targeted customers. The simple fact is that consumers are at the heart of all selling, however all consumers are not alike and do not have the same needs, wants, and desires. Therefore, your self-selling efforts must be directed only to those prospects who you think have a need, want, desire, or interest in whatever you are offering. Once you know the needs, wants, desires, and interests of your targeted prospective customers, you can begin to craft your self-selling strategy and determine what need-satisfying offering you might present to these specific customers.

WHO USES SELF-SELLING?

Virtually all people who have something of value that they want to share or exchange with others, use self-selling. Try this: Make a list of all of the different types of industries where people must sell themselves or their services and you'll quickly see the list is very long. Check out Table C-1 for a list to get you started.

Table C-1 People who sell themselves

• Artists	• Book authors
• Celebrities	• Religious leaders
• Supermodels	• Unemployed individuals
• Musicians	• Scientists
• Professional athletes	• Seamstresses
• Political candidates	• Plumbers
• Elected government officials	• Electricians
• Doctors	• Landscape designers
• Dentists	• Personal fitness trainers
• Attorneys	• Real estate agents and brokers
• Accountants	• Consultants
• Financial planners	• Business analysts
• Investment brokers	• Opticians
• Entrepreneurs	• Business leaders
• Philanthropists	• Photographers
• News anchors	• Videographers
• Comedians	• College students

Who's missing from the list in Table C-1? YOU! But not for long, because after reading this Appendix, you will be well positioned to sell yourself and your talents, products, services, leadership skills, and so on.

Check this out! Google Cameron Johnson and you'll learn how an ordinary young man from the Blue Ridge Mountain area of Roanoke, Virginia, managed to become a nationally known and respected entrepreneur and Chief Executive Officer (CEO) by the age of 15. Cameron started his first business when he was a mere nine-year-old boy, and by the time he was 19 years old he had started nearly a dozen profitable businesses and had received a lucrative offer of $10 million in venture capital. He earned his first million before graduating from high school and bought his own house at age 20. Incredible? Absolutely! Possible? You bet! Cameron learned that if you have passion, believe in yourself, set goals, and have the will to put yourself out there, you can achieve great success. Cameron believes that the most fundamental part of your business is you and, first and foremost, you must be able to sell yourself.[1]

Self-selling can help you, a college or university student, to prepare yourself for the highly competitive world that awaits you after graduation. Knowing how to sell yourself can empower you with both selling knowledge and the professional skills (poise, polish, preparedness) needed to be successful in internships, graduate programs, careers, and life. Are you ready to prepare yourself for success? Are you eager to learn some self-selling strategies and tactics? If so, read on!

Figure C-1 Self-selling process

HOW DO YOU SELL YOURSELF?

As Figure C-1 reveals, you can successfully sell yourself by implementing a four-stage process which includes assessment, preparation, communication, and implementation. Let's briefly examine each of these stages.

Stage 1: Assessing yourself

This step requires some soul searching on your end to determine what goal, objective, ambition, or measure of success you want to achieve. Dream big and don't be afraid to take chances. You only live once! That said, it's important to put your ambitions or goals in writing so you can develop a plan to achieve your goals. Refer back to Chapter 2 to ensure that the goals you create are SMART. In your self-assessment, you might also complete a personal situational analysis, commonly known as a 'SWOT' analysis. This will enable you to reflect on your current situation while envisioning the future. Figure C-2 provides the SWOT analysis template that you can use to itemize (in bullet-point fashion) each of your current strengths and weaknesses, along with your future opportunities and potential threats.

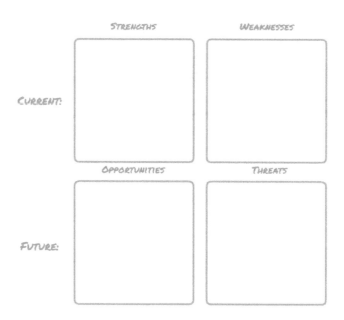

Figure C-2   SWOT analysis template

Self-assessment may also include reaching out to other people to help you to better understand what others think of you – your personal image and reputation. The information you gather may serve as a reality check and provide the insight needed to adjust some of your behaviors in an attempt to project the most desirable or ideal image of yourself. Once you've completed your self-assessment and made personal improvements, you are ready to move forward to stage 2.

Stage 2: Preparing your sales materials and yourself

When creating your personal sales materials, you will need to determine your **unique selling proposition (USP)** which is often referred to as your unique selling point. Your USP is what makes you distinctively different and superior to others.

Determining your USP requires you to also investigate your competitors as you want to be sure to separate yourself from and elevate yourself above your competitors. This includes creating your personal brand which encompasses how you want to be thought of, or what you want to be associated with in the minds of others. You should create a brief personal introduction, often called a 'sound bite' or 'elevator speech,' have it memorized, and be ready to voice it to others during introductions or initial meetings. A sound bite introduction should include your name, your status (such as student, year, school), and your top accomplishment(s) or skills that make you unique and memorable. You want to share something that will set you apart from your peers – your USP.

Savvy self-selling individuals use images and symbols to communicate their branded message in a faster manner. A **personal logo**, which is a unique image or visual sign, symbol, or design can be created that becomes associated with a brand name. These images build awareness of a particular brand and contribute to our perception of that brand. Creating a personal logo can be as easy as using the first letter of your last name. You may also create a **personal slogan** to communicate your USP to your target audiences. Slogans, often referred to as taglines, bylines, catchphrases, or advertising jingles, are the words or phrases that accompany the brand, represent the brand, and distinguish it from other brands.

You should use your logo and slogan consistently in order for them to become associated with you. Images of any given brand must have some degree of consistency. Seeing the same image or tagline again and again builds **brand familiarity** (how well the brand is recognized and accepted by the target audience). Ideally, over time and with consistent usage, your logo and slogan will become recognized and quickly associated with your name and image in a matter of seconds. Think about your personal brand as the synthesis of all the expectations, images, and perceptions it creates in the minds of others when they see or hear your name.[2] Here are some examples:[3]

- Mother Teresa is well known for serving the poor people of the world.
- Albert Einstein is associated with intelligence and innovation – sheer genius.
- Michael Jordan is known as one of the greatest basketball players of all time.
- Professional writer J.K. Rowling will always be associated with the Harry Potter series.

In order to achieve brand consistency, you should place your logo and slogan on all of your self-selling materials. That means you'll likely need to create a resume, personal stationery to use in creating cover letters, notecards to use in sending thank-you notes, and business cards to distribute when networking. Keep in mind that your resume should serve as an introduction to you, and overview your skills and relevant experiences. The three components to an effective resume are: content, format (organization of data), and appearance (layout and design). Your content should contain the following (typically in this order):

- name and contact information
- objective (optional, but if included it should be concise and customized to the desired outcome or career position)
- education (including your year, major or field of study, grade-point-average, and relevant coursework)
- experience (paid, unpaid, internships, career shadowing)
- skills (include proficiency level if appropriate)
- licensures/certifications (if applicable)
- volunteer experience/service projects
- activities/involvement (on-campus and in the community)
- honors/awards/achievements
- study abroad/international experience (if applicable).

The purpose of your cover letter is to persuade your target audience to review your resume or application and give you an interview or a meeting. In your cover letter, you should highlight your strongest qualifications and show your knowledge of the employer's organization and how well you'd fit into its culture. You should not restate what is contained in your resume but instead provide specific details about your experience. Your cover letter should be organized in the following manner:

- your contact information
- the addressee – always include the person's name and title
- the date
- a salutation – 'Dear Mr./Ms./Dr. X'
- first paragraph – purpose for writing the letter
- second paragraph – details of your most relevant experience
- third paragraph – your knowledge of the employer's organization and how you'd fit in
- closing – your plan of action and a sincere 'thank you' for their considering of your application.

You should include your logo and slogan in your email signature line, and include it on all of the social media platforms that you use. Consistency is the key to conveying your personal brand when creating your self-selling materials. Check out Figure C-3 for some ideas on creating a personal logo and slogan, as well as designing a variety of self-selling materials with brand consistency. You should be limited only by your imagination when preparing materials to sell yourself, so be prepared to obtain digital design assistance if needed.

Figure C-3A   Sample A Will Kosko

Figure C-3B   Sample B Ann Stafford

Figure C-3   Personal branding materials

Used with kind permission of Paula Kosko.

Preparing yourself for job hunting involves activities that will build your confidence in your ability to sell yourself. One activity is to conduct research so that you understand your target employer's needs and wants. For example, when applying for a career position with a particular company, you typically start with an online search of the company and browse the company's website to learn as much as possible before you apply for the position (and long before you interview with its associates). Review Chapter 2, which addressed personal preparation and professional business etiquette, to refresh your memory about how to properly prepare for selling before moving on to the next stage.

Stage 3: Communicating

This stage is the action stage where you communicate and interact with others to obtain commitments that help you to move closer to achieving your stated self-selling goals and objectives.

This stage includes both networking and interviewing. Let's discuss each in turn. First, you should always be networking for yourself and making personal connections to build your base of friends and supporters. (Review Chapter 4 to refresh your memory on networking strategies and techniques.)

Networking

A very useful, effective tool for networking is the LinkedIn website. Using LinkedIn can help you to connect with professionals in your chosen field, and well as alumni from your college or university institution.

Let's now discuss how to use LinkedIn to network and sell yourself. To begin, use the following checklist to set up and get started on LinkedIn:

- ✓ Have a professional headshot photo taken and complete your profile as much as possible.
- ✓ Use the city and state in which you hope to secure a career position and/or conduct business.
- ✓ When using keywords, be very clear on what you want to do and make it clear what you are seeking and/or what services you are offering.
- ✓ Reach out to different recruiters and contacts within a particular company and understand and accept the fact that multiple contacts may be needed.
- ✓ Develop personalized, thoughtful, and grammatically correct messaging as conducting individual outreach is the key to success.
- ✓ Indicate whether you are open to relocation or opportunities in other states in your summary statement.
- ✓ Ask for recommendations from professors, former managers, supervisors, etc.
- ✓ List your skills so that others can endorse you.

✓ Set a SMART goal – connect with at least 10 people every day in order to grow your network of customers, potential customers, employers, and potential employers!

Here's how you might conduct alumni networking:

- Once your profile is set up, scroll down and select your university to visit the hyperlinked home page.
- Select 'Alumni' and a screen will emerge displaying all alumni from your institution who have profiles on LinkedIn. For most universities, this will give you direct access to approximately 80–85 percent of your alumni base.
- The default 'search criteria' that appears includes selections for 'Where they live' and 'Where they work,' but you can also use the 'Next' feature to search the list on 'What they do', 'What they studied', 'What they are skilled at' and 'How you are connected.'
- Using these features (and others), you can run very detailed searches to identify alumni with whom you might want to network. See examples below:

  o alumni living in New York City, NY who work in Finance
  o alumni living in Atlanta, GA who are skilled in Adobe Creative Suite
  o alumni who studied Political Science who live in the state of Texas
  o alumni who are First or Second Connections living in London, England
  o alumni who have earned an MBA.

- Once you have identified alumni in your occupation, interest area, skill set, desired geographic region, etc., you can 'request to connect' with them using a customized note or send them a message if you are already connected! See Table C-2 for some sample messages.
- Try to set a goal to send at least 15–20 messages per day and see how quickly your call requests come to fruition!

Table C-2 Sample LinkedIn messages to alumni

Hi Jeff, as a CNU alum, I was hoping we could connect. I'm pursuing a career in a health services setting in the Charlottesville area. You seem to be doing very well in the field and I was wondering if you might be willing to share advice over a brief phone call?

Thank you,

(Name)

(Phone Number)

Hi Jamal, as a CNU alum, I was hoping we could connect! I'm exploring various career paths. I know the Chamber hosts adult education and leadership programs so I was wondering if you might be willing to schedule a call to share a bit about the type of work you do?

Thank you,

(Name)

(Phone Number)

(Continued)

Table C-2 (Continued)

Hi Ms. Nunn, I recognized your name as I recently applied to a nursing recruitment role with Riverside. I am looking through the CNU alumni network and noticed you are a fellow grad! I was hoping we could connect – if you have any advice for me, that would be very helpful!

Thank you,

(Name)

(Phone Number)

Hi Bethany, as a fellow CNU alumni, I was hoping we could connect! I am currently exploring the field of human resources as a career and was wondering if you might be willing to schedule a 15-minute call with me so I can learn more about the field?

Thank you,

(Name)

(Phone Number)

Source: Provided by Monica Hill, Associate Director of Alumni Relations, Christopher Newport University. Used with permission.

Interviewing

Review Chapter 5, which addressed many 'soft skills' you should employ when interviewing, such as establishing rapport, making a good first impression, building credibility and attaining trust, practicing good professional etiquette, communicating effectively via both verbal and non-verbal techniques, adaptive selling, and neuro-linguistic programming.

Know that if you do land an interview, you have already been pre-qualified to make sure that you have the proper educational and/or technical background necessary to perform the job. Everyone interviewing has already been pre-qualified. The mistake people make in interviews is that they keep trying to push the 'hard skills' (education, experiences, technical expertise, etc.) that they have developed in school or through jobs or internships. That is unnecessary. During the interview, employers are trying to determine whether you have developed the appropriate soft skills that are needed for the position. Beyond those mentioned above, this may include: problem solving, thinking outside of the box, being able to multi-task, staying cool under pressure, overcoming adversity, being able to handle challenging people, being able to work in a group setting, and being resilient – meaning that, no matter what, you don't give up until you find a solution.

Your goal when interviewing is to show how you have developed these soft skills from your educational, work, and life experiences. You should do this by sharing a story about your experience and what you learned from it. For instance, if the interviewer says, 'Tell me about a time you had to overcome a major obstacle,' you first tell them what the situation was, then what you did, the outcome of the situation, and the skills that you developed as a result. Basically, the formula to answering these behavior-type questions is to follow the 'STAR' method that was presented in Chapter 7. To review, STAR stands for:

Situation: Describe the scene in which you found yourself.

Task: State what you were challenged to do.

Activity: Briefly explain the activities you carried out.

Results: Provide the outcome or results.

Here's how you can apply the STAR method when sharing brief stories to answer behavioral questions during your interview: This was the challenge. This is what I did. This was the result. Then, provide the moral to the story: This is what I learned. This is how I grew stronger from it. And/or this is how I can apply this learning for your company. When you give the moral to the story, you are showing what soft skills you have developed. What you did is nice to know. What you learned is what they hire.

Stage 4: Implementing and delivering

This is the stage where you fulfill the commitments and promises you've made along the way. Once your target audience responds, you will need to jump into action. This is the where the customer or prospect's need is fulfilled and delivery of the requested product, service, or information is provided directly to that customer or prospect. Sound familiar? This stage aligns well with the 'post-sales' activities we covered in Chapter 10. Take a few minutes to review that chapter as needed.

Once you have created and communicated your personal brand image, you must live that image in order for people to authentically associate your brand image with you. By branding your abilities, talents, and all that makes you unique and different – superior – to others, you are defining your public image and setting expectations for your future behavior. Putting your self-selling strategies into action is the last stage of the process, but without implementation, all of your assessing, preparing, creating, and articulating are of little value. Implementing your self-selling process is critical. Put it to work. Be fearless. Take a chance. You may have heard of the old saying, *nothing ventured, nothing gained*; well, it rings true in this case. So, go for it and see what success lies ahead!

Best wishes in successfully selling yourself!

NOTES

1. Cameron Johnson (2007) *You Call the Shots*. New York: Free Press, p. 15.
2. Hubert K. Rampersad (2008) 'A new blueprint for powerful and authentic personal branding,' *Performance Improvement*, 47(6), 34.
3. Ibid.

GLOSSARY

Account management   a post-sales role that focuses on nurturing client relationships.

Account managers   the employees in charge of overseeing client accounts once a salesperson has closed the business deal.

Account plan   the output or document that is created on the basis of the account planning process.

Account planning   a company-wide collaborative effort toward conducting in-depth assessments of current relationships and activity with customers, as well as with future prospects, to determine where value can be added.

Active listening   making a concentrated, conscious effort to hear and understand the words and sounds in a conversation; then, responding to and remembering that conversation.

Adaptive selling   salespeople recognizing and changing their selling message and behavior based on the unique characteristics of each customer or prospect and the selling situation.

Appeal   message content that addresses consumers' rational or emotional needs, wants, or interests, and entices them to action.

Approaching   salespeople making the initial contact with prospective customers.

Authenticity   something that is legitimate or real and not phony or contrived; there is substance and supporting details that can be confirmed.

Auto-responder   an email or emails that have been set up to be sent automatically when triggered by a predetermined variable or some particular event.

Bargaining   the back-and-forth communication needed to arrive at the terms of a purchase, agreement, or contract.

Beat   the smallest part of a story that still retains the essence of the story itself.

Beliefs   the standards by which people choose to live their lives.

Blog   a Web log that contains informally written information and journal-like entries.

Body language   communication conveyed by certain body movements and expressions, such as facial expressions, poise, and posture.

Budget   a formal written plan used to allocate scarce resources and to measure and evaluate success against performance goals.

Business development   the tasks of generating new business opportunities for salespeople.

Business environment the internal and external factors that influence a company's operating situation, including the issues of human resources, corporate culture, and power and politics.

Business intelligence (BI) gathering, evaluating, and distributing descriptive information to help make decisions for an organization.

Business-to-business (B2B) selling a type of selling in which companies sell to other businesses (formal entities, organizations, associations, or groups who purchase products for further production, use in business operations, or for resale).

Business-to-consumer (B2C) selling a type of selling in which companies sell to final consumers (individuals who purchase products for personal, family, or household consumption).

Buyer journey the first three of the stages in the customer journey – awareness, consideration, and decision to purchase.

Buyer objection any hesitation or reluctance that may block successful selling.

Cadence management the process of prioritizing, structuring, timing, and conducting account interactions.

Call-back a future appointment to meet with the customer to ensure their satisfaction with the purchase, delivery, and post-purchase experience.

Channel a passageway, a means of access for the transfer of a product, an idea, or a communication.

Character sketch an overview description of the character, to provide some depth so readers can identify with them.

Climax the most intense or exciting point in a story.

Closing the act of obtaining commitments.

Coaching a process of empowering sales employees to exceed established performance standards by identifying areas for improvement and praising what they have done well.

Cold calling making an unsolicited call to a potential sales lead or prospect with whom the salesperson has had no prior contact nor gathered any lead qualification information, also known as cold canvassing.

Cold canvassing making an unsolicited call to a potential sales lead or prospect with whom the salesperson has had no prior contact nor gathered any lead qualification information, also known as cold calling.

Commitment in selling, a strategy to continually move the prospect closer to buying, which is typically achieved in progressive steps throughout the sales cycle.

Conflict the behaviors or feelings that one or both of the parties have when the other party has the potential to or actually obstructs, interferes with, or makes less effective a party's behaviors associated with reaching their goals in a relationship.

Conflict management diagnostic processes, interpersonal styles, and negotiation strategies that are designed to avoid unnecessary conflict and reduce or resolve excessive conflict.

Congruence when a person's body language, words, and tonality of voice are all aligned and in sync with one another.

Consultative selling partnership selling where salespeople are focused on selling long-term value and creating long-term relationships with each prospect and customer as opposed to providing products and services.

Consumer touchpoints transactional moments where data can be collected, as well as critical interactions in the customer journey that may either build or erode trust with consumers.

Continuity selling where consumers purchase on a regular basis, e.g. weekly, monthly – also known as 'club offers' or 'subscription offers.'

Cookie an electronic tag or identifier that is placed on a personal computer that allows recognition of the web user again, after they have interacted with a marketer's website once.

Cross-selling selling current customers products and services that are related (and even unrelated) to the products/services they currently purchase from the company.

Customer engagement a measure of a company's interaction with its customers across all touchpoints throughout their lifecycle.

Customer engagement value the set of metrics that describe customers who value the brand and contribute to the firm through purchase activities, referrals, positive influence on other customers, and feedback provided to the company.

Customer journey the set of experiences that a customer goes through from the moment they become aware of a company or brand through the lifetime of the customer relationship.

Customer journey map a visual depiction of every interaction and experience a customer has with a company or an organization throughout the entire customer journey.

Customer relationship management (CRM) an integrated system that delivers a single-source transactional database of up-to-date customer information throughout an entire organization to maximize the total value of the customer relationship.

Data mining using statistical and mathematical techniques to extract knowledge from data contained within a database.

Database analytics the process by which customer information housed within the customer database is analyzed to draw inferences about an individual customer's needs.

Demographics identifiable and measurable statistics that describe the consumer, including variables such as age, gender, education level, income level, and occupation.

Direct channels   sales channels that do not include the use of middlemen or any third party such as wholesalers, distributors, or retailers when selling products/services to consumers.

Direct selling   where products/services are sold directly to consumers via salespeople in non-retail and nontraditional settings.

Distributive bargaining   a type of bargaining where the goals of one party are in direct conflict with the goals of another party, and resources are fixed and limited.

Distributive negotiation   where two negotiating parties use strategies and tactics to attain their respective goals and to maximize their share of the outcome to the detriment of another party, also known as competitive bargaining.

Emotional appeal   an appeal that focuses on a consumer's desires and feelings, targeting consumer's wants such as social status, prestige, power, recognition, and acceptance.

Emotional intelligence   the capability that people have to identify, assess, and manage their emotions.

Financial budget   a budget that consists of the capital budget, the cash budget, the budgeted balance sheet, and the budgeted statement of cash flows. Financial budgets reveal the impact of the planned operations on the company's overall financial position at year end.

Framework   a set of assumptions, concepts, values, and practices that constitutes a way of viewing reality.

Fulfillment   the act of carrying out a customer's expectations.

Geographic information system (GIS)   a computer system capable of capturing, storing, analyzing, and displaying geographically referenced information identified according to location.

Global positioning system (GPS)   an electronic geographic segmentation tool that associates latitude and longitude coordinates with street addresses.

Goals   the specified, desired outcomes to be achieved.

Inbound calls   telephone calls where the customer originates the call.

Indirect channels   sales channels that use a network of channel partners when selling products/services to consumers.

Indoctrinating   the process of teaching a new employee certain ideas, attitudes, cognitive strategies, or professional methodologies.

Influencer marketing   a form of content-driven marketing where the content shared is akin to an endorsement or a testimonial by a third party or potential consumer.

Influencer theory   a concept that states that a small number of consumers are able to sway the mass market.

Inside selling   where salespeople locate potential customers and guide them through the sales process remotely, instead of face to face.

Interests   things that people want to satisfy or do at the present time.

Key account management   the process of building long-term relationships with the company's most valuable client accounts.

Key account manager   the manager who is responsible for turning a company's most valuable clients into business partners via dedicated resources, unique offerings, and periodic meetings.

Key performance indicators (KPIs)   significant factors that companies measure and monitor their own performance against.

Lead generation   the method of getting inquiries from potential customers.

Logline   a single compelling sentence that explains the content of a presentation in a manner that hooks the prospective customer.

Market penetration   a measure of the extent to which a product or service is being used within a defined population or 'universe.'

Marketing automation   software platforms and technologies designed to effectively carry out email blasts.

Marketing qualified lead (MQL)   a sales lead whose engagement levels suggest that they are likely to become a customer.

Mental space   the level of conscious nervousness that is present in salespeople's minds as they approach giving a sales presentation.

Mentor   a trusted friend, counselor, or teacher, usually a more experienced person who is willing to assist others in their professional development.

Mentoring   an interpersonal exchange between a senior-level or experienced person and a less experienced person in which the mentor provides support, direction, and feedback regarding career plans and personal development.

Mirroring   the process of matching certain behaviors, such as a person's tone or tempo of voice, body posture, gestures, facial expressions, and breathing patterns.

Narrative   an explanation of the events happening in a story.

Negotiation   a process whereby two parties are seeking to find a mutually acceptable solution or outcome to a complex conflict.

Negotiation mentor   an experienced negotiator in the same field that salespeople can learn from and interact with as they develop their negotiation skills.

Netiquette   the etiquette of electronic communications.

Networking   using a supportive system for sharing information and services among individuals and groups that have a common interest.

Neuro-linguistic programming (NLP)   a technique for enhancing one's ability to detect personality types through an increased awareness of verbal and physical cues.

Nonverbal skills unspoken aspects of a conversation that influence meaning, such as eye contact, gestures, posture, and body language.

Objectives sub-goals that are smaller and more easily attained than goals.

Offer the value proposition to prospects or customers, stating what they will receive in return for taking the action salespeople are requesting.

Onboarding a strategic management process to empower new employees with the necessary knowledge, skills, tools, and behaviors to become effective organizational members and insiders.

Operating budget a financial representation of the short-term plans of an organization across all functions.

Optimization the process of improving website traffic by using search engines.

Organizational consumer any formal entity that purchases a product or service for further production, use in its operations, or for resale; also known as a business consumer.

Organizational culture the shared set of assumptions, values, and beliefs that employees hold.

Orientation an operationally driven process where new employees are introduced and welcomed to a company, provided information about its history, acquainted with its culture, and asked to complete employment paperwork.

Outbound calls telephone calls where the customer is on the receiving end of the call; such as in cold calls.

Outside selling where products/services are sold when salespeople meet with prospects face to face at business meetings, trade shows, conferences, industry events, or other locations (also called 'field sales' or 'channel sales' when indirect channels are used).

Passive listening hearing what is being said, but not concentrating on what it means at all.

Performance metrics measures of a business' or employees' tasks and activities, which are often quantifiable and can be tracked.

Personal selling the interpersonal communication between sellers and buyers or prospective buyers in the exchange of product, services, or something of value, to the mutual benefit of both parties.

Personal space the amount of space between the salesperson and the prospect, also known as proxemics.

Physical space the environment or venue in which the sales presentation will be delivered.

Post-sales activities the collection of sales, marketing, and operations processes that occur after closing a sale with a customer.

Power   the capacity to control or direct change.

Predicament   the problem, challenge, or opportunity that the main character faces in a story.

Principled negotiation   deciding issues on their merits rather than through a haggling process focused on what each side says it will and won't do, also called consultative negotiation.

Proactive listening   where a listener is so deeply present, focused, and engaged with their audience that they are no longer listening *to* someone but are listening *for* select information, also known as intentional listening.

Probing   when a question or a series of questions is asked to uncover a more detailed response.

Prospecting   engaging in activities or conversations with a suspect to inquire, assess, discover, educate, and determine whether there's a fit and a relationship that are worth pursuing which may lead to an opportunity to deliver value and earn a commitment.

Prospects   'hand-raisers' who have identified themselves to a company or an organization.

Proxemics   the amount of space between the salesperson and the prospect, also known as personal space.

Psychographics   the study of the lifestyles, habits, attitudes, beliefs, interests, and value systems of individuals.

Rapport   a close and harmonious relationship in which the people or groups concerned are 'in sync' with each other, understand each other's feelings or ideas, and communicate smoothly.

Rational appeal   an appeal that presents facts in a logical, rational manner and targets basic needs such as those for food, shelter, clothing, and safety.

Recency/frequency/monetary (RFM) assessment   specific transaction data that includes what products each customer has purchased, how recently (recency), how often (frequency), and how much the customer spends (monetary).

Reference groups   those people a consumer turns to for reinforcement, also called 'peer groups.'

Reference individual   a person a consumer turns to for advice.

Relationship selling   those activities that aim to develop and nurture mutually satisfying relationships with customers that last a lifetime.

Request for proposal (RFP)   a formal announcement issued by companies or organizations specifying a particular project for which they are outsourcing and seeking potential bids for a contract to be awarded for its completion.

Sales analytics   identifying, modeling, understanding, and predicting sales trends and outcomes while aiding sales management in understanding where salespeople can improve.

Sales budget   a quantified expectation of the total sales revenues that will be achieved during a given period of time.

Sales compensation plan   the strategy that businesses use to pay salespeople and drive their performance in a way that will help the business become more profitable.

Sales dashboard   a tools that provides a comprehensive overview of key performance indicators (KPIs) and shows how sales teams are tracking towards goals and revenue targets.

Sales deck   a slide presentation summary of a selling company and what it can do for the specific audience for whom the slides have been created.

Sales employee turnover rate   the percentage of employees who leave a company's sales department in a given amount of time, calculated by dividing the number of sales employees who leave the organization in a given period of time by the total number of sales employees working during that same period.

Sales enablement   where the salesperson's role is more that of being a guide than a primary leader as the consumer moves through the buyer journey.

Sales enablement tool   a platform or system that provides visibility across the sales content lifecycle.

Sales forecast   a quantified expectation of estimated future sales along with specific details about what products/services are to be sold during a specific time period.

Sales forecasting   the process of estimating future sales.

Sales funnel   a graphic that shows that many prospective buyers enter the sales cycle as sales leads, fewer of these progress to prospects once their needs/wants are qualified, and an even smaller number convert to customers once they make the buying commitment (also known as sales cycle).

Sales hand-off   the transition period between the sales cycle and the 'becoming a customer' portion of the client relationship.

Sales lead   an individual or a business that is suspected to have an interest in the products or services being sold.

Sales leadership   activities undertaken by those in a sales organization that motivate others to pursue common goals for the collective good of the organization.

Sales qualified lead (SQL)   a sales lead that indicates immediate interest in a company's products or services.

Sales report   a static, historical descriptive account of sales data.

Sales territory   the regional, industry, or account type assigned to a specific salesperson or sales team.

Sales territory management   the process of creating, managing, and optimizing sales territories and the salespeople that are responsible for them.

Self-assessment the process of identifying one's values, interests, personality traits, knowledge, skills, behavior/social style, and emotional intelligence.

Social listening monitoring social media platforms to learn what is being said about a particular company's brand, what topics are relevant to the company, and what insight can be gained from the content communicated by that company.

Strategy a course of action or an action plan that details what activity needs to occur in order to achieve an objective.

Style flexing adjusting one's behavior to mirror or match another person's social style, to interact more effectively with that individual.

Subscription offer/model an offer that requires consumers to pay an up-front subscription price in order to receive regular delivery of or access to certain products/services for a specified period of time.

Suspect someone who may have a need or want for a company's products or services.

System a set of assumptions, concepts, values, and practices that constitutes a way of viewing reality.

Tactics the resources or tools used to implement a strategy.

Team selling a collaborative sales strategy where two or more members work together to achieve buying commitments.

Thesis a statement of the main point or the premise of a story.

Transactional selling a form of selling that focuses solely on completing a deal.

Trial close a question asked during a sales presentation to get feedback from the prospect and to build momentum toward a positive outcome.

Unique selling proposition (USP) one key benefit to a product or service that is distinctively better than and different from all other competitors vying for the same customers.

Up-selling the suggestion of more expensive products/services over the product/service originally discussed or purchased.

Value the relative worth, utility, or importance of something compared to its cost of acquisition.

Values the beliefs and standards by which people choose to live their lives.

Variance analysis comparing the actual results with the expected figures to determine how accurate the budgeting and forecasting activities were.

Verbal skills the way in which one speaks and the words they choose to use.

Versatility the ability to understand differences in communication styles and preferences, and to adapt to make interactions more productive.

Vocal skills   the rate, pitch, tone, and articulation of one's speech.

Warm call   a call made by a salesperson who knows that the prospect is already aware of the salesperson's organization and its benefits.

Webinar   an online presentation held via the Internet, usually in real time.

Web scraping   a technique used to extract structured data from websites; also called web harvesting or web data extraction.

Web scraping API (WSAPI)   a platform that enables companies to extend their existing web-based system to their clients using an application programming interface (API), and provides companies with fresh structured data which is integrated into their system.

Willing to Buy (WTB)   a framework to help both the sales professional and the sales manager discover and face the reality of a potential sale, using criteria that enable consumers to come to a decision.

Worldview   a term referring to the rules, values, beliefs, and biases that an individual person brings to a situation.

INDEX

Page numbers in *italics* refer to figures; page numbers in **bold** refer to tables.

integrity, 10
intentional listening (proactive listening), 212–217, **214**
interests, 40, 54, **54**
intermediate metrics, 460
interpersonal behavior, 61–63
interpersonal conflict, 286–287
interrogation, 327
intimacy, 10

Jamieson, R., 283
Jester, J. de, 454
job interviews, 395–397, **396–397**, 510–511
job promotion opportunities, 413
Johnson, C., 503
Jones, G. Jr., 34
Jones Stone Quarry (case study), 315–317
Judy, R., 85, 380–381, *381*, 427
Jung, C., 182

Kabatznick, S., 120
K.A.R.E. framework, 365
Kemp, A., 109
Kennedy, D., 123, 178–179
key account management, 367–369, **368**
key performance indicators (KPIs)
    closing strategies and, 342–344
    customer and prospect research and, 47
    recruitment and, 395
    sales analytics and, 463
    salesforce and, 414
    strategic planning and, 97–98
    See also sales dashboards
kinesthetic (K) people, 187–189, **188–189**. *See also* Visual-Auditory-Kinesthetic (VAK) model
Knight, B., 5
Kosko, P., 68–70, *69*, 264, *265*, 283, 483–488
Kumar, V., 375

lead generation. *See* prospecting (stage 1)
leadership skills, 172
leadership styles, 404–406, **406**. *See also* sales leadership
Lifestyle Selector, 41
Lim, T., 206
line graphs, 249, *249*
LinkedIn, 135–136, *135*, 508–509, **509–510**
list rental, 123–125, *124*
listening (stage 3)
    concept and importance of, 18, 207–208
    active listening and, 63, 171–172, 180–181, 212–217, **214**
    buyer journey and, 217–220, *217*
    case study: IBM, 232–234
    effective questioning and, 208–212, **211**
    people, practices and perspectives on, 205–206
    willingness to buy (WTB) and, 220–228, 232–234

L.L. Bean, 261–262
loglines, 259
long-term goals, 81
Lyons, C., 174

manufacturing sales representatives, 499
market penetration, 471–472, *472*
marketing automation, 130–131
marketing qualified leads (MQLs), 116
Marston, W., 183, *184–186*
Mattersight, 361
McKee, R., 260
McKenna, M., 5
McKinsey, 468
McPhaden, I., 455
McPhaden, K., 158
medical sales executives, 498
mental space, 257–258, *258*
mentoring, 114, 302, 392–393, 407, 409–410
Merrill, D., 182, *182*
milestone goals, 81, 82
mirroring, 189
mobile technology tools, 252–255, **253–254**
modern selling
    careers in, 21–22, 495–499, **496**
    case study: pharmaceutical sales, 26–28
    different methods of selling in, 12–16, *13*, **16**
    ethical behavior in, 10–12
    importance of relationships in, 7–10
    people, practices and perspectives on, 4–6
    sales funnel and, 6–7, *7*
    sales metrics in, 22–23
    selling process and, 16–22, *17*, 434. *See also specific stages*
multivariable statistical analysis, 439–441
Myers-Briggs Type Indicator, 182

narratives, 266
needs discovery conversation (NDC), 18, 42, 43, 47–48, 207–208, 243. *See also* listening (stage 3)
negotiation
    concept and importance of, 19, 284, 296–299
    bargaining skills and, 307–310
    case study: Jones Stone Quarry (JSQ), 315–317
    metrics and, 310–311
    planning and preparation for, 299–303, *300*, **303**
    process of, 304–306
negotiation mentors, 302
Neighborhood Change Database (NCDB), 38
Netflix, 340
netiquette, 180
networks and networking, 57–59, 110–114, 120–121, 122–123, 508–510, **509–510**
neuro-linguistic programming (NLP), 186–189, **187–189**, *189*, *191*
NextMark, 123–124, *124*
nonverbal skills, 63, *173*, 174–176, *175–176*